SpringBoard®

Senior English

English Textual Power™

CollegeBoard
inspiring minds.™

THE COLLEGE BOARD
inspiring minds™

About the College Board

The College Board is a mission-driven not-for-profit organization that connects students to college success and opportunity. Founded in 1900, the College Board was created to expand access to higher education. Today, the membership association is made up of more than 5,900 of the nation's leading educational institutions and is dedicated to promoting excellence and equity in education. Each year, the College Board helps more than seven million students prepare for a successful transition to college through programs and services in college readiness and college success — including the SAT® and the Advanced Placement Program®. The organization also serves the education community through research and advocacy on behalf of students, educators and schools.

For further information, visit www.collegeboard.com.

ISBN: 0-87447-918-5
ISBN: 978-0-87447-918-8

3 4 5 6 7 8   11 12 13 14
Printed in the United States of America

Acknowledgments

The College Board gratefully acknowledges the outstanding work of the classroom teachers and writers who have been integral to the development of this revised program. The end product is testimony to their expertise, understanding of student learning needs, and dedication to rigorous but accessible language arts education.

Susie Challancin
English Teacher
Bellevue School District 405
Bellevue, Washington

Paul De Maret
English Teacher
Poudre School District
Fort Collins, Colorado

Suzie Doss
District English/ Language Arts
    Coordinator
Hobbs Municipal Schools
Hobbs, New Mexico

John Golden
English Teacher
Grant High School
Portland, Oregon

Nancy Gray
English Teacher
West Shore Junior/Senior High School
Melbourne, Florida

Ellen Greig
English Teacher, Consultant
Charlotte, North Carolina

Karen Hanson
Exceptional Student Teacher
Volusia Public Schools
DeLand, Florida

Cheryl Harris
English Teacher Consultant
Bedford, Texas

Susie Lowry
English Teacher
Volusia Public Schools
DeLand, Florida

Julie Manley
Middle School Language Arts
    Tech-Curriculum Coach and
    Humanities Teacher
Bellevue School District 405
Bellevue, Washington

Joely Negedly
Secondary Reading and
    Language Arts Specialists
Volusia Public Schools
DeLand, Florida

JoEllen Victoreen
Instructional Specialist,
    SpringBoard
San Jose, California

Douglas Waugh
Administrative Coach,
    SpringBoard
Bellevue, Washington

Nina Wooldridge
Instructional Specialist,
    SpringBoard
Los Angeles, California

Advisors, Reviewers, Special Feature Writers

The following teachers and writers provided invaluable assistance in creating special features and reviewing manuscript. We gratefully acknowledge their contributions to this revised edition.

Gary Cowan
English/Language Arts Coordinator
Metro Nashville Public Schools
Nashville, Tennessee

Nicki Junkins
Administrative Coach,
    SpringBoard
DeLand, Florida

Jeanneine Jones
Professor, Departments of Middle,
    Secondary, and K-12 Education
University of North Carolina
Charlotte, North Carolina

William McBride
Emeritus Professor of English
Colorado State University
Fort Collins, Colorado

Daniel Millet
English Teacher
Weld county School District
    Re-8
Fort Lupton, Colorado

Melanie Sangalli
English Teacher
Irving Public Schools
Irving, Texas

Special Acknowledgments

The College Board wishes especially to acknowledge the writers of the original *Pacesetter* program. Much of their work continues in use today. The result of their efforts was a program that helped both teachers and students succeed. With its roots in Pacesetter, the current program had an excellent foundation on which to build.

Willie Mae Crews
Educator
Birmingham, Alabama

R. Steven Green, Ed.D.
Educator
Kansas City, Missouri

Ellen Greenblatt
University High School
San Francisco, California

Alice Kawazoe
Educational Consultant, California Academic
   Partnership Program
San Carlos, California

Jenny Oren Krugman
Vice President, Southern Region
College Board
Miami, Florida

William McBride, Ph.D.
Emeritus Professor of English
Colorado State University
Fort Collins, Colorado

Robert Scholes, Ph.D.
Research Professor, Brown University
Providence, Rhode Island

In addition, we wish to acknowledge the educators and writers whose work on prior editions helped to continue the *Pacesetter* excellence and to establish the high expectations for which the College Board's SpringBoard program is known.

Lance Balla
Bellevue, Washington

Bryant Crisp
Charlotte, North Carolina

Nancy Elrod
Atlanta, Georgia

Ann Foster
Melbourne, Florida

Ana Gandara
Edinburg, Texas

Alex Gordin
Portland, Oregon

Kenyatta Graves
Washington, DC

Don Keagy
Poultney, Vermont

Don Kirk
Poultney, Vermont

Dana Mebane
Baltimore, Maryland

Bob Messinger
Providence, Rhode Island

Debi Miller
Miami, Florida

Melanie Ross Mitchell
Atlanta, Georgia

Lisa Rehm
DeLand, Florida

Penny Riffe
Palm Bay, Florida

Rick Robb
Clarksville, Maryland

Sue Rodriguez
Miami, Florida

Research and Planning Advisors

We also wish to thank the members of our SpringBoard Advisory Council, the SpringBoard Language Arts Trainers, and the many educators who gave generously of their time and their ideas as we conducted research for the program. Their suggestions and reactions to ideas helped immeasurably as we planned the revisions. We gratefully acknowledge the teachers and administrators in the following districts:

Broward County Public Schools
Fort Lauderdale, Florida

Cherry Creek School District
Cherry Creek, Colorado

Chicago Public Schools
Chicago, Illinois

DeKalb County School System
DeKalb County, Georgia

Duval County Public Schools
Jacksonville, Florida

Guilford County Schools
Greensboro, North Carolina

Hillsborough County Public Schools
Tampa, Florida

Hobbs Municipal Schools
Hobbs, New Mexico

Indianapolis Public Schools
Indianapolis, Indiana

Miami-Dade County Public Schools
Miami, Florida

Metropolitan Nashville Public Schools
Nashville, Tennessee

The City School District of New Rochelle
New Rochelle, New York

Orange County Public Schools
Orlando, Florida

School District of Palm Beach County
Palm Beach, Florida

Peninsula School District
Gig Harbor, Washington

Pinellas County Schools
Largo, Florida

San Antonio Independent School District
San Antonio, Texas

Spokane Public Schools
Spokane, Washington

Volusia County Schools
DeLand, Florida

Editorial Leadership

The College Board gratefully acknowledges the expertise, time, and commitment of the language arts editorial manager.

Betty Barnett
Educational Publishing Consultant

Senior English Contents

To the Student viii

Instructional Units

To the Student

Welcome to the SpringBoard program. We hope you will discover how SpringBoard can help you achieve high academic standards, reach your learning goals, and prepare for success in your study of literature and language arts. The program has been created with you in mind: the content you need to learn, the tools to help you learn, and the critical-thinking skills that help you build confidence in your own knowledge and skills.

The College Board publishes the SpringBoard program as a complete language arts curriculum that prepares you for Advanced Placement and college-level study. SpringBoard maps out what successful students should know and be able to do at each grade level to develop the language, reading, writing, and communication skills needed for success. College Board also publishes the SAT and Advanced Placement exams—exams that you are likely to encounter in your high school years.

Connection to Advanced Placement

The College Board's Advanced Placement program provides the opportunity to complete college-level courses while in high school. In addition to receiving college credits, participation in AP courses helps you develop the skills and knowledge that add to your confidence and ease the transition from high school to college.

The SpringBoard program assists you in preparing for AP-level courses in several ways:

▶ Exposing you to the same types of tasks as on the AP Language and Literature exams; for example, close reading of fiction and nonfiction texts, responding to writing prompts, writing under timed conditions, and writing for multiple purposes (persuasion, argumentation, literary analysis, and synthesis).

▶ Introducing you to AP strategies, such as TP-CASTT and SOAPSTone, that help you analyze literary and other texts, giving you the tools you need to independently analyze any text.

▶ Preparing you for higher-order skills and behaviors required for college-level work through ongoing practice in key skills such as generating and organizing ideas, analysis of different types of texts, synthesis and explanation of concepts, and original writing in a variety of modes.

What Is the Foundation for SpringBoard?

The foundation of SpringBoard is the College Board Standards for College Success, which set out the knowledge and critical-thinking skills you should acquire to succeed in high school and in future college-level work.

The English Language Arts College Board Standards are divided into five categories: reading, writing, speaking, listening, and media literacy.

Your success as a reader depends on many factors, including your interest and motivation to read, the amount of time you spend reading, understanding the purpose for reading, knowledge about a topic, and knowledge about how to read different kinds of text.

Your success as a writer depends on learning many words and how to use those words effectively to communicate a story or information for others to read and understand. Successful writers determine their purpose for writing, such as to explore, inform, express an opinion, persuade, entertain, or to share an experience or emotion. As they write, they also consider their audiences and choose the language that will help them communicate with that audience. Writing is a process that involves several steps, and you will have many opportunities in this program to learn the process and to improve your own writing.

Your success as a speaker is based on how well you communicate orally. What is your message, what words will best communicate it, how do you prepare, or rehearse, for a speech? Good speakers also consider the audience and what they know about a specific topic. They can then deliver a message that uses a shared understanding, or develops one based on common knowledge, with their listeners.

Being a good listener is the other part of effective communication. Communication includes the speaker, listener, message, feedback, and noise (the conditions surrounding the communication). You'll have opportunities throughout the program to practice both your speaking and listening skills.

Finally, being media literate means that you can interpret, analyze, and evaluate the messages you receive daily from various types of media. Being media literate also means that you can use the information you gain to express or support a point of view and influence others.

As you complete the activities in this text, you will develop your skills and knowledge in all of these areas.

How Is SpringBoard Unique?

SpringBoard is unique because it provides instruction with hands-on participation that involves you and your classmates in daily discussions and analysis of what you're reading and learning. The book is organized into multiple activities that invite participation by providing adequate space for taking notes and writing your own thoughts and analyses about texts you're reading or questions you're answering. Among the key features that make SpringBoard a unique learning experience are:

▶ Activities that thoroughly develop topics, leading to deep understanding of the concepts and enabling you to apply learning in multiple situations.

▶ Extensive opportunities to explore a variety of texts—both fiction and nonfiction—that introduce you to many different ways of thinking, writing, and communicating.

▶ Questions that help you examine writing from the perspective of a reader and a writer and the techniques that good writers use to communicate their messages effectively.

▶ Built-in class discussions and collaborative work that help you explore and express your own ideas while integrating the ideas of others into your base of knowledge.

▶ Integrated performance-based assessments that give you practice in showing what you know and can do, not just repeating what you've read.

▶ Assessments that help you decipher tasks and plan how to accomplish those tasks in timed situations like those for standardized tests.

Strategies for Learning

As you complete the activities in this text, you will work on many reading, writing, and oral presentation assignments. You will often work in groups and pairs. To help you do your best, you and your teacher will use a variety of reading, writing, and collaborative learning strategies.

Reading strategies give you specific tools to help you improve your skills in reading and making meaning from text. These strategies will help you improve your ability to analyze text by developing skills in using context clues, finding meaning for unfamiliar words, or organizing your responses to what you read. As you learn to use different reading strategies, it's important to think about which ones work best for you and why.

Writing strategies help you focus on your purpose for writing and the message you want to communicate to your readers. Using writing strategies will help you analyze your own writing for specific purposes and identify how to improve that writing using better word choices or punctuating differently or using sentence structure in different ways.

You and your classmates will use *collaborative strategies* to explore concepts and answer text-related questions as you work in pairs or in groups to discuss the work you're doing and to learn from each other.

Performance Portfolio

You will learn to use language in both written and spoken forms in this course. You are encouraged to keep your work in a Working Folder from which you can choose examples to show where you started and how you are growing in your skills and knowledge during the year. Presenting your best work in a Portfolio not only helps you evaluate your own work and improvement, but also helps you explore your unique style and analyze how your work can best represent you.

Presenting your portfolio provides direction as you revisit, revise, and reflect on your work throughout the year. Your teacher will guide you as you include items in your portfolio that illustrate a wide range of work, including examples of reading, writing, oral literacy, and collaborative activities. As you progress through the course, you will have opportunities to revisit prior work, revise it based on new learning, and reflect on the learning strategies and activities that help you be successful. The portfolio:

▶ Gives you a specific place to feature your work and a way to share it with others.

▶ Provides an organized, focused way to view your progress throughout the year.

▶ Allows you to reflect on the new skills and strategies you are learning.

▶ Enables you to measure your growth as a reader, writer, speaker, and performer.

▶ Encourages you to revise pieces of work to incorporate new skills.

As you move through each unit, your teacher will instruct you to include certain items in your portfolio. Strong portfolios will include a variety of work from each unit, such as first drafts, final drafts, quickwrites, notes, reading logs, audio and video examples, and graphics that represent a wide variety of genre, forms, and media created for a variety of purposes.

We hope you enjoy using the SpringBoard program. It will give you many opportunities to explore your own and others' ideas about becoming effective readers, writers, and communicators.

English Textual Power, Senior English, introduces the use of multiple literary theories as filters through which to interpret texts. Throughout the year, you will learn about and apply Reader Response Criticism, Cultural Criticism, Archetypal Criticism, Marxist Criticism, Feminist Criticism, and Historical Criticism. Analyzing texts through these lenses will develop your awareness of a writer's perspective and the skills to evaluate text for potential biases.

Preview the Unit

Essential Questions pose questions to help you think about the "big ideas" and make connections between what you learn and how you apply that learning.

Unit Overview sets the stage by:

▶ Providing a bridge from what you know to what you'll be learning in the unit.

▶ Outlining the big ideas in the unit and how the book's theme is connected from unit to unit.

Unit Contents give a snapshot of the unit activities and identify the texts and genres you'll explore in the unit.

▶ **Goals**–skills and knowledge you'll learn in the unit.

▶ **Academic Vocabulary**–key terms to use in the unit and to help you gain the vocabulary needed for AP courses and college.

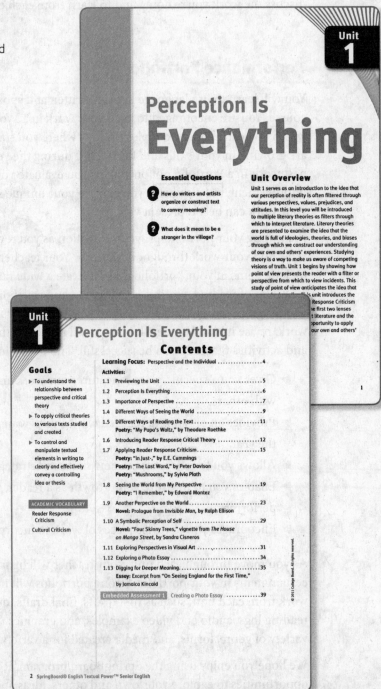

Unit 1

Perception Is Everything

Essential Questions

? How do writers and artists organize or construct text to convey meaning?

? What does it mean to be a stranger in the village?

Unit Overview

Unit 1 serves as an introduction to the idea that our perception of reality is often filtered through various perspectives, values, prejudices, and attitudes. In this level you will be introduced to multiple literary theories as filters through which to interpret literature. Literary theories are presented to examine the idea that the world is full of ideologies, theories, and biases through which we construct our understanding of our own and others' experiences. Studying theory is a way to make us aware of competing visions of truth. Unit 1 begins by showing how point of view presents the reader with a filter or perspective from which to view incidents. This study of point of view anticipates the idea that ... this unit introduces the ... Response Criticism ... the first two lenses ... literature and the ... opportunity to apply ... our own and others'

Unit 1

Perception Is Everything
Contents

Goals

▶ To understand the relationship between perspective and critical theory

▶ To apply critical theories to various texts studied and created

▶ To control and manipulate textual elements in writing to clearly and effectively convey a controlling idea or thesis

ACADEMIC VOCABULARY

Reader Response Criticism

Cultural Criticism

Preparing for Learning

Learning Focus connects what you already know with what you'll learn in the unit and why it's important.

▶ Highlights key terms.

▶ Connects learning from unit to unit.

▶ Introduces concepts for the unit.

Previewing the Unit helps you identify the expectations for knowledge and skills you'll need to learn in the unit by asking you to read and respond to:

▶ **Essential Questions**

▶ **Unit Overview–Learning Focus**

▶ **Embedded Assessment and Scoring Guide**

Starting with the End in Mind
Graphic organizer helps you:

▶ Map out the skills and knowledge you'll need for the Embedded Assessments.

▶ Read the assignment and the Scoring Guide (see page xvi) and outline what you'll need to do.

▶ Identify skills and knowledge to be assessed.

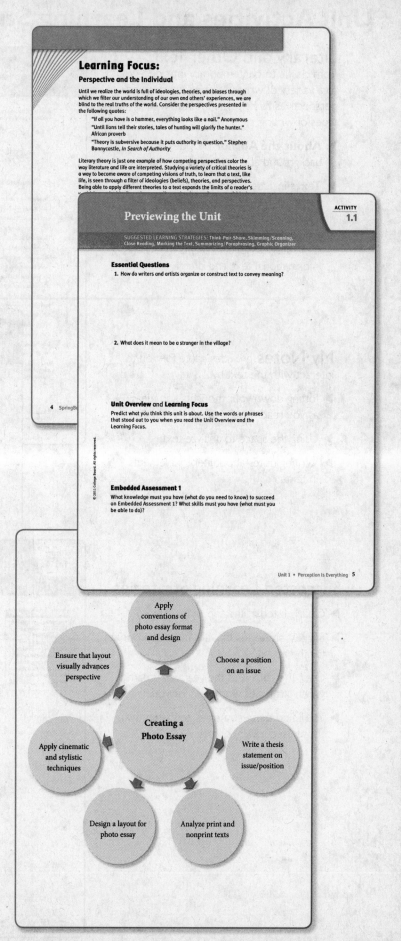

Unit Activities and Learning Strategies

Literary and Other Texts

from classic to contemporary introduce you to a variety of writers, stories, themes, and perspectives to help you interact with all types of writing.

▶ **About the Author** provides author's background and insights about the text.

▶ **Texts** include examples from a variety of genres, including poetry, film, autobiography, essay, print and online articles, folk tales, myths, fables, memoir, short stories, novel excerpts, interviews, Informational text, and drama.

My Notes provides space for you to interact with the text by:

▶ Jotting down your thoughts and ideas as you read.

▶ Using the space to analyze text.

▶ Writing notes about literary elements in texts.

Suggested Learning Strategies

▶ Clearly listed at the top of the page.

▶ Suggest strategies that are most appropriate for the activity.

▶ Over the course of the year, you'll learn which strategies work best for you.

▶ You'll find these strategies consistent with those used in AP courses.

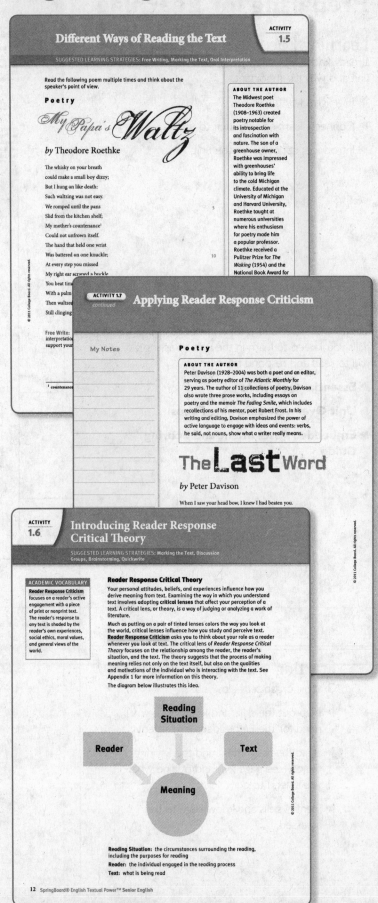

Integrated Language Skills

Vocabulary and Word Study

▶ **Academic Vocabulary** highlights key words you'll need to know for the unit and to expand your vocabulary for AP and college.

▶ **Literary Terms** define key words as you encounter them in your reading and analysis of text.

▶ **Word Connections** help you use context clues from Latin and other roots, understand analogies, and identify words with multiple meanings.

Grammar & Usage

▶ Offers tips about points of grammar and how to avoid common errors.

▶ Shows how writers use various grammatical constructions to clarify their text and to convey meaning for readers.

▶ Helps both speakers <u>and</u> writers use grammar to make their text or message more effective.

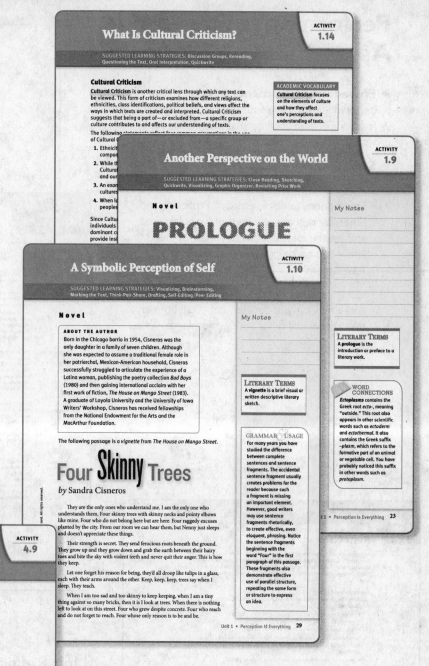

Writing

▶ **Writing Process** is defined and practiced through opportunities to draft, revise, edit, and prepare publishable writing.

▶ **Writing Prompts & Timed Writings** provide practice in identifying specific writing tasks and writing under timed conditions.

▶ **Portfolios** are encouraged to collect your writing throughout the year to show your progress.

Performance-Based Assessment

▶ **Embedded Assessments** provide opportunities to demonstrate your knowledge and your skills in applying that knowledge in a variety of assessments.

▶ **Scoring Guide** walks you through the expectations for performance.

- Descriptions under Exemplary, Proficient, and Emerging describe the level of work required and set the expectations for what you need to know and do <u>before</u> you start the Embedded Assessment.

- Using the descriptions for Exemplary, Proficient, and Emerging, you decide what you'll do and take responsibility for your performance.

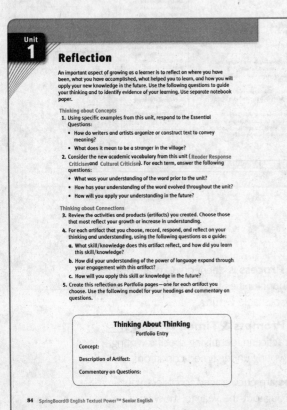

Embedded Assessment 2

Writing a Reflective Essay

SUGGESTED LEARNING STRATEGIES: Brainstorming, Drafting, Self-Editing/Peer Editing

Assignment

Your assignment is to write a reflective essay that illustrates an event in which you or someone you know felt like a "stranger in the village" or was perceived as "strange" by some group.

Steps

Prewriting

1. Generate a list of events that capture the thematic concept of "stranger in the village" by considering a time in which you felt like an outsider, witnessed someone else who was made to feel like an outsider, and/or made someone else feel like an outsider. Select two or three events from your list to share with a partner, and explain how your event addresses the thematic concept.

2. Select the strongest topic of interest to you and use a prewriting strategy to capture ideas and explore your memory of the event.

3. Review the organizational structure of a reflective essay (e.g., event, response, and reflection) by revisiting the two literary examples presented in this unit — "Shooting an Elephant" and "Stranger in the Village." Note the differences between them in terms of the recursive pattern of event, response, and reflection.

Embedded Assessment 2 *continued*

Writing a Reflective Essay

SCORING GUIDE

Scoring Criteria	Exemplary	Proficient	Emerging
Ideas	The reflective essay thoroughly demonstrates a perceptive understanding of the relationship between the chosen event and thematic concept. Use of specific and well-chosen details yields incontrovertible support and creates an extraordinarily convincing text.	The reflective essay demonstrates a solid understanding of the relationship between the chosen event and thematic concept. Use of specific details yields support and creates a convincing text.	The reflective essay demonstrates a superficial understanding of the relationship between the chosen event and thematic concept. Details are underutilized and do little to create a convincing text.
Organization	The essay's effective organization aptly reinforces the writer's ideas. Successful use of transitions enhances overall coherence and connects ideas smoothly and comfortably.	The essay's clear organization supports the ideas. Transitions provide connection between ideas.	The essay's lack of organization detracts from the ideas, making the essay difficult to follow. It may move too rapidly between ideas and may lack transitions.
Use of Language	Diction, syntax, and other stylistic devices are notable and appropriate for the subject, purpose, and audience. Few errors in standard writing conventions are present.	Diction, syntax, and other stylistic devices are appropriate for the subject, purpose, and audience. Errors in standard writing conventions, if present, are minor and do not interfere with meaning.	Diction, syntax, and other stylistic devices are less effective for the subject, purpose, and audience. Errors in standard writing conventions seriously interfere with meaning.
Evidence of Writing Process	The writing demonstrates thoughtful planning, significant revision, and careful editing for grammar and conventions in preparing a publishable draft.	The writing demonstrates planning, revision, and editing for grammar and conventions in preparing a publishable draft.	The writing lacks evidence of planning, revision, and/or editing for grammar and conventions. The draft is not ready for publication.

Unit 1

Reflection

An important aspect of growing as a learner is to reflect on where you have been, what you have accomplished, what helped you to learn, and how you will apply your new knowledge in the future. Use the following questions to guide your thinking and to identify evidence of your learning. Use separate notebook paper.

Thinking about Concepts

1. Using specific examples from this unit, respond to the Essential Questions:
   - How do writers and artists organize or construct text to convey meaning?
   - What does it mean to be a stranger in the village?

2. Consider the new academic vocabulary from this unit (*Reader Response Criticism* and *Cultural Criticism*). For each term, answer the following questions:
   - What was your understanding of the word prior to the unit?
   - How has your understanding of the word evolved throughout the unit?
   - How will you apply your understanding in the future?

Thinking about Connections

3. Review the activities and products (artifacts) you created. Choose those that most reflect your growth or increase in understanding.

4. For each artifact that you choose, record, respond, and reflect on your thinking and understanding, using the following questions as a guide:
   a. What skill/knowledge does this artifact reflect, and how did you learn this skill/knowledge?
   b. How did your understanding of the power of language expand through your engagement with this artifact?
   c. How will you apply this skill or knowledge in the future?

5. Create this reflection as Portfolio pages — one for each artifact you choose. Use the following model for your headings and commentary on questions.

> **Thinking About Thinking**
> Portfolio Entry
>
> Concept:
>
> Description of Artifact:
>
> Commentary on Questions:

Unit Reflection helps you to take ownership of your learning by stopping at regular points to think about:

▶ What you've learned.

▶ What strategies and tools helped you learn.

▶ What you still need to work on in the future.

Perception Is
Everything

Essential Questions

? How do writers and artists organize or construct text to convey meaning?

? What does it mean to be a stranger in the village?

Unit Overview

Unit 1 serves as an introduction to the idea that our perception of reality is often filtered through various perspectives, values, prejudices, and attitudes. In this level you will be introduced to multiple literary theories as filters through which to interpret literature. Literary theories are presented to examine the idea that the world is full of ideologies, theories, and biases through which we construct our understanding of our own and others' experiences. Studying theory is a way to make us aware of competing visions of truth. Unit 1 begins by showing how point of view presents the reader with a filter or perspective from which to view incidents. This study of point of view anticipates the idea that perspective is reality. This unit introduces the literary theories of Reader Response Criticism and Cultural Criticism as the first two lenses through which we interpret literature and the world. You will have the opportunity to apply these literary theories to your own and others' writing.

Unit 1

Perception Is Everything

Contents

Goals

▶ To understand the relationship between perspective and critical theory

▶ To apply critical theories to various texts studied and created

▶ To control and manipulate textual elements in writing to clearly and effectively convey a controlling idea or thesis

ACADEMIC VOCABULARY

Reader Response Criticism

Cultural Criticism

Texts not included in these materials.

Learning Focus:

Perspective and the Individual

Until we realize the world is full of ideologies, theories, and biases through which we filter our understanding of our own and others' experiences, we are blind to the real truths of the world. Consider the perspectives presented in the following quotes:

> "If all you have is a hammer, everything looks like a nail." Anonymous

> "Until lions tell their stories, tales of hunting will glorify the hunter." African proverb

> "Theory is subversive because it puts authority in question." Stephen Bonnycastle, *In Search of Authority*

Literary theory is just one example of how competing perspectives color the way literature and life are interpreted. Studying a variety of critical theories is a way to become aware of competing visions of truth, to learn that a text, like life, is seen through a filter of ideologies (beliefs), theories, and perspectives. Being able to apply different theories to a text expands the limits of a reader's worldview and adds dimension to reading and understanding a text. Critical theory highlights the fact that there is no one, simple vision of the truth. Truth is a complicated product of multiple perspectives.

Reader Response Critical Theory is the first of six literary critical theories you will study. **Reader Response Criticism** focuses on a reader's engagement with a specific text and the dynamics that emerge as meaning is created between the text presented by the author and the reader's interpretation of it. This theory highlights the idea that individuals often read and interpret the same texts differently, allowing texts to be challenged, evaluated, and critiqued.

See Appendix 1 in the back of your book for descriptions of all six literary critical theories. You will want to refer to this information for definitions, characteristics, and examples of different literary perspectives. This list is not intended to be an exhaustive representation of these complex theoretical perspectives, but rather a brief introduction. Your teacher may expect you to do further research on one or more of these literary theories.

Independent Reading: In this unit, you will be reading several texts with the primary focus of self-perception and the role that one's culture plays in defining one's sense of self. For independent reading, look for works of fiction that focus on multiple perspectives. Authors you may want to explore are Amy Tan, Albert Camus, Robert A. Heinlein, Jamaica Kincaid, and Barbara Kingsolver.

Previewing the Unit

SUGGESTED LEARNING STRATEGIES: Think-Pair-Share, Skimming/Scanning, Close Reading, Marking the Text, Summarizing/Paraphrasing, Graphic Organizer

Essential Questions

1. How do writers and artists organize or construct text to convey meaning?

2. What does it mean to be a stranger in the village?

Unit Overview and Learning Focus

Predict what you think this unit is about. Use the words or phrases that stood out to you when you read the Unit Overview and the Learning Focus.

Embedded Assessment 1

What knowledge must you have (what do you need to know) to succeed on Embedded Assessment 1? What skills must you have (what must you be able to do)?

Perception Is Everything

LITERARY TERMS
Perception is a mental
concept or point of view.

An **aphorism** is a succinct statement expressing an opinion, **perception**, or general truth. Choose five aphorisms that you especially like from the following list. In your group, paraphrase the quotes you have chosen, and explain how the quotes relate to the ideas of seeing and understanding.

- "What you see and hear depends a good deal on where you are standing; it also depends on what sort of person you are." — C. S. Lewis

- "The voyage of discovery is not in seeking new landscapes but in having new eyes." — Marcel Proust

- "You can complain because roses have thorns, or you can rejoice because thorns have roses." — Tom Wilson

- "All photographs are accurate. None of them is the truth." — Richard Avedon

- "There are things known and there are things unknown, and in between are the doors of perception." — Aldous Huxley

- "The eye sees only what the mind is prepared to comprehend." — Henri Bergson

- "Better keep yourself clean and bright; you are the window through which you must see the world." — George Bernard Shaw

- "Whilst part of what we perceive comes through our senses from the object before us, another part (and it may be the larger part) always comes out of our own mind." — William James

- "Language forces us to perceive the world as men present it to us." — Julia Penelope

- "If we spoke a different language, we would perceive a somewhat different world." — Ludwig Wittgenstein

Timed Writing: Choose one quote from the list and write a response about the truth it conveys. You will have 15 minutes. Use prewriting strategies to structure your ideas quickly. Remember to use appropriate rhetorical devices and effective transitions to maintain the flow of ideas and to convey meaning to your readers. Then create an original aphorism expressing your perception or a general truth about the world.

Importance of Perspective

Everyone views the world with a unique perspective. That perspective can be influenced by a number of factors, including life experiences, education, significant people, occupations, political affiliations, and numerous other elements that serve to help shape individual attitudes.

Take something as simple as music. Think of one of your favorite songs. Why do you like that song? Does it address an issue that is important to you? Does it feature an instrument that you especially enjoy? Do you merely enjoy it for the rhythm it contains? Your answers to these questions depend on your unique perspective, a perspective that has been influenced in many ways over the course of your life.

In order to illustrate this idea, consider the following **scenario**:

> *On your way to school, you see another student who has been pulled over by a police officer. You see the student's frustration as the officer writes out what appears to be a traffic ticket.*

Complete the graphic organizer on the following page, imagining the response of each individual in the situation. Consider these points when responding:

- Each person described in the scenario will have a distinctly different perspective on the situation.

- Each person described in the scenario will have a different level of connection to the consequences of the situation, which in turn will influence the response. For example, someone will have to pay for the ticket.

- Each person described in the scenario will also be subject to a variety of factors unrelated to the ticket that will also influence the response. For example, if the traffic is moving more slowly due to the ticket distraction, someone may be late for work.

> ### LITERARY TERMS
> A **scenario** is an outline, a brief account, or a synopsis of events.

Importance of Perspective

Individual Perspective	Thoughts Running Through This Person's Mind	Possible Factors Influencing How This Person Is Responding	Primary Goal or Objective of This Person
Student Being Ticketed			
Officer Writing the Ticket			
Parent of Student Being Ticketed Who Happens to Be Driving By			
Favorite Teacher Driving by			
Best Friend of Student Being Ticketed			
You			

Different Ways of Seeing the World

Scan the words listed below, and use the following coding system to rate your level of understanding with the media production elements of photography.

(Q): Signals a question—I have never heard of this word before.

(H): Signals familiarity—I have heard of the word before and here is the context in which I have heard it.

(T): Signals knowledge—I know what this word means, and here is an example.

WORD CONNECTIONS

Choose the appropriate response to complete the analogy.

cropping : photograph :: _____.

a. frame : oil painting
b. editing : film
c. baking : pie
d. chainsaw : timber

_____ 1. Frame   _____ 5. Image

_____ 2. Subject   _____ 6. Composition

_____ 3. Cropping   _____ 7. Space

_____ 4. Lighting

LITERARY TERMS

The *mise en scène* is the composition, or setting, of an image.

Consult your peers to discuss and gain meaning for unfamiliar words. For words you know (the "T" words), share examples and verify understanding. For words you have heard of (the "H" words), use words you know to describe your understanding. Ask peers to share their knowledge of the meaning of words for which you have a question.

Writing Prompt: Study the photograph suggested by your teacher, and use the space below to write a brief description that reflects the *mise en scène,* or composition, of the image. Be sure to use newly acquired words in your response.

Different Ways of Seeing the World

Analyzing Visuals/Art: Using the OPTIC Strategy

Brief Description of OPTIC Steps	Literal Detailed Observations	Interpretation of Observations
Overview: Conduct a brief overview of the visual by examining it carefully. Note the details: images, colors, shapes, position or angle in the frame.		
Parts: Key in on the parts of the visual by reading all labels, images, and symbols, noting any additonal details that seem important.		
Title/Text: Read the title and any text within the visual so that you are clear on the subject. Read all labels and consider how they add to your interpretation.		
Interrelationships: Use the title as your theory and the parts of the visual as your clues to detect and identify the interrelationships in the visual/art.		
Conclusions: Draw conclusions about the visual as a whole.		

Different Ways of Reading the Text

Read the following poem multiple times and think about the speaker's point of view.

Poetry

My Papa's Waltz

by Theodore Roethke

The whisky on your breath
could make a small boy dizzy;
But I hung on like death:
Such waltzing was not easy.

We romped until the pans   5
Slid from the kitchen shelf;
My mother's countenance[1]
Could not unfrown itself.

The hand that held one wrist
Was battered on one knuckle;   10
At every step you missed
My right ear scraped a buckle.

You beat time on my head
With a palm caked hard by dirt,
Then waltzed me off to bed   15
Still clinging to your shirt.

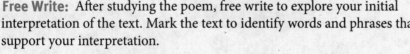

Free Write: After studying the poem, free write to explore your initial interpretation of the text. Mark the text to identify words and phrases that support your interpretation.

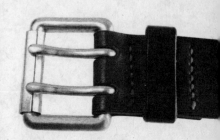

ABOUT THE AUTHOR
The Midwest poet Theodore Roethke (1908–1963) created poetry notable for its introspection and fascination with nature. The son of a greenhouse owner, Roethke was impressed with greenhouses' ability to bring life to the cold Michigan climate. Educated at the University of Michigan and Harvard University, Roethke taught at numerous universities where his enthusiasm for poetry made him a popular professor. Roethke received a Pulitzer Prize for *The Waking* (1954) and the National Book Award for the collection *Words for the Wind* (1957).

---

[1] **countenance:** facial expression

Introducing Reader Response Critical Theory

SUGGESTED LEARNING STRATEGIES: Marking the Text, Discussion Groups, Brainstorming, Quickwrite

ACADEMIC VOCABULARY

Reader Response Criticism focuses on a reader's active engagement with a piece of print or nonprint text. The reader's response to any text is shaded by the reader's own experiences, social ethics, moral values, and general views of the world.

Reader Response Critical Theory

Your personal attitudes, beliefs, and experiences influence how you derive meaning from text. Examining the way in which you understand text involves adopting **critical lenses** that affect your perception of a text. A critical lens, or theory, is a way of judging or analyzing a work of literature.

Much as putting on a pair of tinted lenses colors the way you look at the world, critical lenses influence how you study and perceive text. **Reader Response Criticism** asks you to think about your role as a reader whenever you look at text. The critical lens of *Reader Response Critical Theory* focuses on the relationship among the reader, the reader's situation, and the text. The theory suggests that the process of making meaning relies not only on the text itself, but also on the qualities and motivations of the individual who is interacting with the text. See Appendix 1 for more information on this theory.

The diagram below illustrates this idea.

Reading Situation

Reader

Text

Meaning

Reading Situation: the circumstances surrounding the reading, including the purposes for reading

Reader: the individual engaged in the reading process

Text: what is being read

In the Reading Situation – Reader – Text model, the reader constructs meaning as a result of the interaction among all of these individual factors. Consider the following examples:

- **Scenario 1:** A senior is assigned to read a chapter from the book he is studying in English class. The senior has tickets to see a show that night but knows that there will be a quiz on the chapter the next day. He is a strong reader but has not enjoyed the book the class is studying. What factors are influential on the reader, situation, and text? How would these factors impact the student's ability to make meaning of that chapter?

- **Scenario 2:** A senior is part of a group of four students preparing a presentation about optical illusions. She volunteered to do Internet research to find information to bring back to the rest of the group. She is a computer whiz and fascinated by the topic, and spends several hours on the Internet finding examples of optical illusions, but hasn't done much real reading or investigating of the information about optical illusions. The next day in class the group is expecting some material to read, but the senior brings a collection of optical illusions to show them instead. How did the reader, situation, and text impact the ability to make meaning?

> **LITERARY TERMS**
> **Literary theory** attempts to establish principles for interpreting and evaluating literary texts.

Introducing Reader Response Critical Theory

The Elements of Reader Response Criticism

The Reader

One significant factor in Reader Response Critical Theory is that it takes into account the person doing the reading. This model takes the reader into account in a number of ways, including, but not limited to, the individual's opinions, attitudes, beliefs, and background knowledge. Consider some of the ways in which your personality, attitudes, and personal goals influence you every time you are looking at text. For example, what do you read on your own? Do you read novels, or do you read sports magazines? If you read quite a few novels, then being asked to read 30 pages in a single session might not seem difficult. This is just one way in which you influence the reading process.

The Reading Situation

The reading situation includes *why* you are engaged in reading, *when* you are reading, and *where* you are reading. Some of these factors are within your control, but others are not. Anytime that you read a text because someone else told you to read it, the choice has been made for you. How much you are supposed to read is also often decided for you. However, where and when you choose to read the text can be up to you. If you decide to sit in a comfortable stuffed chair at midnight to read your book, you might tend to lose concentration and drift off to sleep. The last few pages you read before falling asleep might be a little less clear than pages you read at your desk earlier in the evening.

The Text

The text is defined as whatever is being read. Textual features vary, depending on the source. For example, a textbook will present text differently than a magazine or a pamphlet. Numerous other factors influence the text, from level of difficulty to the typefaces and illustrations.

Quickwrite: With a small group, create a summary statement of all that you have learned about Reader Response Critical Theory. Share your responses and choose the clearest, most comprehensive summary statement.

SUGGESTED LEARNING STRATEGIES: Discussion Groups, Sketching, Quickwrite, Rereading, Marking the Text, Metacognitive Markers, TP-CASTT

Poetry

in Just-

by E.E. Cummings

in Just-
spring   when the world is mud-
luscious the little
lame balloonman

whistles   far   and wee   5

and eddieandbill come
running from marbles and
piracies and it's
spring

when the world is puddle-wonderful   10

the queer
old balloonman whistles
far   and   wee
and bettyandisabel come dancing

from hop-scotch and jump-rope and   15
it's
spring
and
     the
          goat-footed   20

balloonMan   whistles
far
and
wee

ABOUT THE AUTHOR
E. E. Cummings (1894–1962) became known for poems that experimented with form, style, and punctuation. During his career, Cummings examined traditional themes such as love and childhood, but he explored these themes with innovative methods, such as incorporating typography into the poem's meaning, or using words such as *if* and *because* as nouns. His awards included the Bollingen Prize in Poetry (1958) and the Charles Eliot Norton Professorship at Harvard.

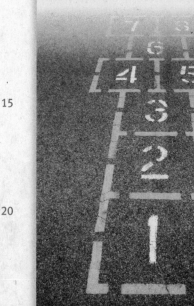

My Notes

Poetry

ABOUT THE AUTHOR

Peter Davison (1928–2004) was both a poet and an editor, serving as poetry editor of *The Atlantic Monthly* for 29 years. The author of 11 collections of poetry, Davison also wrote three prose works, including essays on poetry and the memoir *The Fading Smile*, which includes recollections of his mentor, poet Robert Frost. In his writing and editing, Davison emphasized the power of active language to engage with ideas and events: verbs, he said, not nouns, show what a writer really means.

The Last Word

by Peter Davison

When I saw your head bow, I knew I had beaten you.
You shed no tear—not near me—but held your neck
Bare for the blow I had been too frightened
Ever to deliver, even in words. And now,
5   In spite of me, plummeting it came.
Frozen we both waited for its fall.

Most of what you gave me I have forgotten
With my mind but taken into my body,
But this I remember well: the bones of your neck
10 And the strain in my shoulders as I heaved up that huge
Double blade and snapped my wrists to swing
The handle down and hear the axe's edge
Nick through your flesh and creak into the block.

LITERARY TERMS

Free verse is poetry without a fixed pattern of meter and rhyme. In contrast, **fixed form** is poetry in which the length and pattern are determined by established usage or tradition, such as a sonnet.

Mushrooms

by Sylvia Plath

Overnight, very
Whitely, discreetly,
Very quietly

Our toes, our noses
Take hold on the loam,   5
Acquire the air.

Nobody sees us,
Stops us, betrays us;
The small grains make room.

Soft fists insist on   10
Heaving the needles,
The leafy bedding,

Even the paving.
Our hammers, our rams,
Earless and eyeless,   15

Perfectly voiceless,
Widen the crannies,
Shoulder through holes. We

Diet on water,
On crumbs of shadow,   20
Bland-mannered, asking

Little or nothing.
So many of us!
So many of us!

We are shelves, we are   25
Tables, we are meek,
We are edible.

Nudgers and shovers
In spite of ourselves.
Our kind multiplies: 30

We shall by morning
Inherit the earth.
Our foot's in the door.

ABOUT THE AUTHOR
Sylvia Plath (1932–1963) captured the intensity of her turbulent life in an autobiographical novel and personal, revealing poetry. An accomplished scholar and writer, Plath won many awards as a young woman, including a scholarship to Smith College and a Fulbright fellowship to Newnham College in Cambridge University. In 1956, she married poet Ted Hughes. As their marriage dissolved, Plath produced poems of striking pain and power. These poems were published in the collection *Ariel* (1965), which appeared after her suicide in 1963.

Applying Reader Response Criticism

A **symbol** is something (a person, place, or thing) that stands for something else. A **symbolic representation** makes use of symbols to represent an idea or concept.

Use the following chart to sketch a symbolic representation of the poem you read in your small group. Your sketch should be in the form of a three-panel narrative.

Panel 1	Panel 2	Panel 3

Your Interpretation

Seeing the World from My Perspective

1. Select a memory of a place, event, or time in your life of significance to you, and brainstorm a list of images that this memory generates for you. Try to evoke all five senses in your list.

> **LITERARY TERMS**
> **Imagery** is the verbal expression of sensory experience. **Sensory details** are details that appeal to or evoke one or more of the five senses: sight, touch, smell, hearing, and taste.

2. **Free write** on the memory you have chosen, using *imagery* to convey all the *sensory details* that it evokes.

3. Expand on your writing by **looping**: circle key images in your free write above. Choose an image, and expand your ideas below by including sensory details to capture a vivid description of the image for your readers.

My Notes

Poetry

I Remember

by Edward Montez

From Calafia: The California Poetry Project
Ishmael Reed, Project Director

I remember the scent of acorn soup cooking and deer meat frying in quiet evenings of summer.

And shivering under thin blankets in winter and watching the wallpaper dance to the force of the winter winds outside.

I remember the cry of an owl in the night and I knew it was an ominous warning, a cry of death.

I remember running in the dust behind the medicine truck when it came to the reservation, lifesavers was a free treat.

And grandpa sitting in his favorite resting chair under his favorite shade tree with his dog "Oly" by his side.

I remember running naked and screaming with my aunt in hot pursuit, a stick in her hand, she always caught me.

And every summer we would swim in the river and let the sun bake us until we were a shade less than purple, basking on the riverbank, undisturbed, at peace.

And I remember grandma toiling in the bean fields while I played with my army truck on the fender of a "49" Plymouth.

I remember going to the movies in town on Saturday nights with fifty cents in my pocket, thirty-five cents for the ticket and the rest was mine.

Eating popcorn and drinking water from a discarded coke cup and rooting for the Indians to win, and they never did, but that was yesterday.

Analyzing Evidence of an Author's Perspective

Imagery: The imagery a writer uses can be key to the writer's perspective. Identify the language from Montez's poem that appeals to your senses, and complete the chart below.

Visual Images (sight)	Auditory Images (hearing)	Tactile Images (touch)	Olfactory Images (smell)	Gustatory Images (taste)

What effect is the author trying to convey with these images?

Detail: Details—such as specific facts, observations, and/or incidents—are also evidence of an author's perspective. Identify details from Montez' poem that reveal his perspective on his subject, and complete the chart below.

	Subject	Setting	Speaker
Identify specific details included in the poem "I Remember."			
Discuss how these details contribute to meaning and effect.			
What do these details reveal about each category?			

Seeing the World from My Perspective

Diction: The words an author uses, carefully chosen to evoke emotions and communicate ideas, also reveal perspective. Identify key examples of **diction**, the writer's choice of words, and examine the impact of those choices within the text and on the reader.

Key Word or Phrase	Feeling Evoked by Word or Phrase	Effect on the Meaning of the Sentence	Effect on the Reader

Writing Prompt: Revisit your initial free write about a memory from childhood, and revise your drafts to refine your use of imagery, diction, and detail. Annotate your drafts, identifying the stylistic techniques you used to create particular effects.

Novel

PROLOGUE

by Ralph Ellison

From **Invisible Man**

I am an invisible man. No, I am not a spook like those who haunted Edgar Allan Poe; nor am I one of your Hollywood-movie ectoplasms.[1] I am a man of substance, of flesh and bone, of fiber and liquids—and I might even be said to possess a mind. I am invisible, understand, simply because people refuse to see me. Like the bodiless heads you see sometimes in circus sideshows, it is as though I have been surrounded by mirrors of hard, distorting glass. When they approach me they see only my surroundings, themselves, or figments of their imagination—indeed, everything and anything except me.

Nor is my invisibility exactly a matter of a biochemical accident to my epidermis. That invisibility to which I refer occurs because of a peculiar disposition of the eyes of those with whom I come in contact. A matter of the construction of their inner eyes, those eyes with which they look through their physical eyes upon reality. I am not complaining, nor am I protesting either. It is sometimes advantageous to be unseen, although it is most often rather wearing on the nerves. Then too, you're constantly being bumped against by those of poor vision. Or again, you often doubt if you really exist. You wonder whether you aren't simply a phantom in other people's minds. Say, a figure in a nightmare which the sleeper tries with all his strength to destroy. It's when you feel like this that, out of resentment, you begin to bump people back.

And, let me confess, you feel that way most of the time. You ache with the need to convince yourself that you do exist in the real world, that you're a part of all the sound and the anguish, and you strike out with your fists, you curse and you swear to make them recognize you. And, alas, it's seldom successful.

My Notes

LITERARY TERMS

A **prologue** is the introduction or preface to a literary work.

WORD CONNECTIONS

Ectoplasms contains the Greek root *ecto-*, meaning "outside." This root also appears in other scientific words such as *ectoderm* and *ectothermal*. It also contains the Greek suffix *–plasm*, which refers to the formative part of an animal or vegetable cell. You have probably noticed this suffix in other words such as *protoplasm*.

---

[1] **ectoplasms:** spiritual energy associated with the formation of ghosts

Another Perspective on the World

GRAMMAR & USAGE

Good writing includes variety in sentence length. A series of sentences of more or less the same length becomes monotonous and boring. Such sentences may also lack clarity, failing to show relationships and the progression from one idea to the next. Notice the difference in length between the last two sentences in the Prologue to *Invisible Man*. Consider also the way Ellison conveys relationships among the ideas within the longer sentence (a **compound-complex** sentence) as well as between the two sentences.

ABOUT THE AUTHOR

Though Ralph Ellison's (1914–1994) novelistic output was small, its influence was huge. Ellison is best known for his novel *Invisible Man* (1952). In his masterpiece, an unnamed narrator struggles against racism and urban alienation to find an identity. Ellison employs an all-embracing style—combining elements of African-American folklore, Native American mythology, and classical allusions—which he likened to a jazz musician's improvisation on traditional themes. Though Ellison detested being labeled a black writer, he accepted the label *minority writer*, because, as he put it, "the individual is a minority."

Sketch Images: Review the sketches you made to capture the images and/or ideas in Ellison's Prologue. Refine and arrange them to capture the essence of Ellison's Prologue in the space below or on separate paper.

Using the following model of the structure of Ellison's Prologue, describe your perception of yourself.

I am _____.

No, I am not _____; nor am I

_____.

I am _____,

and _____ —and I

might even be said to

_____.

Quickwrite: Elaborate on the self-perception you presented above, explaining it to your readers.

Another Perspective on the World

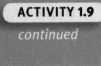

PUNCTUATION: improves clarity, reinforces meaning, constructs effect, and expresses the writer's voice

Punctuation: Purpose and Function	Examining the Craft of a Model Sentence:	Revising Your Sentence
The **dash** marks a sudden change in thought or tone, sets off a brief summary, or sets off a parenthetical part of the sentence. A dash often conveys a casual tone.	Find a sentence using a dash from Ellison's prologue and explain how he has used the dash and how it conveys tone.	Revise a sentence from your quickwrite or create a new sentence that uses a dash similar to the model sentence studied.
The **semicolon** gives equal weight to two or more independent clauses in a sentence. The syntactical balance reinforces parallel ideas and imparts equal importance to the clauses.	Find a sentence using a semi-colon from Ellison's prologue and explain how it conveys tone.	Revise a different sentence from your quickwrite or create a new sentence using a semicolon similar to the model sentence studied.

SYNTAX: the way words are arranged to form phrases, clauses, and sentences

Elements of Syntax: Purpose and Function	Examining the Craft of a Model Sentence	Revising Your Sentence
Sentence Pattern : A **periodic sentence** is one that makes sense only when the end of the sentence is reached: e.g., After a drenching rainstorm that started off as overcast and a light drizzle, the sun came out and warmed us.	Identify a periodic sentence. Explain how it is used to advance the tone or theme of the text. How does the punctuation add to the voice?	Revise a sentence from your quickwrite or create a new periodic sentence emulating the model sentence.
Sentence Pattern: A **complex sentence** contains one independent clause and one or more subordinate clauses.	Identify a complex sentence. Explain its function in the prologue and how is it used to advance the tone or theme of the text.	Revise a sentence from your quickwrite or create a new complex sentence emulating the model sentence studied.
Sentence Pattern: A **parallel structure** uses the same pattern of words to show that two or more ideas have the same level of importance.	Identify a sentence with parallel structure. Explain its function and how it advances the tone or theme of the text.	Revise a sentence from your quickwrite or create a new sentence with parallel structure, emulating the model sentence studied.

Another Perspective on the World

Writing Prompt: Use the space below to revisit your quickwrite and revise it to emulate Ellison's style.

Create a visual representation of your self-perception. Consider your *mise en scène* and arrange images strategically to enhance ideas presented in your text.

Writing Prompt: Now that you have visual images representing yourself, write an essay that you might use as a college application describing yourself, your preparation for college, and your goals. Include convincing reasons why the college should accept you as a student. Remember to include relevant questions or other techniques to engage your readers and address their potential misunderstandings or problems with your application. Use word processing software, and format your essay appropriately through your choice of typefaces, use of boldface, use of white space, and headings if appropriate.

A Symbolic Perception of Self

SUGGESTED LEARNING STRATEGIES: **Visualizing, Brainstorming, Marking the Text, Think-Pair-Share, Drafting, Self-Editing/Peer Editing**

Novel

ABOUT THE AUTHOR

Born in the Chicago barrio in 1954, Cisneros was the only daughter in a family of seven children. Although she was expected to assume a traditional female role in her patriarchal, Mexican-American household, Cisneros successfully struggled to articulate the experience of a Latina woman, publishing the poetry collection *Bad Boys* (1980) and then gaining international acclaim with her first work of fiction, *The House on Mango Street* (1983). A graduate of Loyola University and the University of Iowa Writers' Workshop, Cisneros has received fellowships from the National Endowment for the Arts and the MacArthur Foundation.

The following passage is a *vignette* from *The House on Mango Street*.

Four Skinny Trees

by Sandra Cisneros

They are the only ones who understand me. I am the only one who understands them. Four skinny trees with skinny necks and pointy elbows like mine. Four who do not belong here but are here. Four raggedy excuses planted by the city. From our room we can hear them, but Nenny just sleeps and doesn't appreciate these things.

Their strength is secret. They send ferocious roots beneath the ground. They grow up and they grow down and grab the earth between their hairy toes and bite the sky with violent teeth and never quit their anger. This is how they keep.

Let one forget his reason for being, they'd all droop like tulips in a glass, each with their arms around the other. Keep, keep, keep, trees say when I sleep. They teach.

When I am too sad and too skinny to keep keeping, when I am a tiny thing against so many bricks, then it is I look at trees. When there is nothing left to look at on this street. Four who grew despite concrete. Four who reach and do not forget to reach. Four whose only reason is to be and be.

My Notes

LITERARY TERMS

A **vignette** is a brief visual or written descriptive literary sketch.

GRAMMAR & USAGE

For many years you have studied the difference between complete sentences and sentence fragments. The accidental sentence fragment usually creates problems for the reader because such a fragment is missing an important element. However, good writers may use sentence fragments rhetorically, to create effective, even eloquent, phrasing. Notice the sentence fragments beginning with the word "Four" in the first paragraph of this passage. These fragments also demonstrate effective use of parallel structure, repeating the same form or structure to express an idea.

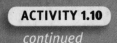
A Symbolic Perception of Self

A Visual Vignette: Create a visual below that represents a symbolic understanding of Cisneros's vignette.

Writing Prompt: Write a literary vignette exploring the memory represented by the photo you brought to class. Then transform your vignette into a free verse poem.

Exploring Perspectives in Visual Art

SUGGESTED LEARNING STRATEGIES: Discussion Groups, Drafting. Activating Prior Knowledge, Graphic Organizer

Shots and Framing

Shot: a single piece of film uninterrupted by cuts.

Establishing Shot: often a long shot or a series of shots that sets the scene. It establishes setting and shows transitions between locations.

Long Shot (LS): a shot from some distance. If filming a person, the full body is shown. It may show the isolation or vulnerability of the character (also called a Full Shot).

Medium Shot (MS): the most common shot. The camera seems to be a medium distance from the object being filmed. A medium shot shows the person from the waist up. The effect is to ground the story.

Close Up (CU): the image takes up at least 80 percent of the frame.

Extreme Close Up: the image is a part of a whole, such as an eye.

Two Shot: a scene between two people shot exclusively from an angle that includes both characters more or less equally. It is used in love scenes where interaction between the two characters is important.

Camera Angles

Eye Level: a shot taken from a normal height; that is, the character's eye level. Ninety to ninety-five percent of the shots seen are eye level, because it is the most natural angle.

High Angle: a shot taken from above the subject. This angle usually has the effect of making the subject look smaller than normal, giving him or her the appearance of being weak, powerless, and trapped.

Low Angle: a shot taken from below the subject. Can make the subject look larger than normal and thus strong, powerful, and threatening.

Lighting

High Key: the scene is flooded with light, creating a bright and open-looking scene.

Low Key: the scene is flooded with shadows and darkness, creating suspense or suspicion.

Bottom or Side Lighting: direct lighting from below or the side, which often makes the subject appear dangerous or evil.

Front or Back Lighting: soft lighting on the actor's face or from behind gives the appearance of innocence or goodness, or a halo effect.

Exploring Perspectives in Visual Art

Analyze the print ad provided, using the OPTIC strategy as outlined below.

Overview:

Parts:

Text/Title:

Interrelationship:

Conclusion:

Working in small groups, use the graphic organizer to continue your discussion and analysis of the print ad. Be sure to incorporate the vocabulary acquired in the unit thus far (e.g., cinematic techniques, OPTIC, rhetoric of photography) to explain with detail the purpose, intent, and effect of the techniques used.

Cinematic Choices Made by the Artistic Director	Effect of Those Choices on the Viewer
Framing: Long, Short, Close Up, Extreme Close Up Shot	
Angle: Eye Level, High, Low Angles	
Strategic Placement of Objects and/or Objects Used as Symbols	

Exploring a Photo Essay

> **LITERARY TERMS**
>
> A **thesis** is the main idea or point of an essay or article.

An essay is an interpretive or analytic composition that reveals the author's perspective on a subject. A *photo essay* reveals the author's perspective on the subject through a collection of photographic images. Just as the words and sentences in a written essay are placed in a specific order, so are the images in a photo essay placed in a specific order to express ideas, convey emotions, and show a progression of thoughts or events.

Analyzing a Photo Essay

As your teacher directs, focus on the following topics as you "read" and analyze a photo essay:

1. Title
2. Sequence of images
3. Content of photographs
4. Captions

Next, consider how you would use the three elements of Reader Response Criticism theory to think about the impact of the photo essay.

After your initial analysis, revisit the photo essay and make interpretations based on your inferences.

1. What issues are presented in the photo essay, and what is the author's position on the issues?

2. What is the purpose of this photo essay?

3. Who is the target audience for this photo essay?

4. How do the images tell a story or progression of events to reveal a particular position?

5. What is your interpretation of the photo essay? Discuss how the composition and arrangement of the photos lead to your interpretation.

Digging for Deeper Meaning

SUGGESTED LEARNING STRATEGIES: **Marking the Text, Discussion Groups, Metacognitive Markers, Diffusing, Close Reading, Graphic Organizer, TWIST, SIFT**

During Reading

Think about the writer's attitude or point of view toward England as revealed in this essay. After reading, you will respond to a writing prompt about her point of view.

Essay

> **ABOUT THE AUTHOR**
> Jamaica Kincaid was born Elaine Potter Richardson in 1949 on the Caribbean island of Antigua. She was a precocious child and a voracious reader. At seventeen, disillusioned by her family's lack of support for her talents, Kincaid moved to New York and later became a staff writer for *The New Yorker*. By 1985, writing under her chosen name, she had earned acclaim for two books: *At the Bottom of the River*, a book of short stories, and *Annie John*, a semi-autobiographical novel. Through deceptively simple and often bitter prose, Kincaid's best-known writings detail the rhythms of everyday life in Antigua.

From

On Seeing England *for* the First Time

by Jamaica Kincaid

When I saw England for the first time, I was a child in school sitting at a desk. The England I was looking at was laid out on a map gently, beautifully, delicately, a very special jewel: it lay on a bed of sky blue—the background of the map—its yellow form mysterious, because though it looked like a leg of mutton, it could not really look like anything so familiar as a leg of mutton[1] because it was England—with shadings of

Chunk 1

[1] **mutton:** the meat of domestic sheep

My Notes

My Notes

GRAMMAR & USAGE

Clauses are groups of words that contain a subject and verb. While dependent clauses cannot stand alone—do not make sense by themselves— independent clauses do. Notice this sentence from Kincaid's essay: "My father, who might have sat next to me at breakfast, was a carpenter and cabinet maker." The dependent clause "who might have sat next to me at breakfast" is an **adjective clause** that modifies the word "father." Notice that the dependent clause is set off by commas because it is not essential to identify *father*. We know who *father* is without this information. A sentence with both an independent clause and a dependent clause is a **complex sentence**. The use of complex sentences enables writers to create sentence variety and establish relationships among ideas.

pink and green, unlike any shadings of pink and green I had seen before, squiggly veins of red running in every direction. England was a special jewel all right, and only special people got to wear it. The people who got to wear England were English people. They wore it well and they wore it everywhere: in jungles, in deserts, on plains, on top of the highest mountains, on all the oceans, on all the seas, in places where they were not welcome, in places they should not have been. When my teacher had pinned this map up on the blackboard, she said, "This is England"—and she said it with authority, seriousness, and adoration, and we all sat up. It was as if she had said, "This is Jerusalem, the place you will go to when you die but only if you have been good." We understood then—we were meant to understand then—that England was to be our source of myth and the source from which we got our sense of reality, our sense of what was meaningful, our sense of what was meaningless—and much about own lives and much about the very idea of us headed that last list.

Chunk 2

At the time I was a child sitting at my desk seeing England for the first time, I was already very familiar with the greatness of it. Each morning before I left for school, I ate breakfast of half a grapefruit, an egg, bread and butter and a slice of cheese, and a cup of cocoa; or half a grapefruit, a bowl of oat porridge, bread and butter and a slice of cheese, and a cup of cocoa. The can of cocoa was often left on the table in front of me. It had written on it the name of the company, the year the company was established, and the words "Made in England." Those words, "Made in England," were written on the box the oats came in too. They would also have been written on the box the shoes I was wearing came in: a bolt of gray linen cloth lying on the shelf of a store from which my mother had bought three yards to make the uniform that I was wearing had written along its edge those three words. The shoes I wore were made in England; so were my socks and cotton undergarments and the satin ribbons I wore tied at the end of two plaits of my hair. My father, who might have sat next to me at breakfast, was a carpenter and cabinet maker. The shoes he wore to work would have been made in England, as were his khaki shirt and brown felt hat. Felt was not the proper material from which a hat that was expected to provide shade from the hot sun should be made, but my father must have seen and admired a picture of an Englishman wearing such a hat in England, and this picture that he saw must have been so compelling that it caused him to wear the wrong hat for a hot climate most of his long life. And this hat—a brown felt hat—became so central to his character that it was the first thing he put on in the morning as he stepped out of bed and the last thing he took off before he stepped back into bed at night. As we sat at breakfast a car might go by. The car, a Hillman or a Zepher, was made in England. The very idea of the meal itself, breakfast, and its substantial quality and quantity was an idea from England; we somehow knew that in England they began the day with this meal called breakfast and a proper breakfast was a big breakfast. No one I knew liked eating so much food so early in the day: it made us feel sleepy, tired. But this breakfast business was Made in England like almost everything else that surrounded us, the exceptions being the sea, the sky, and the air we breathed.

At the time I saw this map—seeing England for the first time—I did not say to myself. "Ah, so that's what it looks like." Because there was no longing in me to put a shape to those three words that ran through every part of my life, no matter how small; for me to have had such a longing would have meant that I lived in a certain atmosphere, an atmosphere in which those three words were felt as a burden. But I did not live in such an atmosphere. My father's brown felt hat would develop a hole in its crown, the lining would separate from the hat itself, and six weeks before he thought that he could not be seen wearing it—he was a very vain man—he would order another hat from England. And my mother taught me to eat my food in the English way: the knife in the right hand, the fork in the left, my elbows held still close to my side, the food carefully balanced on my fork and then brought up to my mouth. When I had finally mastered it, I overheard her saying to a friend, "Did you see how nicely she can eat?" But I knew then that I enjoyed my food more when I ate it with my bare hands, and I continued to do so when she wasn't looking. And when my teacher showed us the map, she asked us to study it carefully, because no test we would ever take would be complete without this statement: "Draw a map of England."

I did not know then that the statement "Draw a map of England" was something far worse than a declaration of war, for in fact a flat-out declaration of war would have put me on alert, and again in fact, there was no need for war—I had long ago been conquered. I did not know then that this statement was part of a process that would result in my erasure, not my physical erasure, but my erasure all the same. I did not know then that this statement was meant to make me feel in awe and small whenever I heard the word "England": awe at its existence, small because I was not from it. I did not know very much of anything then—certainly not what a blessing it was that I was unable to draw a map of England correctly.

Writing Prompt: Write an essay analyzing the author's point of view about England. Write a thesis statement and support your position with details about the author's use of stylistic or rhetorical devices (e.g., diction, imagery, figurative language, tone, symbolism) to convey theme. Identify and analyze the aesthetic effects of Kincaid's use of ambiguities, nuances, and complexities in her essay and their effect in conveying meaning to the reader. Be sure to structure your essay to include appropriate embedded quotations and commentary on how the quotations support your analysis.

Chunk 3

My Notes

Digging for Deeper Meaning

Plan for a Mock Photo Essay
Based on a Thesis About "On First Seeing England"

Thesis:		
Idea for Image 1	**Idea for Image 2**	**Idea for Image 3**
Rationale for Image 1	**Rationale for Image 2**	**Rationale for Image 3**
Image 4	**Image 5**	**Image 6**
Rationale for Image 4	**Rationale for Image 5**	**Rationale for Image 6**
Ideas for Title and Captions		

Creating a Photo Essay

SUGGESTED LEARNING STRATEGIES: Free Writing,
Self-Editing/Peer Editing, Sketching, Sharing and
Responding, Graphic Organizer

Assignment

Your assignment is to create and present a photo essay revealing your
perspective (position) about an issue or topic of importance to you.

Steps

1. Select a topic of interest to you, and then free write and loop to explore
   your position on the issue. If necessary, conduct research to deepen your
   knowledge of the issue. As you plan your photo essay, consider how you
   might use it as a proposal to solicit action on the issue or as support for a
   college application.

2. Generate a working thesis that clearly identifies the issue and your
   position. Use peer response to refine your thesis into a concise
   statement.

3. Use the graphic organizer on page 41 to plan the evidence you will use
   to assert and support your thesis before presenting your position on the
   issue.

   ▶ Generate ideas to support the thesis.

   ▶ Sketch your proposed photo images (at least ten).

   ▶ Include notes about film techniques (shots, angles, *mise en scène*) you
   want to use in your photos.

   ▶ Write a rationale to explain the connection between each proposed
   photograph and your thesis. Format your thesis and rationales with
   headings related to each photo. You will include the final document as
   part of your photo essay.

4. Work collaboratively to plan the layout and format of the photo essay
   so that it advances your argument visually. Anticipate potential
   misunderstandings or problems your readers or viewers may have, and
   include headings or relevant questions that engage readers/viewers and
   address their potential misunderstandings or problems.

5. Plan the process you will use to create appropriate photos for your essay.
   Before you take the photographs, identify the following:

   ▶ The format of the photos.

   ▶ Any resources you will need—equipment, staging, scene
   development, etc.

   ▶ The process for film or digital prints as needed.

   ▶ A schedule for creating the photos and the essay.

6. Once you have your photos in hand, review your original organizational plan. Select and organize your photos to introduce your thesis, provide supporting evidence and details, and provide a conclusion. When citing technical evidence and details to support your position, remember to present them accurately and in language that is accessible and appropriate for your audience.

7. Share the draft layout of your photo essay with your peers and make necessary revisions to ensure clarity of ideas, a clear focus on the thesis, and the support of that thesis. If needed, add brief captions to clarify your argument for your viewers.

8. Next, generate a list of potential titles; select the one that best captures the essence of your photo essay.

9. Assemble your final photo essay. Be sure to include these elements:
   ▶ A captivating title.
   ▶ A numbered arrangement of photos that corresponds to the numbers on the graphic organizer.
   ▶ Your graphic organizer with thesis, description of supporting evidence, and rationale attached to the back of your photo essay.

10. Review the Scoring Guide on page 43. Use that guide to review your photo essay and make sure you have created a strong presentation.

11. On the day of the presentation, you will participate in a gallery walk during which you will use sticky notes to evaluate other photo essays. As you evaluate the essays created by other students, you should attempt to identify the unstated thesis represented in each essay.

12. After your presentation, write a reflection in which you consider the reactions of your classmates in relation to your original intent. Consider the elements of Reader Response Criticism and include any insights you have about how these elements might affect your classmates' responses. Finally, discuss any changes you would make if you were to do this project again.

Planning Your Photo Essay

Use this graphic organizer to develop a plan for your photo essay. First, write the thesis that you refined in Step 2. Then list the supporting ideas you have generated. For each supporting idea, write a description or draw a sketch of the image you think would communicate or represent that idea. Write a rationale explaining how each image helps support the thesis. You must have at least 10 photos.

Thesis Statement:

Supporting Idea	Description/Sketch	Rationale

Supporting Idea	Description/Sketch	Rationale
Conclusion		

SCORING GUIDE

Scoring Criteria	Exemplary	Proficient	Emerging
Ideas	At least 10 photo images expertly convey and support the essay's thesis. Titles and captions creatively convey a clear perspective on the issue. The thesis and rationale graphic organizer is thorough.	At least 10 photo images convey the essay's thesis. Titles and captions communicate a clear perspective on the issue. The thesis and rationale graphic organizer is complete.	Fewer than 10 photo images attempt to convey the essay's thesis. At times the thesis may be unclear. If used, titles and captions do little to provide a clear perspective on the issue. The thesis and rationale graphic organizer is incomplete.
Organization	The layout and design of the essay serve to expertly advance the argument and reflect thoughtful planning.	The layout and design of the essay are appropriate for the argument and reflect adequate planning.	The layout and design of the essay attempts, but does little, to enhance the argument and/or reflect advance thought or planning.
Cinematic Techniques	The photographs skillfully use a variety of media production elements that vividly reveal the image's purpose in connection to the argument.	The photographs adequately use a variety of media production elements that help to reveal the image's purpose in connection to the argument.	The photographs attempt to use a variety of media production elements; however, the purpose of the image in connection to the argument is unclear at times.
Reflection	The reflective text demonstrates a thorough and detailed analysis of the audience's reactions to the photo essay in relation to its original intent and Reader Response Criticism. The reflection includes insightful commentary on potential revisions.	The reflective text demonstrates an adequate analysis of the audience's reactions to the photo essay in relation to its original intent and Reader Response Criticism. The reflection includes clear commentary on potential revisions.	The reflective text demonstrates an inadequate analysis of the audience's reactions to the photo essay in relation to its original intent and in relation to Reader Response Criticism. Commentary on potential revisions is weak or missing.
Additional Criteria			

Comments:

Learning Focus:

Perspective and Culture

Reader Response Criticism puts you, the reader, and your experiences, biases, values, and attitudes as the central factor in your interpretation of what you read and see. This subjective perspective is the starting point for interpreting literature. In order to increase your field of vision or perspective, try seeing and understanding from another perspective. Experience with other points of view or perspectives can help you see things more objectively. The more you move from a strictly subjective point of view, the more objective you can be about your interpretation and understanding of texts and events.

Cultural Criticism examines how differing religious beliefs, ethnicities, class identifications, political beliefs, and individual viewpoints affect how texts are created and interpreted. This critical perspective asks you to examine texts by focusing on how language and culture shape identity and experience.

With this perspective you can begin to understand how culture and language work to include and exclude individuals. This perspective seeks to illuminate the relationship between the individual and the group, between the stranger and the village, and between the dominant culture and the subordinate culture.

Reflecting about yourself within a cultural context helps you gain an awareness of self as the alien, stranger, outsider or as the insider, member, or villager. Such reflection allows you to broaden your perspective to include a consciousness of self within a community.

What Is Cultural Criticism?

SUGGESTED LEARNING STRATEGIES: Discussion Groups, Rereading, Questioning the Text, Oral Interpretation, Quickwrite

Cultural Criticism

Cultural Criticism is another critical lens through which any text can be viewed. This form of criticism examines how different religions, ethnicities, class identifications, political beliefs, and views affect the ways in which texts are created and interpreted. Cultural Criticism suggests that being a part of—or excluded from—a specific group or culture contributes to and affects our understanding of texts.

The following statements reflect four common assumptions in the use of Cultural Criticism as a lens for understanding literature.

1. Ethnicity, religious beliefs, social class, and so on are crucial components in formulating plausible interpretations of text.

2. While the emphasis is on diversity of approach and subject matter, Cultural Criticism is not the only means of understanding ourselves and our art.

3. An examination or exploration of the relationship between dominant cultures and the dominated is essential.

4. When looking at a text through the perspective of marginalized peoples, new understandings emerge.

Since Cultural Criticism examines texts from the position of those individuals who are in some way marginalized or not part of the dominant culture, studying the following poem by Luis Rodriguez will provide insights on this perspective.

> **ACADEMIC VOCABULARY**
>
> **Cultural Criticism** focuses on the elements of culture and how they affect one's perceptions and understanding of texts.

> **WORD CONNECTIONS**
>
> To **marginalize** is relegate or confine to a lower or outer limit (as in social standing).

My Notes

Poetry

> **ABOUT THE AUTHOR**
> An award-winning poet, journalist, and critic, Luis J. Rodriguez was born on the U.S./Mexico border, but grew up in the Watts neighborhood of Los Angeles. As a youth, he joined a gang to gain a sense of belonging and protection, but he found salvation in the Chicano movement and in literature. In prose works like *Always Running: La Vida Loca, Gang Days in L.A.,* and poetry collections like *The Concrete River,* Rodriguez deals with the struggle to survive in a chaotic urban setting.

SPEAKING WITH HANDS

by Luis Rodriguez

There were no markets in Watts.
There were these small corner stores
we called *marketas*
who charged more money
5   for cheaper goods than what existed
in other parts of town.

The owners were often thieves in white coats
who talked to you like animals,
who knew you had no options;
10   who knew Watts was the preferred landfill
of the city.

One time, Mama started an argument
at the cash register.
In her broken English,
speaking with her hands,   15
she had us children stand around her
as she fought with the grocer
on prices & quality & dignity.

Mama became a woman swept
by a sobering madness;   20
she must have been what Moses saw
in the burning bush,
a pillar of fire
consuming the still air
that reeked of overripe fruit   25
and bad meat from the frozen food
section.

She refused to leave
until the owner called the police.
The police came and argued too,   30
but Mama wouldn't stop.
They pulled her into the parking lot,
called her crazy…
and then Mama showed them crazy!

They didn't know what to do   35
but let her go, and Mama took us children
back toward home, tired of being tired.

Quickwrite: Use the elements listed as part of the definition of
Cultural Criticism to write about how this lens or perspective might
help you interpret this text.

Poetic Conversations

SUGGESTED LEARNING STRATEGIES: Graphic Organizer, Predicting, Discussion Groups, Questioning the Text, Quickwrite, SOAPSTone

Use the graphic organizer below to explore the concept of "imperialism."

Paraphrase, or briefly restate in your own words, each definition.

1. the policy of extending the rule or influence of a country over other countries or colonies

2. the political, military, or economic domination of one country over another

Explore connections to the concept of imperialism.

Other Concepts:

Other Ideas:

Other Texts:

Self:

Imperialism

List at least two examples of imperialism.

List at least two non-examples of imperialism.

In order to better understand Cultural Criticism, you will examine two poems. The first poem, by Rudyard Kipling, affirms the concept of imperialism. In contrast, Henry Labouchère's poem, written in response shortly after Kipling's poem was published, questions imperialism. As you read and discuss the two poems, note how the perspective of the speaker, the imaginary voice of the author, influences what the speaker has to say about the concepts of "imperialism" and/or "colonialism."

Poetry

> **ABOUT THE AUTHOR**
> Rudyard Kipling was a British author known for his support of British colonialism and imperialism. Born in Bombay (now Mumbai), India, in 1865, Kipling was educated in England; but he returned to India where he worked for seven years as a journalist. Kipling's poems, novels, and short stories reflect the Anglo-Indian experience. Kipling was awarded the Nobel Prize for Literature in 1907. His children's books, including *Just So Stories* (1902) and *Kim* (1901) are considered classics.

THE WHITE MAN'S BURDEN

by Rudyard Kipling
MCCLURE'S MAGAZINE (12 FEB. 1899)

Take up the White Man's burden—
Send forth the best ye breed—
Go bind your sons to exile
To serve your captives' need;
To wait, in heavy harness,   5
On fluttered folk and wild—
Your new-caught sullen[1] peoples,
Half devil and half child.

Take up the White Man's burden—
In patience to abide,   10
To veil the threat of terror
And check the show of pride;
By open speech and simple,
An hundred times made plain,
To seek another's profit,   15
And work another's gain.

---
[1] **sullen**: moody; sulky

My Notes

Take up the White Man's burden—
The savage wars of peace—
Fill full the mouth of Famine,
20   And bid the sickness cease;
And when your goal is nearest
(The end for others sought)
Watch sloth[2] and heathen[3] Folly
Bring all your hope to naught.

25   Take up the White Man's burden—
No tawdry[4] rule of kings,
But toil of serf and sweeper—
The tale of common things.
The ports ye shall not enter,
30   The roads ye shall not tread,
Go mark them with your living,
And mark them with your dead.

Take up the White Man's burden—
And reap his old reward:
35   The blame of those ye better,
The hate of those ye guard—
The cry of hosts ye humour
(Ah, slowly!) toward the light:—
"Why brought ye us from bondage,
40   Our loved Egyptian night?"

Take up the White Man's burden—
Ye dare not stoop to less—
Nor call too loud on Freedom
To cloak your weariness;
45   By all ye will or whisper,
By all ye leave or do,
The silent, sullen peoples
Shall weigh your God and you.

Take up the White Man's burden!
50   Have done with childish days—
The lightly proffered laurel,[5]
The easy, ungrudged praise:
Comes now, to search your manhood
Through all the thankless years
55   Cold, edged with dear-bought wisdom,
The judgment of your peers!

---

[2] **sloth:** laziness
[3] **heathen:** godless
[4] **tawdry:** flashy
[5] **laurel:** honor

THE BROWN MAN'S BURDEN

by Henry Labouchère
TRUTH (LONDON, FEB. 25, 1899)

> **ABOUT THE AUTHOR**
> A journalist and politician, Henry Du Pré Labouchère (1831–1912) gained notoriety for his wartime dispatches from Paris. From the city besieged during the Franco-Prussian War (1870–1871), Labouchère sent reports by balloon, which later were published in the London *Daily News*. He founded the newspaper *Truth* (1877), which exposed fraud and corruption. Labouchère also served in the British House of Commons.

Pile on the brown man's burden
To gratify your greed;
Go, clear away the "niggers"
Who progress would impede;
Be very stern, for truly   5
'Tis useless to be mild
With new-caught, sullen peoples,
Half devil and half child.

Pile on the brown man's burden;
And, if ye rouse his hate,   10
Meet his old-fashioned reasons
With Maxims[1] up to date.
With shells and dumdum bullets[2]
A hundred times made plain
The brown man's loss must ever   15
Imply the white man's gain.

Pile on the brown man's burden,
compel him to be free;
Let all your manifestoes[3]
Reek with philanthropy[4].   20
And if with heathen folly
He dares your will dispute,
Then, in the name of freedom,
Don't hesitate to shoot.

---

[1] **maxims**: aphorisms; sayings
[2] **dumdum bullets**: bullets that expand on impact
[3] **manifestoes**: declarations
[4] **philanthropy**: charity

LITERARY TERMS
A **parody** is a literary or artistic work that imitates the characteristic style of an author or a work for comic effect or ridicule.

My Notes

WORD CONNECTIONS
Philanthropy derives from the Greek words *phil-* and *anthropos*, meaning "loving mankind." Other words that include *phil-* are *philology* and *philosopher*.

Poetic Conversations

25 Pile on the brown man's burden,
    And if his cry be sore,
    That surely need not irk you—
    Ye've driven slaves before.
    Seize on his ports and pastures,
30 The fields his people tread;
    Go make from them your living,
    And mark them with your dead.

    Pile on the brown man's burden,
    Nor do not deem it hard
35 If you should earn the rancor[5]
    Of those ye yearn to guard.
    The screaming of your Eagle
    Will drown the victim's sob—
    Go on through fire and slaughter.
40 There's dollars in the job.

    Pile on the brown man's burden,
    And through the world proclaim
    That ye are Freedom's agent—
    There's no more paying game!
45 And, should your own past history
    Straight in your teeth be thrown,
    Retort that independence
    Is good for whites alone.

    Pile on the brown man's burden,
50 With equity have done;
    Weak, antiquated scruples[6]
    Their squeamish course have run,
    And, though 'tis freedom's banner
    You're waving in the van[7],
55 Reserve for home consumption
    The sacred "rights of man"!

    And if by chance ye falter,
    Or lag along the course,
    If, as the blood flows freely,
60 Ye feel some slight remorse,
    Hie ye to Rudyard Kipling,
    Imperialism's prop,
    And bid him, for your comfort,
    Turn on his jingo[8] stop.

---

[5] **rancor**: hatred
[6] **scruples**: ethical or moral principles
[7] **van**: forefront
[8] **jingo**: aggressively patriotic

LITERARY TERMS

Satire is a manner of writing that mixes a critical attitude with wit and humor in an effort to improve mankind and human institutions. Satire often uses exaggeration and parody to create its effect.

Questions for Consideration in Socratic Seminars

1. In what ways does the speaker in Kipling's poem affirm or refute the concepts of "colonialism" and "imperialism"? Who is his audience?

2. Why is the speaker's attitude in Labouchère's poem so different from the speaker's attitude in Kipling's poem?

3. In what ways does Labouchère's poem respond to Kipling's poem? How is satire an effective weapon against the self-righteous imperialism of "The White Man's Burden"?

4. What understanding of these poems emerges as you apply the perspective of Cultural Criticism? Who is dominant, and who is marginalized or subordinated?

5. What new insights about these poems emerge as you apply Reader Response Theory?

Other Questions for Socratic Seminar:

Writing Prompt: Choose one of the poems and write about how the Cultural Criticism perspective adds to a broader understanding of the writer's intended or perhaps unintended impact of his poem. Be sure to use a variety of grammatical structures and sentence types and lengths in your response.

Imperialism

Know	Want to Know	How I Will Learn It	Learning...

Rule Britannia!

by James Thomson and Thomas Augustine Arne

When Britain first at Heav'n's command,
Arose from out the azure main,
Arose, arose, arose from out the azure main[1],
This was the charter,
The charter of the land,   5
And guardian angels sang this strain:

(Chorus)
Rule, Britannia! Britannia, rule the waves!
Britons never, never, never shall be slaves.

The nations not so blessed as thee,
Must in their turn, to tyrants fall,
Must in their turn, to tyrants fall,   10
While thou shalt flourish, shalt flourish great and free,
The dread and envy of them all.

(Chorus)
Still more majestic shalt thou rise,
More dreadful from each foreign stroke,   15
More dreadful from each foreign stroke,
As the loud blast that, loud blast that tears the skies,
Serves but to root thy native oak.

(Chorus)

Questions for Consideration

1. What does this song reveal about the attitude of the British toward Britain and the rest of the world when the song was chosen as the national anthem?

2. How might someone who came from one of the countries colonized by Britain view these lyrics?

---

[1] **azure main**: blue ocean

My Notes

A Deeper Understanding of Imperialism

PREVIEWING AND CONNECTING

Life experiences often have a significant influence on a writer's ideas and perception of events. In the next activity, you will be studying George Orwell's essay, "Shooting an Elephant." You will examine the essay from a Cultural Criticism lens in relation to the topic of imperialism. To prepare for that reading, it will be helpful to consider the title of the essay and a few details about the writer's life.

Details about Orwell's Life

- George Orwell (1903–1950), British citizen, was born in colonial India but educated in England.
- He served with the Imperial Police in Burma.
- He became a journalist.
- He was admired for conveying the truth about political events around the world.

Questions

1. How does Orwell's experience appear to relate to the topic of imperialism?

2. Based upon what you know, including the title of the essay, what do you think Orwell's point of view would be—affirming imperialism or refuting it?

3. What would you like to discover as you read the essay?

Organizational Structure of a Reflective Essay

You are about to read George Orwell's "Shooting an Elephant,"
a reflective essay. Most reflective essays are structured in similar
ways, including three parts that are threaded throughout the piece.

Event or Incident: The author describes some incident or set of
circumstances.

Response: The author describes his or her feelings and thoughts
concerning the encounter. This response describes initial reactions
without the benefit of reflection.

Reflection: The author reflects on the incident. This reflection usually
occurs some time after the event or incident. In the reflection, the
author will often transition from describing a situation unique to him
or her to a discussion more universal in nature.

As you read this essay, use a highlighter to identify the various parts
(Event, Response, Reflection) of Orwell's reflective essay that you have
been assigned to track.

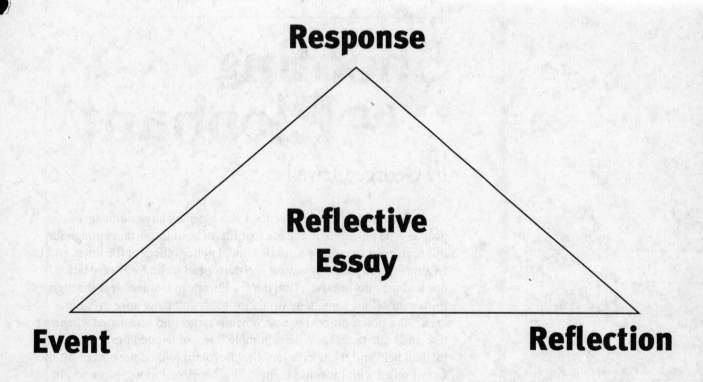

My Notes

Reflective Essay

> **ABOUT THE AUTHOR**
> George Orwell (1903–1950) was born Eric Blair in what was then British India, where his father was a government official. After an education in England, Orwell himself worked in the Indian Imperial Police, though he retired at the age of 24 to turn his hand to writing. Throughout his career, Orwell wrote under his pen name about the poor and working classes in Asia, England, and France. Working for the BBC during and after WWII, he wrote his two most famous works: *Animal Farm*, a satire of collectivism, and *1984*, a stinging critique of totalitarianism. Orwell, who famously said, "Good prose is like a window pane," is considered one of the most influential stylists of the twentieth century. He wrote extensively on the art of prose, which he considered a powerful political tool.

Shooting an Elephant

by George Orwell

Chunk 1

1 In Moulmein, in lower Burma, I was hated by large numbers of people—the only time in my life that I have been important enough for this to happen to me. I was subdivisional police officer of the town, and in an aimless, petty kind of way an anti-European feeling was very bitter. No one had the guts to raise a riot, but if a European woman went through the bazaars alone somebody would probably spit betel juice over her dress. As a police officer I was an obvious target and was baited whenever it seemed safe to do so. When a nimble Burman tripped me up on the football field and the referee (another Burman) looked the other way, the crowd yelled with hideous laughter. This happened more than once. In the end the sneering yellow faces of young men that met me everywhere, the insults hooted after me when I was at a safe distance, got badly on my nerves. The young Buddhist priests were the worst of all. There were several thousands of them in the town and none of them seemed to have anything to do except stand on street corners and jeer at Europeans.

2   All this was perplexing[1] and upsetting. For at that time I had already made up my mind that imperialism was an evil thing and the sooner I chucked up my job and got out of it the better. Theoretically—and secretly, of course—I was all for the Burmese and all against their oppressors, the British. As for the job I was doing, I hated it more bitterly than I can perhaps make clear. In a job like that you see the dirty work of Empire at close quarters[2]. The wretched prisoners huddling in the stinking cages of the lockups, the gray, cowed faces of the long-term convicts, the scarred buttocks of men who had been flogged[3] with bamboos—all these oppressed me with an intolerable sense of guilt. But I could get nothing into perspective. I was young and ill-educated and I had to think out my problems in the utter silence that is imposed on every Englishman in the East. I did not know that the British Empire is dying, still less did I know that it is a great deal better than the younger empires that are going to supplant[4] it. All I knew was that I was stuck between my hatred of the empire I served and my rage against the evil-spirited little beasts who tried to make my job impossible. With one part of my mind I thought of the British Raj as an unbreakable tyranny, as something clamped down, in saecula saeculorum[5], upon the will of prostrate[6] peoples; with another part I thought that the greatest joy in the world would be to drive a bayonet into a Buddhist priest's guts. Feelings like these are the normal by-product of imperialism; ask any Anglo-Indian official, if you can catch him off duty.

3   One day something happened which in a roundabout way was enlightening. It was a tiny incident in itself, but it gave me a better glimpse than I had had before of the real nature of imperialism—the real motives for which despotic governments act. Early one morning the subinspector at a police station the other end of the town rang me up on the phone and said that an elephant was ravaging the bazaar. Would I please come and do something about it? I did not know what I could do, but I wanted to see what was happening and I got onto a pony and started out. I took my rifle, an old .44 Winchester and much too small to kill an elephant, but I thought the noise might be useful *in terrorem*[7]. Various Burmans stopped me on the way and told me about the elephant's doings. It was not, of course, a wild elephant, but a tame one which had gone "must."[8] It had been chained up, as tame elephants always are when their attack of "must" is due, but on the previous night it had broken its chain

Chunk 2

---

[1] **perplexing:** puzzling
[2] **quarters:** range
[3] **flogged:** beaten
[4] **supplant:** replace
[5] **saecula saeculorum:** forever and ever
[6] **prostrate:** overpowered
[7] **in terrorem:** in case of fright or terror
[8] **must:** a condition of dangerous frenzy

WORD CONNECTIONS

Orwell uses the words *close quarters* to mean very near. Among other meanings of *quarters* are coins, four parts, living space, or a part of a year. Research this word to identify additional meanings.

My Notes

My Notes

and escaped. Its mahout[9], the only person who could manage it when it was in that state, had set out in pursuit, but had taken the wrong direction and was now twelve hours' journey away, and in the morning the elephant had suddenly reappeared in the town. The Burmese population had no weapons and were quite helpless against it. It had already destroyed somebody's bamboo hut, killed a cow and raided some fruit stalls and devoured the stock; also it had met the municipal rubbish van and, when the driver jumped out and took to his heels, had turned the van over and inflicted violences upon it.

4   The Burmese subinspector and some Indian constables were waiting for me in the quarter where the elephant had been seen. It was a very poor quarter, a labyrinth of squalid huts, thatched with palm leaf, winding all over a steep hillside. I remember it was a cloudy, stuffy morning at the beginning of the rains. We began questioning the people where the elephant had gone and, as usual, failed to get any definite information. That is invariably the case in the East; a story always sounds clear enough at a distance, but the nearer you get to the scene of events the vaguer it becomes. Some of the people said that the elephant had gone in one direction, some said that it had gone in another, some professed not even to have heard of any elephant. I had made up my mind that the whole story was a pack of lies, when I heard yells a little distance away. There was a loud, scandalized cry of "Go away, child! Go away this instant!" and an old woman with a switch in her hand came round the corner of a hut, violently shooing away a crowd of naked children. Some more women followed, clicking their tongues and exclaiming; evidently there was something the children ought not to have seen. I rounded the hut and saw a man's dead body sprawling in the mud. He was an Indian, a black Dravidian[10] coolie[11], almost naked, and he could not have been dead many minutes. The people said that the elephant had come suddenly upon him round the corner of the hut, caught him with its trunk, put its foot on his back, and ground him into the earth. This was the rainy season and the ground was soft, and his face had scored a trench a foot deep and a couple of yards long. He was lying on his belly with arms crucified and head sharply twisted to one side. His face was coated with mud, the eyes wide open, the teeth bared and grinning with an unendurable agony. (Never tell me, by the way, that the dead look peaceful. Most of the corpses I have seen looked devilish.) The friction of the great beast's foot had stripped the skin from his back as neatly as one skins a rabbit. As soon as I saw the dead man I sent an orderly to a friend's house nearby to borrow an elephant rifle. I had already sent back the pony, not wanting it to go mad with fright and throw me if it smelt the elephant.

---

[9] **mahout:** the keeper and driver of an elephant
[10] **Dravidian:** belonging to an ancient race in India
[11] **coolie:** servant

5 The orderly came back in a few minutes with a rifle and five cartridges, and meanwhile some Burmans had arrived and told us that the elephant was in the paddy fields[12] below, only a few hundred yards away. As I started forward practically the whole population of the quarter flocked out of the houses and followed me. They had seen the rifle and were all shouting excitedly that I was going to shoot the elephant. They had not shown much interest in the elephant when he was merely ravaging their homes, but it was different now that he was going to be shot. It was a bit of fun to them, as it would be to an English crowd; besides they wanted the meat. It made me vaguely uneasy. I had no intention of shooting the elephant—I had merely sent for the rifle to defend myself if necessary—and it is always unnerving to have a crowd following you. I marched down the hill, looking and feeling a fool, with the rifle over my shoulder and an ever growing army of people jostling at my heels. At the bottom, when you got away from the huts, there was a metaled road and beyond that a miry waste of paddy fields a thousand yards across, not yet plowed but soggy from the first rains and dotted with coarse grass. The elephant was standing eight yards from the road, his left side toward us. He took not the slightest notice of the crowd's approach. He was tearing up bunches of grass, beating them against his knees to clean them, and stuffing them into his mouth.

6 I had halted on the road. As soon as I saw the elephant I knew with perfect certainty that I ought not to shoot him. It is a serious matter to shoot a working elephant—it is comparable to destroying a huge and costly piece of machinery—and obviously one ought not to do it if it can possibly be avoided. And at that distance, peacefully eating, the elephant looked no more dangerous than a cow. I thought then and I think now that his attack of "must" was already passing off; in which case he would merely wander harmlessly about until the mahout came back and caught him. Moreover, I did not want in the least to shoot him. I decided that I would watch him a little while to make sure that he did not turn savage again, and then go home.

7 But at that moment I glanced round at the crowd that had followed me. It was an immense crowd, two thousand at the least and growing every minute. It blocked the road for a long distance on either side. I looked at the sea of yellow faces above the garish clothes—faces all happy and excited over this bit of fun, all certain that the elephant was going to be shot. They were watching me as they would watch a conjurer[13] about to perform a trick. They did not like me, but with the magical rifle in my hand I was momentarily worth watching. And suddenly I realized that I would have to shoot the elephant after all. The people expected it of me and I had got to do it; I could feel their two thousand wills

Chunk 3

Chunk 4

---

[12] **paddy fields:** rice fields
[13] **conjurer:** magician

My Notes

GRAMMAR & USAGE

Verbals are verbs that are used as another part of speech. In English, two verbals—**gerunds** and **participles**—are formed by adding *-ing* to the base form of the verb. Gerunds acts as nouns, and participles act as adjectives. The title of this essay, "Shooting an Elephant," is a gerund phrase; all three words act together as a noun. When Orwell writes of the "growing army," he is using the participle "growing" to modify a noun. When he describes himself as "looking and feeling a fool," he is using a participial phrase. Writers use verbals and verbal phrases to add action, as well as precise detail, to their writing.

My Notes

pressing me forward irresistibly. And it was at this moment, as I stood there with the rifle in my hands, that I first grasped the hollowness, the futility of the white man's dominion in the East. Here was I, the white man with his gun, standing in front of the unarmed crowd—seemingly the leading actor of the piece; but in reality I was only an absurd puppet pushed to and fro by the will of those yellow faces behind. I perceived in this moment that when the white man turns tyrant it is his own freedom that he destroys. He becomes a sort of hollow, posing dummy, the conventionalized figure of a sahib[14]. For it is the condition of his rule that he shall spend his life in trying to "impress the natives," and so in every crisis he has got to do what the "natives" expect of him. He wears a mask, and his face grows to fit it. I had got to shoot the elephant. I had committed myself to doing it when I sent for the rifle. A sahib has got to act like a sahib; he has got to appear resolute, to know his own mind and do definite things. To come all that way, rifle in hand, with two thousand people marching at my heels, and then to trail feebly away, having done nothing—no, that was impossible. The crowd would laugh at me. And my whole life, every white man's in the East, was one long struggle not to be laughed at.

Chunk 5

8 But I did not want to shoot the elephant. I watched him beating his bunch of grass against his knees, with that preoccupied grandmotherly air that elephants have. It seemed to me that it would be murder to shoot him. At that age I was not squeamish about killing animals, but I had never shot an elephant and never wanted to. (Somehow it always seems worse to kill a large animal.) Besides, there was the beast's owner to be considered. Alive, the elephant was worth at least a hundred pounds; dead, he would only be worth the value of his tusks, five pounds, possibly. But I had got to act quickly. I turned to the experienced-looking Burmans who had been there when we arrived, and asked them how the elephant had been behaving. They all said the same thing; he took no notice of you if you left him alone, but he might charge if you went too close to him.

9 It was perfectly clear to me what I ought to do. I ought to walk up to within, say, twenty-five yards of the elephant and test his behavior. If he charged I could shoot; if he took no notice of me, it would be safe to leave him until the mahout came back. But I also knew that I was going to do no such thing. I was a poor shot with a rifle and the ground was soft mud into which one would sink at every step. If the elephant charged and I missed him, I should have about as much chance as a toad under a steam roller. But even then I was not thinking particularly of my own skin, only of the watchful yellow faces behind. For at that moment, with the crowd watching me, I was not afraid in the ordinary sense, as I would have been if I had been alone. A white man mustn't be frightened in front of "natives"; and so, in general, he isn't frightened. The thought in my mind

---

[14] **sahib:** native term for a European gentleman

was that if anything went wrong those two thousand Burmans would see me pursued, caught, trampled on, and reduced to a grinning corpse like that Indian up the hill. And if that happened it was quite probable that some of them would laugh. That would never do.

10 There was only one alternative. I shoved the cartridges into the magazine and lay down on the road to get a better aim. The crowd grew very still, and a deep, low, happy sigh, as of people who see the theater curtain go up at last, breathed from innumerable throats. They were going to have their bit of fun after all. The rifle was a beautiful German thing with cross-hair sights. I did not know then that in shooting an elephant one would shoot to cut an imaginary bar running from earhole to earhole. I ought, therefore, as the elephant was sideways on, to have aimed straight at his earhole; actually I aimed several inches in front of this, thinking the brain would be further forward.

11 When I pulled the trigger I did not hear the bang or feel the kick—one never does when a shot goes home—but I heard the devilish roar of glee that went up from the crowd. In that instant, in too short a time, one would have thought, even for the bullet to get there, a mysterious, terrible change had come over the elephant. He neither stirred nor fell, but every line of his body had altered. He looked suddenly stricken, shrunken, immensely old, as though the frightful impact of the bullet had paralyzed him without knocking him down. At last, after what seemed a long time—it might have been five seconds, I dare say—he sagged flabbily to his knees. His mouth slobbered. An enormous senility seemed to have settled upon him. One could have imagined him thousands of years old. I fired again into the same spot. At the second shot he did not collapse but climbed with desperate slowness to his feet and stood weakly erect, with legs sagging and head drooping. I fired a third time. That was the shot that did for him. You could see the agony of it jolt his whole body and knock the last remnant of strength from his legs. But in falling he seemed for a moment to rise, for as his hind legs collapsed beneath him he seemed to tower upward like a huge rock toppling, his trunk reaching skywards like a tree. He trumpeted for the first and only time. And then down he came, his belly toward me, with a crash that seemed to shake the ground even where I lay.

Chunk 6

My Notes

Reading with a Cultural Criticism Lens

My Notes

12 I got up. The Burmans were already racing past me across the mud. It was obvious that the elephant would never rise again, but he was not dead. He was breathing very rhythmically with long rattling gasps, his great mound of a side painfully rising and falling. His mouth was wide open—I could see far down into caverns of pink throat. I waited a long time for him to die, but his breathing did not weaken. Finally I fired my two remaining shots into the spot where I thought his heart must be. The thick blood welled out of him like red velvet, but still he did not die. His body did not even jerk when the shots hit him, the tortured breathing continued without a pause. He was dying, very slowly and in great agony, but in some world remote from me where not even a bullet could damage him further. I felt that I had got to put an end to that dreadful noise. It seemed dreadful to see the great beast lying there, powerless to move and yet powerless to die, and not even to be able to finish him. I sent back for my small rifle and poured shot after shot into his heart and down his throat. They seemed to make no impression. The tortured gasps continued as steadily as the ticking of a clock.

Chunk 7

13 In the end I could not stand it any longer and went away. I heard later that it took him half an hour to die. Burmans were bringing dahs[15] and baskets even before I left, and I was told they had stripped his body almost to the bones by afternoon.

14 Afterwards, of course, there were endless discussions about the shooting of the elephant. The owner was furious, but he was only an Indian and could do nothing. Besides, legally I had done the right thing, for a mad elephant has to be killed, like a mad dog, if its owner fails to control it. Among the Europeans, opinion was divided. The older men said I was right, the younger men said it was a shame to shoot an elephant for killing a coolie, because an elephant was worth more than any Coringhee coolie. And afterwards I was very glad that the coolie had been killed; it put me legally in the right and gave me a sufficient pretext for shooting the elephant. I often wondered whether any of the others grasped that I had done it solely to avoid looking a fool.

---

[15] **dahs:** bowls

Being a Stranger

Stranger in the Village

1 Brainstorm connotative words for "village."

2 What does it mean to be part of the group encountering the unfamiliar—to be part of the village?

3 Brainstorm connotative words for "stranger."

4 What does it mean to be the unfamiliar one, the stranger?

5 View the film clip and consider what the filmmaker does to set the "stranger" apart from the "village."

6 Brainstorm a list of film clips with which you are familiar and for each one discuss: Who is the "stranger" and who or what is the "village"?

7 What does it mean to be a stranger in the village?

Two Different Worlds

Writing Prompt: Think about a time when you were excluded or treated like a stranger. What were your feelings at the time? How did you respond? In what ways did that event shape or change you as an individual? Write an essay in which you examine a time when you were treated like a stranger, explain how you felt at that time, and reflect on the ways in which that event has shaped your life. Begin working on your essay with the activities outlined below.

Webbing to Generate Ideas In the space below, create a web of circles, each containing a key word or concept related to the topic and the questions above.

Writing Your First Draft On your own paper, write a draft paper in response to the prompt above. Use the information in your web to help you organize your paper.

Reading About a Stranger in a Village After completing your first draft, read the following excerpt from *The Joy Luck Club*.

LINDO JONG:
DOUBLE FACE

by Amy Tan

from The Joy Luck Club

ABOUT THE AUTHOR

Born in 1952 in Oakland, California, Amy Tan is author
of several critically acclaimed novels like *The Kitchen
God's Wife* and *The Bonesetter's Daughter*, as well as
short stories and children's books. Her first novel, *The
Joy Luck* Club (1989), was an international best-seller
that became an award-winning film. Tan says her first
important piece of writing, however, was a letter she
wrote in the third grade to raise money for a local library.
Tan's fiction often deals with tensions between Chinese
immigrants and their Americanized children. Praised for
her lucid images and gripping storylines, she believes her
first career as a business writer helped her develop her
simple yet forceful style.

My daughter wanted to go to China for her second honeymoon, but now
she is afraid.

"What if I blend in so well they think I'm one of them?" Waverly asked
me. "What if they don't let me come back to the United States?"

"When you go to China," I told her, "you don't even need to open your
mouth. They already know you are an outsider."

"What are you talking about?" she asked. My daughter likes to speak
back. She likes to question what I say.

"Aii-ya," I said. "Even if you put on their clothes, even if you take off your
makeup and hide your fancy jewelry, they know. They know just watching the
way you walk, the way you carry your face. They know you do not belong."

My daughter did not look pleased when I told her this, that she didn't
look Chinese. She had a sour American look on her face. Oh, maybe ten years
ago, she would have clapped her hands—hurray! as if this were good news.
But now she wants to be Chinese, it is so fashionable. And I know it is too
late. All those years I tried to teach her! She followed my Chinese ways only
until she learned how to walk out the door by herself and go to school.

My Notes

Two Different Worlds

My Notes

So now the only Chinese words she can say are *shsh, houche, chr fan,* and *gwan deng shweijyau.* How can she talk to people in China with these words? Pee-pee, choo-choo train, eat, close light sleep.

How can she think she can blend in? Only her skin and her hair are Chinese. Inside—she is all American-made.

It's my fault she is this way. I wanted my children to have the best combination: American circumstances and Chinese character. How could I know these two things do not mix?

I taught her how American circumstances work. If you are born poor here, it's no lasting shame. You are first in line for a scholarship. If the roof crashes on your head, no need to cry over this bad luck. You can sue anybody, make the landlord fix it. You do not have to sit like a Buddha under a tree letting pigeons drop their dirty business on your head. You can buy an umbrella. Or go inside a Catholic church. In America, nobody says you have to keep the circumstances somebody else gives you.

She learned these things, but I couldn't teach her about Chinese character. How to obey parents and listen to your mother's mind. How not to show your own thoughts, to put your feelings behind your face so you can take advantage of hidden opportunities. Why easy things are not worth pursuing. How to know your own worth and polish it, never flashing it around like a cheap ring. Why Chinese thinking is best.

No, this kind of thinking didn't stick to her: She was too busy chewing gum, blowing bubbles bigger than her cheeks. Only that kind of thinking stuck.

"Finish your coffee," I told her yesterday. "Don't throw your blessings away."

"Don't be so old-fashioned, Ma," she told me, finishing her coffee down the sink. "I'm my own person."

And I think, How can she be her own person? When did I give her up?

GRAMMAR & USAGE

Notice the sentences on this page in which Tan uses direct quotations. Writers use direct quotations to develop characters, to further action, and to add life to their writing.

Direct quotations are always set off from the rest of the text with quotation marks. In addition, they may require other punctuation to convey meaning or to clearly distinguish what is quoted from what is not quoted.

Always start a new paragraph for each speaker. Notice that the narrator has one paragraph for what she says and another paragraph for what her mother says.

Revisiting Your Draft: Reread your initial draft on being a stranger, and identify an appropriate place to revise and add dialogue (e.g., to reveal something about your characters or advance the narrative). Be sure to adhere to the punctuation rules of dialogue.

Understanding the Stranger's Perception of a Village

SUGGESTED LEARNING STRATEGIES: Previewing, Diffusing, Skimming/Scanning, Marking the Text, Think-Pair-Share, Metacognitive Markers

Reflective Essay

My Notes

ABOUT THE AUTHOR

James Baldwin (1924–1987) was born in Harlem, into a poor household headed by his rigid and demanding stepfather, a storefront preacher. Though he had planned to follow in his stepfather's footsteps and had served as a junior minister, he eventually became disillusioned with Christianity and resolved to become a writer. His move to Paris in 1948 helped provide the critical distance he needed to write the autobiographical *Notes of a Native Son* and his first novel, *Go Tell It on the Mountain*—powerful works about the African American experience. After returning to the U.S., he became a leading literary voice for civil rights. While his unsparing view of race issues in the U.S. drew criticism from his African American and white peers alike, he is now viewed as one of the most significant U.S. writers of the twentieth century.

Stranger in the Village

by James Baldwin, 1955

1 From all available evidence no black man had ever set foot in this tiny Swiss village before I came. I was told before arriving that I would probably be a "sight" for the village; I took this to mean that people of my complexion were rarely seen in Switzerland, and also that city people are always something of a "sight" outside of the city. It did not occur to me—possibly because I am an American—that there could be people anywhere who had never seen a Negro.

Chunk 1

2 It is a fact that cannot be explained on the basis of the inaccessibility of the village. The village is very high, but it is only four hours from Milan and three hours from Lausanne. It is true that it is virtually unknown. Few people making plans for a holiday would elect to come here. On the other hand, the villagers are able, presumably, to come and go as they

Chunk 2

Understanding the Stranger's Perception of a Village

My Notes

WORD CONNECTIONS

Baldwin uses an idiom in paragraph 3: "to take the waters," meaning to immerse oneself in the water for potentially healthful benefits.

please—which they do: to another town at the foot of the mountain, with a population of approximately five thousand, the nearest place to see a movie or go to the bank. In the village there is no movie house, no bank, no library, no theater; very few radios, one jeep, one station wagon; and, at the moment, one typewriter, mine, an invention which the woman next door to me here had never seen. There are about six hundred people living here, all Catholic—I conclude this from the fact that the Catholic church is open all year round, whereas the Protestant chapel, set off on a hill a little removed from the village, is open only in the summertime when the tourists arrive. There are four or five hotels, all closed now, and four or five *bistros*[1], of which, however, only two do any business during the winter. These two do not do a great deal, for life in the village seems to end around nine or ten o'clock. There are a few stores, butcher, baker, *epicerie*[2], a hardware store, and a money-changer—who cannot change travelers' checks, but must send them down to the bank, an operation which takes two or three days. There is something called the *Ballet Haus*, closed in the winter and used for God knows what, certainly not ballet, during the summer. There seems to be only one schoolhouse in the village, and this for the quite young children; I suppose this to mean that their older brothers and sisters at some point descend from these mountains in order to complete their education—possibly, again, to the town just below. The landscape is absolutely forbidding, mountains towering on all four sides, ice and snow as far as the eye can reach. In this white wilderness, men and women and children move all day, carrying washing, wood, buckets of milk or water, sometimes skiing on Sunday afternoons. All week long boys and young men are to be seen shoveling snow off the rooftops, or dragging wood down from the forest in sleds.

3   The village's only real attraction, which explains the tourist season, is the hot spring water. A disquietingly high proportion of these tourists are cripples, or semi-cripples, who come year after year—from other parts of Switzerland, usually—to take the waters. This lends the village, at the height of the season, a rather terrifying air of sanctity, as though it were a lesser Lourdes[3]. There is often something beautiful, there is always something awful, in the spectacle of a person who has lost one of his faculties, a faculty he never questioned until it was gone, and who struggles to recover it. Yet people remain people, on crutches or indeed on deathbeds; and wherever I passed, the first summer I was here, among the native villagers or among the lame, a wind passed with me—of astonishment, curiosity, amusement and outrage. That first summer I stayed two weeks and never intended to return. But I did return in the winter, to work; the village offers, obviously, no distractions whatever and has the further advantage of being extremely cheap. Now it is winter

[1] **bistro:** French, for restaurant
[2] **epicerie:** French, for grocery store
[3] **Lourdes:** a place of Christian pilgrimage in France

again, a year later, and I am here again. Everyone in the village knows my name, though they scarcely ever use it, knows that I come from America—though this, apparently, they will never really believe: black men come from Africa—and everyone knows that I am the friend of the son of a woman who was born here, and that I am staying in their chalet. But I remain as much a stranger today as I was the first day I arrived, and the children shout *Neger! Neger!* as I walk along the streets.

4 It must be admitted that in the beginning I was far too shocked to have any real reaction. In so far as I reacted at all, I reacted by trying to be pleasant—it being a great part of the American Negro's education (long before he goes to school) that he must make people "like" him. This smile-and-the-world-smiles-with-you routine worked about as well in this situation as it had in the situation for which it was designed, which is to say that it did not work at all. No one, after all, can be liked whose human weight and complexity cannot be, or has not been, admitted. My smile was simply another unheard-of phenomenon which allowed them to see my teeth—they did not, really, see my smile and I began to think that, should I take to snarling, no one would notice any difference. All of the physical characteristics of the Negro which had caused me, in America, a very different and almost forgotten pain were nothing less than miraculous—or infernal—in the eyes of the village people. Some thought my hair was the color of tar, that it had the texture of wire, or the texture of cotton. It was jocularly[4] suggested that I might let it all grow long and make myself a winter coat. If I sat in the sun for more than five minutes some daring creature was certain to come along and gingerly put his fingers on my hair, as though he were afraid of an electric shock, or put his hand on my hand, astonished that the color did not rub off. In all of this, in which it must be conceded there was the charm of genuine wonder and in which there was certainly no element of intentional unkindness, there was yet no suggestion that I was human: I was simply a living wonder.

5 I knew that they did not mean to be unkind, and I know it now; it is necessary, nevertheless, for me to repeat this to myself each time that I walk out of the chalet. The children who shout *Neger!* have no way of knowing the echoes this sound raises in me. They are brimming with good humor and the more daring swell with pride when I stop to speak with them. Just the same, there are days when I cannot pause and smile, when I have no heart to play with them; when, indeed, I mutter sourly to myself, exactly as I muttered on the streets of a city these children have never seen, when I was no bigger than these children are now: *Your* mother was a *nigger.* Joyce[5] is right about history being a nightmare—but it may be the nightmare from which no one *can* awaken. People are trapped in history and history is trapped in them.

Chunk 3

---

[4] **jocularly:** jokingly
[5] **Joyce:** James Joyce, Irish author of *Ulysses*

My Notes

Understanding the Stranger's Perception of a Village

6 There is a custom in the village—I am told it is repeated in many villages—of "buying" African natives for the purpose of converting them to Christianity. There stands in the church all year round a small box with a slot for money, decorated with a black figurine, and into this box the villagers drop their francs. During the carnaval which precedes Lent, two village children have their faces blackened—out of which bloodless darkness their blue eyes shine like ice—and fantastic horsehair wigs are placed on their blond heads; thus disguised, they solicit among the villagers for money for missionaries in Africa. Between the box in the church and blackened children, the village "bought" last year six or eight African natives. This was reported to me with pride by the wife of one of the *bistro* owners and I was careful to express astonishment and pleasure at the solicitude shown by the village for the souls of black folks. The *bistro* owner's wife beamed with a pleasure far more genuine than my own and seemed to feel that I might now breathe more easily concerning the souls of at least six of my kinsmen.

Chunk 4

7 I tried not to think of these so lately baptized kinsmen, of the price paid for them, or the peculiar price they themselves would pay, and said nothing about my father, who having taken his own conversion too literally never, at bottom, forgave the white world (which he described as heathen) for having saddled him with a Christ in whom, to judge at least from their treatment of him, they themselves no longer believed. I thought of white men arriving for the first time in an African village, strangers there, as I am a stranger here, and tried to imagine the astounded populace touching their hair and marveling at the color of their skin. But there is a great difference between being the first white man to be seen by Africans and being the first black man to be seen by whites. The white man takes the astonishment as tribute, for he arrives to conquer and to convert the natives, whose inferiority in relation to himself is not even to be questioned; whereas I, without a thought of conquest, find myself among a people whose culture controls me, has even, in a sense, created me, people who have cost me more in anguish and rage than they will ever know, who yet do not even know of my existence. The astonishment with which I might have greeted them, should they have stumbled into my African village a few hundred years ago, might have rejoiced their hearts. But the astonishment with which they greet me today can only poison mine.

8 And this is so despite everything I may do to feel differently, despite my friendly conversations with the *bistro* owner's wife, despite their three-year-old son who has at last become my friend, despite the *saluts* and *bonsoirs* which I exchange with people as I walk, despite the fact that I know that no individual can be taken to task for what history is doing, or has done. I say that the culture of these people controls me—but they can scarcely be held responsible for European culture. America comes out of Europe, but these people have never seen America, nor have most of

them seen more of Europe than the hamlet at the foot of their mountain. Yet they move with an authority which I shall never have; and they regard me, quite rightly, not only as a stranger in their village but as a suspect latecomer, bearing no credentials, to everything they have—however unconsciously—inherited.

9 For this village, even were it incomparably more remote and incredibly more primitive, is the West, the West onto which I have been so strangely grafted. These people cannot be, from the point of view of power, strangers anywhere in the world; they have made the modern world, in effect, even if they do not know it. The most illiterate among them is related, in a way that I am not, to Dante, Shakespeare, Michelangelo, Aeschylus, Da Vinci, Rembrandt, and Racine; the cathedral at Chartres says something to them which it cannot say to me, as indeed would New York's Empire State Building, should anyone here ever see it. Out of their hymns and dances come Beethoven and Bach. Go back a few centuries and they are in their full glory—but I am in Africa, watching the conquerors arrive.

10 The rage of the disesteemed is personally fruitless, but it is also absolutely inevitable: this rage, so generally discounted, so little understood even among the people whose daily bread it is, is one of the things that makes history. Rage can only with difficulty, and never entirely, be brought under the domination of the intelligence and is therefore not susceptible to any arguments whatever. This is a fact which ordinary representatives of the *Herrenvolk*[6], having never felt this rage and being unable to imagine it, quite fail to understand. Also, rage cannot be hidden it can only be dissembled[7]. This dissembling deludes the thoughtless, and strengthens rage and adds, to rage, contempt. There are, no doubt, as many ways of coping with the resulting complex of tensions as there are black men in the world, but no black man can hope ever to be entirely liberated from this internal warfare—rage, dissembling, and contempt having inevitably accompanied his first realization of the power of white men. What is crucial here is that, since white men represent in the black man's world so heavy a weight, white men have for black men a reality which is far from being reciprocal; and hence all black men have toward all white men an attitude which is designed, really, either to rob the white man of the jewel of his naïveté[8] or else to make it cost him dear.

11 The black man insists, by whatever means he finds at his disposal, that the white man cease to regard him as an exotic rarity and recognize him as a human being. This is a very charged and difficult moment, for there is a great deal of will power involved in the white man's naïveté. Most people are not naturally reflective any more than they are naturally malicious,

Chunk 5

My Notes

WORD CONNECTIONS

In paragraph 10, look at Baldwin's use of the word *disesteemed*. Using the prefix *dis-* adds a layer of meaning that the prefix *un-* does not, although both mean "not."

---

[6] **Herrenvolk:** German, for master race
[7] **dissembled:** concealed
[8] **naïveté:** innocence

My Notes

WORD CONNECTIONS

Attribute comes from the Latin word *attribuere*, which means "to assign." It is related to the word *tribute*, which comes from the Latin word *tribuere*, *which also means* "to assign, allot, or pay."

and the white man prefers to keep the black man at a certain human remove because it is easier for him thus to preserve his simplicity and avoid being called to account for crimes committed by his forefathers, or his neighbors. He is inescapably aware, nevertheless, that he is in a better position in the world than black men are, nor can he quite put to death the suspicion that he is hated by black men therefore. He does not wish to be hated, neither does he wish to change places, and at this point in his uneasiness he can scarcely avoid having recourse to those legends which white men have created about black men, the most usual effect of which is that the white man finds himself enmeshed, so to speak, in his own language which describes hell, as well as the attributes which lead one to hell, as being as black as night.

12 Every legend, moreover, contains its residuum[9] of truth, and the root function of language is to control the universe by describing it. It is of quite considerable significance that black men remain, in the imagination, and in overwhelming numbers in fact, beyond the disciplines of salvation; and this despite the fact that the West has been "buying" African natives for centuries. There is, I should hazard[10], an instantaneous necessity to be divorced from this so visibly unsaved stranger, in whose heart, moreover, one cannot guess what dreams of vengeance are being nourished; and, at the same time, there are few things on earth more attractive than the idea of the unspeakable liberty which is allowed the unredeemed. When, beneath the black mask, a human being begins to make himself felt one cannot escape a certain awful wonder as to what kind of human being it is. What one's imagination makes of other people is dictated, of course, by the laws of one's own personality and it is one of the ironies of black-white relations that, by means of what the white man imagines the black man to be, the black man is enabled to know who the white man is.

13 I have said, for example, that I am as much a stranger in this village today as I was the first summer I arrived, but this is not quite true. The villagers wonder less about the texture of my hair than they did then, and wonder rather more about me. And the fact that their wonder now exists on another level is reflected in their attitudes and in their eyes. There are the children who make those delightful, hilarious, sometimes astonishingly grave overtures of friendship in the unpredictable fashion of children; other children, having been taught that the devil is a black man, scream in genuine anguish as I approach. Some of the older women never pass without a friendly greeting, never pass, indeed, if it seems that they will be able to engage me in conversation; other women look down or look away or rather contemptuously smirk. Some of the men drink with me and suggest that I learn how to ski—partly, I gather, because they cannot imagine what I would look like on skis—and want to know if I am married, and ask questions about my *métier*[11]. But some of the

---

[9] **residuum:** something left over or remaining
[10] **hazard:** presume

men have accused *le sale negre*—behind my back—of stealing wood and there is already in the eyes of some of them the peculiar, intent, paranoiac malevolence which one sometimes surprises in the eyes of American white men when, out walking with their Sunday girl, they see a Negro male approach.

14 There is a dreadful abyss between the streets of this village and the streets of the city in which I was born, between the children who shout *Neger!* today and those who shouted *Nigger!* yesterday—the abyss is experience, the American experience. The syllable hurled behind me today expresses, above all, wonder: I am a stranger here. But I am not a stranger in America and the same syllable riding on the American air expresses the war my presence has occasioned in the American soul.

Chunk 6

15 For this village brings home to me this fact: that there was a day, and not really a very distant day, when Americans were scarcely Americans at all but discontented Europeans, facing a great unconquered continent and strolling, say, into a marketplace and seeing black men for the first time. The shock this spectacle afforded is suggested, surely, by the promptness with which they decided that these black men were not really men but cattle. It is true that the necessity on the part of the settlers of the New World of reconciling their moral assumptions with the fact—and the necessity—of slavery enhanced immensely the charm of this idea, and it is also true that this idea expresses, with a truly American bluntness, the attitude which to varying extents all masters have had toward all slaves.

16 But between all former slaves and slave-owners and the drama which begins for Americans over three hundred years ago at Jamestown, there are at least two differences to be observed. The American Negro slave could not suppose, for one thing, as slaves in past epochs had supposed and often done, that he would ever be able to wrest the power from his master's hands. This was a supposition[12] which the modern era, which was to bring about such vast changes in the aims and dimensions of power, put to death; it only begins, in unprecedented fashion, and with dreadful implications, to be resurrected today. But even had this supposition persisted with undiminished force, the American Negro slave could not have used it to lend his condition dignity, for the reason that this supposition rests on another: that the slave in exile yet remains related to his past, has some means—if only in memory—of revering and sustaining the forms of his former life, is able, in short, to maintain his identity.

Chunk 7

17 This was not the case with the American Negro slave. He is unique among the black men of the world in that his past was taken from him, almost literally, at one blow. One wonders what on earth the first slave found to say to the first dark child he bore. I am told that there

---

[11] **métier:** profession
[12] **supposition:** belief

My Notes

are Haitians able to trace their ancestry back to African kings, but any American Negro wishing to go back so far will find his journey through time abruptly arrested by the signature on the bill of sale which served as the entrance paper for his ancestor. At the time—to say nothing of the circumstances—of the enslavement of the captive black man who was to become the American Negro, there was not the remotest possibility that he would ever take power from his master's hands. There was no reason to suppose that his situation would ever change, nor was there, shortly, anything to indicate that his situation had ever been different. It was his necessity, in the words of E. Franklin Frazier[13], to find a "motive for living under American culture or die." The identity of the American Negro comes out of this extreme situation, and the evolution of this identity was a source of the most intolerable anxiety in the minds and the lives of his masters.

18 For the history of the American Negro is unique also in this: that the question of his humanity, and of his rights therefore as a human being, became a burning one for several generations of Americans, so burning a question that it ultimately became one of those used to divide the nation. It is out of this argument that the venom of the epithet *Nigger!* is derived. It is an argument which Europe has never had, and hence Europe quite sincerely fails to understand how or why the argument arose in the first place, why its effects are so frequently disastrous and always so unpredictable, why it refuses until today to be entirely settled. Europe's black possessions remained—and do remain—in Europe's colonies, at which remove they represented no threat whatever to European identity. If they posed any problem at all for the European conscience, it was a problem which remained comfortingly abstract: in effect, the black man, *as a man*, did not exist for Europe. But in America, even as a slave, he was an inescapable part of the general social fabric and no American could escape having an attitude toward him. Americans attempt until today to make an abstraction of the Negro, but the very nature of these abstractions reveals the tremendous effects the presence of the Negro has had on the American character.

19 When one considers the history of the Negro in America it is of the greatest importance to recognize that the moral beliefs of a person, or a people, are never really as tenuous as life—which is not moral—very often causes them to appear; these create for them a frame of reference and a necessary hope, the hope being that when life has done its worst they will be enabled to rise above themselves and to triumph over life. Life would scarcely be bearable if this hope did not exist. Again, even when the worst has been said, to betray a belief is not by any means to have put oneself beyond its power; the betrayal of a belief is not the same thing as ceasing to believe. If this were not so there would be no moral standards in the

---

[13] **E. Franklin Frazier:** American sociologist who studied race relations

world at all. Yet one must also recognize that morality is based on ideas and that all ideas are dangerous—dangerous because ideas can only lead to action and where the action leads no man can say. And dangerous in this respect: that confronted with the impossibility of remaining faithful to one's beliefs, and the equal impossibility of becoming free of them, one can be driven to the most inhuman excesses. The ideas on which American beliefs are based are not, though Americans often seem to think so, ideas which originated in America. They came out of Europe. And the establishment of democracy on the American continent was scarcely as radical a break with the past as was the necessity, which Americans faced, of broadening this concept to include black men.

20 This was, literally, a hard necessity. It was impossible, for one thing, for Americans to abandon their beliefs, not only because these beliefs alone seemed able to justify the sacrifices they had endured and the blood that they had spilled, but also because these beliefs afforded them their only bulwark[14] against a moral chaos as absolute as the physical chaos of the continent it was their destiny to conquer. But in the situation in which Americans found themselves, these beliefs threatened an idea which, whether or not one likes to think so, is the very warp and woof[15] of the heritage of the West, the idea of white supremacy.

21 Americans have made themselves notorious by the shrillness and the brutality with which they have insisted on this idea, but they did not invent it; and it has escaped the world's notice that those very excesses of which Americans have been guilty imply a certain, unprecedented uneasiness over the idea's life and power, if not, indeed, the idea's validity. The idea of white supremacy rests simply on the fact that white men are the creators of civilization (the present civilization, which is the only one that matters; all previous civilizations are simply "contributions" to our own) and are therefore civilization's guardians and defenders. Thus it was impossible for Americans to accept the black man as one of themselves, for to do so was to jeopardize their status as white men. But not so to accept him was to deny his human reality, his human weight and complexity, and the strain of denying the overwhelmingly undeniable forced Americans into rationalizations so fantastic that they approached the pathological.

22 At the root of the American Negro problem is the necessity of the American white man to find a way of living with the Negro in order to be able to live with himself. And the history of this problem can be reduced to the means used by Americans—lynch law and law, segregation and legal acceptance, terrorization and concession—either to come to terms with this necessity, or to find a way around it, or (most usually) to find a way of doing both these things at once. The resulting spectacle,

---

[14] **bulwark:** defense
[15] **warp and woof:** foundation

My Notes

at once foolish and dreadful, led someone to make the quite accurate observation that "the Negro-in-America is a form of insanity which overtakes white men."

23 In this long battle, a battle by no means finished, the unforeseeable effects of which will be felt by many future generations, the white man's motive was the protection of his identity; the black man was motivated by the need to establish an identity. And despite the terrorization which the Negro in America endured and endures sporadically until today, despite the cruel and totally inescapable ambivalence of his status in his country, the battle for his identity has long ago been won. He is not a visitor to the West, but a citizen there, an American; as American as the Americans who despise him, the Americans who fear him, the Americans who love him—the Americans who became less than themselves, or rose to be greater than themselves by virtue of the fact that the challenge he represented was inescapable. He is perhaps the only black man in the world whose relationship to white men is more terrible, more subtle, and more meaningful than the relationship of bitter possessed to uncertain possessors. His survival depended, and his development depends, on his ability to turn his peculiar status in the Western world to his own advantage and, it may be, to the very great advantage of that world. It remains for him to fashion out of his experience that which will give him sustenance, and a voice. The cathedral at Chartres, I have said, says something to the people of this village which it cannot say to me; but it is important to understand that this cathedral says something to me which it cannot say to them. Perhaps they are struck by the power of the spires, the glory of the windows; but they have known God, after all, longer than I have known him, and in a different way, and I am terrified by the slippery bottomless well to be found in the crypt, down which heretics[16] were hurled to death, and by the obscene, inescapable gargoyles jutting out of the stone and seeming to say that God and the devil can never be divorced. I doubt that the villagers think of the devil when they face a cathedral because they have never been identified with the devil. But I must accept the status which myth, if nothing else, gives me in the West before I can hope to change the myth.

24 Yet, if the American Negro has arrived at his identity by virtue of the absoluteness of his estrangement from his past, American white men still nourish the illusion that there is some means of recovering the European innocence, of returning to a state in which black men do not exist. This is one of the greatest errors Americans can make. The identity they fought so hard to protect has, by virtue of that battle, undergone a change: Americans are as unlike any other white people in the world as it is possible to be. I do not think, for example, that it is too much to suggest that the American vision of the world—which allows so little reality,

---

16 **heretics:** nonbelievers

generally speaking, for any of the darker forces in human life, which tends until today to paint moral issues in glaring black and white—owes a great deal to the battle waged by Americans to maintain between themselves and black men a human separation which could not be bridged. It is only now beginning to be borne in on us—very faintly, it must be admitted, very slowly, and very much against our will—that this vision of the world is dangerously inaccurate, and perfectly useless. For it protects our moral high-mindedness at the terrible expense of weakening our grasp of reality. People who shut their eyes to reality simply invite their own destruction, and anyone who insists on remaining in a state of innocence long after that innocence is dead turns himself into a monster.

25 The time has come to realize that the interracial drama acted out on the American continent has not only created a new black man, it has created a new white man, too. No road whatever will lead Americans back to the simplicity of this European village where white men still have the luxury of looking on me as a stranger. I am not, really, a stranger any longer for any American alive. One of the things that distinguishes Americans from other people is that no other people has ever been so deeply involved in the lives of black men, and vice versa. This fact faced, with all its implications, it can be seen that the history of the American Negro problem is not merely shameful, it is also something of an achievement. For even when the worst has been said, it must also be added that the perpetual challenge posed by this problem was always, somehow, perpetually met. It is precisely this black-white experience which may prove of indispensable value to us in the world we face today. This world is white no longer, and it will never be white again.

Chunk 8

Writing a Reflective Essay

SUGGESTED LEARNING STRATEGIES: **Brainstorming, Drafting, Self-Editing/Peer Editing**

Assignment

Your assignment is to write a reflective essay that illustrates an event in which you or someone you know felt like a "stranger in the village" or was perceived as "strange" by some group.

Steps

Prewriting

1. Generate a list of events that capture the thematic concept of "stranger in the village" by considering a time in which you felt like an outsider, witnessed someone else who was made to feel like an outsider, and/or made someone else feel like an outsider. Select two or three events from your list to share with a partner, and explain how your event addresses the thematic concept.

2. Select the strongest topic of interest to you and use a prewriting strategy to capture ideas and explore your memory of the event.

3. Review the organizational structure of a reflective essay (e.g., event, response, and reflection) by revisiting the two literary examples presented in this unit— "Shooting an Elephant" and "Stranger in the Village." Note the differences between them in terms of the recursive pattern of event, response, and reflection.

4. Consider a structure that would work well for your event and create a graphic organizer to generate a rhetorical plan that expands ideas from your prewrite and organizes the information.

5. Refine your rhetorical plan by considering your subject, purpose, target audience, and tone.

Drafting

6. Use your rhetorical plan to generate a first draft that develops points within the preliminary organizational structure, addresses the thematic concept, and incorporates stylistic devices (e.g., voice, diction, detail, figurative language, syntax, etc.).

Revising

7. Read through your draft and revise it for clarity, to achieve the rhetorical purpose outlined in the assignment, and to maintain a consistent tone appropriate for your audience.

8. Use a strategy to refine ideas, improve organization (e.g., SOAPSTone, marking the text for elements of a reflective essay, annotation, etc.), and achieve consistency of tone within your text before you present it to your peers.

9. In a small group, review the Scoring Guide criteria for this assignment. Share your draft and evaluate it using the scoring criteria as a guide for revision (e.g., organizational structure, thematic concept, stylistic techniques). Within your groups, solicit feedback for revision and brainstorm strategies to refine drafts presented.

10. Evaluate the revision suggestions from your peers, and consider which ones you want to incorporate in your draft. Revise your essay accordingly, and share changes to your draft with your peers.

Publishing

11. Compose a title for your piece by generating a list of possible titles stemming from ideas, topics, or words or phrases within your text. Review and rank your list. Select the most gripping title that captures the essence of your text.

12. Reread your essay silently and edit it to correct errors in spelling, conventions, grammar, style, and/or formatting. Consult editing tools (spell-check, dictionary, thesaurus, style manual, grammar references, etc.) to create a technically sound text and publish a final draft.

Writing a Reflective Essay

SCORING GUIDE

Scoring Criteria	Exemplary	Proficient	Emerging
Ideas	The reflective essay thoroughly demonstrates a perceptive understanding of the relationship between the chosen event and thematic concept. Use of specific and well-chosen details yields incontrovertible support and creates an extraordinarily convincing text.	The reflective essay demonstrates a solid understanding of the relationship between the chosen event and thematic concept. Use of specific details yields support and creates a convincing text.	The reflective essay demonstrates a superficial understanding of the relationship between the chosen event and thematic concept. Details are underutilized and do little to create a convincing text.
Organization	The essay's effective organization aptly reinforces the writer's ideas. Successful use of transitions enhances overall coherence and connects ideas smoothly and comfortably.	The essay's clear organization supports the ideas. Transitions provide connection between ideas.	The essay's lack of organization detracts from the ideas, making the essay difficult to follow. It may move too rapidly between ideas and may lack transitions.
Use of Language	Diction, syntax, and other stylistic devices are notable and appropriate for the subject, purpose, and audience. Few errors in standard writing conventions are present.	Diction, syntax, and other stylistic devices are appropriate for the subject, purpose, and audience. Errors in standard writing conventions, if present, are minor and do not interfere with meaning.	Diction, syntax, and other stylistic devices are less effective for the subject, purpose, and audience. Errors in standard writing conventions seriously interfere with meaning.
Evidence of Writing Process	The writing demonstrates thoughtful planning, significant revision, and careful editing for grammar and conventions in preparing a publishable draft.	The writing demonstrates planning, revision, and editing for grammar and conventions in preparing a publishable draft.	The writing lacks evidence of planning, revision, and/or editing for grammar and conventions. The draft is not ready for publication.

SCORING GUIDE

Scoring Criteria	Exemplary	Proficient	Emerging
Additional Criteria			

Comments:

Reflection

An important aspect of growing as a learner is to reflect on where you have been, what you have accomplished, what helped you to learn, and how you will apply your new knowledge in the future. Use the following questions to guide your thinking and to identify evidence of your learning. Use separate notebook paper.

Thinking about Concepts

1. Using specific examples from this unit, respond to the Essential Questions:

   • How do writers and artists organize or construct text to convey meaning?

   • What does it mean to be a stranger in the village?

2. Consider the new academic vocabulary from this unit (Reader Response Criticism and Cultural Criticism). For each term, answer the following questions:

   • What was your understanding of the word prior to the unit?

   • How has your understanding of the word evolved throughout the unit?

   • How will you apply your understanding in the future?

Thinking about Connections

3. Review the activities and products (artifacts) you created. Choose those that most reflect your growth or increase in understanding.

4. For each artifact that you choose, record, respond, and reflect on your thinking and understanding, using the following questions as a guide:

   a. What skill/knowledge does this artifact reflect, and how did you learn this skill/knowledge?

   b. How did your understanding of the power of language expand through your engagement with this artifact?

   c. How will you apply this skill or knowledge in the future?

5. Create this reflection as Portfolio pages—one for each artifact you choose. Use the following model for your headings and commentary on questions.

Thinking About Thinking
Portfolio Entry

Concept:

Description of Artifact:

Commentary on Questions:

The Collective Perspective

Essential Questions

? How does applying a critical perspective affect an understanding of text?

? How does a new understanding of a text gained through interpretation help or hinder your enjoyment of it?

Unit Overview

Unit 2 provides an opportunity to continue your focus on critical perspectives, giving attention to Marxist, Feminist, and Archetypal literary theory. You will focus your attention on characters, characterizations, and the relationships between and among individuals and groups in a variety of texts including drama, film, and nonfiction. You will deepen your interpretation and discussion of text by considering the social and cultural implications of presenting a text from a particular perspective. By studying texts this way, you will start to understand various textual readings and reflect on whether or not the understanding of these perspectives enhances or limits your enjoyment of them.

The Collective Perspective
Contents

Goals

▶ To enhance critical thinking by studying the Feminist, Marxist, and Archetypal critical perspectives

▶ To apply multiple critical perspectives to drama, nonfiction, and non-print texts

▶ To engage in the writing process to generate a play script and an analytical response

Archetypal Criticism

Marxist Criticism

Feminist Criticism

Texts not included in these materials.

Learning Focus:

How Is My Perspective Shaped?

Reading and viewing are never passive activities. You bring certain levels of engagement to your reading and viewing, just as you bring biases, experiences, and prejudices to any text you read. As a matter of fact, it is difficult to truly get "lost in a text" because as a reader you bring so much to the interaction between reader and text.

Reading drama is especially demanding because most often there is no narrative point of view to help the reader understand the action. Viewers and readers have to be attentive to the usual literary elements, as well as dramatic elements such as stage directions, dialogue, action, subtext, costume, and set design, to infer meaning. At the same time, you can layer on a critical perspective or lens through which to interpret and understand the larger ideas of the drama. In this way you can form, challenge, and critique the ideas and opinions presented in the drama. Examining texts through multiple literary theories provides you the opportunity to sharpen your analytical skills as you consider alternative ways to view texts. In the last unit you worked with Reader Response Criticism and Cultural Criticism. In this unit, you will explore three new theories: Marxist Criticism, Archetypal Criticism, and Feminist Criticism. The first half of the unit will focus on Marxist Criticism and Archetypal Criticism, and the second half will focus on Feminist Criticism.

Archetypal Criticism

Archetypal Criticism deals with the similarities of patterns in the literature of widely diverse cultures. For example, most cultures have stories that present a hero's journey.

The following are common assumptions in the use of Archetypal Criticism:

▶ Certain images that share a common interpretation recur in texts from diverse cultures—water, sun, colors, the tree, settings such as the garden, the desert.

▶ Certain characters recur—the hero, the trickster, the great mother, the wise old man, the prodigal son.

▶ Certain motifs and patterns recur—creation stories, the quest, voyage to the underworld, journey, initiation.

Independent Reading: In this unit, you will be reading texts that share common archetypes—i.e., images, characters, motifs, and patterns. For independent reading, look for novels whose reading can be enhanced by an understanding of Marxist, archetypal, or feminist critical theories. Some possibilities for each theory are novels by Ayn Rand (Marxist); *Song of Solomon*, by Toni Morrison (archetypal), or novels by Margaret Atwood (feminist).

Marxist Criticism

Marxist Criticism asserts that economics is the foundation for all social, political, and ideological reality. The presence of economic inequalities is a power structure that drives history and influences differences in religion, race, ethnicity, and gender.

The following are common assumptions in the use of Marxist Criticism:

▶ All aspects of humanity are based on the struggle for economic power.

▶ The basic struggle in human society is between the "haves" and the "have nots."

Feminist Criticism

Feminist Criticism focuses on relationships between genders. It examines the patterns of thought, behavior, values, enfranchisement[1], and power in relations between and within the sexes. For example, a Feminist reading of *The Great Gatsby* may take into account the idea of power relationships between the men and women of the novel.

The use of Feminist Criticism includes these common assumptions:

▶ A pervasively patriarchal[2] society conveys the notion of male dominance through the images of women in its texts.

▶ Many literary texts lack complex female figures and deem the female reader as an outsider, or require her to assume male values in terms of perception, feelings, and actions.

▶ Issues of gender are central to artistic expression.

▶ Fictional portrayals of female characters often reflect and create stereotypical social and political attitudes toward women.

▶ Texts authored by women may have different viewpoints than texts authored by men.

---

[1] **enfranchisement:** having rights of citizenship, such as the right to vote
[2] **patriarchal:** society in which the male is head of the household and holds authority over women and children

Previewing the Unit

Essential Questions

1. How does applying a critical perspective affect an understanding
   of text?

2. How does a new understanding of a text gained through
   interpretation help or hinder your enjoyment of it?

Unit Overview and Learning Focus

Predict what you think this unit is about. Use the words or phrases
that stood out to you when you read the Unit Overview and the
Learning Focus.

Embedded Assessment 1

What knowledge must you have (what do you need to know) to succeed
on Embedded Assessment 1? What skills must you have (what must you
be able to do)?

A Close Reading of Film

You are about to view a series of film clips that will expose you to key thematic elements surrounding the critical perspectives in this unit. You will watch each clip twice. After the first viewing, you will complete a quickwrite by noting your impressions of a specific character in the film. Following the second viewing, you will answer a series of questions that will help you to begin thinking about different critical perspectives.

The Manchurian Candidate

First Screening: Compose a quickwrite that describes your initial response to the character, Mrs. Iselin. Conclude your quickwrite by listing several adjectives that describe Mrs. Iselin.

WORD CONNECTIONS

Choose a relationship closest to this pair of words: pervasive : widespread :: _____.

a. theoretical : practical
b. loathe : love
c. stereotypical : conventional
d. seeing : believing

Second Screening: What is the relationship between Mrs. Iselin and her son, Raymond Shaw? Cite specifics from the film clip in your response.

What does the staging of the characters (where they are physically located, how they move) in this scene suggest to you?

What is the power relationship between these two characters? Who is powerful? Who is in control?

How do you believe Raymond will react in the scenes that follow?

How does Mrs. Iselin differ from female villains you may have encountered previously?

These questions help examine the film from a(n) _____ critical perspective. Explain.

A Close Reading of Film

Nine to Five

First Screening: Compose a quickwrite that describes your feelings about "corporate" work. Generally, are careers in corporate settings considered desirable? Why or why not?

Second Screening: How might Judy describe her initial impressions of the consolidated organization?

Why is Eddie resentful of Judy's hiring?

What is Violet's role in this office? What appear to be her ambitions?

Do any of the characters appear to be happy with their jobs? What role does happiness play in selecting and maintaining a career?

Why do people work? What is the function of employment in our society?

These questions help examine the film from a(n) _____ critical perspective. Explain.

The Legend of Bagger Vance

First Screening

Compose a quickwrite that describes Bagger's role in this scene. Conclude your quickwrite by listing several adjectives that describe Bagger Vance.

Second Screening

What in the clip may indicate that Bagger is more than a regular golf caddy?

How does Hardy Greaves respond to Bagger? Does Hardy ever question Bagger's wisdom or advice?

What is the deeper meaning of Bagger's advice to Hardy?

What is the significance of Bagger's role in this clip?

Why can't helpers just dispense the information needed? Why is it important for the protagonist to find the needed information—"the one true authentic swing"—for herself or himself?

These questions help examine the film from a(n) _____ critical perspective. Explain.

From an Archetypal Perspective

ACADEMIC VOCABULARY

Archetypes are universal symbols—images, characters, motifs, or patterns—that recur in the myths, dreams, oral traditions, songs, literature, and other texts of peoples widely separated by time and place. **Archetypal Criticism** deals with the similarities of these patterns in the literature of widely diverse cultures.

LITERARY TERMS

A **motif** is a word, character, object, image, or idea that recurs in a literary work or works. A motif is almost always related to the theme of a work of literature.

The theory of **Archetypal Criticism** suggests that the study of literature can and should examine archetypes to derive meaning from and to understand literature. In this activity, you will examine the concept of "archetype" in preparation for your study of Archetypal Criticism.

1. Read and discuss the definitions for archetype and Archetypal Criticism.

2. In small groups, list ten of the following common archetypes on a large piece of poster paper. Then brainstorm examples and characteristics that you are already familiar with for each of the archetypes, adding the results of your brainstorming to your poster.

   - IMAGES—fire, rose, snake, water, sun, colors, the tree, settings such as the garden, the desert

   - CHARACTERS—the hero, the sidekick, the villain, the trickster, the great mother, the wise old man, the prodigal son

   - MOTIFS AND PATTERNS—creation stories, the quest, voyage to the underworld, journey, initiation, pursuit of revenge, damsel in distress, loss of innocence

3. With your group, illustrate and label your poster, highlighting the archetypes and their characteristics.

4. Be prepared to share your poster with the entire class.

Viewing the Subjects

SUGGESTED LEARNING STRATEGIES: Predicting, Graphic Organizer, Notetaking

You will engage in a gallery walk, viewing a collection of photos from a film version of a play you will be reading. Take notes on the following elements for each of the photos.

- Write down the identifying letter or number for each photo.
- Make note of the *mise en scène* (scene composition) of the photo. Consider where the characters are in relation to one another and within the setting of the photo.
- Describe the subject (character) or subject(s). Take into consideration costume, facial expression, and body language. You should view the characters' names and describe them.

PHOTO #	Description of *Mise en Scène*	Description of Character(s)

Viewing the Subjects

Based on your observations of the photos in the gallery, make some predictions about the play on a separate sheet of paper.

What is the story's setting?

What is the play about?

What kind of characters are in the play?

What are the relationships between the various characters?

Can you tell which characters have power and which do not?

Are there hints as to why they have that power?

As your classmates present their predictions about the play, engage in a discussion about connections and/or differences between their predictions and your group's predictions.

Use the following prompts to make further predictions about the play.

• After reviewing the publicity stills and discussing them with my peers I think this play is about...

• Understanding what this play is about, I could likely apply _____ Criticism, because....

Introducing *Pygmalion*

SUGGESTED LEARNING STRATEGIES: Marking the Text, Drafting, Paraphrasing/Summarizing, Graphic Organizer, Notetaking, Brainstorming

The Pygmalion myth is one of the sources for George Bernard Shaw's play, *Pygmalion*. As you read this myth, look for archetypal characters: the creative person, the object of his affection, and the being who grants his wish.

Myth

ABOUT THE AUTHOR

The Roman poet Ovid (43 BC–AD 18) is best known for *Metamorphoses,* a collection of myths describing transformation. Ovid is notable for his skillful construction of verse, including not only the hexameters of the *Metamorphoses,* but also the elegiacs of *Ars Amatoria,* three books that explore the art of love. The poet was exiled around AD 8; the collection of poems called *Tristia* explores his grief.

> **LITERARY TERMS**
>
> A **myth** is a traditional story, one passed down from generation to generation, that explains something in human life and in the world.

My Notes

ORPHEUS SINGS: PYGMALION AND THE STATUE

by Ovid

From Metamorphoses, Book X: 243-297 (~1850)

'Pygmalion had seen them, spending their lives in wickedness, and, offended by the failings that nature gave the female heart, he lived as a bachelor, without a wife or partner for his bed. But, with wonderful skill, he carved a figure, brilliantly, out of snow-white ivory, no mortal woman, and fell in love with his own creation. The features are those of a real girl, who, you might think, lived, and wished to move, if modesty did not forbid it. Indeed, art hides his art. He marvels: and passion, for this bodily image, consumes his heart. Often, he runs his hands over the work, tempted as to whether it is flesh or ivory, not admitting it to be ivory. He kisses it and thinks his kisses are returned; and speaks to it; and holds it, and imagines that his fingers press into the limbs, and is afraid lest bruises appear from the pressure. Now he addresses it with compliments, now brings it gifts that please girls, shells and polished pebbles, little birds, and many-coloured flowers, lilies and tinted

My Notes

beads, and the Heliades's[1] amber tears, that drip from the trees. He dresses the body, also, in clothing; places rings on the fingers; places a long necklace round its neck; pearls hang from the ears, and cinctures[2] round the breasts. All are fitting: but it appears no less lovely, naked. He arranges the statue on a bed on which cloths dyed with Tyrian murex are spread, and calls it his bedfellow, and rests its neck against soft down, as if it could feel.

The day of Venus's festival came, celebrated throughout Cyprus, and heifers, their curved horns gilded, fell, to the blow on their snowy neck. The incense was smoking, when Pygmalion, having made his offering, stood by the altar, and said, shyly: "If you can grant all things, you gods, I wish as a bride to have..." and not daring to say "the girl of ivory" he said "one like my ivory girl." Golden Venus, for she herself was present at the festival, knew what the prayer meant, and as a sign of the gods' fondness for him, the flame flared three times, and shook its crown in the air. When he returned, he sought out the image of his girl, and leaning over the couch, kissed her. She felt warm: he pressed his lips to her again, and also touched her breast with his hand. The ivory yielded to his touch, and lost its hardness, altering under his fingers, as the bees' wax of Hymettus softens in the sun, and is molded, under the thumb, into many forms, made usable by use. The lover is stupefied, and joyful, but uncertain, and afraid he is wrong, reaffirms the fulfillment of his wishes, with his hand, again, and again.

It was flesh! The pulse throbbed under his thumb. Then the hero, of Paphos[3], was indeed overfull of words with which to thank Venus, and still pressed his mouth against a mouth that was not merely a likeness. The girl felt the kisses he gave, blushed, and, raising her bashful eyes to the light, saw both her lover and the sky. The goddess attended the marriage that she had brought about, and when the moon's horns had nine times met at the full, the woman bore a son, Paphos, from whom the island takes its name.

Quickwrite: Many stories from different world cultures feature elements of this myth. Why do you think this myth permeates world cultures? What is it in human nature that inspires in us a desire to create life?

---

[1] **Heliades**: daughters of Helios, turned into poplar trees
[2] **cincture**: a belt or sash
[3] **Paphos**: mythical birthplace of Aphrodite

Ladies and Gentlemen

SUGGESTED LEARNING STRATEGIES: Quickwrite, Predicting, Marking
the Text, Think-Pair-Share, Graphic Organizer, Discussion Groups

Reflecting on Act 1 of *Pygmalion*

"THE NOTE TAKER. You see this creature with her kerbstone English:
the English that will keep her in the gutter to the end of her days.
Well, sir, in three months I could pass that girl off as a duchess at an
ambassador's garden party."   from *Pygmalion, Act I*

Quickwrite: What does this boast say about the note taker? What does
it say about the flower girl?

Making Predictions

Based on what you have learned about the note taker and the flower
girl, make two predictions about how their roles and situations might
relate to Marxist and Feminist Criticism.

Prediction 1:

Prediction 2:

Ladies and Gentlemen

LITERARY TERMS

Characterization is the process a writer uses to develop a character.

Identify characteristics for each of the characters. Provide textual support (evidence from the play) for your ideas. Consider the following elements of characterization:

- What they say (dialogue).
- What they do (actions).
- What they think (interior monologue).
- The people with whom they associate.
- What others say about them.

	Characteristics	Textual Support
ELIZA		
HIGGINS		
PICKERING		
MRS. PEARCE		

How is Eliza made to conform at Professor Higgins's home?

Does social class play a significant role in characterization?

Compare Eliza's situation to Baldwin's in "Stranger in the Village."

Rules of Etiquette

Higgins and Pickering have worked Eliza day and night, teaching her
proper speech and manners, but it appears they have more work to do
in the area of social graces. Reread the scene in Act III when Eliza visits
Mrs. Higgins on her at-home day.

> **LITERARY TERMS**
>
> A **satire** is a literary work
> that ridicules human
> weakness or folly to bring
> about social reform.

What social blunders does Eliza commit?

How is Shaw satirizing society in this scene?

How do the guests try to make what they see and what they are hearing
go together? Would they do the same for Eliza the flower girl? Why or
why not?

Think about a time when you committed a social blunder. What
happened?

Why do we find social blunders humorous?

Rules of Etiquette

Play scripts usually follow a particular pattern to establish a context for the story. Review the genre conventions of a play script and then respond to the quickwrite below.

- **Form:** Scripts begin with a title and are followed by a list of characters accompanied by a brief description. Next, an explanation of the setting is provided to set the stage for the dialogue that follows.

- **Dialogue:** Conversation is the key to successful play writing because it is how the audience learns about the problem. The characters' dialogue reveals conflict and moves the action through the stages of a plotline: exposition, rising action, climax, falling action, and resolution.

- **Problem:** Usually a play script revolves around an interesting conflict that complicates the lives of the characters involved before the problem is resolved.

- **Stage Directions:** Indicate the time and place of the action, entrances, exits, movement, subtext, etc. through stage directions. Stage directions also indicate what the characters are doing on stage as well as provide clues to voice or delivery of lines. Stage directions should be used strategically. Often, when a writer decides not to include them, it is because he or she is placing emphasis on the characters' words.

Quickwrite: Think about the social blunder you identified on the previous page. Write a brief dialogue with at least two characters and your blunder as the problem.

Reading Between the Lines

Performance 1

The following chart contains the text of a dialogue between two characters, known as A and B. As you watch the performance, try to identify the subtext of each part of the dialogue. For dialogue, *subtext* is the situational context in which the dialogue is spoken.

> **LITERARY TERMS**
> The **subtext** is an underlying theme or idea that lies below the surface text.

Text	Subtext	What clues help you figure out the subtext?
A: Well, here it is.		
B: Is that what I think it is?		
A: I think so.		
B: Are you sure?		
A: See for yourself, if you don't believe me.		
B: Okay, what now?		

Reading Between the Lines

Performance 2

This chart is just like the one on the previous page. Use it to take notes on the subtext as you listen to the second performance.

Text	Subtext	What clues help you figure out the subtext?
A: Well, here it is.		
B: Is that what I think it is?		
A: I think so.		
B: Are you sure?		
A: See for yourself, if you don't believe me.		
B: Okay, what now?		

Examining Eliza's Options

SUGGESTED LEARNING STRATEGIES: Summarizing/Paraphrasing,
Think-Pair-Share, Sharing and Responding, Graphic Organizer, Drafting

Act III ends with Eliza, Higgins, and Pickering leaving the ball. Imagine
the conversation that might take place when they get home. With a
small group, you will take one of the three characters and explore
answers to the following questions.

The Character _____

How does the character typically behave and speak?	How does the character feel now that the ball is over?

Now that you have discussed and taken notes on one of the characters
with your small group, you will work with another group to create a
dialogue with all three characters. Remember that the subtext is often
even more important than the words that are actually spoken, so
include any subtext that seems appropriate by noting it in parentheses
at the end of the corresponding line.

Examining Eliza's Options

WORD CONNECTIONS

Complete the analogy.

dialogue : monologue ::

_____

a. dimeter : monometer
b. prologue : epilogue
c. diatribe : diamante
d. logos : pathos

1. After you have read Act IV, compare how the conversation Shaw created is similar to and different from the one you and your group created.

2. In Act IV, Eliza asks, "Where am I to go? What am I to do? What's to become of me?" What are Eliza's options, given the setting of the play? Create a bubble cluster or other graphic organizer on which you brainstorm Eliza's options and the pros and cons of each.

Transformations

1. In Act V, we are reacquainted with Eliza's father, Alfred Doolittle. Like Eliza, Doolittle has been transformed. Use a Venn diagram or other graphic organizer to compare and contrast these two transformations. You should consider these points, as well as any others that occur to you:

   - What, specifically, about each character has changed?
   - How did the transformation occur?
   - How active was each character in the transformation?
   - How may the transformation impact each character's future?
   - What is each character's attitude toward the transformation?
   - What role does social class play in each of their transformations?

2. Answer the questions below after closely rereading the end of *Pygmalion* (beginning when Pickering and Doolittle exit for the wedding, leaving Higgins and Eliza alone).

When is Higgins in control?	When is Eliza in control?
How does he get control?	How does she get control?
How does he use his control?	How does she use her control?

What does each want from the other? How do you think they really feel? In other words, what is the subtext of their lines?

The play ends with Higgins laughing at the thought of Eliza marrying Freddy. Based on Shaw's portrayal of these characters, what do you imagine becomes of Eliza and Higgins?

I Feel a Song Coming On

LITERARY TERMS

Tone is the writer's attitude toward a character, a subject, or the reader.

Reader Response: What do you know about musicals? How are they similar to, and different from, plays and other forms of movies?

In the 1950s, Alan Jay Lerner and Frederick Loewe wrote *My Fair Lady*, their version of *Pygmalion*, for the musical theater. In the 1960s the story underwent another transformation, to the film of the same name. The stage and film versions incorporate many of Shaw's lines, but they also depart from Shaw's play in significant ways. As you watch parts of the film, consider the following questions.

Eliza's Future

What is the overall tone of this scene?	What in the film creates this tone?
How does Eliza feel about Higgins?	How can you tell?
How does Higgins feel about Eliza?	How can you tell?
Who is in control?	How can you tell?

"Without You"

What is the overall tone of this scene?	What in the film creates this tone?
How does Eliza feel about Higgins?	How can you tell?
How does Higgins feel about Eliza?	How can you tell?
Who is in control?	How can you tell?

On a separate sheet of paper, respond to the following:

"I've Grown Accustomed to Her Face"

This song serves as an interior monologue, showing Higgins's conflicting feelings. Describe the contrasts presented in the song.

"Where the Devil?"

When Higgins goes into his home, the tone of the scene changes. Describe the tone now. What film elements convey that tone? Why do you think the director wanted to set this particular tone?

Read carefully the last few shots of the film. What does the film suggest becomes of Eliza and Higgins? What details from the film text tell you this?

What Does Eliza Do?

SUGGESTED LEARNING STRATEGIES: **Visualizing, Notetaking, Brainstorming**

GRAMMAR & USAGE

Think about the sentence: "Unless Freddy is biologically repulsive to her, and Higgins biologically attractive to a degree that overwhelms all her other instincts, she will...marry Freddy." The commas before "and" and after "instincts" are not required, so why does Shaw include them? Try reading the sentence first without, and then with, those two commas. Writers sometimes add punctuation to slow the reader down, thus forcing the reader to pay more attention to certain parts of a sentence.

Consider the following quotation from Shaw's sequel to *Pygmalion*:

> This being the state of human affairs, what is Eliza fairly sure to do when she is placed between Freddy and Higgins? . . . Unless Freddy is biologically repulsive to her, and Higgins biologically attractive to a degree that overwhelms all her other instincts, she will, if she marries either of them, marry Freddy.

> And that is just what Eliza did.

Note below the parts of the sequel that you are able to visualize most clearly (the parts that appeal to your imagination).

Writing Prompt: Choose a part of the sequel that you were able to visualize clearly and transform the prose into drama. Use the space below to brainstorm ideas for your script.

Title and List of Characters	
Setting	
Problem/Dialogue	
Stage Directions	

Examining the Archetypes

Read and analyze the following excerpts from Shaw's *Pygmalion*, considering how each excerpt does or does not represent the archetype established in Ovid's myth. Consider the following elements: the character of the creator, the character of the created, the nature of the transformation, the relationship between the creator and the created. Make notes on your analysis of each excerpt.

My Notes

1 THE NOTE TAKER. You see this creature with her kerbstone English: the English that will keep her in the gutter to the end of her days. Well, sir, in three months I could pass that girl off as a duchess at an ambassador's garden party. I could even get her a place as a lady's maid or shop assistant, which requires better English. (Act I)

2 HIGGINS. Yes, you squashed cabbage leaf, you disgrace to the noble architecture of these columns, you incarnate insult to the English language: I could pass you off as the Queen of Sheba. (Act I)

3 HIGGINS. [*carried away*] Yes: in six months—in three if she has a good ear and a quick tongue— I'll take her anywhere and pass her off as anything. We'll start today: now! this moment! Take her away and clean her, Mrs. Pearce. (Act II)

4 HIGGINS. [*deftly retrieving the handkerchief and intercepting her on her reluctant way to the door*] You're an ungrateful wicked girl. This is my return for offering to take you out of the gutter and dress you beautifully and make a lady of you. (Act II)

5 HIGGINS. What! That thing! Sacred, I assure you. [*Rising to explain*] You see, she'll be a pupil; and teaching would be impossible unless pupils were sacred. I've taught scores of American millionairesses how to speak English: the best looking women in the world. I'm seasoned. They might as well be blocks of wood. *I* might as well be a block of wood. (Act II)

6 HIGGINS. Oh, I can't be bothered with young women. My idea of a lovable woman is something as like you as possible. I shall never get into the way of seriously liking young women: some habits lie too deep to be changed. [*Rising abruptly and walking about, jingling his money and his keys in his trouser pockets*] Besides, they're all idiots. (Act III)

GRAMMAR & USAGE

When Shaw writes, "I shall never get into the way of seriously liking you women: some habits lie too deep to be changed," he creates a compound sentence. **Compound sentences** have two or more independent clauses; and, in this case, the two clauses are joined by a colon. Independent clauses can also be joined by a semicolon, by a comma and a coordinating conjunction, and by a comma and a conjunctive adverb.

7 ELIZA. [*continuing*] It was just like learning to dance in the fashionable way: there was nothing more than that in it. But do you know what began my real education?

PICKERING. What?

ELIZA. [*stopping her work for a moment*] Your calling me Miss Doolittle that day when I first came to Wimpole Street. That was the beginning of self-respect for me. [*She resumes her stitching*] And there were a hundred little things you never noticed, because they came naturally to you. Things about standing up and taking off your hat and opening doors—(Act V)

8 ELIZA. I know. I am not blaming him. It is his way, isn't it? But it made such a difference to me that you didn't do it. You see, really and truly, apart from the things anyone can pick up (the dressing and the proper way of speaking, and so on), the difference between a lady and a flower girl is not how she behaves, but how she's treated. I shall always be a flower girl to Professor Higgins, because he always treats me as a flower girl, and always will; but I know I can be a lady to you, because you always treat me as a lady, and always will. (Act V)

9 ELIZA. You never thought of the trouble it would make for me.

HIGGINS. Would the world ever have been made if its maker had been afraid of making trouble? Making life means making trouble. There's only one way of escaping trouble; and that's killing things. Cowards, you notice, are always shrieking to have troublesome people killed. (Act V)

10 HIGGINS. [*wondering at her*] By George, Eliza, I said I'd make a woman of you; and I have. I like you like this. (Act V)

Writing Prompt: Using your notes, write an analysis of Shaw's use of the Pygmalion archetype as established in Ovid's Pygmalion myth. Focus your analysis on the extent to which Shaw adhered to or departed from the Pygmalion archetype. You should include all of the following:

a. A claim that identifies to what extent Shaw adheres to or departs from the archetype.

b. Examples from the text (the above quotes or other examples from the text) to support your claim.

c. How recognizing the archetype advances or complicates the reading.

d. Effective introductory and concluding paragraphs, a variety of sentence structures, effective use of rhetorical devices, and appropriate internal and external transitions to maintain coherence.

From a Marxist Perspective

Anticipation Guide

Review these statements about the importance of money, power, and social class, and then circle the responses that most nearly reflect your beliefs.

Being wealthy is a burden.	Strongly Agree	Agree	Disagree	Strongly Disagree
Middle-class people are happier than wealthy or poor people.	Strongly Agree	Agree	Disagree	Strongly Disagree
You can change your social standing if you try hard enough.	Strongly Agree	Agree	Disagree	Strongly Disagree
I would rather marry someone I love than someone who is rich.	Strongly Agree	Agree	Disagree	Strongly Disagree
Fame equals power.	Strongly Agree	Agree	Disagree	Strongly Disagree
People are more important than things.	Strongly Agree	Agree	Disagree	Strongly Disagree
Wealth is a reflection of how hard a person works.	Strongly Agree	Agree	Disagree	Strongly Disagree
People of different social classes can be close friends.	Strongly Agree	Agree	Disagree	Strongly Disagree
The love of money is the root of all evil.	Strongly Agree	Agree	Disagree	Strongly Disagree
People who have power have earned it and deserve to enjoy it.	Strongly Agree	Agree	Disagree	Strongly Disagree

Which statement brings out the strongest reaction in you? Explain your viewpoint.

From a Marxist Perspective

ACADEMIC VOCABULARY

Marxist Criticism asserts that economics provides the foundation for all social, political, and ideological reality. The presence of economic inequalities is a power structure that drives history and influences differences in religion, race, ethnicity, and gender.

Marxist Criticism

Read the description of **Marxist Criticism** at the left. Marxist Criticism is based on the theories of German philosopher, Karl Marx, who proposed that social conditions are a result of economic and political conditions. To Marxist critics, the economic conditions are the influencing factor in a culture's literature. The use of Marxist Criticism to analyze literature assumes the following:

- All aspects of humanity are based on the struggle for economic power.
- The basic struggle in human society is between the "haves" and the "have nots."

Read the lyrics for Tracy Chapman's song, "Talkin' Bout a Revolution." As you use SOAPSTone to analyze the lyrics, consider the perspective of Marxist Criticism.

SPEAKER	
OCCASION	
AUDIENCE	
PURPOSE	
SUBJECT	
TONE	

Karl Marx lived from 1818 to 1883. During his life, he was a philosopher, economist, political theorist, historian, and published author whose work was focused on the struggle between social classes and how the accumulation of wealth and power enables an economic minority to dominate a working class majority. Marxist Literary Criticism looks at ways in which a text reveals the oppression of the working class or poor by a dominant economic elite. Among questions that might be asked when looking at a text through a Marxist Criticism lens are the following:

1. Whose viewpoint is represented in the text (the poor, middle class, or weathy); i.e., whose story gets told?

2. What values are represented for each of the social classes (poor, middle class, weathy)?

3. What economic/social values are held by the main character(s)?

4. Who is the audience, and what does the text suggest about their values?

Research: Marxist Criticism considers characters' perspectives based on economic and social status. It looks at the "hidden rules" that are characteristic of each economic and social class. Conduct research to describe attitudes of each of these groups toward topics in the following graphic organizer.

	Poor	Middle Class	Wealthy
Money			
Use of Time			
Education			
Family Structure			
Social Behavior and Goals			

1. Based on your research, what are the "hidden rules" for each social/ economic class? Do you agree that these rules are hidden? Why or why not?

2. What would Marxist Criticism say about these rules? To what extent does a struggle for economic equality cause or perpetuate these differences?

3. Are these differences archetypal or stereotypical?

Money, Power, and Class in *Pygmalion*

Now that you have finished reading *Pygmalion*, it may be useful to think about the drama from the perspective of Marxist Criticism, looking at the relationships among power, money, and social class. As a part of a small group, you will analyze one of the three following topics and prepare a presentation for the class.

1 Power

Create a graphic to illustrate the hierarchy of power in *Pygmalion*. In other words, visually represent a ranking of who has the most power to who has the least power. In addition to the major characters (Higgins, Pickering, and Eliza), be sure to include the minor characters, such as Mrs. Pearce, Mrs. Higgins, Mr. Doolittle, Freddy, Clara, and Mrs. Eynsford Hill. Include on your graphic an explanation as to why some of the characters have power, while others do not.

2 Social Classes

Create a graphic to illustrate the social class structure in *Pygmalion*. First, consider what social classes are and how they are related to power and money. Identify the social classes represented in *Pygmalion*. Who is in each class? What do you think Shaw thought of social class divisions? What in the text makes you think this?

3 Money

Create a graphic to illustrate the hierarchy of economic status in *Pygmalion*. What is the economic status of each character? What are the thoughts of each of these characters toward their economic status? Be sure to include Eliza, Doolittle, Pickering, Higgins, and Freddy. As you think about Eliza and Doolitte, consider their thoughts and feelings both before and after their transformations.

Reflection

As you read *Pygmalion*, you thought about how this drama reflects the Pygmalion archetype it is named for. Today you have changed perspectives, looking at the drama with attention to economic and political issues such as money, power, and social class. What impact has this new way of looking at the play had on your understanding of it?

Illuminating *Pygmalion*

SUGGESTED LEARNING STRATEGIES: **Skimming/Scanning, Brainstorming, Self-Editing/Peer Editing**

Assignment

Your assignment is to work with a partner to write a script that transforms a scene from *Pygmalion*, so that it reflects a critical perspective. You will also write a reflection analyzing and evaluating your process and product.

Steps

1. Review with your partner the critical perspectives you have encountered so far: Reader Response Criticism, Cultural Criticism, Archetypal Criticism, and Marxist Criticism. As a team, discuss the guiding questions for each.

2. Choose one criticism that you and your partner think you would like to work with for this assignment.

3. Skim *Pygmalion* and identify scenes that would allow you to convey the criticism you have chosen in a clear and interesting way.

4. Brainstorm ways that the criticism you have chosen would change the drama; also, brainstorm how you would stage this scene in order to highlight the criticism most effectively.

5. Create a two-column page: the script you write goes on the left side, and the subtext, where appropriate, goes on the right side.

6. Review the genre conventions of a play script and work with your partner to draft the script for the transformed scene and the corresponding subtext.

7. In preparation for publishing your final draft, evaluate, revise and edit your script. As you revise, look for ways to improve your draft's organization, parallel structures, and use of appropriate techniques such as inverted word order or repetition to enhance meaning and add interest to your script. Reread your final draft and correct errors in spelling, conventions, grammar, style, and/or formatting. Consult appropriate references to create a technically sound final draft.

8. Reflect on your process and product, and write a response that addresses the following points:

   ▶ The process you, as a team, used to create your final product.

   ▶ Why you chose the scene and the criticism.

   ▶ How you transformed the scene to reflect the criticism you chose.

   ▶ How looking at the scene through another perspective affected your understanding of the drama.

⌐**TECHNOLOGY TIP** You may want to use word processing software to create your script. Remember to format your script appropriately, identifying actors, dialogue, and stage directions in different fonts. Use the program's font library to preview and choose appropriate fonts for each type of text.

You will be exploring four kinds of criticism, trying them out to see which one you and your partner agree will allow for the most interesting transformation of the drama. Understand that there may be some overlapping among the critical theories, but emphasize the differences. Begin by reviewing important characteristics of each criticism and decide which one to choose.

Criticism: (Write important characteristics and guiding questions under each.)	Scene from *Pygmalion*	What element of the play will you transform?	How will this affect the scene?
Reader Response Criticism			
Cultural Criticism			
Archetypal Criticism			
Marxist Criticism			

SCORING GUIDE

Scoring Criteria	Exemplary	Proficient	Emerging
Ideas of Transformation	The choice of scene and its transformation through a particular criticism reveals a sophisticated understanding of both the drama and the elements of the chosen criticism.	The scene is chosen and changed in a way that indicates a clear understanding of the chosen criticism.	The scene is not changed in a way that shows understanding of a particular criticism.
Organization of Transformation	Uses stage directions and subtext to reveal a mature understanding of the complexities and subtleties of scenes and characters, and of the drama itself.	Appropriate use of stage directions and subtext shows focused analysis of the scene and characters.	Stage directions and/or subtext do not add insight into the characters or scene.
Reflective Text	Reflection offers thorough explanation of choices made and provides a thoughtful discussion of how this different perspective affects understanding of the drama.	Reflection addresses choices made as well as how this different perspective affects understanding of the drama.	Reflection provides limited discussion of choices made and shows a vague grasp of how this different perspective affects understanding of the drama.
Evidence of the Writing Process	The script and reflection demonstrate thoughtful planning, significant revision, and careful editing for grammar and conventions in preparing a publishable draft.	The script and reflection demonstrate adequate planning, revision, and editing for grammar and conventions in preparing a publishable draft.	The script and/or the reflection lack evidence of planning, revision, and editing for grammar and conventions. The draft is not ready for publication.
Additional Criteria			

Comments:

Learning Focus:

Can I Still Enjoy A Movie?

After examining and transforming a text considering archetypes, power struggles, and wealth, you have been able to analyze text as well as consider the social and cultural implications of presenting a text from a particular perspective. In the second part of this unit, you will expand your toolbox of critical theories by adding a new critical perspective. In addition, you will encounter examples of how that theory is applied to a familiar story and a film, as models for applying that perspective to a work of literary merit.

Feminist Criticism: Feminist interpretation focuses on relationships between genders. It examines the patterns of thought, behavior, values, enfranchisement, and power in relations between and within the sexes. For example, a feminist reading of *Pygmalion* may take into account the idea of power relationships between the men and women of the play. Following are some common assumptions in Feminist Criticism:

▶ A pervasively patriarchal society conveys the notion of male dominance through the images of women in its texts.

▶ Many literary texts lack complex female figures and deem the female reader as an outsider, or require her to assume male values in terms of perception, feelings, and actions.

▶ Issues of gender and sexuality are central to artistic expression.

▶ Fictional portrayals of female characters often reflect and create stereotypical social and political attitudes toward women.

▶ Texts authored by women may have different viewpoints from those in texts authored by men.

You have worked with film as text before and know that **cinematic elements** are used by filmakers to create certain effects and manipulate viewers' perspectives. These elements should also be taken into consideration as you apply critcial theory to the story content and cinematic techniques of film production. Viewing a film through the lens of Marxist or Archetypal or Feminist Critical theory can significantly alter your understanding and appreciation of a film.

A Reversal of Fortune

The following essay is an example of literary criticism. As you read it, consider the critical perspective the author takes toward the Cinderella legend.

Nonfiction

ABOUT THE AUTHOR

An author, educator, and activist, Madonna Kolbenschlag (1935–2000) wrote six books on feminism and spirituality. A member of the Catholic Sisters of Humility, Kolbenschlag earned Ph.Ds in both literature and clinical psychology. *Kiss Sleeping Beauty Goodbye* (1979) uses fairy tale and myth to explore contemporary female psychology. *Eastward Toward Eve* (1996) explores the connections between gender, culture, and psychology.

Cinderella, THE LEGEND

From *Kiss Sleeping Beauty Goodbye* by Madonna Kolbenschlag

Cinderella, the best-known and probably best-liked fairy tale, is above all a success story. The rags-to-riches theme perhaps explains its equal popularity among boys as well as girls. It is a very old fairy tale having at least 345 documented variants and numerous unrecorded versions. The iconic[1] focus of the tale on the lost slipper and Cinderella's "perfect fit" suggest that the story may have originated in the Orient where the erotic significance of tiny feet has been a popular myth since ancient times.

The basic motifs of the story are well-known: an ill-treated heroine, who is forced to live by the hearth; the twig she plants on her mother's grave that blossoms into a magic tree; the tasks demanded of the heroine; the magic animals that help her perform the tasks and provide her costume for the ball; the meeting at the ball; the heroine's flight from the ball; the lost slipper; the shoe test; the sisters' mutilation of their feet; the discovery of the true bride and the happy marriage. The variants retain the basic motifs; while differing

My Notes

LITERARY TERMS
Allusion is a reference to a well-known person, event, or place from history, music, art, or another literary work.

GRAMMAR & USAGE
Note the first sentence in the second paragraph. It has a list introduced by a colon. When creating a list followed by a colon, you typically separate items in the list with commas. However, as in this list, it is necessary to use a semicolon to separate the items if any of the individual items have commas within them. Note, for example, that the first item in the list has a comma within it, to separate the descriptive clause from the word it modifies. To make that distinction clear, all subsequent items in the list are separated by semicolons.

---

[1] **iconic:** an object or concept with great cultural significance to a wide cultural group

WORD CONNECTIONS

This essay contains several words that may be unfamiliar to you. Find definitions for these words to help you make meaning from the text:

aspiration, seminal, abasement, servitude, paradigm, sojourn, deus ex machina, docility, domesticity, virulence, icon, Teutonic.

My Notes

WORD CONNECTIONS

Virtue comes from the Anglo-French *vertu*, meaning "moral strength or excellence." Other related words include *virtuoso* and *virtuosity*, which both refer to technical skill as a sign of worth.

considerably in detail, they range more widely in their origins than any other fairy tale: Asiatic, Celtic, European, Middle-Eastern and American Indian versions numbered among them.

The Horatio Alger quality of the story helps to explain its special popularity in mercantile[2] and capitalistic societies. As a parable of social mobility it was seized upon by the writers of the new "literature of <u>aspiration</u>" in the seventeenth and eighteenth centuries as a basic plot for a new kind of private fantasy—the novel. Our literary world has not been the same since Pamela and all her orphaned, governess sisters. Most Anglo-American novels, early and late, are written in the shadow of Pamela and the Cinderella myth. Even Franklin's *Autobiography*, the <u>seminal</u> work in the success genre, owes much to the myth. The primary "moral" of the fairy tale—that good fortune can be merited—is the every essence of the Protestant Ethic.

At the personal and psychological level, Cinderella evokes intense identification. It is a tale of sibling rivalry (and subliminally, of sex-role stereotyping)—a moral fable about socialization. Very few themes could be closer to the inner experience of the child, an emerging self enmeshed[3] in a family network. ...

The personality of the heroine is one that, above all, accepts *abasement* as a prelude to and precondition of *affiliation*. That abasement is characteristically expressed by Cinderella's <u>servitude</u> to menial[4] tasks, work that diminishes her. This willing acceptance of a condition of worthlessness and her expectation of rescue (as reward for her virtuous suffering) is a recognizable <u>paradigm</u> of traditional feminine socialization. Cinderella is deliberately and systematically excluded from meaningful achievements. Her stepmother assigns her to meaningless tasks; her father fails her as a helpful mentor. Her sisters, inferior in quality of soul, are preferred before her. ...

Like most fairy tales, Cinderella dramatizes the passage to maturity. Her <u>sojourn</u> among the ashes is a period of grieving, a transition to a new self. On the explicit level of the story, Cinderella is literally grieving for her dead mother. Grimm's version of the tale preserves the sense of process, of growth that is symbolized in the narrative. Instead of a fairy godmother—<u>deus ex machina</u>—Cinderella receives a branch of hazel bush from her father. She plants the twig over her mother's grave and cultivates it with her prayers and tears. This is her contact with her past, her roots, her essential self. Before one can be transformed one must grieve for the lost as well as the possible selves, as yet unfulfilled—Kierkegaard's existential anguish. ...

---

[2] **mercantile:** engage in trade and commerce
[3] **enmeshed:** entangled or caught in some situation or trap
[4] **menial:** lowly and sometimes degrading

The Perrault version places great emphasis on the "midnight" prohibition given to Cinderella. The traditional connotation would, of course, associate it with the paternal mandate of obedience, and a threat: if the heroine does not return to <u>domesticity</u> and <u>docility</u> at regular intervals she may lose her "virtue" and no longer merit her expected one. Like the old conduct manuals for ladies, the moral of the tale warns against feminine excursions as well as ambition. Too much time spent "abroad" may result in indiscreet sex or unseemly hubris, or both. …

The slipper, the central <u>icon</u> in the story, is a symbol of sexual bondage and imprisonment in a stereotype. Historically, the <u>virulence</u> of its significance is born out in the twisted horrors of Chinese footbinding practices. On another level, the slipper is a symbol of power—with all of its accompanying restrictions and demands for conformity.[5] When the Prince offers Cinderella the lost slipper (originally a gift of the magic bird), he makes his kingdom hers.

We know little of Cinderella's subsequent role. In Grimm's version she is revenged by the birds which pluck out the eyes of the envious sisters. But Perrault's version celebrates Cinderella's kindness and forgiveness. Her sisters come to live in the palace and marry two worthy lords. In the Norse variant of the tale, Aslaug, the heroine, marries a Viking hero, bears several sons, and wields a good deal of power in <u>Teutonic</u> style. (She is the daughter of Sigurd and Brynhild.) But in most tales Cinderella disappears into the vague region known as the "happily ever after." She changes her name, no doubt, and—like so many women—is never heard of again.

Writing Prompt: After discussing the essay in class, write a sentence that you think states the thesis of Kolbenschlag's essay. Then write a letter to Kolbenschlag in which you refute, confirm, or extend her thesis as you understand it.

---

[5] **conformity:** compliance with prevailing social standards, attitudes, and practices

My Notes

My Notes

Folk Tale

> **ABOUT THE AUTHOR**
> A folklorist, anthropologist, and novelist, Zora Neale
> Hurston (1891–1960) was an important voice of the
> Harlem Renaissance. She studied anthropology at
> Barnard University, collecting folk tales in the rural
> South that were published in *Mules and Men* (1935) and
> *Tell My Horse* (1938), a fictional work that included her
> field studies of voodoo in Haiti. Hurston also completed
> four novels, of which the best known is *Their Eyes Were
> Watching God* (1937). During her career, Hurston also
> taught at North Carolina College for Negroes and worked
> at the Library of Congress.

Why Women Always Take Advantage of Men

from Men and Mules
by Zora Neale Hurston

Chunk 1

"Don't you know you can't git de best of no woman in de talkin' game? Her tongue is all de weapon a woman got," George Thomas chided Gene. "She could have had mo' sense, but she told God no, she'd ruther take it out in hips. So God give her her ruthers. She got plenty hips, plenty mouf and no brains."

"Oh, yes, womens is got sense too," Mathilda Moseley jumped in. "But they got too much sense to go 'round braggin' about it like y'all do. De lady people always got de advantage of mens because God fixed it dat way."

"Whut ole black advantage is y'all got?" B. Moseley asked indignantly. "We got all de strength and all de law and all de money and you can't git a thing but whut we jes' take pity on you and give you."

"And dat's jus' de point," said Mathilda triumphantly. "You *do* give it to us, but how come you do it?" And without waiting for an answer Mathilda began to tell why women always take advantage of men.

You see in de very first days, God made a man and a woman and put 'em in a house together to live. 'Way back in them days de woman was just as strong as de man and both of 'em did de same things. They useter get to fussin' 'bout who gointer do this and that and sometime they'd fight, but they was even balanced and neither one could whip de other one.

Chunk 2

One day de man said to hisself, "B'lieve Ah'm gointer go see God and ast Him for a li'l mo' strength so Ah kin whip dis 'oman and make her mind. Ah'm tired of de way things is." So he went on up to God.

"Good mawnin', Ole Father."

"Howdy man. Whut you doin' 'round my throne so soon dis mawnin'?"

"Ah'm troubled in mind, and nobody can't ease mah spirit 'ceptin' you."

God said: "Put yo' plea in de right form and Ah'll hear and answer."

"Ole Maker, wid de mawnin' stars glitterin' in yo' shinin' crown, wid de dust from yo' footsteps makin' worlds upon worlds, wid de blazin' bird we call de sun flyin' out of yo' right hand in de mawnin' and consumin' all day de flesh and blood of stump-black darkness, and comes flyin' home every evenin' to rest on yo' left hand, and never once in all yo' eternal years, mistood de left hand for de right,

Ah ast you *please* to give me mo' strength than dat woman you give me, so Ah kin make her mind. Ah know you don't want to be always comin' down way past de moon and stars to be straightenin' her out and its got to be done. So give me a li'l mo' strength, Ole Maker and Ah'll do it."

"All right, Man, you got mo' strength than woman."

So de man run all de way down de stairs from Heben till he got home. He was so anxious to try his strength on de woman dat he couldn't take his time. Soon's he got in de house he hollered "Woman! Here's yo' boss. God done tole me to handle you whichever way Ah please. Ah'm yo' boss."

Chunk 3

De woman flew to fightin' 'im right off. She fought 'im frightenin' but he beat her. She got her wind and tried 'im agin but he whipped her agin. She got herself together and made de third try on him vigorous but he beat her every time. He was so proud he could whip 'er at last, dat he just crowed over her and made her do a lot of things she didn't like. He told her, "Long as you obey me, Ah'll be good to yuh, but every time yuh rear up Ah'm gointer put plenty wood on yo' back and plenty water in yo' eyes."

De woman was so mad she went straight up to Heben and stood befo' de Lawd. She didn't waste no words. She said, "Lawd, Ah come befo' you mighty mad t'day. Ah want back my strength and power Ah useter have."

My Notes

WORD CONNECTIONS

Even though *dis-incouraged* is not a word you'll find in the dictionary, we can still trace its roots. The Latin root *cur* means "heart" and is the base of the word *courage.* By adding the prefix *dis-* which means "deprive," we create a word meaning "to deprive of hope or courage." By adding the prefix *en-*, which means "to make" or "to cause", we create a word with the opposite meaning—*encourage.* Hurston has added both prefixes, creating a word this has a more complex meaning.

My Notes

"Woman, you got de same power you had since de beginnin.'"

"Why is it then, dat de man kin beat me now and he useter couldn't do it?"

"He got mo' strength than he useter have. He come and ast me for it and Ah give it to 'im. Ah gives to them that ast, and you ain't never ast me for no mo' power."

"Please suh, God, Ah'm astin' you for it now. Jus' gimme de same as you give him."

God shook his head. "It's too late now, woman. Whut Ah give, Ah never take back. Ah give him mo' strength than you and no matter how much Ah give you, he'll have mo.'"

Chunk 4

De woman was so mad she wheeled around and went on off. She went straight to de devil and told him what had happened.

He said, "Don't be dis-incouraged, woman. You listen to me and you'll come out mo' than conqueror. Take dem frowns out yo' face and turn round and go right on back to Heben and ast God to give you dat bunch of keys hangin' by de mantel-piece. Then you bring 'em to me and Ah'll show you what to do wid 'em."

So de woman climbed back up to Heben agin. She was mighty tired but she was more out-done that she was tired so she climbed all night long and got back up to Heben agin. When she got befo' de throne, butter wouldn't melt in her mouf.

"O Lawd and Master of de rainbow, Ah know yo' power. You never make two mountains without you put a valley in between. Ah know you kin hit a straight lick wid a crooked stick."

"Ast for whut you want, woman."

"God, gimme dat bunch of keys hangin' by yo' mantel-piece."

"Take 'em."

So de woman took de keys and hurried on back to de devil wid 'em. There was three keys on de bunch. Devil say, "See dese three keys? They got mo' power in 'em than all de strength de man kin ever git if you handle 'em right. Now dis first big key is to de do' of de kitchen and you know a man always favors his stomach. Dis second one is de key to de bedroom and he don't like to be shut out from dat neither and dis last key is de key to de cradle and he don't want to be cut off from his generations at all. So now you take dese keys and go lock up everything and wait till he come to you. Then don't you unlock nothin' until he use his strength for yo benefit and yo' desires."

De woman thanked 'im and tole 'im, "If it wasn't for you, Lawd knows whut us po' women folks would do."

She started off but de devil halted her. "Jus' one mo' thing: don't go home braggin' 'bout yo' keys. Jus' lock up everything and say nothin' until you git asked. And then don't talk too much."

De woman went on home and did like de devil tole her. When de man come home from work she was settin' on de porch singin' some song 'bout "Peck on de wood make de bed go good."

When de man found de three doors fastened what useter stand wide open he swelled up like pine lumber after a rain. First thing he tried to break in cause he figgered his strength would overcome all obstacles. When he saw he couldn't do it, he ast de woman, "Who locked dis do'?"

She tole 'im, "Me."

"Where did you git de key from?"

"God give it to me."

He run up to God and said, "God, woman got me locked 'way from my vittles, my bed and my generations, and she say you give her the keys."

God said, "I did, Man, Ah give her de keys, but de devil showed her how to use 'em!"

"Well, Ole Maker, please gimme some keys jus' lak 'em so she can't git de full control."

"No, Man, what Ah give Ah give. Woman got de key."

"How kin Ah know 'bout my generations?"

"Ast de woman."

So de man come on back and submitted hisself to de woman and she opened de doors.

He wasn't satisfied but he had to give in. "Way after while he said to de woman, "Le's us divide up. Ah'll give you half of my strength if you lemme hold de keys in my hands."

De woman thought dat over so de devil popped and tol her, "Tell 'im, naw. Let 'im keep his strength and you keep yo' keys."

So de woman wouldn't trade wid 'im and de man had to mortgage his strength to her to live. And dat's why de man makes and de woman takes. You men is still braggin' 'bout yo' strength and de women is sittin' on de keys and lettin' you blow off till she git ready to put de bridle on you.

B. Moseley looked over at Mathilda and said, "You just like a hen in de barnyard. You cackle so much you give de rooster de blues."

Mathilda looked over at him archly and quoted:

Stepped on a pin, de pin bent

And dat's de way de story went.

Chunk 5

My Notes

Battle of the Sexes

Think about the gender issues raised by the authors of the essay "Cinderella, the Legend" and the folk tale "Why Women Always Take Advantage of Men." Use a Venn diagram to compare and contrast the issues raised by each author individually and those shared by both. Share the information in your diagram with the rest of your group in a discussion.

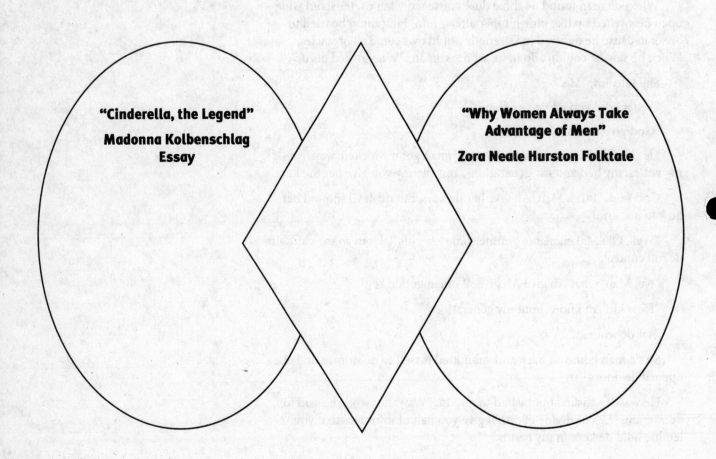

"Cinderella, the Legend"

Madonna Kolbenschlag Essay

"Why Women Always Take Advantage of Men"

Zora Neale Hurston Folktale

Summarize the significant points of your group's discussion. Include areas where the group reached consensus as well as the most important points of dissension, if any.

From a Feminist Perspective

SUGGESTED LEARNING STRATEGIES: Rereading, Graphic Organizer, Quickwrite

Think about the description of **Feminist Criticism** in the Learning Focus on page 120 and in the vocabulary at the right. Then answer the following questions about the general assumptions of this critical perspective.

1. If a matriarchal society is the opposite of a patriarchal society, what is the basis of the difference?

2. What is one assumption of Feminist Criticism about patriarchal societies?

3. What point of view does Feminist Criticism take toward the treatment of female characters in many literary texts?

4. How can a literary character both reflect and create stereotypes?

5. What assumption does Feminist Criticism make about texts authored by men versus those authored by women?

ACADEMIC VOCABULARY

Feminist Criticism focuses on relationships between genders. It examines the patterns of thought, behavior, values, enfranchisement, and power in relations between and within the sexes.

From a Feminist Perspective

WORD CONNECTIONS

The Latin root of the word *assumption* is *sumere*, meaning "take." When we *assume*, or make an *assumption*, we take on a responsibility, an idea, etc.

Consider some of the common assumptions in the use of Feminist Criticism. Based on your reading and discussion of "Cinderella, the Legend" and "Why Women Always Take Advantage of Men," decide whether Madonna Kolbenschlag and Zora Neale Hurston would tend to agree or disagree with the common assumptions below. Then decide whether you agree or disagree with the same statements and record your thinking in the last column.

Common Assumptions in the Use of a Feminist Critical Perspective	Kolbenschlag		Hurston		You	
	Agree	Disagree	Agree	Disagree	Agree	Disagree
Images of women support a patriarchal society.						
The female reader is an outsider who must assume male values.						
Gender issues are central.						
Fictional portrayals of women are stereotypical.						
Texts authored by women may have different viewpoints from those authored by men.						

Feminist Critique: The Tree of Life

SUGGESTED LEARNING STRATEGIES: Summarizing/Paraphrasing, Graphic Organizer, Quickwrite

A cornerstone of Feminist Criticism is the examination of the portrayal of gender roles and relationships between men and women. Use the following questions to apply a Feminist Critical Perspective to Shel Silverstein's *The Giving Tree*.

WORD CONNECTIONS

Complete the analogy.

matriarchal : patriarchal ::

_____

- • How are women presented in the text? How are men presented in the text?

- • How is the relationship between men and women presented?

- • To what extent does the portrayal of men and women support a patriarchal view of the world?

a. matricide : patricide
b. patrilineal : matrilineal
c. patrimony : matrimony
d. pater : mater

Use the following graphic organizer to analyze the story. Write a passage in the left column, and, using the questions above, write your analysis in the right column. Your teacher will model the completion of the first two or three passages.

Passage	Answers to Questions and Analysis

Feminist Critique: The Tree of Life

Passage	Answers to Questions and Analysis

Quickwrite: Consider the final line of the story: "And the tree was happy." Do you agree that the tree is happy? How could a Feminist reading of this story give the reader a new or different perspective on understanding this story?

View from a Lens: A Review of Film Terms

SUGGESTED LEARNING STRATEGIES: **Marking the Text, Summarizing/ Paraphrasing, Brainstorming**

The following are film terms you will need in the next few activities. The ones followed by an asterisk are the ones you learned in Unit 1 (page 31).

Shots

Shot: A single piece of film uninterrupted by cuts.*

Establishing Shot (ES): Often a long shot or a series of shots that sets the scene. This shot is used to establish setting and to show transitions between locations.*

Framing

Long Shot: (LS): A shot from some distance. If filming a person, the full body is shown. It may show the isolation or vulnerability of the character (also called a **Full Shot**).*

Medium Shot (MS): The most common shot. The camera seems to be a medium distance from the object being filmed. A medium shot shows the person from the waist up. The effect is to ground the story.

Close-Up (CU): The image being shot takes up at least 80 percent of the frame.*

Extreme Close-Up (ECU): The image being shot is a part of a whole, such as an eye or a hand.*

Two Shot: A scene between two people shot exclusively from one angle that includes both characters more or less equally. It is used in love scenes, arguments, or scenes where interaction between the two characters is important.*

Mise en Scène: The arrangement of performers and properties on a stage for a theatrical production or before the camera in a film.*

Camera Angles

Eye Level: A shot taken from a normal height, that is, the character's eye level; 90 to 95 percent of the shots seen are eye level because it is the most natural angle.*

High Angle: Camera is above the subject. This usually has the effect of making the subject look smaller than normal, giving him or her the appearance of being weak, powerless, and trapped.*

Low Angle: Camera shoots subject from below. This usually has the effect of making the subject look larger than normal, and therefore strong, powerful, and threatening.

Camera Movements

Pan: Stationary camera that moves side to side. Panning is used to create a source of tension or to provide information.

Tilt: Pivoting up or down along a vertical axis.

Zoom: Stationary camera where the lens moves to make an object seem to move closer to or farther away from the camera. With this technique, moving into a character is often a personal or revealing movement, while moving away distances or separates the audience from the character.

Dolly/Tracking: Camera is on a track that allows it to move with the action. It may be used to follow in front, behind, or next to a character as he or she walks or runs.

Boom/Crane: Camera is on a crane over the action; used to create overhead shots.

Lighting

High Key: Scene is flooded with light, creating a bright and open-looking scene.*

Low Key: Scene is flooded with shadows and darkness, creating suspense or suspicion.*

Bottom Lighting: Direct lighting from below, often making the subject appear dangerous or evil.*

Side Lighting: Direct lighting from one side. This may indicate a split personality or moral ambiguity.

Front Lighting: Soft lighting on the actor's face. It gives the appearance of innocence or goodness, or a halo effect.*

Back Lighting: Strong light behind the subject.*

Editing Techniques

Cut: Most common editing technique. Two pieces of film are sliced together to "cut" to another image.

Dissolve: A kind of fade in which one image is slowly replaced by another. It can create a connection between images.

Wipe: A new image wipes off the previous image. A wipe is more fluid than a cut and quicker than a dissolve.

Flashback: Cut or dissolve to action that has happened in the past.

Shot-Reverse-Shot: a shot of one subject, then another, then back to the first. It is often used for conversation or reaction shots and is also used with eye-line match.

Cross Cutting: Cut into action that is happening simultaneously. This is also called *parallel editing*.

Point of View: Shows what things look like from the perspective of someone or something in the scene. It may be juxtaposed with shots of the actor's face in order to make a connection with the viewer.

Eye-Line-Match: Cut to an object, then to a person. This technique shows what a person seems to be looking at.

Fade: Can be to or from black or white. A fade begins in darkness and gradually assumes full brightness (fade-in) or the image gradually gets darker (fade-out). A fade often implies that time has passed.

Sound

Diegetic: Sound that would be logically heard by the characters in the film.

Nondiegetic: Sound that could not be heard by the characters but is designed for audience reaction. An example might be ominous music for foreshadowing.

Applying Film Terms to *Rear Window*

The Opening Montage

In this activity, you will view a portion of Alfred Hitchcock's *Rear Window* and apply the film terms you have learned. The first segment you will view is the opening montage, or sequence of images.

As you view the segment, note the images you see. What story do these images tell?

> **LITERARY TERMS**
>
> A **montage** is a composite picture that is created by bringing together a number of images and arranging them to create a connected whole.

Image	Analysis and Interpretation

Applying Film Terms to *Rear Window*

The Apartment House Segment

This segment shows the apartment houses outside Jeff's window as the occupants are waking up.

The list of characters you will encounter is as follows:

A Dancer   A Sculptor

A Songwriter   Miss Lonelyheart

A Man and his Wife   Newlyweds

A Couple who sleep on the fire escape

What do you know about these characters?	How do you know? (Examples)

Identify the film techniques used in the scenes you have viewed, as well as the effects of those techniques.

Scene	Film Technique	Effect
Opening Montage/Apartment Shots		
Jeff watching the newlyweds entering their apartment		
Lisa introducing herself		
Miss Lonelyhearts' imaginary date		
Argument between Thorwald and wife		
Argument between Jeff and Lisa		
Jeff spying on Thorwald		

Rear Window: Screening Day 1

As you watch the first part of the film again, take notes relating to the following elements:

What film techniques underscore/portray the dominant patriarchal culture?

Film Techniques
Shots/Framing/Camera Angles/Camera Movements/ Sound/Editing/ Lighting

How are women presented?
How are men presented?
How is their relationship presented?

Cinematic Elements
Dialogue/Vocal Delivery/Props/Sets/Costumes/Makeup

Writing Prompt: A pervasively patriarchal society conveys the notion of male dominance through the images of women in its texts. To what extent does the portrayal of women in *Rear Window* convey the notion of male dominance in a patriarchal society?

Rear Window: Screening Day 2

SUGGESTED LEARNING STRATEGIES: Notetaking, Graphic Organizer, Think-Pair-Share, Self-Editing/Peer Editing

As you watch the second part of *Rear Window*, take notes relating to the following elements:

What film techniques underscore/portray the dominant patriarchal culture?

Film Techniques
Shots/Framing/Camera Angles/Camera Movements/ Sound/Editing/ Lighting

How are women presented?
How are men presented?
How is their relationship presented?

Cinematic Elements
Dialogue/Vocal Delivery/Props/Sets/Costumes/Makeup

Writing Prompt: Many literary texts lack complex female figures and deem the female reader to be an outsider or require her to assume male values in terms of perception, feelings, and actions. How does this assumption of Feminist Criticism apply to the second part of *Rear Window*?

Rear Window: Screening Day 3

As you watch the third part of *Rear Window*, take notes relating to the
following elements:

What film techniques underscore/portray the dominant patriarchal culture?

Film Techniques

Shots/Framing/Camera Angles/Camera Movements/ Sound/Editing/ Lighting

How are women presented?
How are men presented?
How is their relationship presented?

Cinematic Elements

Dialogue/Vocal Delivery/Props/Sets/Costumes/Makeup

Writing Prompt: Fictional portrayals of female characters often reflect
and create stereotypical social and political attitudes toward women.
Are female characters in this portion of *Rear Window* portrayed in a
way that supports this assumption of Feminist Criticism? Write an
interpretation of this portion of the film. Support your interpretation
with examples from the film. Anticipate and respond to readers'
contradictory views and information. Also anticipate and respond to
readers' questions about your interpretation and how your examples
support your assertions.

Looking Back Through *Rear Window*

In *Rear Window*, Hitchcock skillfully draws the viewers into Jeff's world, a world that Jeff sees through the lens of his camera. Each apartment Jeff watches becomes, in a way, its own movie or story. What if we portrayed those "movies" with a feminist lens on the camera?

Analyzing Subplot and Characters

With a small group, choose three subplots you would like to explore in more detail. For each subplot, consider the focus questions below. For example, what would a Feminist Critical Perspective say about Ms. Lonelyheart and her problems? Is she sad because she does not have a man? How is she presented with a man present versus when she is alone? To what extent does this portrayal present a patriarchal view of her? Analyze each subplot using a feminist perspective.

Feminist Critique

How are women presented? How are men presented?

What is the relationship between men and women? Are women's opinions ignored? Who has the power?

To what extent does the portrayal of men and women support a patriarchal (or male centered) view of the world?

When you complete your analysis, work together as a group to perform the following tasks:

1. Use a piece of paper or poster board.

2. Sketch a diagram of three of the windows of the apartments Jeff watches.

3. Next, cut out slips of paper the same size as the windows you have drawn. These will represent the shades that Jeff's neighbors (with the exception of the newlyweds) never seem to close. Tape or glue the "shades" only to the top of the windows.

4. On the outside of each shade, write the name and/or description of the person or people who live there: the dancer, the sculptor, the composer, Miss Lonelyhearts, Mr. and Mrs. Thorwald, the newlyweds, the couple with the little dog, etc.

5. Underneath the shade, so that you can read it if you lift the flap, write a brief description and analysis of the story of that apartment, using the critical perspective of your preceding analysis.

6. Share your poster as your teacher directs, and enjoy viewing those created by your classmates. How were they similar to or different from your own?

Analyzing the Main Plot and Character

As intriguing as these subplots may be, they are still just that—subplots. Now turn the camera inward, so that you are viewing Jeff's own apartment. As Stella says, "What people ought to do is get outside their own house and look in for a change."

Writing Prompt: Write a brief synopsis of Jeff's story and then analyze it from two of the critical perspectives you have studied so far. This analysis should include a thoughtful thesis, a coherent analysis using the two perspectives, and an insightful conclusion.

Before beginning your paper, you may want to review the assumptions of the three critical perspectives presented in this unit and those presented in Unit 1. See questions related to the feminist assumptions on the previous page and questions related to the archetypal and Marxist assumptions below.

Archetypal Critique

- Do you identify universal symbols (images, characters, motifs, and patterns) that are similar across widely diverse cultures?

- Are these archetypes complete? Why or why not?

- How does the archetype advance or complicate your reading?

Marxist Critique

- Are there "haves" and "have-nots?"

- Are there economic inequities that create a power struggle?

- What causes these inequities? Why does the author focus on these inequities?

Applying a Critical Perspective

SUGGESTED LEARNING STRATEGIES: **Graphic Organizer, Drafting, Self-Editing/Peer Editing, Revising**

Assignment

Your assignment is to write an analytical essay applying the Feminist Critical Perspective to a short story. Include a brief synopsis of the text.

Steps

1. Read the short stories listed below and choose the story that best resonates with you on a personal level (both stories are included on the following pages). Use that story for your analytical essay.

   a. "The Story of An Hour" by Kate Chopin

   b. "A Rose For Emily" by William Faulkner

2. Reread your selected story applying a Feminist Critical Perspective. Consider the focus questions you have used throughout this unit for guidance. These may include:

   ▶ How are women presented in the text? How are men presented in the text?

   ▶ How is the relationship between men and women presented?

   ▶ To what extent does the portrayal of men and women support a patriarchal (or male centered) view of the world?

   ▶ What ambiguities, nuances, and complexities does the author present, and how do they guide the reader to form an interpretation?

3. Generate a graphic organizer to record textual evidence and quotations that support your critique. For each example or quotation you record, formulate analytical commentary synthesizing your feminist criticism.

4. Use a prewriting strategy to generate, evaluate, and critique your ideas. Next develop a preliminary organizational structure for the most important ideas that you have generated from your multiple close readings. Make notes about your rhetorical purpose and specific devices you want to include.

5. Draft your essay making sure to include the following:

   ▶ A brief synopsis of the story.

   ▶ A thoughtful thesis with an effective introductory paragraph.

   ▶ A coherent analysis from a Feminist Critical Perspective.

   ▶ Quotations from the text with appropriate commentary.

   ▶ Paragraphs that include effective use of rhetorical devices, a variety of sentence structures, and effective internal and external transitions.

   ▶ An insightful conclusion.

6. In preparation for sharing your draft with peers, review your text to anticipate and respond to readers' questions and misconceptions. Review and analyze views and information that contradict your thesis and evaluate the evidence supporting them. Revise your draft for clarity and to address these concerns.

7. Find a partner or group of partners who used the same story. Read each other's drafts and use the following guiding questions to provide feedback:

   ▶ Did the author provide a brief and thoughtful synopsis?

   ▶ Did he/she use feminist criticism effectively?

   ▶ Were the examples clear and the analysis appropriate?

   ▶ Does he/she include an insightful conclusion?

8. Revise your essay using your peer feedback from Step 6. Review your next draft and refine it for clarity, to achieve your rhetorical purpose, to use a variety of sentence structures, to maintain a consistent tone appropriate to your audience, and to include effective internal and external transitions.

9. After you have refined your essay based on your peer's evaluation, consult the Scoring Guide and review your essay to assess yourself in each category. Mark your essay to indicate where you can revise in order to move from one benchmark to another. Further refine your essay for ideas, organization, and use of language.

10. Reread your draft silently and correct errors in spelling, conventions, and grammar. Consult editing tools available (spell-check, dictionary, thesaurus, etc.) to create a technically sound text and publish a final draft.

Short Story

ABOUT THE AUTHOR

A native of St. Louis, Missouri, Katherine O'Flaherty
Chopin (1850–1904) became a keen observer of New
Orleans culture after her marriage to Oscar Chopin of
Louisiana. She depicted the regional flavor and racial
tensions of Creole and Cajun people in the short story
collections *Bayou Folk* (1894) and *A Night in Acadie*
(1897). Her best-known work is *The Awakening* (1899), a
novel that explores the emotional growth of a dissatisfied
New Orleans wife and mother. Contemporary critics
condemned *The Awakening* for its frank treatment of
sexuality and women's independence.

The Story of an Hour

by Kate Chopin

Knowing that Mrs. Mallard was afflicted with a heart trouble, great care
was taken to break to her as gently as possible the news of her husband's
death.

It was her sister Josephine who told her, in broken sentences; veiled hints
that revealed in half concealing. Her husband's friend Richards was there, too,
near her. It was he who had been in the newspaper office when intelligence
of the railroad disaster was received, with Brently Mallard's name leading the
list of "killed." He had only taken the time to assure himself of its truth by a
second telegram, and had hastened to forestall any less careful, less tender
friend in bearing the sad message.

She did not hear the story as many women have heard the same, with a
paralyzed inability to accept its significance. She wept at once, with sudden,
wild abandonment, in her sister's arms. When the storm of grief had spent
itself she went away to her room alone. She would have no one follow her.

There stood, facing the open window, a comfortable, roomy armchair.
Into this she sank, pressed down by a physical exhaustion that haunted her
body and seemed to reach into her soul.

She could see in the open square before her house the tops of trees that were all aquiver with the new spring life. The delicious breath of rain was in the air. In the street below a peddler was crying his wares. The notes of a distant song which someone was singing reached her faintly, and countless sparrows were twittering in the eaves.

There were patches of blue sky showing here and there through the clouds that had met and piled one above the other in the west facing her window.

She sat with her head thrown back upon the cushion of the chair, quite motionless, except when a sob came up into her throat and shook her, as a child who has cried itself to sleep continues to sob in its dreams.

She was young, with a fair, calm face, whose lines bespoke repression and even a certain strength. But now there was a dull stare in her eyes, whose gaze was fixed away off yonder on one of those patches of blue sky. It was not a glance of reflection, but rather indicated a suspension of intelligent thought.

There was something coming to her and she was waiting for it, fearfully. What was it? She did not know; it was too subtle and elusive to name. But she felt it, creeping out of the sky, reaching toward her through the sounds, the scents, the color that filled the air.

Now her bosom rose and fell tumultuously. She was beginning to recognize this thing that was approaching to possess her, and she was striving to beat it back with her will—as powerless as her two white slender hands would have been. When she abandoned herself a little whispered word escaped her slightly parted lips. She said it over and over under her breath: "free, free, free!" The vacant stare and the look of terror that had followed it went from her eyes. They stayed keen and bright. Her pulses beat fast, and the coursing blood warmed and relaxed every inch of her body.

She did not stop to ask if it were or were not a monstrous joy that held her. A clear and exalted perception enabled her to dismiss the suggestion as trivial. She knew that she would weep again when she saw the kind, tender hands folded in death; the face that had never looked save with love upon her, fixed and gray and dead. But she saw beyond that bitter moment a long procession of years to come that would belong to her absolutely. And she opened and spread her arms out to them in welcome.

There would be no one to live for during those coming years; she would live for herself. There would be no powerful will bending hers in that blind persistence with which men and women believe they have a right to impose a private will upon a fellow-creature. A kind intention or a cruel intention made the act seem no less a crime as she looked upon it in that brief moment of illumination.

And yet she had loved him—sometimes. Often she had not. What did it matter! What could love, the unsolved mystery, count for in the face of this possession of self-assertion which she suddenly recognized as the strongest impulse of her being!

"Free! Body and soul free!" she kept whispering.

Josephine was kneeling before the closed door with her lips to the keyhole, imploring for admission. "Louise, open the door! I beg; open the door—you will make yourself ill. What are you doing, Louise? For heaven's sake open the door."

"Go away. I am not making myself ill." No; she was drinking in a very elixir of life through that open window.

Her fancy was running riot along those days ahead of her. Spring days, and summer days, and all sorts of days that would be her own. She breathed a quick prayer that life might be long. It was only yesterday she had thought with a shudder that life might be long.

She arose at length and opened the door to her sister's importunities. There was a feverish triumph in her eyes, and she carried herself unwittingly like a goddess of Victory. She clasped her sister's waist, and together they descended the stairs. Richards stood waiting for them at the bottom.

Someone was opening the front door with a latchkey. It was Brently Mallard who entered, a little travel-stained, composedly carrying his grip-sack and umbrella. He had been far from the scene of the accident, and did not even know there had been one. He stood amazed at Josephine's piercing cry; at Richards' quick motion to screen him from the view of his wife.

When the doctors came they said she had died of heart disease—of the joy that kills.

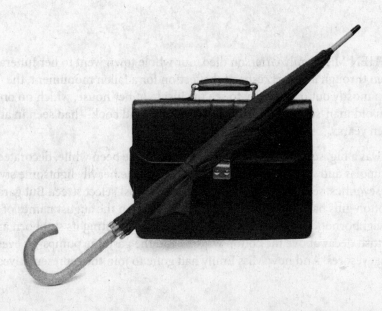

Short Story

> **ABOUT THE AUTHOR**
> William Faulkner (1897–1962) captured the atmosphere and poignancy of the American South in novels such as *The Sound and the Fury* (1929) and *Absalom, Absalom!* (1936). Raised in Oxford, Mississippi, Faulkner did not finish high school and drifted through several inconsequential jobs. His first novel, *Soldier's Pay* (1926), drew on his experience as a pilot training in Canada's British Royal Air Force. In subsequent novels, Faulkner created Yoknapatawpha County, a fictional Mississippi county with recurring families, landscapes, and histories. Faulkner won the Nobel Prize for Literature in 1949.

A Rose for Emily

by William Faulkner

> **WORD CONNECTIONS**
>
> The Latin root of **obliterated** is *littera*, meaning "letter." The prefix *ob-* means "opposed to" or "against." The meaning of *obliterate* is "to blot out or destroy." Words with the same root include *literate, literacy, literary,* and *literally.*

I

WHEN Miss Emily Grierson died, our whole town went to her funeral: the men through a sort of respectful affection for a fallen monument, the women mostly out of curiosity to see the inside of her house, which no one save an old man-servant—a combined gardener and cook—had seen in at least ten years.

It was a big, squarish frame house that had once been white, decorated with cupolas and spires and scrolled balconies in the heavily lightsome style of the seventies, set on what had once been our most select street. But garages and cotton gins had encroached and obliterated even the august names of that neighborhood; only Miss Emily's house was left, lifting its stubborn and coquettish decay above the cotton wagons and the gasoline pumps-an eyesore among eyesores. And now Miss Emily had gone to join the representatives of those august names where they lay in the cedar-bemused cemetery among the ranked and anonymous graves of Union and Confederate soldiers who fell at the battle of Jefferson.

Alive, Miss Emily had been a tradition, a duty, and a care; a sort of hereditary obligation upon the town, dating from that day in 1894 when Colonel Sartoris, the mayor—he who fathered the edict that no Negro woman should appear on the streets without an apron—remitted her taxes, the dispensation dating from the death of her father on into perpetuity. Not that Miss Emily would have accepted charity. Colonel Sartoris invented an involved tale to the effect that Miss Emily's father had loaned money to the town, which the town, as a matter of business, preferred this way of repaying. Only a man of Colonel Sartoris' generation and thought could have invented it, and only a woman could have believed it.

When the next generation, with its more modern ideas, became mayors and aldermen, this arrangement created some little dissatisfaction. On the first of the year they mailed her a tax notice. February came, and there was no reply. They wrote her a formal letter, asking her to call at the sheriff's office at her convenience. A week later the mayor wrote her himself, offering to call or to send his car for her, and received in reply a note on paper of an archaic shape, in a thin, flowing calligraphy in faded ink, to the effect that she no longer went out at all. The tax notice was also enclosed, without comment.

They called a special meeting of the Board of Aldermen. A deputation waited upon her, knocked at the door through which no visitor had passed since she ceased giving china-painting lessons eight or ten years earlier. They were admitted by the old Negro into a dim hall from which a stairway mounted into still more shadow. It smelled of dust and disuse—a close, dank smell. The Negro led them into the parlor. It was furnished in heavy, leather-covered furniture. When the Negro opened the blinds of one window, they could see that the leather was cracked; and when they sat down, a faint dust rose sluggishly about their thighs, spinning with slow motes in the single sun-ray. On a tarnished gilt easel before the fireplace stood a crayon portrait of Miss Emily's father.

They rose when she entered, a small, fat woman in black, with a thin gold chain descending to her waist and vanishing into her belt, leaning on an ebony cane with a tarnished gold head. Her skeleton was small and spare; perhaps that was why what would have been merely plumpness in another was obesity in her. She looked bloated, like a body long submerged in motionless water, and of that pallid hue. Her eyes, lost in the fatty ridges of her face, looked like two small pieces of coal pressed into a lump of dough as they moved from one face to another while the visitors stated their errand.

GRAMMAR & USAGE

A **complex sentence** has one independent clause and one or more dependent clauses. Using such a sentence structure enables a writer to show complex relationships between and among ideas. Examine the ideas Faulkner has connected in the last sentence of the fourth paragraph.

Independent Clause: *her eyes, lost in the fatty ridges of her face, looked like two small pieces of coal pressed into a lump of dough*

Dependent Clause: *as they moved from one face to another*

Dependent Clause: *while the visitors stated their errand*

Applying a Critical Perspective

She did not ask them to sit. She just stood in the door and listened quietly until the spokesman came to a stumbling halt. Then they could hear the invisible watch ticking at the end of the gold chain.

Her voice was dry and cold. "I have no taxes in Jefferson. Colonel Sartoris explained it to me. Perhaps one of you can gain access to the city records and satisfy yourselves."

"But we have. We are the city authorities, Miss Emily. Didn't you get a notice from the sheriff, signed by him?"

"I received a paper, yes," Miss Emily said. "Perhaps he considers himself the sheriff . . . I have no taxes in Jefferson."

"But there is nothing on the books to show that, you see. We must go by the—"

"See Colonel Sartoris. I have no taxes in Jefferson."

"But, Miss Emily—"

"See Colonel Sartoris." (Colonel Sartoris had been dead almost ten years.) "I have no taxes in Jefferson. Tobe!" The Negro appeared. "Show these gentlemen out."

II

So SHE vanquished them, horse and foot, just as she had vanquished their fathers thirty years before about the smell.

That was two years after her father's death and a short time after her sweetheart—the one we believed would marry her—had deserted her. After her father's death she went out very little; after her sweetheart went away, people hardly saw her at all. A few of the ladies had the temerity to call, but were not received, and the only sign of life about the place was the Negro man—a young man then—going in and out with a market basket.

"Just as if a man—any man—could keep a kitchen properly, "the ladies said; so they were not surprised when the smell developed. It was another link between the gross, teeming world and the high and mighty Griersons.

A neighbor, a woman, complained to the mayor, Judge Stevens, eighty years old.

"But what will you have me do about it, madam?" he said.

"Why, send her word to stop it," the woman said. "Isn't there a law? "

"I'm sure that won't be necessary," Judge Stevens said. "It's probably just a snake or a rat that nigger of hers killed in the yard. I'll speak to him about it."

The next day he received two more complaints, one from a man who came in diffident deprecation. "We really must do something about it, Judge. I'd be the last one in the world to bother Miss Emily, but we've got to do something." That night the Board of Aldermen met—three graybeards and one younger man, a member of the rising generation.

"It's simple enough," he said. "Send her word to have her place cleaned up. Give her a certain time to do it in, and if she don't...."

"Dammit, sir," Judge Stevens said, "will you accuse a lady to her face of smelling bad?"

So the next night, after midnight, four men crossed Miss Emily's lawn and slunk about the house like burglars, sniffing along the base of the brickwork and at the cellar openings while one of them performed a regular sowing motion with his hand out of a sack slung from his shoulder. They broke open the cellar door and sprinkled lime there, and in all the outbuildings. As they recrossed the lawn, a window that had been dark was lighted and Miss Emily sat in it, the light behind her, and her upright torso motionless as that of an idol. They crept quietly across the lawn and into the shadow of the locusts that lined the street. After a week or two the smell went away.

That was when people had begun to feel really sorry for her. People in our town, remembering how old lady Wyatt, her great-aunt, had gone completely crazy at last, believed that the Griersons held themselves a little too high for what they really were. None of the young men were quite good enough for Miss Emily and such. We had long thought of them as a tableau, Miss Emily a slender figure in white in the background, her father a spraddled silhouette in the foreground, his back to her and clutching a horsewhip, the two of them framed by the back-flung front door. So when she got to be thirty and was still single, we were not pleased exactly, but vindicated; even with insanity in the family she wouldn't have turned down all of her chances if they had really materialized.

When her father died, it got about that the house was all that was left to her; and in a way, people were glad. At last they could pity Miss Emily. Being left alone, and a pauper, she had become humanized. Now she too would know the old thrill and the old despair of a penny more or less.

The day after his death all the ladies prepared to call at the house and offer condolence and aid, as is our custom Miss Emily met them at the door, dressed as usual and with no trace of grief on her face. She told them that her father was not dead. She did that for three days, with the ministers calling on her, and the doctors, trying to persuade her to let them dispose of the body. Just as they were about to resort to law and force, she broke down, and they buried her father quickly.

We did not say she was crazy then. We believed she had to do that. We remembered all the young men her father had driven away, and we knew that with nothing left, she would have to cling to that which had robbed her, as people will.

III

SHE WAS SICK for a long time. When we saw her again, her hair was cut short, making her look like a girl, with a vague resemblance to those angels in colored church windows—sort of tragic and serene.

The town had just let the contracts for paving the sidewalks, and in the summer after her father's death they began the work. The construction company came with riggers and mules and machinery, and a foreman named Homer Barron, a Yankee—a big, dark, ready man, with a big voice and eyes lighter than his face. The little boys would follow in groups to hear him cuss the riggers, and the riggers singing in time to the rise and fall of picks. Pretty soon he knew everybody in town. Whenever you heard a lot of laughing anywhere about the square, Homer Barron would be in the center of the group. Presently we began to see him and Miss Emily on Sunday afternoons driving in the yellow-wheeled buggy and the matched team of bays from the livery stable.

At first we were glad that Miss Emily would have an interest, because the ladies all said, "Of course a Grierson would not think seriously of a Northerner, a day laborer." But there were still others, older people, who said that even grief could not cause a real lady to forget *noblesse oblige*—without calling it noblesse oblige. They just said, "Poor Emily. Her kinsfolk should come to her." She had some kin in Alabama; but years ago her father had fallen out with them over the estate of old lady Wyatt, the crazy woman, and there was no communication between the two families. They had not even been represented at the funeral.

WORD CONNECTIONS

The term *noblesse oblige* comes from the French and means literally "nobility obligates." Writers use the term to refer to an assumption that those of noble birth, or high rank, are obliged to act honorably.

And as soon as the old people said, "Poor Emily," the whispering began. "Do you suppose it's really so?" they said to one another. "Of course it is. What else could . . ." This behind their hands; rustling of craned silk and satin behind jalousies closed upon the sun of Sunday afternoon as the thin, swift clop-clop-clop of the matched team passed: "Poor Emily."

She carried her head high enough—even when we believed that she was fallen. It was as if she demanded more than ever the recognition of her dignity as the last Grierson; as if it had wanted that touch of earthiness to reaffirm her imperviousness. Like when she bought the rat poison, the arsenic. That was over a year after they had begun to say "Poor Emily," and while the two female cousins were visiting her.

"I want some poison," she said to the druggist. She was over thirty then, still a slight woman, though thinner than usual, with cold, haughty black eyes in a face the flesh of which was strained across the temples and about the eyesockets as you imagine a lighthouse-keeper's face ought to look. "I want some poison," she said.

"Yes, Miss Emily. What kind? For rats and such? I'd recom—"

"I want the best you have. I don't care what kind."

The druggist named several. "They'll kill anything up to an elephant. But what you want is—"

"Arsenic," Miss Emily said. "Is that a good one?"

"Is . . . arsenic? Yes, ma'am. But what you want—"

"I want arsenic."

The druggist looked down at her. She looked back at him, erect, her face like a strained flag. "Why, of course," the druggist said. "If that's what you want. But the law requires you to tell what you are going to use it for."

Miss Emily just stared at him, her head tilted back in order to look him eye for eye, until he looked away and went and got the arsenic and wrapped it up. The Negro delivery boy brought her the package; the druggist didn't come back. When she opened the package at home there was written on the box, under the skull and bones: "For rats."

IV

So THE NEXT day we all said, "She will kill herself"; and we said it would be the best thing. When she had first begun to be seen with Homer Barron, we had said, "She will marry him." Then we said, "She will persuade him yet," because Homer himself had remarked—he liked men, and it was known that he drank with the younger men in the Elks' Club—that he was not a marrying man. Later we said, "Poor Emily" behind the jalousies as they passed on Sunday afternoon in the glittering buggy, Miss Emily with her head high and Homer Barron with his hat cocked and a cigar in his teeth, reins and whip in a yellow glove.

Then some of the ladies began to say that it was a disgrace to the town and a bad example to the young people. The men did not want to interfere, but at last the ladies forced the Baptist minister—Miss Emily's people were Episcopal— to call upon her. He would never divulge what happened during that interview, but he refused to go back again. The next Sunday they again drove about the streets, and the following day the minister's wife wrote to Miss Emily's relations in Alabama.

So she had blood-kin under her roof again and we sat back to watch developments. At first nothing happened. Then we were sure that they were to be married. We learned that Miss Emily had been to the jeweler's and ordered a man's toilet set in silver, with the letters H. B. on each piece. Two days later we learned that she had bought a complete outfit of men's clothing, including a nightshirt, and we said, "They are married." We were really glad. We were glad because the two female cousins were even more Grierson than Miss Emily had ever been.

So we were not surprised when Homer Barron—the streets had been finished some time since—was gone. We were a little disappointed that there was not a public blowing-off, but we believed that he had gone on to prepare for Miss Emily's coming, or to give her a chance to get rid of the cousins. (By that time it was a cabal, and we were all Miss Emily's allies to help circumvent the cousins.) Sure enough, after another week they departed. And, as we had expected all along, within three days Homer Barron was back in town. A neighbor saw the Negro man admit him at the kitchen door at dusk one evening.

And that was the last we saw of Homer Barron. And of Miss Emily for some time. The Negro man went in and out with the market basket, but the front door remained closed. Now and then we would see her at a window for a moment, as the men did that night when they sprinkled the lime, but for almost six months she did not appear on the streets. Then we knew that this was to be expected too; as if that quality of her father which had thwarted her woman's life so many times had been too virulent and too furious to die.

When we next saw Miss Emily, she had grown fat and her hair was turning gray. During the next few years it grew grayer and grayer until it attained an even pepper-and-salt iron-gray, when it ceased turning. Up to the day of her death at seventy-four it was still that vigorous iron-gray, like the hair of an active man.

From that time on her front door remained closed, save for a period of six or seven years, when she was about forty, during which she gave lessons in china-painting. She fitted up a studio in one of the downstairs rooms, where the daughters and granddaughters of Colonel Sartoris' contemporaries were sent to her with the same regularity and in the same spirit that they were sent to church on Sundays with a twenty-five-cent piece for the collection plate. Meanwhile her taxes had been remitted.

Then the newer generation became the backbone and the spirit of the town, and the painting pupils grew up and fell away and did not send their children to her with boxes of color and tedious brushes and pictures cut from the ladies' magazines. The front door closed upon the last one and remained closed for good. When the town got free postal delivery, Miss Emily alone refused to let them fasten the metal numbers above her door and attach a mailbox to it. She would not listen to them.

Daily, monthly, yearly we watched the Negro grow grayer and more stooped, going in and out with the market basket. Each December we sent her a tax notice, which would be returned by the post office a week later, unclaimed. Now and then we would see her in one of the downstairs windows—she had evidently shut up the top floor of the house—like the carven torso of an idol in a niche, looking or not looking at us, we could never tell which. Thus she passed from generation to generation—dear, inescapable, impervious, tranquil, and perverse.

And so she died. Fell ill in the house filled with dust and shadows, with only a doddering Negro man to wait on her. We did not even know she was sick; we had long since given up trying to get any information from the Negro.

He talked to no one, probably not even to her, for his voice had grown harsh and rusty, as if from disuse.

She died in one of the downstairs rooms, in a heavy walnut bed with a curtain, her gray head propped on a pillow yellow and moldy with age and lack of sunlight.

V

THE NEGRO met the first of the ladies at the front door and let them in, with their hushed, sibilant voices and their quick, curious glances, and then he disappeared. He walked right through the house and out the back and was not seen again.

The two female cousins came at once. They held the funeral on the second day, with the town coming to look at Miss Emily beneath a mass of bought flowers, with the crayon face of her father musing profoundly above the bier and the ladies sibilant and macabre; and the very old men—some in their brushed Confederate uniforms—on the porch and the lawn, talking of Miss Emily as if she had been a contemporary of theirs, believing that they had danced with her and courted her perhaps, confusing time with its mathematical progression, as the old do, to whom all the past is not a diminishing road but, instead, a huge meadow which no winter ever quite touches, divided from them now by the narrow bottle-neck of the most recent decade of years.

Already we knew that there was one room in that region above stairs which no one had seen in forty years, and which would have to be forced. They waited until Miss Emily was decently in the ground before they opened it.

The violence of breaking down the door seemed to fill this room with pervading dust. A thin, acrid pall as of the tomb seemed to lie everywhere upon this room decked and furnished as for a bridal: upon the valance curtains of faded rose color, upon the rose-shaded lights, upon the dressing table, upon the delicate array of crystal and the man's toilet things backed with tarnished silver, silver so tarnished that the monogram was obscured. Among them lay a collar and tie, as if they had just been removed, which, lifted, left upon the surface a pale crescent in the dust. Upon a chair hung the suit, carefully folded; beneath it the two mute shoes and the discarded socks.

The man himself lay in the bed.

For a long while we just stood there, looking down at the profound and fleshless grin. The body had apparently once lain in the attitude of an embrace, but now the long sleep that outlasts love, that conquers even the grimace of love, had cuckolded him. What was left of him, rotted beneath what was left of the nightshirt, had become inextricable from the bed in which he lay; and upon him and upon the pillow beside him lay that even coating of the patient and biding dust.

Then we noticed that in the second pillow was the indentation of a head. One of us lifted something from it, and leaning forward, that faint and invisible dust dry and acrid in the nostrils, we saw a long strand of iron-gray hair.

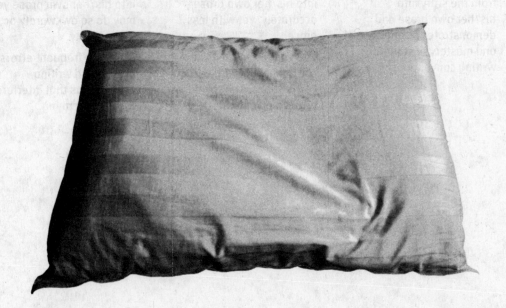

SCORING GUIDE

Scoring Criteria	Exemplary	Proficient	Emerging
Ideas	The essay demonstrates a thorough understanding of the short story and a perceptive application of feminist criticism to create a thorough analysis using specific and well-chosen examples as support for the thesis.	The essay demonstrates an understanding of the short story and a suitable application of feminist criticism to create a complete analysis using appropriate examples to support the thesis.	The essay demonstrates a superficial understanding of the short story and/or an underdeveloped application of feminist criticism. Analysis may depend on too few examples or may be replaced by summary.
Organization	The essay's organization is exceptional. Ideas move smoothly and comfortably with effective use of transitions enhancing the essay's coherence.	The essay's organization is clear and easy to follow. Transitions are used to move between ideas.	The essay is difficult to follow. It may lack transitions and jump too rapidly between ideas.
Use of Language	Stylistic choices in language serve to enhance the author's analysis and consistently convey an academic voice appropriate for the discourse. The writer successfully weaves textual evidence from the story into his/her own prose and demonstrates strong control and mastery of standard writing conventions.	Stylistic choices in language communicate the author's analysis clearly and demonstrate an academic voice appropriate for the discourse. The writer weaves textual evidence from the novel into his/her own prose accurately, yet with less grace. The writer demonstrates control of standard writing conventions. Though some errors may appear, they do not seriously impede readability.	Stylistic choices in language are less mature and do little to create an academic voice appropriate for the discourse. At times, the writer attempts to incorporate textual evidence from the novel into his/her own prose yet may do so awkwardly or inaccurately. There are frequent errors in standard writing conventions that interfere with the meaning.

SCORING GUIDE

Scoring Criteria	Exemplary	Proficient	Emerging
Evidence of the Writing Process	The essay demonstrates thoughtful planning, significant revision, and careful editing for grammar and conventions in preparing a publishable draft.	The essay demonstrates adequate planning, revision, and editing for grammar and conventions in preparing a publishable draft.	The essay lacks evidence of planning, revision, and/or editing for grammar and conventions. The draft is not ready for publication.
Additional Criteria			

Comments:

Reflection

An important aspect of growing as a learner is to reflect on where you have been, what you have accomplished, what helped you to learn, and how you will apply your new knowledge in the future. Use the following questions to guide your thinking and to identify evidence of your learning. Use separate notebook paper.

Thinking about Concepts

1. Using specific examples from this unit, respond to the Essential Questions:

   • How does applying a critical perspective affect an understanding of text?

   • How does a new understanding of a text gained through interpretation help or hinder your enjoyment of it?

2. Consider the new academic vocabulary from this unit (Archetypal Criticism, Marxist Criticism, Feminist Criticism) as well as academic vocabulary from previous units, and select 2–3 terms of which your understanding has grown. For each term, answer the following questions:

   • What was your understanding of the term before you completed this unit?

   • How has your understanding of the term evolved throughout the unit?

   • How will you apply your understanding in the future?

Thinking about Connections

3. Review the activities and products (artifacts) you created. Choose those that most reflect your growth or increase in understanding.

4. For each artifact that you choose, record, respond to, and reflect on your thinking and understanding, using the following questions as a guide:

   a. What skill/knowledge does this artifact reflect, and how did you learn this skill/knowledge?

   b. How did your understanding of the power of language expand through your engagement with this artifact?

   c. How will you apply this skill or knowledge in the future?

5. Create this reflection as Portfolio pages—one for each artifact you choose. Use the model in the box for your headings and commentary on questions.

Thinking About Thinking
Portfolio Entry

Concept:

Description of Artifact:

Commentary on Questions:

Evolving
Perspectives

Essential Questions

? How can a dramatic performance reflect a critical perspective?

? What role does literature play in the examination of recurring societal issues?

Unit Overview

In Units 1 and 2, you explored how your perception of a text could change when you examined it using a particular critical perspective. In this unit, you will deepen your understanding of critical perspectives as you apply Reader Response, Feminist, Marxist, Cultural, and Archetypal Criticism to scenes from a drama. William Shakespeare's *The Tragedy of Othello, the Moor of Venice* has inspired various critical interpretations over the centuries. The many interpretations are, in some ways, as compelling as the drama itself; thus, *Othello* offers the ideal opportunity for introducing Historical Critical Perspective.

Contents

Texts not included in these materials.

Goals

▶ To interpret multiple representations of a Shakespearean tragedy

▶ To examine critical perspectives as they apply to drama

▶ To plan and perform dramatic interpretations of selected scenes

▶ To analyze the ways in which historical contexts have influenced performances of the play

ACADEMIC VOCABULARY

Historical Criticism

Learning Focus:

A Tragedy for All Time

If Shakespeare could see what people have done with his plays over the last 400 years, what would he think? This question has been posed repeatedly by critics of stage and film interpretations of the Bard's works. We cannot know, of course, but we do know that the way directors, actors, and audiences have responded to *Othello* has changed over time, reflecting the norms and beliefs of their times.

Shakespeare's plays have consistently been reimagined and reinvented over the more than 400 years they have existed. It is a tribute to the enduring popularity and timelessness of Shakespeare's characters, plots, and themes that his plays continue to be produced all over the globe. While modern producers, directors, and actors try to make a play such as *Othello* or *Hamlet* timely, it is important to understand the historical, social, and cultural context in which the plays were written and set and produced and how these factors influence how the play is received and perceived today.

Historical Criticism gives us a lens by which to examine how the context within which a literary work is created and set affects interpretation. This element is especially significant with dramatic productions because the time periods in which the dramas are produced and reimagined adds another layer of interpretation based on historical significance. Producing *Othello*, a drama about an interracial marriage, in South Africa before apartheid was abolished was an act of social, cultural, and historical significance.

Historical Criticism

While acknowledging the importance of the literary text, Historical Criticism recognizes the significance of historical information in interpreting literature. This perspective assumes that texts both influence and are influenced by the times in which they were created. For example, an interpretation of *Things Fall Apart by* Chinua Achebe may be enhanced by an understanding of the effects of colonialism in present-day African life.

The use of Historical Criticism includes these assumptions:

▶ A text cannot be separated from its historical context, which is a web of social, cultural, personal, and political factors.

▶ An understanding of a text is enhanced by the study of beliefs and artifacts such as diaries, films, paintings, and letters in existence when the text was created.

Independent Reading: In this unit, you will be reading drama and applying Historical Criticism theory to one of Shakespeare's plays. For independent reading, look for contemporary critical reviews of one or more film versions of *Othello*.

Previewing the Unit

Essential Questions

1. How can a dramatic performance reflect a critical perspective?

2. What role does literature play in the examination of recurring societal issues?

Unit Overview and Learning Focus

Predict what you think this unit is about. Use the words or phrases that stood out to you when you read the Unit Overview and the Learning Focus.

Embedded Assessment 1

What knowledge must you have (what do you need to know)? What skills must you have (what will you need to do to complete the Embedded Assessment successfully)? Write your responses below.

1. In Shakespeare's day, acting companies named themselves, sometimes honoring their patron. Shakespeare belonged first to the Lord Chamberlain's Men and later the King's Men.

   Your acting company should come up with a name that represents your group. You may want to incorporate something you have learned about Shakespeare, the Renaissance, Elizabethan theater, or *Othello* into your company's name.

2. Work with your acting company to make a preliminary scene choice. Do not let gender dictate your casting choices.

3. Also make preliminary decisions about who will assume the following three roles within each acting company:

   - **Director:** Leads the rehearsals, working collaboratively with the group. Assumes responsibility for all of the theatrical elements: a set diagram, a plan for lighting and sound, props, and a complete script of the scene. Writes and memorizes an engaging introduction to the performance and delivers it on performance day.

   - **Dramaturge:** Conducts research to support the critical perspective the group is applying to the scene and answers questions about the scene. Writes and memorizes a concluding statement about the scene that explains how the group applied a critical perspective and how research supported the performance, and delivers it on performance day.

   - **Actors:** Study the play, paying particular attention to their characters, and take notes. Collaborate with the director and the other actors to plan a performance. During the performance, use appropriate vocal delivery, facial expression, gestures and movement, props, and costumes to convey nuances of their characters.

4. Once you have come to an agreement, sign and turn in a contract to your teacher. Here is a template:

   We, the _____ (name of acting company),

   pledge to plan, rehearse, and perform

   _____ (act and scene) **from William**

   Shakespeare's *The Tragedy of Othello*.

   Cast:

   (Name of student) **as** (name of character)

   Director:

   Dramaturge:

ABOUT THE AUTHOR
William Shakespeare (1564-1616) is considered one of the most gifted and perceptive writers in the English Language. He left his home in Stratford-upon-Avon for London, where he pursued a career as an actor. He was more successful as a playwright and poet, however, producing more than three dozen plays that are still performed centuries after his death.

Creating Acting Companies

Scene	Description	Characters	First Line and Approximate Length
Act I, Scene 1	Iago and Roderigo awaken Brabantio and inform him that his daughter has eloped.	Iago Roderigo Brabantio	RODERIGO Tush, never tell me! 206 lines (Companies could opt to do only part of the scene.)
Act I, Scene 3 Lines 197–335	Desdemona admits her love for Othello; the Duke dispatches them to Cyprus.	Duke Desdemona Othello First senator* * only one line	DUKE I think this tale would win my daughter too. 139 lines
Act I, Scene 3 Lines 344–447	Iago continues to take advantage of Roderigo's affection for Desdemona.	Roderigo Iago	RODERIGO Iago— IAGO What say'st thou, noble heart? 104 lines
Act II, Scene 1 Lines 197–307	Desdemona welcomes Othello to Cyprus; Iago convinces Roderigo to attack Cassio.	Othello Desdemona Iago Roderigo	OTHELLO O my fair warrior! 111 lines
Act II, Scene 3 Lines 14–124	With Iago's encouragement, Cassio gets drunk.	Cassio Iago Montano Gentleman* *only one line, which could be given to Montano	CASSIO Welcome, Iago. We must to the watch. 111 lines
Act II, Scene 3 Lines 125–265	A drunken brawl ends with Othello demoting Cassio.	Iago Montano Cassio Roderigo	IAGO [*to Montano*] You see this fellow that is gone before. 141 lines

Scene	Description	Characters	First Line and Approximate Length
Act III, Scene 3 Lines 1–99	Desdemona tries to convince Othello to reinstate Cassio.	Desdemona Emilia Cassio Othello Iago	DESDEMONA Be thou assured, good Cassio …. 99 lines
Act III, Scene 3 Lines 100–240	Iago plants the seed of doubt in Othello's mind.	Othello Iago	OTHELLO Excellent wretch! 141 lines
Act III, Scene 4 Lines 39–115	Othello demands to see the handkerchief, while Desdemona tries to change the subject by pleading Cassio's case.	Othello Desdemona	OTHELLO How do you, Desdemona? 77 lines
Act IV, Scene 2 Lines 128–201	Desdemona seeks advice from Iago, while Emilia curses the person who planted the thought of infidelity in Othello's mind.	Iago Desdemona Emilia	IAGO What is your pleasure, madam? 75 lines
Act IV, Scene 3 Lines 11–117	Desdemona and Emilia discuss infidelity.	Desdemona Emilia	EMILIA How goes it now? 107 lines
Act V, Scene 1 Lines 1–151	Roderigo attacks Cassio.	Iago Roderigo Cassio Gratiano Lodovico Bianca Emilia	IAGO Here, stand behind this bulk. 151 lines
Act V, Scene 2 131–301	Emilia tells Othello the truth.	Emilia Othello Desdemona Montano	OTHELLO What's the matter with thee now? 171

Guess Who's in Love

Directions: Your teacher will play a song and give you the lyrics so you can follow along. Listen and think about the words and the music.

1. **Quickwrite:** Using Reader Response as your critical lens, quickwrite your thoughts about the text. Consider your values, experiences, and your community as you form opinions.

WORD CONNECTIONS

The word *components* contains the Latin prefix *com-*, which means "with" or "together." The Latin root of *component* is *ponere*, which means "to place." Related words include *comport*, *compose*, *composer*, and *composite*.

2. Now, review the principles of Cultural Criticism below.

"Cultural Criticism examines how differing religious beliefs, ethnicities, class identifications, political beliefs, and individual viewpoints affect how texts are created and interpreted. What it means to be a part of—or excluded from—a specific group contributes to and impacts our understanding of texts in relation to culture."

The use of Cultural Criticism includes these assumptions:

- Ethnicity, religious beliefs, political beliefs, and so on are crucial components in formulating plausible interpretations of text.

- While the emphasis is on diversity of approach and subject matter, Cultural Criticism is not the only means of understanding ourselves and our art.

- An examination or exploration of the relationship between dominant cultures and the dominated is essential.

3. Think about the song's lyrics and music. What do you think the song is about? Brainstorm the kinds of relationships or situations the lyrics might describe.

4. **Quickwrite:** After your brainstorming session, write a response in which you interpret the song and its lyrics using the principles of Cultural Criticism.

Bringing the Plot to Life

Scenario:	Character 1 tells Character 2 that his or her spouse is cheating on him or her. Character 1 then produces physical evidence as "proof," although the story is *untrue*.
Outcome A	Character 2 does not believe the story.
Outcome B	Character 2 considers the story as a possibility but then decides it is not true.
Outcome C	Character 2 is filled with jealousy and wants revenge.

LITERARY TERMS

Dramatic irony describes a situation in which the reader or audience knows more about the circumstances or future events in a story than the characters within it; as a result, the audience can see a discrepancy between characters' perceptions and the reality they face.

Verbal irony occurs when a character says one thing but means something completely different.

Situational irony is like a surprise ending—your audience expects one thing to happen but something completely different takes place.

1. Now that you have the bare bones of a plot, flesh out the story by writing dialogue between the two characters that conveys the scenario and your assigned outcome. Give the characters names and character traits that seem fitting.

2. Use your imagination to create a **subtext** for this scene; for example, why would Character 1 do such a deceitful thing?

3. Remember that Character 1 must produce physical evidence as "proof." Be imaginative about the prop your character uses as the "evidence."

4. Also, incorporate forms of irony (**verbal, situational,** and **dramatic irony**) in your plot. Dramatic irony particularly applies because your audience knows that the story is not true.

5. After you have presented your dialogue and watched performances by your classmates, write a reflection using the following questions as a starting point:

   • What did you learn (about the play, about writing a dialogue, about performing a short scene)?

   • How realistic were the scenes? Do you think scenarios and outcomes like this can happen in real life?

Cast of Characters: A Close Reading

Examine the cast descriptions, shown below, from the play *Othello*. What relationships exist between characters? In your group, discuss how the character descriptions provide information about the organization of Venetian society.

Using a Marxist Critical Perspective, draft a one-page essay that describes the organizational structure of Venetian society as you have inferred it from reading the cast descriptions below.

Othello

Cast of Characters

- **Othello,** a Moorish general in the Venetian army
- **Desdemona,** a Venetian lady, Othello's wife, Brabantio's daughter
- **Brabantio,** a Venetian senator, Desdemona's father
- **Iago,** Othello's standard-bearer, or "ancient"
- **Emilia,** Iago's wife, Desdemona's attendant
- **Cassio,** Othello's second-in-command, or lieutenant
- **Roderigo,** a Venetian gentleman
- **Duke of Venice**
- **Lodovico** and **Gratiano,** Venetian gentlemen, kinsmen to Brabantio
- **Venetian senators**
- **Montano,** an official in Cyprus
- **Bianca,** a woman in Cyprus in love with Cassio
- **Clown,** a comic servant to Othello and Desdemona
- **Gentlemen of Cyprus**
- **Sailors**

Servants, Attendants, Officers, Messengers, Herald, Musicians, Torchbearers

⤤**TECHNOLOGY TIP** You may wish to create your essay using word processing software. You will be sharing your essay in Activity 3.17, and using software will help you create a legible copy and also make it easier for you to revise.

A Father's Reaction

My Notes

In Act I, Scene1, Iago and Roderigo deliver to Brabantio the news that his daughter has eloped with Othello. Reread the lines from the end of Act 1 below. As you read, visualize Brabantio, a father awakened in the middle of the night to discover that his only child is missing. Picture his vulnerability as he comes down to the street in his nightgown. One emotional state that a director may decide to have Brabantio express is a broken heart.

You may notice that there are several dashes in Brabantio's speeches; these indicate where he changes to whom he is speaking.

Follow along as your teacher models how to annotate the text on this page in order to guide an actor delivering Brabantio's lines. Then annotate the text on the following pages to indicate to whom Brabantio is speaking. Also add notes about how the actor should move and sound in order to convey the character's heartbreak.

WORD CONNECTIONS

The Latin root *notare*, meaning "note" or "mark" and the prefix *ad-*, meaning "to," form the base of the word *annotate*. The noun form of the verb *annotate* is formed by adding the suffix, *-tion*. Words formed the same root include *notary*, *notable*, and *notation*.

Drama

From

THE TRAGEDY OF
OTHELLO,
THE MOOR OF VENICE

by William Shakespeare

BRABANTIO: It is too true an evil. Gone she is;

And what's to become of my despised time

Is naught but bitterness.

—Now, Roderigo,

Where didst thou see her?—O, unhappy girl!—

With the Moor, say'st thou?—Who would be a father?—

How didst thou know 'twas she?—O, she deceives me

Past thought!—What said she to you?—Get more tapers.

Raise all my kindred.—Are they married, think you?

RODERIGO: Truly I think they are.

BRABANTIO: O heaven! How got she out? O treason of the blood!

Fathers, from hence trust not your daughters' minds

By what you see them act.—Is there not charms

By which the property of youth and maidhood

May be abused? Have you not read, Roderigo,

Of some such thing?

RODERIGO: Yes, sir, I have indeed.

BRABANTIO: Call up my brother.—O, would you had had her!—

Some one way, some another.—Do you know where we may apprehend her and the Moor?

RODERIGO: I think I can discover him, if you please

To get good guard and go along with me.

BRABANTIO: Pray you lead on. At every house I'll call.

I may command at most.—Get weapons, ho!

And raise some special officers of night.—

On, good Roderigo. I will deserve your pains.

My Notes

_____

_____

_____

_____

_____

_____

GRAMMAR & USAGE

Even though the English of Shakespeare's day was somewhat different from the language we use today, much of the sentence structure remains the same. Note Roderigo's sentence: *I think I can discover him, if you please to get good guard and go along with me.* This sentence is **complex,** beginning with an independent clause and ending with the dependent clause that starts with the subordinating conjunction "if." The subordinate clause modifies the verb and is thus an adverb clause. An **adverb clause** generally tells *how, when, where, why, how much, to what extent,* or *under what condition* the action of the verb occurs.

_____

_____

A Father's Reaction

My Notes

What if Brabantio's response to Roderigo's news is anger instead of heartbreak? Imagine that Brabantio has a different reaction—one of fury at his daughter's impudence. Annotate the text to indicate how you would have your actor playing Brabantio convey anger.

BRABANTIO: It is too true an evil. Gone she is,

And what's to become of my despised time

Is naught but bitterness.—Now, Roderigo,

Where didst thou see her?—O, unhappy girl!—

With the Moor, say'st thou?—Who would be a father?—

How didst thou know 'twas she?—O, she deceives me

Past thought!-What said she to you?—Get more tapers.

Raise all my kindred.—Are they married, think you?

RODERIGO: Truly, I think they are.

BRABANTIO: O heaven! How got she out? O treason of the blood!

Fathers, from hence trust not your daughters' minds

By what you see them act.—Is there not charms

By which the property of youth and maidhood

May be abused? Have you not read, Roderigo,

Of some such thing?

RODERIGO: Yes, sir, I have indeed.

BRABANTIO: Call up my brother.—O, would you had had her!—

Some one way, some another.—Do you know

Where we may apprehend her and the Moor?

RODERIGO: I think I can discover him, if you please

To get good guard and go along with me.

BRABANTIO: Pray you lead on. At every house I'll call.

I may command at most.—Get weapons, ho!

And raise some special officers of night.—

On, good Roderigo. I will deserve your pains.

My Notes

The Moor

WORD CONNECTIONS

The word *derogatory* includes *de-* "away" and *rogare* "ask, question, propose." The word means disparaging or belittling.

Throughout the first scene, no character uses Othello's name, although all three characters refer to him several times. Collect all the terms used to describe Othello in Act I, Scene 1. Try to decide what the speaker is suggesting about Othello by using a specific term. Is it a complimentary term or a derogatory one? Also, decide what the descriptive terms tell you about the speaker in each case.

Reference to Othello	Who is speaking? (line number)	What does the reference suggest about Othello?	What does the reference suggest about the speaking character?
Example: "his Moorship's"	Iago (line 35)	He's compared to royalty.	Iago uses verbal irony here; we know he doesn't truly think of Othello as royalty.

Most characters in the play are referred to by their name when other characters make mention of them. What cultural motivations may be influencing how characters refer to Othello in Act 1?

As you read Act I, Scene 2, make note of Othello's responses to the accusation(s) made against him.

Accusation	Accuser	Othello's Response	What does Othello's response say about him?

On a separate sheet of paper, compose a character sketch that describes Othello, based on the information you have so far. Draft your character sketch from a Cultural Critical Perspective.

As a model for your writing, use the following character sketch of the Reverend Jonathan Hale, an expert in witchcraft, from Arthur Miller's drama *The Crucible*.

> [The Reverend] Mr. Hale is nearing forty, a tight-skinned, eager-eyed intellectual. This is a beloved errand for him; on being called here to ascertain witchcraft he felt the pride of the specialist whose unique knowledge has at last been publicly called for. Like almost all men of learning, he spent a good deal of his time pondering the invisible world, especially since he had himself encountered a witch in his parish not long before. That woman, however, turned into a mere pest under his searching scrutiny, and the child she had allegedly been afflicting recovered her normal behavior after Hale had given her his kindness and a few days of rest in his own house. However, that experience never raised a doubt in his mind as to the reality of the underworld or the existence of Lucifer's many-faced lieutenants. And his belief is not to his discredit. Better minds than Hale's were—and still are—convinced that there is a society of spirits beyond our ken. . . .

GRAMMAR & USAGE

The last sentence in this excerpt from *The Crucible* provides an example of a common use of the dash, to amplify or explain. In this example sentence, a pair of dashes is needed to set off the explanatory element. If the element comes at the beginning or the end of the sentence, only one dash is needed. Commas, parentheses, or a colon may perform a similar function.

A Husband's Response

My Notes

Using the My Notes space, write the letters of SOAPSTone and add responses to guide you through an analysis of Othello's speech before the Duke and the Senate in Act I, Scene 3, lines 149–196.

Her father loved me; oft invited me;

Still questioned me the story of my life

From year to year—the battles, sieges, fortunes

That I have passed.

I ran it through, even from my boyish days

To the very moment that he bade me tell it.

Wherein I spake of most disastrous chances,

Of moving accidents by flood and field;

Of hairbreadth scapes i' th' imminent deadly breach;

Of being taken by the insolent foe

And sold to slavery; of my redemption thence

And portance in my travel's history:

Wherein of antres vast and deserts idle,

Rough quarries, rocks, and hills whose heads touch heaven

It was my hint to speak—such was the process;

And of the Cannibals that each other eat,

The Anthropophagi and men whose heads

Do grow beneath their shoulders. This to hear

Would Desdemona seriously incline:

But still the house-affairs would draw her thence:

Which ever as she could with haste dispatch,

She'd come again, and with a greedy ear

Devour up my discourse. Which I observing,

Took once a pliant hour, and found good means

To draw from her a prayer of earnest heart

That I would all my pilgrimage dilate,

Whereof by parcels she had something heard,

But not intentively. I did consent,

And often did beguile her of her tears,

When I did speak of some distressful stroke

That my youth suffered. My story being done,

She gave me for my pains a world of sighs.

She swore, in faith, 'twas strange, 'twas passing strange,

'Twas pitiful, 'twas wondrous pitiful.

She wished she had not heard it; yet she wished

That heaven had made her such a man. She thank'd me;

And bade me, if I had a friend that loved her,

I should but teach him how to tell my story.

And that would woo her. Upon this hint I spake.

She loved me for the dangers I had passed,

And I loved her that she did pity them.

This only is the witchcraft I have used.

Here comes the lady: let her witness it.

In your acting group, using your SOAPSTone analysis of the written text, discuss how you would have Othello deliver these lines. Keep in mind the other characters in the scene; with whom, and how, would Othello interact? How would the other characters respond to Othello?

A Husband's Response

As you view different interpretations of Othello's speech, take notes on the following elements of the scene.

Film Version 1:		Film Version 2:
	Delivery of lines	
	Actions/gestures/facial expressions	
	Interactions among characters	
	Props/costumes	
	Set	
	Cinematic/theatrical elements	

Writing Prompt: Compose an essay that compares and contrasts the two filmed interpretations. Include an evaluation of which version is more effective. You may want to use a Venn diagram as a prewriting organizer.

Knavery's Plain Face

SUGGESTED LEARNING STRATEGIES: Summarizing, Close Reading, TP-CASTT, Marking the Text, Predicting, Rereading, Graphic Organizer

Act 1, Scene 3, lines 377-404

IAGO

It is merely a lust of the blood and a permission of the will. Come, be a man! Drown thyself? Drown cats and blind puppies! I have professed me thy friend, and I confess me knit to thy deserving with cables of perdurable toughness. I could never better stead thee than now. Put money in thy purse. Follow thou the wars; defeat thy favor with an usurped beard. I say, put money in thy purse. It cannot be that Desdemona should long continue her love to the Moor — put money in thy purse — nor he his to her. It was a violent commencement, and thou shalt see an answerable sequestration. Put but money in thy purse. These Moors are changeable in their wills. Fill thy purse with money. The food that to him now is as luscious as locusts shall be to him shortly as bitter as coloquintida. She must change for youth. When she is sated with his body she will find the error of her choice. She must have change, she must. Therefore put money in thy purse. If thou wilt needs damn thyself, do it a more delicate way than drowning. Make all the money thou canst. If sanctimony and a frail vow betwixt an erring barbarian and a supersubtle Venetian be not too hard for my wits and all the tribe of hell, thou shalt enjoy her. Therefore make money. A pox of drowning thyself! It is clean out of the way. Seek thou rather to be hanged in compassing thy joy than to be drowned and go without her.

> **GRAMMAR & USAGE**
>
> The last sentence in Iago's speech contains two **infinitive phrases**. An infinitive is a verb form that can be used as a noun, adjective, or adverb. The infinitive phrases in this example are nouns, direct objects of *seek*. Most infinitives begin with the word "to." The infinitives in this sentence are in the passive voice—*to be hanged* and *to be drowned*. Active voice would omit the word "be"—*to hang* and *to drown*.

Closely read the passage above to discover Iago's character. Use SOAPSTone to guide your thinking as you consider responses to these questions.

- What is Iago's purpose?
- To whom is he speaking?
- What is his tone?

A Historical Look at the Moor

ACADEMIC VOCABULARY

While acknowledging the importance of the literary text, **Historical Criticism** recognizes the significance of historical information in interpreting literature. This perspective assumes that texts both influence and are influenced by the times in which they were created.

Previously you have learned about critical theories and used them to understand and interpret various texts. Now you will learn about **Historical Criticism** and use it to interpret and perform scenes from *Othello*.

Historical Criticism

While acknowledging the importance of the literary text, Historical Criticism draws on the significance of historical context of literature. This theory assumes that texts both influence and are influenced by the times in which they were written. For example, an interpretation of *The Crucible*, which is set in seventeenth-century New England, may be enhanced by an understanding of political developments in the 1950s when Arthur Miller wrote the play.

The use of Historical Criticism assumes that:

- Text cannot be separated from its historical context: a web of social, cultural, personal, and political factors.

- The understanding of a text is enhanced by the study of beliefs and artifacts such as diaries, films, paintings, and letters in existence when the text was created.

1. Show your understanding by paraphrasing each of these assumptions of Historical Criticism.

2. Your teacher will lead a guided reading of an excerpt from "The Moor in English Renaissance Drama." After reading and discussing the excerpt, locate textual evidence from Act I of *Othello* that confirms or negates D'Amico's assertions.

Excerpt from

The Moor in English Renaissance Drama

by Jack D'Amico

Relations between England and Morocco were extremely complex, and the opinions generated by those relations were as varied. What we find is not one image of the Moroccan, but many images, from the dangerously inscrutable[1] alien to the exotically attractive ally. I have reviewed the experiences of these men in this chapter because, it seems to me, theater has the ability to re-create for its audience the encounter with an alien culture and to force an imaginative assessment of likeness and difference. Through this kind of experience some prejudices may be confirmed, while in other ways spectators may come to see themselves and their world differently.

The positive and negative characterizations that emerge from the first fifty years of trade and diplomacy can with ease be related to the specific historical perspectives of trade, war, and diplomacy. But traditional images of the Moor as black devil, Islamic infidel, or oriental despot were certainly drawn on to articulate what the traders and diplomats experienced. Optimistic prospects, disappointment and frustrations, and strong prejudices against Catholic Spain were by turn equally strong. Dramatic contexts, too, reflect a give-and-take of opinion, a frequent counter-balancing of prejudices, the interplay of abstract stereotypes and the more complex shadings of experience.

The theatrical representation of the Moor, while shaped in part by the traditional anti-Islam polemic[2], or the characterization of the black man as devil, also reshapes those traditions. Along with the stereotypes we will find subtler explorations of the problems that beset individuals from different cultures as they attempt to judge one another. Stereotypes often provide a convenient mask the dramatist can use to identify a character. But under the pressure of dramatic experience that character will move often closer to the context of the observer's world, exhibiting the same needs, frustrations, and perceptions that shape "our" experience. As with the diversity of opinion about Moors and Morocco represented by the reports of traders and diplomats, we must follow the complex, and at times tangled, dramatic interplay of ideas, opinions, stereotypes, and fresh characterizations within the plays. Even if the spectator does not come away from the dramatic experience with a fuller understanding

1

2

3

My Notes

GRAMMAR & USAGE

Note the underlined phrase in this sentence: "But under the pressure of dramatic experience that character will often move closer to the context of the observer's world, <u>exhibiting the same needs, frustrations, and perceptions that shape "our" experience</u>. This phrase, a present participle, is acting as a free modifier. Free modifiers, which can appear at the end or the beginning of a sentence, say something about the subject of the closest verb. Free modifiers are effectively used by good writers to extend the content of a sentence without creating a series of awkward phrases and clauses.

---

[1] **inscrutable**: mysterious
[2] **polemic**: controversial argument

My Notes

of another culture and its people, in most instances seeing the familiar world set in a different perspective leads to an expansion of imaginative experience. (39–40)

* * *

4   Yet the representation of the Moor could also lead the dramatist and the audience beyond a comfortable sense of superiority or the superficial titillation[3] provided by a darkly alien villain. The Moor could become a dramatic symbol of the many stereotypes and masks that divide society and alienate the individual. The process by which a character is reduced to a type and the consequences of that reduction became a central dramatic issue. The representation of the Moor, whether motivated by a desire to make theatrical capital of a famous event, such as the Battle of Alcazar, or by a desire to discover and explore difference, opened up the question of what resulted from the contact between different cultures, religions, and races.

5   Dramatic interest also seemed naturally to focus on the question of the kind of power the isolated individual sought within a society of others. Power could mean destroying or mastering that society, controlling its women and tricking its men into acts of blind self-destruction. Or power could be sought in ways acceptable to society, as was the case for Othello, who could seem "fair" both within his dark exterior and within the Venetian state because of his military prowess[4]. Audiences and dramatists were drawn to the Moor as a type because the character provided a way to examine some of the most difficult questions of division and alienation. The audience that witnessed the struggle for self-control and the insidious[5] powers that transform Othello would confront the destructiveness of its own collective perceptions of race, religion, and cultural difference. In this case, the audience would engage in an exchange of something other than a coin for the sight of a dead Indian; the living character required that the audience engage in an emotional and intellectual exchange. And that giving, which is the life of theater, certainly drew the audience into some understanding of the tragic divisions within their own world as mirrored in the story of a character such as Othello, the Moor of Venice.

6   Our imaginative journey into the dramatic world of these plays fosters respect for the willingness and ability of Renaissance dramatists to do more than trade in dead stereotypes. Most of the plays created for their audience a complex dramatic encounter with the Moor. The audience identified the otherness of the type and to the extent that individual members of that audience saw difference as essential to human experience, they were connected to the outsider. Working within the conventions of Western theater and poetry, the dramatist could use

---

GRAMMAR & USAGE

Infinitives can function as adjectives and adverbs as well as nouns. The infinitive phrases "to make theatrical capital…" and "to discover and explore difference" are adjective phrases, both modifying *desire* in paragraph 4.

In paragraph 7, the infinitive phrase "to create an important political perspective…" is an adverb modifying the verb *used*.

---

3 **titillation**: excitement
4 **prowess**: exceptional ability
5 **insidious**: stealthy, deceitful

the open stage of Shakespeare's age to explore inner perspectives and challenge easy assumptions about difference and inferiority. The poet-dramatist was provided with a further connection between the Moor, or the alien, and the role of the artist within society. (212–213)

7 Shakespeare more than any other dramatist of the English Renaissance used theater to create an important political perspective that framed the encounter between different cultures. On the Moor he focused the problems that any state would face when it moved from a relatively closed condition to the open expansion that generates contact and conflict with other civilizations. Around the Moor he built those conflicts which test a society's sense of the natural rightness of its particular cultural traditions. He saw that with the kind of political expansion that characterized Renaissance Venice and ancient Rome came the problem of absorbing the outsider and the fear of being absorbed. The opposition between Roman reason and the darkly feminine otherness and fertility of Egypt is but one variation on this conflict between different conceptions of power and order. Shakespeare could also identify with a Moor of military *virtú* who is fearful of the erotic femininity of Venice, a European city as exotic for him as Alexandria was for the Romans. For the modern, cosmopolitan state that thrives on the exchange of goods and images with other nations and cultures, this conflict persists in the struggle between a closed national identity and the need for intercourse with others.

8 …Shakespeare wrote for a society that saw its contact with other people increase, while it struggled to define for itself the kind of government and religion it would have. Traditional definitions of Western norms and of the others who deviated from those norms provided a groundwork for curiosity, or a base of operations for exploration and exploitation[6]. But the ground was and always is shifting as experience and traditional values interact. What may have seemed strange turns out to be familiar, as when Clem finds that courts in Morocco and England are much the same; and what is native may, upon closer examination, turn out to be more monstrous than the strangest alien. As we have seen with Tamburlaine[7], an outsider who became a projection of new political ambition, the imaginative contact with the outsider became a way of dramatizing the need to create new categories. The Moor's difference was something established by tradition, and the Moor was a sign of spatial distance, a creature from a distant place. But for the English Renaissance stage the Moor could also be identified with the newness of discovery, exploration, and trade. This experience, real or theatrical, might confirm or challenge the tradition. Since the Moor was often portrayed as isolated and in rebellion against Western society, the type might conveniently

---

[6] **exploitation**: the use of someone or something for profit
[7] **Tamburlaine**: a character who had high political aspirations, from the play of the same name by Christopher Marlowe.

WORD CONNECTIONS
The word *cosmopolitan* contains the Greek prefix *cosmo-*, meaning "world" or "universe." Someone who is *cosmospolitan* is not bound by any local or national customs or prejudices. Other words beginning with this prefix include *cosmonaut*, *cosmology*, and *cosmopolis*.

My Notes

My Notes

channel opposition to traditional structures. If the old definitions fixed the character in safe inferiority, the new experience created an emotionally and intellectually charged encounter with a figure who required the audience to reflect on and to question its own values.

9   The plays certainly trade in what were, and still are, trusted assumptions about the Moor, Islam, and cultural difference. And they also draw upon our fascination with how another culture can make the familiar world seem strange. It is unsettling and also exciting to feel the ground of assumptions shift, as is the case in travel, when the norm is not your norm, when dress, speech, food, and the details of life reflect a difference that places you at the margin, reduced to a sign of deviation from the norm. That sense of disorientation was projected into an Eleazar[8] who speaks of the finger of scorn pointed at him, or Othello who fears the accusing gesture that will destroy his reputation. What is most disturbing for the outsider is the sense that the secret, unwritten codes are being used to degrade one's true image. As a group, sharing language, a national and racial identity, and an inherited set of theatrical conventions, the audience would have been like those Venetians or Spaniards who share a culture the Moor can never understand. And yet the individual spectator might retain a sense of separateness and know what it is like to be the object of open scorn, or what is worse, to feel the unspoken isolation of one who is reduced to a mere sign of the abnormal. (214–215)

---

[8] **Eleazar**: a villainous Moor in an English Renaissance drama called *Lust's Dominion*.

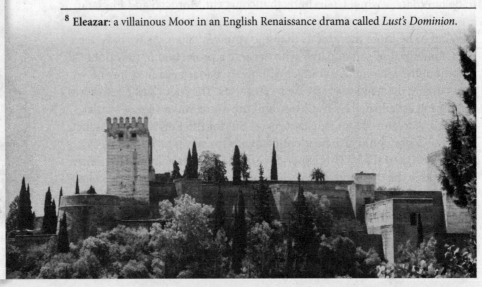

Friendly Banter or Pointed Comments?

SUGGESTED LEARNING STRATEGIES: Double-Entry Journal, Skimming/
Scanning, Marking the Text, Diffusing

As you read Act II, Scene 1, lines 108–179, pay attention to the ways
women are referred to in the text. As you encounter a character's
perception of women that agrees or differs from your own, record the
quotation in your dialectical, or double-entry, journal below, including
the line number. Then write a response.

Reread the scene silently while classmates orally perform and interpret
the scene. Continue to respond in your journal as you listen.

Quotation	Response

Honest Iago

1. *Dramatic irony* occurs when the audience knows something that the characters do not. For example, in *Othello*, everyone seems to think Iago is honest, but the audience knows that he is untrustworthy. We discover his duplicity in his conversations with Roderigo and in his asides and soliloquies.

   Asides and **soliloquies** are dramatic conventions in which a character reveals his or her thoughts to the audience. *Asides* are usually brief pieces of dialogue; often other actors may be present on the stage, but it is clear to the audience that the aside cannot be heard by the other actors. A *soliloquy* is usually a speech that an actor delivers while alone on the stage. A director could have an actor present a soliloquy in three ways:

   • Directly to the audience, or to the camera if filmed.

   • As if the character is simply talking to himself.

   • As a voice-over, while the actor appears to be lost in thought.

2. With your acting companies, you will do a close reading of one of Iago's asides or soliloquies. On a separate sheet of paper, take notes on your discussion about the meaning of the speech as well as its importance in the play as a whole.

   Act II, Scene _____, lines _____ — _____

   • Set the scene: what has happened before this speech?

   • Paraphrase the speech.

   • What is the significance of the speech in the plot of the drama?

   • What about Iago's character is revealed in the speech?

3. Now that you have analyzed the speech, work as a group to decide how to present the speech. Take these questions into consideration as you plan your presentation:

   • What does the set look like?

   • Is this an aside or a soliloquy?

   • Are any other actors on the stage? If so, what are they doing?

   • What do you want the audience to understand about the play and about Iago?

   • How will you convey this understanding?

Emilia's Secret

SUGGESTED LEARNING STRATEGIES: Marking the Text, Graphic
Organizer, Drafting, Close Reading

A handkerchief is the most innocuous of objects, yet it holds
tremendous importance in *Othello*. Use the space below to create a
graphic organizer exploring the significance of the handkerchief to
the various characters (Othello, Desdemona, Emilia, Iago, Cassio, and
Bianca) and to the plot of the play through the end of Act III. Include line
numbers as textual support.

In Act III, Scene 3, appear the critical stage directions "*The handkerchief
falls, unnoticed.*" Emilia, who is nearby when the handkerchief falls,
picks it up and then gives it to her "wayward" husband. Why would she
give Iago Desdemona's first gift from Othello, knowing how dear it is to
Desdemona? Brainstorm a list of reasons.

Emilia's Secret

To understand Emilia's deception, it is important to make sense of the nature of the relationship between Emilia and Iago. Directors and actors have presented a number of interpretations of the characters' relationship. As you watch two of these interpretations, take notes in the format of the charts below.

Film Version 1—Title:
Director:

	Emilia	Iago
Delivery of lines (pace, volume, emphasis, tone of voice, etc.)		
Actions/gestures/facial expressions		
What is the nature of this relationship?		
How can you tell?		
In this interpretation, why does Emilia give Iago the handkerchief?		

Film Version 2—Title:

Director:

Emilia		Iago
	Delivery of lines (pace, volume, emphasis, tone of voice, etc.)	
	Actions/gestures/facial expressions	
	What is the nature of this relationship?	
	How can you tell?	
	In this interpretation, why does Emilia give Iago the handkerchief?	

Writing Prompt: After viewing and discussing at least two film versions of this scene, write an essay in which you evaluate which interpretation presents the most plausible explanation for Emilia's deception. Explain how your preference could be affected by a critical perspective.

Who's That Girl?

Read closely the scene assigned to your group. After reading, decide what the scene reveals about Emilia. You may begin to make your determinations about this character by questioning the text. How is she characterized? What is her relationship to other characters? What are her motivations?

Scene	What the Scene Reveals About Emilia	Textual Evidence
Act III, Scene 1, lines 46–64, Emilia & Cassio (Begins with EMILIA: Good morrow... and goes to the end of Act I)		
Act III, Scene 3, lines 344–368, Emilia & Iago (Begins with IAGO: How now? What do you here alone? and ends when Emilia exits.)		
Act III, Scene 4, lines 23–34, Emilia & Desdemona (Begins with DESDEMONA: Where should I lose that handkerchief, Emilia? and ends when Othello enters.)		

Use multiple critical perspectives to question the text (Archetypal, Cultural, Historical, Feminist, Reader Response, or Marxist Perspective). Draft one literal, one interpretive, and one universal question. Include at least two different critical perspectives in your questions.

Critical Perspectives/Scenes:

Levels of Questioning	Your Questions
Literal	
Interpretive	
Universal question	

Staging Iago's Lies

Revisit Activity 3.4, "Bringing the Plot to Life." Now that you are reading *Othello*, you should understand that the scenario and outcomes in the earlier activity were based on the play. Discuss with your acting company, and take notes on the connections.

> **Scenario:** Character 1 tells Character 2 that his or her spouse is cheating on him or her. Then Character 1 produces physical evidence as "proof," although the story is untrue.

Outcomes	How My Acting Company (or Another Company in My Class) Presented the Outcome	How *Othello*, the Play, Presents the Situation
Outcome A: Character 2 does not believe the story.		
Outcome B: Character 2 considers the story as a possibility but then decides it is untrue.		
Outcome C: Character 2 is filled with jealousy and wants revenge.		

1. Based on what you have read so far, predict what Iago will need to do to convince Othello that Desdemona is unfaithful.

LITERARY TERMS

In a drama, **blocking** refers to how actors position themselves in relation to one another, the audience, and the objects on the stage.

2. Based on the summary you've read or your teacher has presented, what are the key events in Act IV, Scene 1?

3. The moment when Othello falls into a trance is important, but it can be challenging to stage. This is *not* a moment when you want the audience laughing. How did your acting company decide to present Othello's trance?

4. Summarize lines 89 (IAGO: Stand you apart awhile.) to 120 (IAGO: How do you now, lieutenant?).

5. The conversation that follows can be tricky to stage. Othello must be visible to the audience but not to Cassio. The audience needs to see how Othello could misinterpret Cassio's comments about Bianca. The audience knows, of course, how Iago has orchestrated this misunderstanding; Bianca's surprise appearance is "the icing on the cake" for Iago's plan, at least.

   Draw your set diagram on separate paper. Use X's and arrows to indicate the characters' movements, or blocking.

6. Watch a film version and a filmed stage production of this scene. What is the difference between a film version and a stage production on film?

- What advantages might a film version have?

- What advantages might a stage version have?

Film Version—Director:	How is it presented?	What is the effect?
Dialogue between Iago and Othello, up to the trance		
The trance		
Dialogue between Iago and Cassio, observed by Othello		
Dialogue between Cassio and Bianca, observed by Othello		
Dialogue between Othello and Iago, after Cassio and Bianca exit		
Othello striking Desdemona		

Filmed Stage Version—Director:	How is it presented?	What is the effect?
Dialogue between Iago and Othello, up to the trance		
The trance		
Dialogue between Iago and Cassio, observed by Othello		
Dialogue between Cassio and Bianca, observed by Othello		
Dialogue between Othello and Iago, after Cassio and Bianca exit		
Othello striking Desdemona		

Shifting Perspectives

In Act IV, Scene 2, Othello confronts Emilia and Desdemona about his wife's meetings with Cassio. Examine this scene through each critical perspective.

Critical Perspective	How does this critical perspective apply to this scene?
Archetypal criticism would suggest that an archetype such as the fatal woman or temptress (a woman who uses her power—intellect, magic, or beauty—to make men weak) is essential to our understanding of this scene.	
Feminist criticism would suggest that the male-female power relationships that come into play in this scene are the most important influence on our understanding of it.	
Marxist criticism would suggest that we must examine the issues of class or social standing in order to fully understand this scene.	
Reader response criticism would suggest that what you bring to the scene will determine its significance.	
Cultural criticism would suggest that we must consider such issues as ethnicity, religious beliefs, social class, and so on to understand of this scene.	
Historical criticism would suggest that the historical context plays a significant role in a modern reader's understanding of the scene.	

Which critical perspective do you think provides the most interesting lens for the scene? Explain.

1. In American society, we tend to classify people into three primary socioeconomic classes: lower class, middle class, and upper class. One can argue that such categorizations lack authenticity, as the philosophies and commonalities shared by individuals within a classification differ. Grouping individuals into lower-, middle-, and upper-class socioeconomic categories is often oversimplified and without nuance.

2. Revisit your own or another student's essay, a close reading of the cast of characters in *Othello*, written for Activity 3.5. Examine the essays and then think about the characters as you have encountered them in *Othello*. With your group members, create an organizational structure that identifies categories into which the characters can be grouped, based on the socioeconomic power relationships evident in the text. The creation of the categories may not be random. You may not use "lower class, middle class, and upper class" as valid categories. Your group must justify the categories you have created by listing the philosophies and commonalities of each category. You must have a minimum of three different categories.

3. Use the graphic organizer on the next page to write your organizational structure.

WORD CONNECTIONS

The suffix *–ity* in **authenticity** is commonly used in English to indicate a state of being or condition. Adding this suffix to an adjective, such as *authentic, possible*, or *scarce*, creates a noun form.

Revisiting the Cast of Characters

Category	Characters	Philosophies of the Category	Commonalities

"Talk You of Killing?"

Act V, Scene 2 of *Othello* is the climax of the tragedy. As you reread Desdemona's last conversation with her husband, try to visualize it.

- What does the set look like?
- What costumes are the characters wearing?
- How does each character behave?
- What are the lighting and music like?

Describe:	Title: Director: Year:	Title: Director: Year:
The set		
Othello's costume		
Desdemona's costume		
Othello's actions		
Desdemona's actions		
Lighting		
Music		
Other theatrical or cinematic elements		

Writing Prompt: Write a comparison of the two interpretations of Desdemona's death. Include your ideas as to why the directors may have made the choices that they did. Consider the critical perspectives you have studied and whether any of them seem to be presented in these interpretations.

SUGGESTED LEARNING STRATEGIES: Chunking the Text,
Discussion Groups, Graphic Organizer, Guided Reading, Marking
the Text, Skimming and Scanning, Summarizing/Paraphrasing

My Notes

Essay

> **ABOUT THE AUTHOR**
> Sylvan Barnet has served as an English professor, editor
> of classical Shakespeare editions, and writer of numerous
> articles on Shakespeare and his works. He has also edited
> several textbooks and written books on teaching and
> writing about art.

Othello ON STAGE AND SCREEN

by Sylvan Barnet

The earliest mention of a performance of *Othello*, in an account of 1604,
reports only that the play was acted before James I at Whitehall Palace. Next
come two references to performances in 1610, one telling us that it was acted
at the Globe in April, the other telling us that it was acted in September at
Oxford. The reference to the Oxford production is especially valuable, since
it provides one of the very few glimpses we have of early seventeenth-century
acting and of an audience's response to a performance. The relevant passage,
in Latin, may be translated thus:

> In their tragedies they acted with appropriate decorum; in these they
> caused tears not only by their speaking, but also by their action. Indeed
> Desdemona, although greatly successful throughout, moved us especially
> when at last, lying on her bed, killed by her husband, she implored the
> pity of the spectators in her death with her face alone.

This may not seem like much, but it is more than we have for all but a few
of Shakespeare's other plays, and it is especially valuable as a reminder that
the Renaissance boy actors—a boy played Desdemona—were highly skilled
performers.

There are only a few additional references to performances in the first
half of the seventeenth century, but a very large number of rather general
references to the play (as opposed to specific performances) allows us to
conclude that the play must have been popular on the stage. From 1642 to

My Notes

1660 the theaters were closed by act of Parliament, but when the theaters reopened in 1660, Othello was staged almost immediately. Samuel Pepys saw it in 1660:

> To the Cockpit to see *The Moor of Venice*, which was well done. [Nathaniel] Burt acted the Moor: by the same token, a very pretty lady that sat by me called out, to see Desdemona smothered.

He saw it again in 1669, this time with less pleasure:

> To the King's playhouse, and there in an upper box . . . did see *The Moor of Venice*: but ill acted in most parts; [Michael] Mohun which did a little surprise me not acting Iago's part by much so well as [Walter] Clun used to do . . . nor, indeed, Burt doing the Moor's so well as I once thought he did.

During this period, the great interpreter of the title role was Thomas Betterton, who performed it from 1684 to 1709. Although he was the leading Othello of the period and was much praised, the only informative contemporary account of his performance in the role tells us little more than that his

> aspect was serious, venerable[1], and majestic.... His voice was low and grumbling, though he could lime[2] it by an artful climax, which enforced attention. . . . He kept this passion under, and showed it most.

Betterton's successor as Othello was James Quin, who played the part from 1722 to 1751. Wearing a white wig and the white uniform (including white gloves) of a British officer, he was said to have presented an impressive appearance, but his acting was characterized as statuesque, even stiff, lacking in tenderness, pathos, fire, and any suggestion of inner pain. Quin was eclipsed in 1745 by David Garrick, whose Othello was quite different: the complaint now was that this Othello lacked dignity. The accusation was not merely a glance at Garrick's relatively short stature (he sought to compensate for his height by adding a turban to the costume of an officer in the British army), or even at his bold restoration of the fainting episode (4.1.45), which had been cut by his predecessors. Rather, it was directed at Garrick's violent gestures, which suggested to one critic that Othello seemed afflicted with St. Vitus dance.[3] Garrick defended his interpretation by arguing that Shakespeare

> had shown us white men jealous in other pieces, but that their jealousy had limits, and was not so terrible... .[In] Othello he had wished to paint that passion in all its violence, and that is why he chose an African in whose being circulated fire instead of blood, and whose true or imaginary character could excuse all boldness of expression and all exaggerations of passion.

---

[1] **venerable (adj.):** commanding respect
[2] **lime (v.):** join together
[3] **St. Vitus dance:** a disease characterized by frenzied movements

My Notes

Garrick's rival, Quin, was not convinced. Of Garrick's Othello, Quin said: "Othello!... psha! no such thing. There was a little black boy ... fretting and fuming about the stage; but I saw no Othello."

A reader can scarcely overlook the racism in these remarks, and something should be said about attitudes toward Moors. There is no doubt that most Elizahethans regarded Moors as vengeful—largely because they were not Christians. That Moors were black—the color of the devil—was thought to be a visible sign of their capacity for endless evil. (In fact, Shakespeare specifies that Othello is a Christian, and this is only one of several ways in which Othello departs from the stereotype.) Othello's physical blackness, by the way, seems not to have been doubted until the early nineteenth century. Certainly Quin and Garrick played him in blackface, and presumably so did their predecessor Betterton. And there is no doubt that on the Elizabethan stage Othello was very black. The only contemporary illustration of a scene from Shakespeare shows another of Shakespeare's Moors, Aaron in *Titus Andronicus*, as having an inky complexion. But in the early nineteenth century one finds expressions of distinct discomfort at the thought that Othello is black rather than, say, bronzed, or (to use an even loftier metaphor) golden. Even the best critics were not exempt from the racist thinking of their times. Thus, in 1808 Charles Lamb, picking up Desdemona's assertion that she judged Othello by his mind rather than by his color, argued that although we can share her view when we read the play, we cannot do so when we see a black Othello on the stage:

She sees Othello's color in his mind. But upon the stage, when the imagination is no longer the ruling faculty, but we are left to our poor unassisted senses, I appeal to every one that has seen Othello played, whether he did not, on the contrary, sink Othello's mind in his color; whether he did not find something extremely revolting in the courtship and wedded caresses of Othello and Desdemona, and whether the actual sight of the thing did not over-weigh all that beautiful compromise which we make in reading. . . .

At about the time that Lamb offered his comment on Othello, Lamb's friend Coleridge made some notes to the effect that Shakespeare could not possibly have thought of Othello as a black:

Can we suppose [Shakespeare] so utterly ignorant as to make a barbarous *negro* plead royal birth? Were negroes then known but as slaves; on the contrary, were not the Moors the warriors? . . . No doubt Desdemona saw Othello's visage in his mind; yet, as we are constituted, and most surely as an English audience was disposed in the beginning of the seventeenth century, it would he something monstrous to conceive this beautiful Venetian girl falling in love with a veritable negro. It would argue a disproportionateness, a want of balance in Desdemona, which Shakespeare does not appear to have in the least contemplated.

Given Coleridge's certainty that Othello could not possibly have been black, it is well to reiterate that the Elizabethans thought of Moors as black. True, there are a few references in Elizabethan literature to "tawny" Moors, but there is no evidence that the Elizabethans distinguished between tawny and black Moors, and in any case, if they did, various passages in *Othello* indicate that the protagonist is surely a black Moor. Admittedly, most of the references to Othello's Negroid features are made by persons hostile to him— Roderigo calls him "the thick-lips" (1.1.63), for instance, and Iago speaks of him as "an old black ram" (1.1 .85)—but Othello himself says that his name "is now begrimed and black / As mine own face" (3.3 .384—5). Of course "black" is sometimes used in the sense of brunette, hut there really cannot be any doubt that Othello is black in the most obvious modern sense, and to call him tawny or golden or bronzed, or to conceive of him as something of an Arab chieftain, is to go against the text of the play.

When Spranger Barry, the actor who displaced Garrick as Othello in the middle of the eighteenth century (he was said to have not only the passion of Garrick but also the majesty that in Quin was merely stiffness), the question of color seems not to have come up, nor did it come up when the role in effect belonged to John Philip Kemble, the chief Othello at the turn of the eighteenth century (he played his first Othello in 1785, his last in 1805). Kemble, tall and stately, acted in what can be called a classic rather than romantic manner, a style suited more to, say, Brutus than to Othello. His interpretation of the role was criticized for its superabundance of dignity and for its lack of variety and fire, but not for its blackness. But when Edmund Kean played the role in 1814 he is said to have used a light brown makeup in place of the usual burnt cork. Oddly, there is some uncertainty about this— most critics of the period did not comment on the novelty—but putting aside the question of who made the change, and exactly when, about this time the color changed. By 1827 Leman Thomas Rede's *The Road to the Stage* (a book on makeup) could report that "A tawny tinge is now the color used for the gallant Moor." Here it is evident that the makeup no longer uses burnt cork. Most of the Othellos of the rest of the century were tawny, their bronze skin suggesting that they were sons of the desert, but Henry Irving's Othello of 1881 was conspicuously dark (darker than his "bronze" Othello of 1876), and, as we shall see, in the twentieth century dark Othellos have been dominant, especially in our own generation, when American blacks have often played the part.

My Notes

Putting aside the point that Kean's Othello was lighter than usual, it was exceptional for its power and its pathos. If Kemble is the paradigm of classical acting, Kean— passionate, even spasmodic—is the paradigm of romantic acting. Coleridge wrote: "Seeing [Kean] act was like reading Shakespeare by flashes of lightning." Another great romantic writer, William Hazlitt, at first found Kean too passionate. In the following passage Hazlitt complains that the fault in the performance is not in the color of Kean's face, or in Kean's relatively short stature:

Othello was tall, but that is nothing; he was black, but that is nothing. But he was not fierce, and that is everything. It is only in the last agony of human suffering that he gives way to his rage and despair. . . . Mr. Kean is in general all passion, all energy, all relentless will. . . . He is too often in the highest key of passion, too uniformly on the verge of extravagance, too constantly on the rack.

Kean later moderated the passion, perhaps under Hazlitt's influence, but, curiously, Hazlitt regretted the change, remarking: "There is but one perfect way of playing Othello, and that was the way . . . he used to play it." Equally compelling is the tribute to Kean offered by the American actor Junius Brutus Booth, who in England in 1817–18 played Iago to Kean's Othello. Booth said that "Kean's Othello smothered Desdemona and my Iago too." Kean's triumph in the role was undoubted, but in 1825, two weeks after he had been proved guilty of adultery, public opinion turned against him, denouncing the hypocrisy of an adulterer who dared to play the outraged husband lamenting his wife's infidelity. Still, he continued in the role, playing Othello almost to the day of his death. His last performance was in this role, in 1833, when he collapsed on the stage and died a few weeks later.

Other nineteenth-century actors have made their mark in the role—for instance William Macready (he sometimes played Iago against Kean's Othello) and Samuel Phelps— but here there is space to mention only four, Ira Aldridge, Edwin Booth, Tommaso Salvini, and Henry Irving. Aldridge, a black, was born in New York in 1807. As a very young man he determined to be an actor, but seeing no possibility of a career as an actor in America, he went to London in 1824 and never returned to the United States, At least one black actor, James Hewlett, had already played Othello in America, but that was with the all-black African Company, and Aldridge's ambition was to be accepted as an actor, not as a black actor, an ambition impossible to fulfill in the United States, where there were no interracial companies. He performed throughout the British Isles and also on the Continent, playing not only Othello but also (with white makeup) such roles as Richard III, Shylock, Hamlet, Macbeth, and Lear.

In America, Edwin Booth (son of Junius Brutus Booth) acted Othello almost annually from 1826 to 1871. From time to time he changed his performance, sometimes working in the violent style associated with Tommaso Salvini, hurling his Iago to the ground, but sometimes he played with restraint—occasionally he even omitted striking Desdemona at IV.i.240—and he was especially praised for his tender passion. Most critics, however, preferred his Iago, which seemed genial, sincere, and terrifyingly evil; he was widely regarded as the greatest Iago of the later nineteenth century. (Among the performers with whom he alternated the roles of Othello and Iago were Henry Irving and James O'Neill, Eugene O'Neill's father; and he played Iago to Salvini's Othello. Here is his advice on how to play Iago:

> Don't *act* the villain, don't *look* it or *speak* it (by scowling and growling, I mean), but *think* it all the time. Be genial, sometimes jovial, always gentlemanly. Quick in motion as in thought; lithe and sinuous as a snake. A certain bluffness (which my temperament does not afford) should be added to preserve the military flavor of the character; in this particular I fail utterly, my Iago lacks the soldierly quality.

Henry Irving played Othello only in 1876 and 1881. Although he had already achieved success in the roles of Hamlet, Macbeth, and Lear, his Othello did not find equal favor. It was not especially violent, but it was said to lack dignity (apparently there was much lifting up of hands and shuffling of feet), and after the attempt in 1881 Irving decided to drop the role. Still, some things about the 1881 performance should be mentioned. The makeup was very black, the costume exotic (a white jeweled turban, an amber robe), and the killing of Desdemona very solemn—until Desdemona tried to escape, at which point he flung her on the bed. The play ended with Othello's suicide, the curtain descending as he fell at Gratiano's feet. Iago (played by Booth) stood by, smiling malignantly.

By common consent the greatest Othello of the later nineteenth century was Tommaso Salvini, who acted in Italian—even when in England or the United States, with the rest of the company speaking English. Some Victorians regarded Salvini as too savage, too volcanic, too terrifying to arouse pity—he seized Iago by the throat and hurled him to the floor, and put his foot on Iago's neck, and of course he did not hesitate to strike Desdemona—but most audiences were deeply moved as well as terrified by his performance. We are told that especially in the first three acts, where some of the love play seemed almost to be high comedy, his Othello was "delightful' and "delicate." Still, the overall effect was that of enormous energy, though not of mere barbarism. Henry James was among Salvini's greatest admirers:

> It is impossible to imagine anything more living, more tragic, more suggestive of a tortured soul and of generous, beneficent strength changed

My Notes

My Notes

to a purpose of destruction. With its tremendous force, it is magnificently quiet, and from the beginning to the end has not a touch of rant or crudity.

Actors of note who played Othello or Iago in the early twentieth century include Johnston Forbes-Robertson, Oscar Asche, and Beerbohm Tree, but none of these was widely regarded as great. Indeed, the standard opinion is that the twentieth century did not have a great Othello until Paul Robeson, an African American, played the role in 1943. But Robeson was not primarily an actor. As a college student at Rutgers he distinguished himself not to theatrics but in athletics (all-American end in football in 1918, and letters in several varsity sports) and in scholarship (Phi Beta Kappa). He next prepared for a career in the law, taking a law degree at Columbia University, but while at Columbia in 1921 he performed in his first amateur production. He soon began to appear in some professional productions, including *Showboat*, where his singing of "Ol' Man River" led to a career as a concert singer, especially of spirituals and work songs, though he returned to the stage to play Othello in 1930 in England, in 1942 in Cambridge, Boston, and Princeton, in 1943 in New York, and in 1959 at Stratford-upon-Avon. Observers agree that the 1959 performance was poor; Robeson had been weakened by an attack of bronchitis, his political beliefs had been shaken (earlier he had praised Stalin, but now the crimes of the Stalin era were evident), and, perhaps worst of all, the director's presence was too strongly felt, for instance in a distracting fog that supposedly was the result of the storm at Cyprus. Many scenes were so dark that spectators could not see the actors' faces, and there seems no reason to doubt the accuracy of those reviewers who accused the director of obliterating the principal actors.

Robeson's first Othello—indeed, his first performance in a play by Shakespeare, in 1930—was much more enthusiastically received. The London *Morning Post* said: "There has been no Othello on our stage for forty years to compare with his dignity, simplicity, and true passion." But not all of the reviewers were entirely pleased. James Agate, the leading theater critic of the period, said that Robeson lacked the majesty that Shakespeare insists on early in the play, for instance in such lines as

> I fetch my life and being
>
> From men of royal siege,   (1.2.20–21)

and

> Were it my cue to fight, I should have known it
> Without a prompter,   (82–83)

and

> Keep up your bright swords, for the dew will
> rust them.   (58)

The majesty displayed in such passages, Agate said, tells us how Othello must behave when he puts down Cassio's drunken brawl, but according to Agate, Robeson (despite his height—six feet, three inches) lacked this majesty. Thus, when Robeson's Othello said "Silence that dreadful bell! It frights the isle / From her propriety" (2.3.174–75), he showed personal annoyance rather than the "passion for decorum" (Agate's words) that the line reveals. Agate found Robeson best in the third and fourth acts, where he captured the jealousy of the part, but weak (lacking in dignity) in the last act, where he failed to perform the murder with a solemn sense of sacrifice.

Despite the reservations of Agate and others, there was some talk of bringing the production to the United States, but nothing came of it, doubtless because of uncertainty about how American audiences (and perhaps performers?) would respond to a company that mixed whites and blacks. In 1938 Margaret Webster again raised the topic, but she was discouraged by the Americans with whom she talked. It was acceptable for a black actor—a real black man, not a white man in blackface—to kiss a white girl in England, but not in the United States. Fortunately, however, Webster later persuaded the Theatre Guild to invite Robeson to do *Othello* in the United States in 1942, if not on Broadway at least as summer stock, with José Ferrer as Iago and Uta Hagen as Desdemona. The production was enthusiastically received, but Robeson's concert commitments prevented it from going to New York until the fall of 1943. When it did open in New York, the reviews were highly favorable, but some of them contained reservations about Robeson's ability to speak blank verse and to catch the grandeur of the role. In any case, the production was an enormous success, running for 296 continuous performances. The previous record for a New York *Othello* had been 57.

Robeson inevitably was asked to discuss his conception of the role; equally inevitably, he said different things at different times, and perhaps sometimes said what reporters wanted to hear—or perhaps the reporters heard only what they wanted to hear. Sometimes he was reported as saying that the matter of color is secondary, but on other occasions he is reported as saying: "The problem [of *Othello*] is the problem of my own people. It is a tragedy of racial conflict, a tragedy of honor, rather than of jealousy."

Until Robeson, black actors in the United States were in effect limited to performing in all-black companies. With Robeson, a black actor played Othello with an otherwise white company. His appearance as Othello in 1943 was an important anticipation of the gains black actors were to make in later decades. Earle Hyman, Moses Gunn, Paul Winfield, William Marshall, and James Earl Jones are among the black actors who have played impressive Othellos in mixed-race companies. More important however, as the careers of these actors show, a black may now also play a role other than Othello, as

My Notes

My Notes

Ira Aldridge did a hundred and fifty years ago, though he had to cross the Atlantic to do it.

Before looking at Laurence Olivier's Othello in 1964, mention should be made of Olivier's Iago in a production of 1937, directed by Tyrone Guthrie at the Old Vic. Olivier and Guthrie talked to Ernest Jones, friend of Sigmund Freud, and came away with the idea that Iago's hatred for Othello was in fact based on a subconscious love for Othello. That Iago protests "I hate the Moor" means nothing, for he is unaware of his true emotions. Ralph Richardson was Othello in this production, but Guthrie and Olivier decided not to shock him (remember, this was 1937) by any such unconventional idea, and so, the story goes, Richardson could never quite understand what Olivier was making out of the role. (What Olivier apparently made out of it was something like this: Iago is manic because he cannot face his true feelings.) The critics, like Richardson and the general public, were in the dark, and the production was poorly reviewed. Guthrie himself later called the production "a ghastly, boring hash," and Olivier has said that he no longer subscribes to Jones's interpretation.

In 1964 Olivier played Othello, with Frank Finlay as Iago, and Maggie Smith as Desdemona, in production directed by John Dexter. (This production was later filmed, and most of what is true of the stage production is true also of the film.) Far from suggesting that Othello was some sort of desert chief, Olivier emphasized the Negroid aspects, or at least the white man's stock ideas of' Negroid aspects. Thus, Othello's skin was very dark, his lips were red and sensuous, and his lilting voice had something of a West Indian accent. He rolled his eyes a good deal, and he walked (barefooted and adorned with ankle bracelets) with a sensuous sway. More important (worse, some viewers felt), was the idea behind this Othello, which was indebted to some thoughts by T. S. Eliot and F. R. Leavis. For Eliot (in an essay called "Shakespeare and the Stoicism of Seneca," first published in 1927) and for Leavis (in an essay first published in a journal in 1937 but more readily available, in reprinted form, in Leavis's *The Common Pursuit*), Othello is not so much a heroic figure—the noble Moor who gains our sympathy despite the terrible deed he performs—as a fatuous[4] simpleton,[5] a man given to egotistical self-dramatizing. The playbill included some passages from Leavis's essay, which the director in effect summarized when he told the cast that

> Othello is a pompous[6], word-spinning, arrogant black general. . . . The important thing is not to accept him at his own valuation. . . . He isn't just a righteous man who's been wronged. He's a man too proud to think he could ever be capable of anything as base as jealousy. When he learns he can be jealous, his character changes. The knowledge destroys him, and he goes berserk.

---

[4] **fatuous:** foolish, silly
[5] **simpleton:** foolish or ignorant person
[6] **pompous:** self-important

Thus, Olivier delivered "Farewell the tranquil mind" (3.3.345)—a speech customarily delivered reflectively—in a frenzy. It's probably fair to say that the gist of the idea underlying this production is fairly odd: Othello is a barbarian with a thin veneer of civilization. Thus, the early speeches were delivered with easy confidence because Othello had no understanding of how simple and how volatile he really was. The change from civilized man to barbarian was marked by Othello tearing off a crucifix he wore, an effective enough bit of business but one at odds with two aspects of the end of Shakespeare's play: Othello (who just before he kills Desdemona is careful to urge her to make her peace with God; "I would not kill thy soul" (5.2.32) murders Desdemona partly because he believes she has been false to the highest ideals. Second, when he comes to understand the horror of his action he executes justice upon himself. Still, although much in the conception could be faulted, it was widely agreed that Olivier's acting was a triumph—a triumph won, among other things, at the expense of an unprepossessing Iago and a negligible Desdemona.

The film with Olivier (1965), directed by Stuart Burge, was made in a sound studio, using sets that were essentially those of the stage production— even for scenes set out-of-doors—but it was not simply a filmed version of what a spectator sitting in the third row center would have seen. For instance, because close-ups are used for all of Iago's soliloquies, Iago becomes considerably more prominent in the film than he was on the stage.

Olivier said that the backgrounds in the film were minimal because he was concerned with "offering as little visual distraction as possible from the intentions of Shakespeare—or our performance of them." For a film of the opposite sort, a film that does not hesitate to introduce impressive visual effects not specified in the text, one should look at Orson Welles's *Othello*, a black and white film begun in 1951 and completed and released in 1955, with Welles in the title role. The film was shot on location, chiefly in Morocco and Venice, but what especially strikes a viewer is not that the camera gives us a strong sense of the real world, but that the camera leads us into a strange, shadowy world of unfamiliar and puzzling appearance. The film begins with Welles reading a passage from Shakespeare's source while we see a shot of the face of the dead Othello. The camera rises above the bier, which is carried by pallbearers, and we then see Desdemona's body, also being borne to the grave. We see the two funeral processions converge, and then we see Iago, in chains, thrust into a cage and hoisted above the crowd. From above—Iago's viewpoint—we look down on the bodies of Othello and Desdemona. All of this is presented before we see the credits for the film. The film ends with a dissolve from the dying Othello to a shot of the funeral procession and then to shots of the fortress at Cyprus, the cage, and Venetian buildings and ships. Between this highly cinematic beginning and ending, other liberties are taken with the text. The murder of Roderigo, for instance, is set in a steamy bathhouse. Welles had intended to shoot the scene in a street, but because he had run out of money and didn't have costumes, he set it in a steam bath, where a few towels were all the clothing that was needed. In short, Welles's *Othello* is not for the Shakespeare purist (too much is cut and too much is added), but it is imaginative and it often works. Admirers will want to see also *Filming "Othello,"* a film memoir (1978) in which Welles and others discuss the work.

The BBC television version of *Othello*, directed by Jonathan Miller and released in 1981, is, like Olivier's film, somewhat in the Eliot-Leavis tradition. In the introduction to the printed text of the BBC version, Miller says that the play does not set forth "the spectacle of a person of grandeur falling." Rather,

> what's interesting is that it's not the fall of the great but the disintegration of the ordinary, of the representative character. It's the very ordinariness of Othello that makes the story intolerable.

Miller is insistent, too, that the play is not about race. "I do not see the play as being about color but as being about jealousy—which is something we are all vulnerable to." In line with this emphasis on the ordinary, Othello (Anthony Hopkins) is relatively unheroic, though he is scarcely as commonplace as Miller suggests, since he is full of energy and rage. More successful is Iago (Bob Hoskins), a bullet-headed hood who delights in Othello's anguish. The sets, in order to reduce any sense of heroism or romance, are emphatically domestic; no effort was made to take advantage of the camera's ability to record expansive space. Interestingly, however, the domestic images on the screen are by no means ordinary; notably beautiful, they often remind us of Vermeer.

During the course of this survey it has been easy to notice racist implications in the remarks of certain actors and critics. And it was racism, of course, that kept blacks from acting in Othello and in other plays) along with whites. One point that has not been raised till now is this: Does it matter if a black plays Othello? When Robeson played the part, some theatergoers found that the play made more sense than ever before, partly because Robeson (whatever his limitations as an actor) was a black. Others found that it was distracting for a black to play the part; it brought into the world of Othello irrelevant issues of twentieth-century America. Jonathan Miller, holding the second position, puts it thus:

> When a black actor does the part, it offsets the play, puts it out of balance. It makes it a play about blackness, which it is not. . . . The trouble is, the play was hijacked for political purposes.

Many things can be said against this view, for instance that when the white actor Olivier played Othello he expended so much energy impersonating a black that a spectator was far more conscious of the performer's blackness than one is of, say, James Earl Jones's. In any case, Miller has not said the last word on this topic, which will continue to be debated.

Bibliographic Note: For a modern edition of *Othello* prefaced with a long stage history, and equipped with abundant footnotes telling how various actors delivered particular lines, see Julie Hankey, *Othello* (1987), a volume in a series entitled *Plays in Performance*.

For a survey of *Othello* on the stage, see Marvin Rosenberg, *The Masks of "Othello"* (1961); for a brief study of five recent productions (including Robeson in 1943, Olivier in 1964, and the BBC television version of 1981), see Martin L. Wine, *"Othello": Text and Performance* (1984). Errol Hill's *Shakespeare in Sable* (1984), a history of black actors of Shakespeare, contains much information about *Othello*. Other items especially relevant to the productions discussed above include: Arthur Colby Sprague, *Shakespearian Players and Performances* (1953), for Kean's Othello and Edwin Booth's Iago; Daniel J. Watermeier, "Edwin Booth's Iago," *Theatre History Studies* 6 (1986): 32–55; Kenneth Tynan, ed., *"Othello" by William Shakespeare: The National Theatre Production* (1966), on Olivier; *The BBC TV Shakespeare: "Othello"* (1981), on the version directed by Jonathan Miller. On Robeson, see Susan Spector, "Margaret Webster's *Othello*," *Theatre History Studies* 6 (1968): 93–108. For film versions, see Jack J. Jorgens, *Shakespeare on Film* (1977), and, for Welles's film only, see Michael MacLiammoir, *Put Money in Thy Purse* (1952).

My Notes

Writing an Analysis

SUGGESTED LEARNING STRATEGIES: **Outlining, Drafting, Self-Editing**

Assignment

Your assignment is to choose one critical perspective and compose an argumentative essay in response to a prompt, while working under specific time constraints. You should use the same prewriting and drafting strategies that you would normally employ in a writing situation with unlimited time.

Steps

1. The ability to interpret a writing prompt and to plan and execute the writing in a short period of time is an essential skill for college-bound students, as well as for graduates who immediately enter the workforce. Remember that the point of a timed writing is to assess your ability to organize and develop ideas quickly and to experience your "writing voice." Each of the writing assignments that you have completed in this unit's activities has prepared you for a task such as this.

2. Carefully read the argumentative essay writing prompt that your teacher will provide. Ensure that you are responding to the requirements of the prompt by marking it for important language. The paraphrase will ensure that you accurately comprehend the writing task you have been given.

3. Construct a brief outline or perform some other prewriting strategy (e.g., graphic organizer, list, notes) to structure ideas in a sustained and persuasive way and to ensure that your essay is planned and organized.

4. You will have 45 minutes to read the prompt and plan and compose the essay.

5. Be sure that your essay has an organizing principle. It should include a thesis statement that takes a definite position and builds strong support for that position. Be sure to include rhetorical devices to convey meaning and enhance your argument.

6. You may use references from sports, history, art, literature, science, film, or your personal experiences and observations to support your position.

7. Your essay will be assessed as a first draft. Do not spend time editing, revising, and rewriting unless you have completed the essay in full and have some time remaining.

8. Your teacher will inform you when you have ten minutes remaining.

SCORING GUIDE

Scoring Criteria	Exemplary	Proficient	Emerging
Ideas	The essay insightfully and thoroughly uses Historical, Cultural, or Feminist critical perspective. The essay is exceptionally focused. The thesis is clearly defined. Supporting details and commentary are relevant.	The essay adequately uses a Historical, Cultural, or Feminist critical perspective in its argument. The essay is clear, with an identifiable thesis. Supporting details or commentary are present but may require some inference.	The essay does not clearly use a critical perspective in its argument. The essay's focus is weak; it may not contain a coherent thesis. Supporting details and commentary are superficial or missing.
Organization	The essay's organization is exceptional. Ideas move smoothly and comfortably with effective use of transitions enhancing the essay's coherence.	The essay's organization is clear and easy to follow. Transitions help readers move between ideas.	The essay is difficult to follow. It may lack transitions and jump too rapidly between ideas.
Evidence of Planning	The essay demonstrates evidence of multiple prewriting strategies.	The essay demonstrates evidence of outlining, marking the text of the prompt, or some other prewriting strategy.	The essay lacks evidence of prewriting attempts.
Additional Criteria			

Comments:

Learning Focus:

Drama Is Performance

"He was not of an age, but for all time!"

Ben Jonson

As Shakespeare's contemporary, Ben Jonson predicted that Shakespeare's words would long outlive their author. In this unit, you have examined the complex production history of *Othello*. You know that Shakespeare's plays were meant to be performed, that the vision of actors and directors can breathe life into Shakespeare's words. You have also learned how to use theatrical elements to convey your interpretation of a scene. You have considered, too, how different critical perspectives present opportunities for interesting interpretations of the play. Now is your chance to bring all of this learning together in your presentation of a scene from *Othello* that reflects a critical perspective and shows that Shakespeare's tragedy is still relevant in your time.

Bringing a drama to life on the stage is a complex, collaborative effort in which all members of the team or acting group must plan, organize, rehearse, and perform together, even as they have separate roles and responsibilities for a successful production.

A staging notebook becomes an important tool for acting groups to keep a record of their decisions about theatrical elements such as costume, set design, props, blocking, lighting and sound, as well as script notations for actors' gestures, movements, and vocal delivery of dialogue. These notes should reflect your group's performance plan based on a particular interpretation of the scene. Rehearsals and performances must adhere to your plan in order to successfully convey the specific interpretation your group has created using the theatrical elements typical of all stage productions.

The Hero's Adversary

SUGGESTED LEARNING STRATEGIES: Summarizing, Graphic Organizer, KWL Chart

The Hero's Adversary

Audiences of Shakespeare are familiar with the concept of the **tragic hero** or **protagonist**. Shakespeare's hero is the character with whom audiences become emotionally invested. He is derived from the flawed heroes of Greek tragedy; he has a flaw that makes him vulnerable to a tragic death or downfall.

Generally, the Shakespearean hero's greatest obstacle (after himself) is the villain, **antagonist,** or **adversary** who is adept at perceiving the hero's flaw and exploiting it. The adversary also elicits a significant emotional response from the audience. Frequently, the behavior of the villain is unjustified or unexplained; it exists for the sole purpose of being cunning, deceitful, or evil. The hero may be forced to reckon with the adversary (or his evil deeds) on more than one occasion, as perseverance is a trait the character must exhibit to be worthy of the title "hero." One might describe the experiences of the hero's adversary as devolution[1] in three phases: the flashpoint, the flourishing, and the foil.

The Flashpoint—a period in which the anger of the adversary explodes, even if that explosion is controlled or subtle. During this phase, the deviant inclinations of the hero's adversary are revealed.

The Flourishing—a period of relative success for the hero's adversary after he has injured the hero physically or emotionally. During this phase, the adversary is often able to entice others (especially one who is trusted or beloved by the hero) into the service of his or her cunning plans.

The Foil—a period where the adversary or the adversary's schemes are exposed. The hero finds courage or strength to triumph over the adversary mentally or physically. During this phase, the adversary's exposure ultimately causes his or her downfall or defeat, even in circumstances where the hero is bested.

WORD CONNECTIONS

The Latin root of the word *perseverance*, meaning "steady persistence," is *serverus*, meaning "severe." Related words include *persevere* and *severance.*

---

[1] **devolution:** descent through successive stages

The Hero's Adversary

Iago: The Hero's Adversary

Phase	Dramatic Moments in the Plot	Character Developments
The Flashpoint		
The Flourishing		
The Foil		

Staging an Interpretation

SUGGESTED LEARNING STRATEGIES: **Group Discussion, Close Reading, Drafting, Rehearsal**

Assignment

Your assignment is to interpret a scene from *Othello* using one of the critical perspectives you have studied and then plan, rehearse, and perform the scene.

Steps

Planning

1. With your acting company, select a scene from *Othello* that lends itself to an engaging interpretation based on one of the critical perspectives you have studied.

2. When you formed your acting companies, you selected a scene from the play to perform for the class. Revisit that scene.

3. Read through the scene in parts several times to clarify meaning. Assign responsibilities. Your acting company identified the director, dramaturge, and cast on the contract you made for Activity 3.2, but you may make changes with your teacher's approval.

4. As you get to know the scene better through close reading and discussion, think about how one of the critical perspectives might apply to the scene and how your acting company could bring the critical perspective to life. You may delete lines or make other changes, such as to the setting, stage directions, or gender of the characters, in order to apply your selected critical perspective.

5. Staging notebooks play an important part in preparing for performances. Each member of your acting company should complete a staging notebook, although the entries will be different for directors, dramaturges, and actors.

6. Create a copy of the script so that you can mark blocking, facial expressions, gestures, and so on. It is imperative that you learn the lines so that your performance is not encumbered by notes.

Rehearsing and Refining

7. Begin the rehearsal process by getting comfortable saying the lines and understanding the action in your scene. Try to speak naturally and clearly and with emphasis. Remember that presentations are more formal than informal group discussions and adapt your language and delivery accordingly.

8. As you rehearse, integrate theatrical elements that your acting company intends to use.

9. If possible, videotape one of your rehearsals to help you improve the quality of the performance. Pay attention to your interactions with one another, your position on stage, the pace of your speech, and the volume of your voice. If videotaping is not practical, ask another group to watch your rehearsal and provide feedback on how you might improve your performance. In either case, use the Scoring Guide to provide feedback about the performance.

Presenting and Reflecting

10. Perform your scene. Remember to use good speaking skills by speaking clearly, looking at the audience, and using a tone appropriate for your purpose and your audience. Your teacher may ask other students to use the Scoring Guide to assess your performance.

11. After your performance, describe the process you went through to complete this project, the challenges you faced, how you worked to overcome them, and your evaluation of the final performance. You may want to use your peers' assessments in your self-evaluation.

12. Practice good listening skills during other acting groups' performances. Listen closely, look at the actors, and think about what they are saying and how they are saying it. Pay attention to both verbal and nonverbal communication.

Critical Perspectives Notes

Our scene (Act, Scene, and line numbers):

Cast:

We are going to apply this critical perspective to the scene:

We think this is a good choice because:

We will convey our critical perspective through the following elements:

Acting		
Blocking		
Costumes		
Props		
Set		
Other		

Staging an Interpretation

SCORING GUIDE

Scoring Criteria	Exemplary	Proficient	Emerging
Preparatory Texts	The marked script and critical perspectives notes reveal an insightful analysis and mature understanding of the scene.	The marked script and critical perspectives notes demonstrate a clear analysis and understanding of the scene.	The marked script and critical perspectives notes reveal a limited analysis and understanding of the scene.
Performance	The group's interpretation of the scene and application of the critical perspective are insightful, and the intended effect is clearly communicated to the audience. Participants demonstrate a polished performance by: • skillfully using various theatrical elements; • strategically using elements of vocal delivery to effectively fulfill their role within the acting company; • effectively using elements of visual delivery to create focus and maintain energy for the scene.	The group's interpretation of the scene and application of the critical perspective are plausible, and the intended effect is communicated to the audience. Participants demonstrate a good performance by: • adequately using various theatrical elements; • knowledgably using elements of vocal delivery to portray their characters or to communicate information within the acting company; • using elements of visual delivery to create cohesion for the scene.	The group's interpretation of the scene and application of the critical perspective may be unclear, or the intended effect is not communicated to the audience. Participants demonstrate a disorganized performance and may: • fail to use varied theatrical elements; • use vocal delivery that fails to portray their characters or to communicate information related to their role within the acting company; • use elements of visual delivery that are unclear or detract from the quality of the scene.
Evidence of Collaboration	Throughout the process of planning and presenting, the group cooperates successfully to maintain purpose and to achieve goals. Equal sharing of responsibility is evident.	Throughout the process of planning and presenting, the group works adequately to maintain purpose and achieve goals. Sharing of responsibility is mostly balanced.	Throughout the process of planning and presenting, the group lacks cooperation, which impedes its ability to maintain purpose or achieve goals. Responsibilities are not equally divided.

SCORING GUIDE

Scoring Criteria	Exemplary	Proficient	Emerging
Reflective Text	The reflective text demonstrates a thorough and detailed analysis of the entire process including analyzing, creating, rehearsing, and performing the scene.	The reflective text demonstrates adequate analysis of the process of analyzing, creating, rehearsing, and performing the scene.	The reflective text demonstrates inadequate analysis of the process of analyzing, creating, rehearsing, and performing the scene.
Additional Criteria			

Comments:

Reflection

An important aspect of growing as a learner is to reflect on where you have been, what you have accomplished, what helped you to learn, and how you will apply your new knowledge in the future. Use the following questions to guide your thinking and to identify evidence of your learning. Use separate notebook paper.

Thinking about Concepts

1. Using specific examples from this unit, respond to the Essential Questions:

   • How can a dramatic performance reflect a critical perspective?

   • What role does literature play in the examination of recurring societal issues?

2. Consider the new academic vocabulary from this unit (Historical Criticism) as well as academic vocabulary from previous units and select 2–3 terms of which your understanding has grown. For each term, answer the following questions:

   • What was your understanding of the word before you completed this unit?

   • How has your understanding of the word evolved throughout the unit?

   • How will you apply your understanding in the future?

Thinking about Connections

3. Review the activities and products (artifacts) you created. Choose those that most reflect your growth or increase in understanding.

4. For each artifact that you choose, record, respond to, and reflect on your thinking and understanding, using the following questions as a guide:

   a. What skill/knowledge does this artifact reflect, and how did you learn this skill/knowledge?

   b. How did your understanding of the power of language expand through your engagement with this artifact?

   c. How will you apply this skill or knowledge in the future?

5. Create this reflection as Portfolio pages—one for each artifact you choose. Use the model in the box for your headings and commentary on questions.

Thinking About Thinking
Portfolio Entry

Concept:

Description of Artifact:

Commentary on Questions:

Multiple
Perspectives

Essential Questions

? How can an examination of texts through multiple perspectives affect understanding?

? How do media production elements shape a message?

Unit Overview

In Units 1 through 3, you explored the concept "Perception Is Everything" by learning to apply various critical perspectives to the texts you encountered. Unit 4 expands this understanding by guiding you to apply all of the critical perspectives to a single text; first, you and your class will read and interpret *The Arrival* by Shaun Tan, applying Reader Response, Historical, Feminist, Marxist, and Archetypal Criticism at different points during your study, just as you have practiced in previous units. At the same time, however, you will begin engaging in an ongoing process to help you keep track of how Cultural Criticism enhances your understanding of the entire graphic novel, *The Arrival*. This work will prepare you to explore a novel or play with a small group, choosing which critical perspectives to apply and evaluating how each one helped you make meaning. By the end of the unit, you and your small group should be well prepared to demonstrate how multiple critical perspectives enriched your understanding of the novel or play you chose.

Unit 4

Multiple Perspectives

Contents

Goals

▶ To trace a reading through a critical perspective over the course of an extended text

▶ To analyze two literary works through multiple critical perspectives

▶ To analyze and then utilize text features of a graphic novel

▶ To create a presentation using a performance-based or visual medium

ACADEMIC VOCABULARY

Archetypal Criticism

Cultural Criticism

Feminist Criticism

Historical Criticism

Marxist Criticism

Reader Response Criticism

Texts not included in these materials.

Learning Focus:

New Literacies

New literacies is a term used to denote new types of reading demands that may require new and different skills in the twenty-first century.

If you do research online, connect with friends via an online social networking site, share photos over the Internet, contribute to blogs, or access your homework assignments via webmail, you are using new literacy skills that put you squarely in the forefront of the burgeoning possibilities afforded by new media channels in our daily lives. Even as you create new texts with these new media channels, you are expected to analyze and critically evaluate these new forms of communication also. Your critical evaluation helps you choose how you will communicate and with whom.

Increasingly you must be able to collaborate with others to create an original media communication for a variety of purposes. Your ability to understand your purpose, analyze your audience, and select appropriate production elements is the basis of successful media communications.

The elements that make up a successful media product include **composition, sound** (both diegetic and non-diegetic), **transitions between shots, color, lighting,** and **framing choices**. All of these elements are chosen to suit the purpose and audience.

One form of media product that has begun to emerge as a form of new literacy is the graphic novel. Graphic novels are an emerging genre of media text that should command our respect, and they raise the question of what defines "literary merit." Which books and plays get to be called "Great Literature," and who creates that list? How has the literary canon, the collection of literature held in highest regard, changed over time, and why? You may know that some books that are now considered classics, such as Zora Neale Hurston's *Their Eyes Were Watching God*, are actually recent additions to the canon of American literature. The collection of literary works honored by a society does evolve, and the explosion of new kinds of literacies in today's world keeps these questions relevant. Your study and assessment of this new literacy form gives you a voice in the community of readers who assign value to texts

Independent Reading: In this unit, you will read a graphic novel about the experiences of a man who emigrates to a new country. For your own reading, you might consider short stories or essays on immigrant experiences.

Previewing the Unit

Essential Questions

1. How can an examination of text through multiple perspectives affect understanding?

2. How do media production elements shape a message?

Unit Overview and Learning Focus

Predict what you think this unit is about. Use the words or phrases that stood out to you when you read the Unit Overview and the Learning Focus.

Embedded Assessment 1

What knowledge must you have (what do you need to know) to succeed on Embedded Assessment 1? What skills must you have (what must you be able to do)?

Understanding the Genre

SUGGESTED LEARNING STRATEGIES: Brainstorming, Graphic
Organizer, Think-Pair-Share, Diffusing, Quickwrite

One of the major texts in this unit is a graphic novel. It is important, then, to clarify your understanding of the graphic novel as a genre.

What is a graphic novel? Write your initial ideas as well as those of your classmates.

What questions do you have about graphic novels? Write down any questions generated by you and your classmates.

WORD CONNECTIONS

McCloud uses the word *aesthetic* to describe the way he wants a reader to see his work. This word may have different meanings, such as dealing with beauty or good taste or pleasing to the eye.

How are comics different from graphic novels? Here are two formal definitions. Consider the basic differences.

Comics are "juxtaposed pictorial and other images in deliberate sequence, intended to convey information and/or to produce an aesthetic response in the viewer." (Scott McCloud)

A **graphic novel** is a "book-length sequential art narrative featuring an anthology-style collection of comic art, a collection of reprinted comic book issues comprising a single story line (or arc), or an original, stand-alone graphic narrative." (James Bucky Carter)

Quickwrite: After exploring the genre, compose a quickwrite on these questions: To what extent are visual and graphic media a significant factor in your life now, and how do you interact with them? How might knowledge of visual and graphic media be a twenty-first century skill?

Beginning the Graphic Novel

ABOUT THE AUTHOR
Shaun Tan was born in 1974 near Perth, Australia. He attended the University of Western Australia, graduating in1995 with honors in English Literature and Fine Arts. He began drawing and illustrating for small-press magazines and has since become known for his illustrated books. He has also worked as a concept artist for the films *Horton Hears a Who and WALL-E*. He has received numerous awards including the 2007 World Fantasy Award for Best Artist and the Children's Book Council of Australia Picture Book of the Year Award for two of his books—*The Arrival* and *The Red Tree*.

Previewing the Text

You will be reading Shaun Tan's graphic novel, *The Arrival*. Previewing a text can facilitate your understanding. To preview this novel, scan the following and then predict what you think the novel will be about:

- The front and back covers
- The inside covers
- The title and copyright page

After you make your prediction, continue with the following steps:

- Scan the text to determine the *structure* of the book.
- Analyze and describe the *style* of the author.

Preparing a Book Summary

The Embedded Assessment asks you to summarize a book. After reading Part I, practice writing a succinct, yet complete, summary of the *plot* of Part I.

LITERARY TERMS

The **structure** of a literary work is the way it is organized, the arrangement of its parts.

Style refers to the way writers say what they want to say.

The **plot** is the series of events that make up a story, novel, or play.

Applying Cultural Criticism

One of the critical perspectives you might apply to *The Arrival* is **Cultural Criticism**. Reread the definition of this perspective and its assumptions in Appendix 1.

Now brainstorm a list of elements of culture:

What are some elements of culture that you noticed in Part I?

Beginning the Graphic Novel

Taking Notes on Discussion

As your group discusses the questions you generated about Part I of *The Arrival*, take notes on the graphic organizer. Write ideas shared by members of the group, including you, and summarize the support provided. Record your own responses, even if you do not share them with the group, and/or interesting responses from the group.

Discussion Notes

An Interesting Point Made By a Member of the Discussion Group	Support	Response

Applying Reader Response Criticism

Another way to examine the text is to consider the **Reader Response Critical Perspective**, which you studied in Unit 1. This graphic organizer, which you also saw in Unit 1, can help you organize your thoughts about Part 1 of *The Arrival* as seen from this perspective.

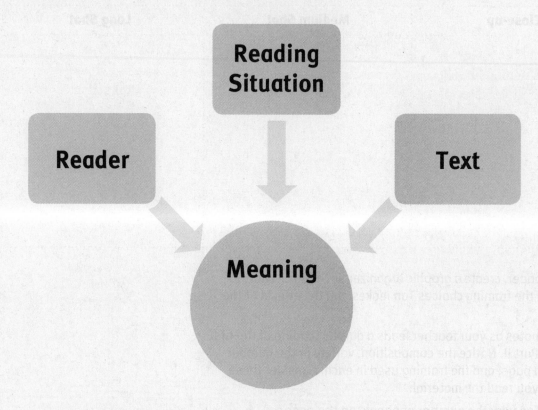

Writing Prompt: Draft a response to Part 1 of *The Arrival*, considering and including the following ideas in your response:

- Whether the cultural elements in Part 1 are familiar or unfamiliar, based on what you bring to the text.

- How the reading situation, such as sharing a book and reading in the classroom, influenced your understanding of the text.

- How the graphic novel genre influences your understanding and appreciation of *The Arrival*.

Reviewing Part I

What title could you give to Part I that would capture the essence of the text? How does Shaun Tan's *The Arrival* match up with your notes about graphic novels?

Framing the Narrative

The author/illustrator of a graphic novel makes deliberate choices about framing (how close or far away the subject of the picture seems to be) and about the size of each panel on a page.

1. Sketch stick figures to illustrates these framing options:

Close-up	Medium Shot	Long Shot

2. On separate paper, create a graphic organizer such as a T-chart to take notes on the framing choices Tan makes and the effects of the choices.

3. Add to these notes as your teacher leads a guided reading of the first few pages of Part II. Notice the composition, variety in the number of panels on a page, and the framing used in each. Consider these questions as you read the material:

- How does Tan vary the number of panels on the page?

- Why might an author vary the size of the panels in this way?

- How would you describe the people on the ship?

- What might the folded paper bird indicate?

- What might the flock of birds indicate?

- What might the people on the ship be thinking when they see the two giant statues shaking hands in the harbor?

- What do you know about practices at points of entry for immigrants to the United States?

4. The protagonist makes a bird from paper, which may remind you of a paper bird you saw in Part I. Reread those illustrations with the understanding that the paper bird is a motif that will appear again and again in the book. What role has it played so far? Try to predict future uses of this image.

5. As you continue reading Part II, continue to pay attention to framing and effects.

   • How many panels are on a page?

   • Are the panels close-up, medium shots, or long shots?

   • Which panels seem the most interesting? Why?

6. Reread the pages that show the protagonist's experiences as he enters the new land.

   • Consider how his experiences align with your prior knowledge about the processes for entering a new country.

   • Examine the protagonist's experiences through a Historical Critical Perspective.

WORD CONNECTIONS

The word **protagonist** is made from the Greek prefix *proto-*, meaning "first," and the Greek word *agōnistēs*, meaning "actor." Other words using the prefix *proto-* include *prototype*, *proton*, and *protozoan*.

7. Use this graphic organizer to examine how Cultural Criticism can help you make meaning from the portion of *The Arrival*, Part II, that you just read. If you notice additional elements of culture, feel free to add them to the list.

Tracing a Critical Perspective

Title of Text	Author	Genre	Critical Perspective
Definition in your own words:		Common assumptions:	

Location in the text	Element of Culture	Is this element of culture familiar, alien, or in between to the protagonist? How does the author capture the response?	What do you think is the significance of this element of culture?

Transitioning to a New Land

SUGGESTED LEARNING STRATEGIES: Graphic Organizer, Think-Pair-Share, Discussion Groups

Scott McCloud has created an illustrated explanation of the six techniques used to create transitions in comics and graphic novels. As you read and consider his explanation, which begins on the next page, complete the graphic organizer below. Because *The Arrival* does not contain the sixth technique, *non sequitur*, it has been omitted from this chart.

Transition Technique	Example from *The Arrival*	Effect of Transition
Moment to moment		
Action to action		
Subject to subject		
Scene to scene		
Aspect to aspect		

Transitioning to a New Land

Nonfiction

From Making Comics

by Scott McCloud

CONSIDER WHAT YOU WANT FROM EACH PART OF YOUR STORY: DO YOU WANT TO JUMP AHEAD TO A **KEY EVENT**? DO YOU WANT TO PUT ON THE BRAKES AND FOCUS ON **SMALLER MOMENTS**? DO YOU WANT TO DRAW ATTENTION TO **CONVERSATIONS** AND **FACES**?

DEPENDING ON YOUR ANSWERS, YOU'LL FIND THAT CERTAIN TYPES OF TRANSITIONS **BETWEEN** PANELS MAY GET THE JOB DONE BETTER THAN OTHERS.

THESE PANEL TO PANEL **TRANSITIONS** COME IN **SIX** VARIETIES*, INCLUDING:

 1. MOMENT TO MOMENT

A SINGLE ACTION PORTRAYED IN A SERIES OF MOMENTS.

 **2. ACTION TO ACTION**

A SINGLE SUBJECT (PERSON, OBJECT, ETC...) IN A SERIES OF ACTIONS.

 3. SUBJECT TO SUBJECT

A SERIES OF CHANGING SUBJECTS WITHIN A SINGLE SCENE.

 4. SCENE TO SCENE

TRANSITIONS ACROSS SIGNIFICANT DISTANCES OF TIME AND/OR SPACE.

 5. ASPECT TO ASPECT

 TRANSITIONS FROM ONE ASPECT OF A PLACE, IDEA OR MOOD TO ANOTHER.

 6. NON SEQUITUR

 A SERIES OF SEEMINGLY NONSENSICAL, UNRELATED IMAGES AND/OR WORDS.

Reading and Analyzing Part II, *The Arrival*

Looking at Sensory Images: You have identified sensory images in poetry and other genres, but you might not have realized that illustrations can appeal to the senses, too. Read the sequence of seven frames that follow the moment when the protagonist leaves the transportation device and make a list of Tan's illustrations that appeal to the various senses.

Using a Critical Perspective: In the previous activity, you started taking notes about the cultural elements that appear in *The Arrival* on a graphic organizer called "Tracing a Critical Perspective" (page 236). Add to those notes, and then use them as you draft an interior monologue from the protagonist's point of view, describing what you see upon arriving in this new setting.

> **LITERARY TERMS**
> An **interior monologue** is a literary device through which a writer presents a character's internal emotions and thoughts.

Summarizing Events: Examine the sequence of illustrations that show the protagonist finding a place to stay, and summarize how he manages to do it. Include the obstacles he encounters and how he overcomes them, and remember to make your summary succinct yet complete.

LITERARY TERMS

Mood is the atmosphere or general feeling in a literary work.

Considering Mood: After you finish reading Part II, identify the mood at the end. What details in the text create this mood?

Analyzing Establishing Shots: Meet with a discussion group to analyze the establishing shots Tan has used so far. Take notes during the discussion, either copying the notetaking graphic organizer used in Activity 4.3 or devising one of your own.

Creating a Title: Consider what you have learned about Part II, and create an original title that clearly represents the events and their meaning.

Angles and Perspectives

Reading and Analyzing Part III, *The Arrival*

The beginning of Part III offers new experiences for the protagonist as he attempts to navigate this new culture.

1. As you read and review the beginning of Part III, add your observations to the notes about Cultural Criticism that you have been taking for "Tracing a Critical Perspective."

2. The protagonist meets a woman on the boat who shares her story. Locate the beginning of her narrative. What language indicates the kind of transition Tan uses to signal the flashback?

> **LITERARY TERMS**
>
> A **flashback** is a scene that interrupts the narrative to show events that occurred at an earlier time.

3. List the main points of the woman's narrative, using the details in the illustrations as your basis. Write from the woman's point of view (i.e., "I was reading my book").

Angles and Perspectives

4. The woman's narrative may become richer if you read it with another critical perspective. With a partner, reread the woman's story, applying the critical perspective assigned by your teacher. Imagine that you can hear the woman telling her story to the man, like voice-over narration in a film, and draft the voice-over narration in such a way that others should be able to recognize the critical perspective you have applied. As you discuss these readings, use a notetaking guide to capture the ideas. You might use a format you have used already in this unit or try a new one.

Quickwrite: Write a reflection in which you evaluate the two critical perspectives your class has just examined. Which perspective enriches this narrative most for you? Why do you think this is the case?

Marginalized Peoples

SUGGESTED LEARNING STRATEGIES: Notetaking, Previewing, Discussion Groups, Tihnk-Pair-Share

In Part III, the protagonist continues to experience the culture of the new land.

Using the Critical Perspectives

Keep in mind that you are practicing tracing Cultural Criticism through the entire graphic novel, but you can also apply other criticisms to different parts of *The Arrival*. You have discussed feminist and Marxist readings of one of the subplots; now you will apply another criticism. Review Archetypal Critical Perspective and its assumptions. Write a summary of this perspective and its assumptions. You can use the space below.

Applying Archetypes

Reread the couple's narrative, applying the archetypal criticism to the reading. How does this reading enhance your understanding of the couple's narrative? Explain.

Analyzing Themes

You have read the stories of two people that the protagonist encounters, and you may have noticed common themes between the two narratives. On separate paper, create a graphic organizer to help you compare and contrast these two narratives. Use the common assumptions of Cultural Criticism as a guide.

Considering Titles

Now that you have finished reading Part III, create an original title that you feel would be appropriate for the content.

Choosing a Perspective

In Part IV of the *The Arrival*, the protagonist searches for and finds work.

1. The protagonist in *The Arrival*, like all other people, has needs for survival. Brainstorm a list of these needs and mark your list to show which needs the protagonist has managed to meet and what needs he has yet to meet. You can use the space below.

2. On the assembly line, the protagonist meets an elderly man who shares a narrative about going off to war. While you read the old man's narrative, try to visualize the narrative as a film. What diegetic sounds would appear on the soundtrack? What non-diegetic sounds would you add? Identify where each sound you have described would appear, placing sticky notes at the places in the text you have identified.

3. As you read the old man's narrative, you may have been thinking in terms of one of the critical perspectives: Reader Response, Cultural, Historical, Archetypal, Feminist, Marxist. Select a critical perspective that makes sense to you and reread the narrative, applying this perspective. Be prepared to share your understanding with others.

4. Now that you have heard how multiple critical perspectives can be applied to this narrative, choose the one that you think best fits and draft an explanation on separate paper.

5. Continue to add to your notes about "Tracing a Critical Perspective" as you finish reading Part IV. After you finish reading, create an original title for this part of *The Arrival*.

Adapting for an Audience

Reading and Analyzing Part V, *The Arrival*

1. Before you read Part V, brainstorm a list of reasons that people immigrate to new and sometimes unfamiliar places. Use separate paper.

2. Which, if any, of these reasons seems to apply to the protagonist of *The Arrival*?

3. After you finish reading it, create a title for Part V, and then consider Tan's choice to make *The Arrival* a wordless graphic novel. How would your experience of the book be different if it had words? What is the effect of his choice?

4. The protagonist communicates with people he encounters, despite language obstacles. How has Tan shown the protagonist and the people he encounters changing their delivery based on reaction from their audience?

Writing Prompt: You have examined several text features, or media production elements, of graphic novels during this unit: framing and page composition (Activity 4.4), transition, flow, and establishing shots (Activity 4.5), angles (Activity 4.6), color (Activity 4.7) and now text. How well does Shaun Tan employ these tools of the trade? The protagonist has learned to adapt to survive in his new surroundings. What are some of the ways in which he has adapted? On separate paper, draft an assessment of Tan's use of these textual features. To support your assessment, be sure to provide examples from what you have read so far of *The Arrival*.

WORD CONNECTIONS

Complete the analogy.

emigrate : immigrate ::

_____

a. plan : create
b. arrive : stay
c. leave : enter
d. known : unknown

Preparing for the Group Presentation

5. The Embedded Assessment asks you to participate in a group presentation. An important part of speaking in front of an audience is responding to the audience. Read the following Performance Expectation from the Speaking portion of the College Board Standards for College Success:

> Monitors audience feedback; makes inferences about audience engagement, understanding, and agreement; and adjusts delivery and content to achieve purposes and goals. Subsequently reflects on presentation and feedback to determine effectiveness and what changes to make in a future presentation.

Work with your assigned group to make meaning from this standard. What signals can you watch for that can tell you about your audience's level of engagement, understanding, and agreement? How could a speaker adjust the presentation according to the signal?

6. The standard says that the speaker is supposed to adjust delivery and content. To practice this, choose parts in a role play, using one of the texts on the next two pages:

- *Speaker*: Read a poem aloud.

- *Audience*: Send signals to the speaker. Choose from the list your group generated, and plan when and how you will send the signals. Be consistent so that the speaker can practice adjusting delivery in a meaningful way.

- *Observer*: Take notes about the speaker-audience interaction. Provide feedback on your observations without making judgments.

IMMIGRANT SONG

by Led Zeppelin

ABOUT THE AUTHOR
The Led Zeppelin rock band was formed in the late 1960s. The band integrated Delta blues, British folk influences, and modern rock. Their classic recordings include "Whole Lotta Love," "Ramble On," and "Stairway to Heaven."

My Notes

Ah, ah,

We come from the land of the ice and snow,

From the midnight sun where the hot springs blow.

The hammer of the gods

Will drive our ships to new lands,   5

To fight the horde, singing and crying:

Valhalla, I am coming!

On we sweep with threshing oar,

Our only goal will be the western shore.

Ah, ah,   10

We come from the land of the ice and snow,

From the midnight sun where the hot springs blow.

How soft your fields so green,

Can whisper tales of gore,

Of how we calmed the tides of war.   15

We are your overlords.

On we sweep with threshing oar,

Our only goal will be the western shore.

So now you'd better stop and rebuild all your ruins,

For peace and trust can win the day   20

Despite of all your losing

My Notes

Poetry

> **ABOUT THE AUTHOR**
> Emma Lazarus was born in 1849 in New York. She was educated by private tutors and became a prolific reader. She began writing poems as a child and later magazine articles and essays, as well as a five-act drama. Her poem "The New Colossus" grew, at least in part, out of her advocacy for Jewish immigrants.

THE NEW COLOSSUS

by Emma Lazarus

Not like the brazen giant of Greek fame,
With conquering limbs astride from land to land;
Here at our sea-washed, sunset gates shall stand
A mighty woman with a torch, whose flame
5   Is the imprisoned lightning, and her name
Mother of Exiles. From her beacon-hand
Glows world-wide welcome; her mild eyes command
The air-bridged harbor that twice cities frame.
"Keep, ancient lands, your storied pomp" cries she
10 With silent lips. "Give me your tired, your poor,
Your huddled masses yearning to breathe free,
The wretched refuse of your teeming shore.
Send these, the homeless, tempest-tossed to me:
I lift my lamp beside the golden door!"

GRAMMAR & USAGE

"The New Colossus" has several words joined together with hyphens—*sea-washed, world-wide, air-bridged,* and *tempest-tossed.* All of these words are compound adjectives. Always hyphenate a compound adjective when it precedes the noun it modifies: *sea-washed gates, air-bridged harbor,* etc. Some compound adjectives are always hyphenated, whether or not they precede the noun they modify. Check your dictionary to determine whether a compound adjective is always hyphenated.

Designing a Media Communication

SUGGESTED LEARNING STRATEGIES: Discussion Groups, Notetaking, Sharing and Responding, Drafting

Reading and Analyzing Part VI, *The Arrival*

1. The first page of Part VI nearly parallels the first page of Part I. How are they similar? How are they different? What is the effect of Tan's choice to make these Parts nearly parallel?

2. After you have finished reading *The Arrival*, consider why Tan might have chosen this title. Choose prewriting strategies, and then draft an analysis of the title on separate paper.

Applying Cultural Criticism

3. The writing and thinking you have done about *The Arrival* should have helped you to gain a deep understanding of this text. Draft a thematic statement or two that is relevant to *The Arrival*.

4. Review the common assumptions of Cultural Criticism and your notes from "Tracing a Critical Perspective." What are the important issues and ideas in the graphic novel? What issues does a Cultural Critical Perspective highlight?

Creating a Media Presentation

5. You have identified at least one important theme in *The Arrival*. As practice for the Embedded Assessment, you will work with a group to plan and create a media communication to convey one of those important themes. With your group, choose an audience for your media communication, and design a multimedia product that will appeal to that audience. Explore multiple points of view about *The Arrival*, and synthesize information to arrive at a theme or interpretation you will present in your multimedia product. Incorporate sound, graphics, and images that communicate effectively with your chosen audience.

The Author's Perspective

My Notes

If you had the opportunity, what questions would you like to ask Shaun Tan? Would you want to know how he gets his ideas, how he creates his illustrations, what else he has written? As you read his comments below, you may find the answer to some of those questions.

Essay

Comments on The Arrival,
by Shaun Tan

Much of the difficulty involved combining realistic reference images of people and objects into a wholly imaginary world, as this was always my central concept. In order to best understand what it is like to travel to a new country, I wanted to create a fictional place equally unfamiliar to readers of any age or background (including myself). This of course is where my penchant for 'strange lands' took flight, as I had some early notions of a place where birds are merely 'bird-like' and trees 'tree-like'; where people dress strangely, apartment fixtures are confounding and ordinary street activities are very peculiar. This is what I imagine it must be like for many immigrants, a condition ideally examined through illustration, where every detail can be hand-drawn.

That said, imaginary worlds should never be 'pure fantasy', and without a concrete ring of truth, they can easily cripple the reader's suspended disbelief, or simply confuse them too much. I'm always interested in striking the right balance between everyday objects, animals and people, and their much more fanciful alternatives. In the case of 'The Arrival', I drew heavily on my own memories of travelling to foreign countries, that feeling of having basic but imprecise notions of things around me, an awareness of environments saturated with hidden meanings: all very strange yet utterly convincing. In my own nameless country, peculiar creatures emerge from pots and bowls, floating lights drift inquisitively along streets, doors and cupboards conceal their contents, and all around are notices that beckon, invite or warn in loud, indecipherable alphabets. These are all equivalents to some moments I've experienced as a traveller, where even simple acts of understanding are challenging.

GRAMMAR & USAGE

Occasionally a writer finds the use of a series of independent clauses, flowing from one to another within a single sentence, to be an effective language device. In the middle of the second paragraph, Shaun Tan has such a **compound sentence**: "In my own nameless country, peculiar creatures....indecipherable alphabets." Notice that this sentence has four independent clauses. All four of these clauses serve to describe what exists in his "own nameless country." Tan has used commas to separate these independent clauses, probably because they are short. However, semicolons would have worked as well since the last clause has internal commas.

One of my main sources for visual reference was New York in the early 1900s, a great hub of mass-migration for Europeans. A lot of my 'inspirational images' blu-tacked to the walls of my studio were old photographs of immigrant processing at Ellis Island, visual notes that provided underlying concepts, mood and atmosphere behind many scenes that appear in the book. Other images I collected depicted street scenes in European, Asian and Middle-Eastern cities, old-fashioned vehicles, random plants and animals, shopfront signs and posters, apartment interiors, photos of people working, eating, talking and playing, all of them chosen as much for their ordinariness as their possible strangeness. Elements in my drawings evolved gradually from these fairly simple origins. A colossal sculpture in the middle of a city harbour, the first strange sight that greets arriving migrants, suggests some sisterhood with the Statue of Liberty. A scene of immigrants travelling in a cloud of white balloons was inspired by pictures of migrants boarding trains as well as the night-time spawning of coral polyps, two ideas associated by common underlying themes – dispersal and regeneration.

Even the most imaginary phenomena in the book are intended to carry some metaphorical weight, even though they don't refer to specific things, and may be hard to fully explain. One of the images I had been thinking about for years involved a scene of rotting tenement buildings, over which are 'swimming' some kind of huge black serpents. I realised that these could be read a number of ways: literally, as an infestation of monsters, or more figuratively, as some kind of oppressive threat. And even then it is open to the individual reader to decide whether this might be political, economic, personal or something else, depending on what ideas or feelings the picture may inspire.

I am rarely interested in symbolic meanings, where one thing 'stands for' something else, because this dissolves the power of fiction to be reinterpreted. I'm more attracted to a kind of intuitive resonance or poetry we can enjoy when looking at pictures, and 'understanding' what we see without necessarily being able to articulate it. One key character in my story is a creature that looks something like a walking tadpole, as big as a cat and intent on forming an uninvited friendship with the main protagonist. I have my own impressions as to what this is about, again something to do with learning about acceptance and belonging, but I would have a lot of trouble trying to express this fully in words. It seems to make much more sense as a series of silent pencil drawings.

I am often searching in each image for things that are odd enough to invite a high degree of personal interpretation, and still maintain a ring of truth. The experience of many immigrants actually draws an interesting parallel with the creative and critical way of looking I try to follow as an artist. There is a similar kind of search for meaning, sense and identity in an environment that can be alternately transparent

My Notes

> ### WORD CONNECTIONS
>
> The Latin root of **regenerate** is *gignere*, which means "to beget" or "to produce." The Latin prefix *re-* means "back" or "again." Words with the prefix *re-* include *recollect*, *reconcile*, and *record*.

The Author's Perspective

My Notes

and opaque, sensible and confounding, but always open to re-assessment. I would hope that beyond its immediate subject, any illustrated narrative might encourage its readers to take a moment to look beyond the 'ordinariness' of their own circumstances, and consider it from a slightly different perspective. One of the great powers of storytelling is that invites us to walk in other people's shoes for a while, but perhaps even more importantly, it invites us to contemplate our own shoes also. We might do well to think of ourselves as possible strangers in our own strange land. What conclusions we draw from this are unlikely to be easily summarised, all the more reason to think further on the connections between people and places, and what we might mean when we talk about 'belonging.'

Discussion Questions

1. What personal experiences did Tan draw on to create *The Arrival*?

2. How are Tan's ideas about imaginary worlds versus pure fantasy realized in *The Arrival*?

3. Although Tan says he is not "interested in symbolic meaning," what imagery can you point to that seems to function symbolically?

4. How does Tan feel about his readers and their perspective?

Writing Prompt: Write a reflective essay in which you compare your perceptions of *The Arrival* to Tan's explanations of how and why he created it.

Multiple Perspectives on the Graphic Novel

SUGGESTED LEARNING STRATEGIES: Discussion Groups, Graphic Organizer, Notetaking

In Units 1 through 3, you examined several critical perspectives: Archetypal, Feminist, Marxist, Cultural, Reader Response, and Historical. With your group, complete the following graphic organizer as you analyze the graphic novel using one of the perspectives.

The Critical Perspective: _____

Paraphrase the definition and common assumptions of this criticism.	
How does this perspective provide insight into the graphic novel?	
How does thinking about this perspective affect your understanding of the characters?	
How does thinking about this perspective affect your understanding of the setting?	
Which events lend themselves to an interpretation from this critical perspective? Explain.	

Multiple Perspectives on the Graphic Novel

As you listen to your classmates' presentations of the various perspectives, take notes below. These notes will be helpful as you draft your next paper.

Which critical perspective best illuminates the graphic novel for you?

How does this critical perspective add insight to the graphic novel?	Textual support for your ideas:

Independent Reading and Discussion

As you prepare for the Embedded Assessment, you will need to identify a novel or play and work with your discussion group to develop a reading and discussion plan.

Organizing the Group: As you get together with your group, begin your work by identifying the following:

- Group members.
- Title of novel or play.
- Author.
- What you know about this text and/or the author.

Creating a Reading Schedule: Work with your discussion group to create a schedule for reading, making sure that your schedule reflects the timeline provided by your teacher. Your schedule should include the following dates:

- Deadline for completing the reading.
- Date of halfway point.
- Dates of other assessment checkpoints.

Make sure that group members write down the reading schedule in their calendars; it is imperative for each member of the group to maintain the reading schedule in order for discussions to be effective.

Organizing the Reading: Your group should divide the reading into chunks, by chapters, acts, or even page numbers, and agree on which pages you will discuss at each discussion meeting. In addition, you should set the following goals:

- Reread the Embedded Assessment and web graphic organizer you created to identify the skills and knowledge required (from Activity 4.1).
- Identify what you and your group should be doing while you are reading and discussing the text in order to prepare for the Embedded Assessment.
- Apply multiple critical perspectives to the text.

To support productive discussions, work with your new group to agree upon norms, or standards of conduct, for your group discussions.

On the next page you will find a graphic organizer you may use to take notes during group discussions.

Independent Reading and Discussion

Use an organizer such as this to take notes during your group discussions.

Today's Date:	Reading Assignment:
Summary of Today's Reading Assignment	
Our Purposes for Today's Discussion	**How Purposes Support the Embedded Assessment**

An interesting point made by a member of the discussion group	Support	Response

Evaluation of Today's Progress Toward Goals

Exploring Critical Perspectives

SUGGESTED LEARNING STRATEGIES: Discussion Groups, Graphic Organizer

With your group, review the critical perspectives and consider how each critical perspective might apply to your novel or play. You can make notes on each perspective in the chart below.

Reader Response	Cultural
Archetypal	Marxist
Feminist	Historical

With your group, follow these steps to continue the process of applying the critical perspectives:

- Decide which critical perspectives seem most appropriate for your play or novel.
- Identify at least four critical perspectives to trace.
- Identify which perspective each group member will focus on.
- Adapt the organizer you used to apply the Cultural Critical Perspective to *The Arrival* for use with the other perspectives you are applying to your novel or play.

Assessing Perspectives

Writing a Draft Analysis

At this point in your reading and discussion, you should take some time to focus on your own thoughts and analysis. First, carefully consider the critical perspective you have been applying. Next, draft an explanation of how the critical perspective you are tracing has enriched your understanding of the text so far.

Sharing and Responding

After completing your draft analysis, participate in sharing and responding with your group. Discuss how the other critical perspectives being shared during group discussion meetings have given you new ways to think about the text.

You and your group may notice, too, that the relevance of critical perspectives may shift. For example, a particular critical perspective may shed light on the early part of the text but may lose relevance later in the text.

Planning the Next Stage

Based on your sharing and responding, your group has several options to discuss:

- Continue reading with these critical perspectives.
- Add an additional critical perspective that really seems to fit with those you are already tracing.
- Replace a critical perspective that may not be working with one that might make more sense.
- Identify additional options.

As a group, develop a plan to address these options and present it to your teacher for consideration.

As you continue to meet and discuss the text, keep these options in mind. Adjustments may continue to be beneficial and may enrich your understanding of the text.

Presenting a Literary Work Through Multiple Critical Perspectives

SUGGESTED LEARNING STRATEGIES: **Drafting, Discussion Groups, Sketching, Self-Editing/Peer Editing**

Assignment

Your assignment is to work with a group to present a novel or play to an audience of your peers. You will collaboratively write an analysis of the literary work from multiple critical perspectives and present your completed analysis in a performance-based or visual medium of your choice. Your analysis should include a summary of the text in the format of a graphic novel.

Planning

1. With your group, choose prewriting strategies to plan a summary of the novel or play. Consider your audience and determine what background knowledge they need to understand your group's analysis of the work using critical perspectives.

2. Develop a plan for delivering an engaging summary that will not only provide necessary background knowledge, but may also entice your classmates to read the novel or play. Follow Scott McCloud's example as you use the comic format to deliver the summary, and discuss how you will make your product visible to your audience during the presentation.

3. Collect and review the notes that you took while you read the novel or play, the notes in which you interpreted the work according to a particular critical perspective. Also review the notes you took during group discussions and reflect on how your classmates' analyses using critical perspectives deepened your understanding of the work. Individually, prepare an analysis of the novel or play enhanced by a critical perspective. As part of your work, identify and analyze nuances and ambiguities within the text and determine how they affect your critical perspective. Also analyze the author's use of stylistic or rhetorical devices and their aesthetic effect on the reader. Consider how to incorporate representative aesthetic effects in your summary of the text.

4. As a group, agree upon a design for a product in which you synthesize information from multiple points of view. Choose your visual or performance medium. You may use a storyboard with graphics to support your presentation or create a multimedia film or presentation with sound, graphics, and images.

Drafting/Rehearsing

5. Collaboratively draft a summary of the work and then begin planning your frames. Assign roles in the creation of the visual performance medium, and create a schedule for responding and sharing within the group. Remember to give your visual a meaningful title.

6. As individual group members, present to the rest of the group an explanation of how each of you interpreted the book through a critical perspective.

7. Work together to create the graphic or performance-based representation of multiple critical perspectives that you will present to the class. Each group member must have input so that the representation encompasses all of the critical perspectives discussed by the group.

8. Practice presenting your representation of the work through multiple perspectives, considering it from the point of view of your audience. Make sure that your visual representation or performance presents multiple critical perspectives and that each member plays a part in the presentation of the product.

TECHNOLOGY TIP Use available technology to help you create your presentation. If needed, ask for help in learning to use presentation software, video equipment, digital cameras, or graphics programs.

Presenting

9. During your group's presentation, monitor your audience and adjust your delivery as appropriate.

10. Practice effective speaking skills for your presentation, adapting your spoken language appropriately for formal speaking purposes. Practice active listening as your classmates deliver their presentations.

Evaluating

11. Reflect on your group's collaboration as well as on the presentation and the response of the audience to determine the effectiveness of the choices made by you and your group.

TECHNOLOGY TIP If you have resources available, you may want to scan your work into a slide presentation program that you might then project for your presentation to the class. If you have skills using digital drawing programs, you might also create your graphics with such a program.

SCORING GUIDE

Scoring Criteria	Exemplary	Proficient	Emerging
Text Summary	The summary in graphic novel format demonstrates an exceptional understanding of the text. It serves as a platform for analysis and skillfully uses genre conventions to deliver an enticing summary to the audience.	The summary in graphic novel format demonstrates a sufficient understanding of the text. It serves as a platform for analysis and logically uses genre conventions to deliver a clear summary to the audience.	The summary in graphic novel format demonstrates an insufficient understanding of the text. It does little to serve as a platform for analysis and/or uses genre conventions ineffectively to deliver an incomplete summary to the audience.
Text Analysis	The visual or performance medium skillfully uses thought-provoking production elements to convey an adept synthesis of multiple critical perspectives.	The visual or performance medium uses interesting production elements to convey a coherent synthesis of multiple critical perspectives.	The visual or performance medium uses minimal production elements and fails to sufficiently convey a logical synthesis of multiple critical perspectives.
Presentation	Participants achieve an informative and engaging presentation while perceptively monitoring the audience to keenly adjust individual delivery if needed.	Participants achieve an interesting presentation while adequately monitoring the audience to accurately adjust individual delivery if needed.	Participants attempt to achieve a clear presentation; monitoring the audience to adjust individual delivery may be attempted but to a limited degree and with limited success.
Additional Criteria			

Comments:

Reflection

An important aspect of growing as a learner is to reflect on where you have been, what you have accomplished, what helped you to learn, and how you will apply your new knowledge in the future. Use the following questions to guide your thinking and to identify evidence of your learning.

Thinking about Concepts

1. Using specific examples from this unit, respond to the Essential Questions:
   - How can an examination of text through multiple perspectives affect understanding?
   - How do media production elements shape a message?

2. Consider the academic vocabulary from this unit as well as academic vocabulary from previous units (Archetypal Criticism, Cultural Criticism, Feminist Criticism, Historical Criticism, Marxist Criticism, Reader Response Criticism) and select 3–4 terms of which your understanding has grown. For each term, answer the following questions:
   - What was your understanding of the word prior to the unit?
   - How has your understanding of the word evolved?
   - How will you apply your understanding in the future?

Thinking about Connections

3. Review the activities and products (artifacts) you created. Choose those that most reflect your growth in understanding.

4. For each artifact that you chose, record, respond, and reflect on your thinking and understanding. Use the following questions as a guide:
   a. What skill/knowledge does this artifact reflect, and how did you learn this skill/knowledge?
   b. How did your understanding of the power of language expand through your engagement with this artifact?
   c. How will you apply this skill or knowledge in the future?

5. Create this reflection as Portfolio pages—one for each artifact you choose. For each artifact, identify the concept, describe the artifact, and provide commentary on the questions.

Thinking About Thinking
Portfolio Entry

Concept:

Description of Artifact:

Commentary on Questions:

Creating
Perspectives

Essential Questions

❓ How do media sources impact our understanding of the truth and significance of an issue?

❓ How can media texts be constructed to support an agenda or intepretation?

Unit Overview

During this year, you have explored the idea of perspective by learning about and applying various critical lenses to literary texts. All of these perspectives allow you to view texts through a particular set of ideas or assumptions, in effect reading the texts differently depending on the perspective being explored. Looking at real events, rather than literary texts, poses the different but related challenge of discerning which version of reality is closest to the objective truth. This challenge is particularly significant in the context of how the media relate events. From reporting a war in a foreign country to covering a local city council meeting, the media have an obligation to report news events in a manner that is balanced, representing the facts of the story in an objective manner. In this unit, though, you will explore how the meaning of something is seldom limited to its facts. You will be asked to analyze the reporting of events, looking at all aspects of the reports. This unit asks you to become an active rather than passive viewer of journalistic texts, recognizing that journalistic reporting, like a literary text, needs to be read or "decoded" carefully.

Unit 5

Creating Perspectives

Goals

▶ To identify ways in which media shape how and what we know about particular events

▶ To investigate how different media channels communicate information about a particular event

▶ To investigate a variety of perspectives on a single event

▶ To analyze how different critical perspectives shape the reporting and interpreting of events

▶ To create a media text applying multiple lenses to the investigation and representation of an event

ACADEMIC VOCABULARY

Media channel

Contents

Texts not included in these materials.

Learning Focus:

Exposing Perspectives

Gone are the days when Americans relied on just the major national television news networks and local TV news in the United States. Twenty-four-hour news stations have filled the cable channels, and competition for viewers has never been greater. Additionally, countless magazines vie for attention on the racks at supermarkets and in newsstands. Local city newspapers and nationally distributed papers compete for market share. Countless sites devoted to news have cropped up on the Internet, and numerous chat rooms and Web logs (blogs) devoted to current events have been established. With so many sources for news available, individuals have the opportunity to select their news sources. This raises a number of interesting questions, though: How do you know the news from all these sources is true? What drives the selection process? Which sources are most reliable? How can **bias** be detected? Is bias a problem?

We are not passive consumers of media; rather, as active participants we bring our own sets of interests, experiences, assumptions, and biases to what we read, see, and hear, as do those who produce what we read, see, and hear. When we care about an event, we want to know how to determine what is true about the event and how to get close to that truth. However, recognizing our own filters—those personal interests, experiences, assumptions, and biases—and how they significantly impact our ability to discern the truth is important.

Recognizing the filters of the media source is equally important. In earlier levels, you studied how nonfiction visual texts use techniques such as **primary** and **archival footage** to explore their subjects. You also examined how **biased language** and **rhetorical slanters** can be used to construct a representation of a subject. And you also looked at how **cinematic techniques** such as lighting and camera angles influence the representation of a subject in a film. In nonfiction media, the journalist is both camera and director, choosing what to focus on and how to present it. In this way, the journalist has as much power as the film director to shape images and opinion, to create verbal and actual pictures, and to adapt and edit. These choices often consciously reflect or can be read through a particular critical lens. Your job in Embedded Assessment 1 will be to expose how the coverage of an event reflects or is shaped by one such lens. In a sense you will become the journalist, reporting on a critical perspective that shapes or is revealed in the work of others.

Independent Reading: You have read a variety of texts throughout this level. For independent reading for this unit, choose a genre you like and a subject that you would enjoy reading about. Read something just for your enjoyment.

Previewing the Unit

SUGGESTED LEARNING STRATEGIES: Close Reading, KWL Chart, Marking the Text, Skimming/Scanning, Summarizing/Paraphrasing, Think-Pair-Share

Essential Questions

1. How do media sources impact our understanding of the truth and significance of an issue?

2. How can media texts be constructed to support an agenda or intepretation?

Unit Overview and Learning Focus

Predict what you think this unit is about. Use the words or phrases that stood out to you when you read the Unit Overview and the Learning Focus.

Embedded Assessment 1

What knowledge must you have (what do you need to know) to succeed on Embedded Assessment 1? What skills must you have (what must you be able to do)?

How Do You Get Information?

Complete the following graphic organizer with information about
current events.

School Event	Details/Facts I Know About the Event	Information Sources
Local Event	Details/Facts I Know About the Event	Information Sources
National Event	Details/Facts I Know About the Event	Information Sources

Read the following terms and list what you know about the meaning of each term.

Term	Definition
Target Audience	
Circulation	
Perspective	
Agenda	
Bias	
Conservative	
Liberal	
Sound Bite	
Objectivity	

GRAMMAR & USAGE

In general, you should vary the length of your sentences. Too many lengthy sentences tend to wear the reader out. Too many short sentences become dull and monotonous. Now and then, however, a writer can use a series of short sentences to grab readers' attention.

Notice the second paragraph in this article. It is very short compared to all the other paragraphs, and it comprises three very short sentences. Those short sentences set off in a paragraph by themselves stop us, the readers, in our tracks, forcing us to think about what the writer is saying. She is saying, "Pay attention! I am worried ('not laughing') about the way the press's choice of stories and choice of words shape culture."

As you write, think about the lengths of your sentences, not just as a way to create variety, but also as a way to create power and emphasis.

Essay

How the Media Twist the News

by Sheila Gribben Liaugminas

In a most ordinary moment on a normal day at work in the Chicago bureau of a major national newsmagazine, I came to a realization that has bothered me ever since. Everyone knows how much power the press has in shaping the news, how its choice of stories and words influence readers. But one afternoon, talking about a rather silly feature story we were doing on pop culture, someone joked, "You know, we can start a trend just by calling it a trend!"

I stopped dead. It was true. But I was the only one not laughing.

Of course, this was hardly an original insight. Walter Lippman—journalist, military intelligence specialist during World War I, propagandist, political scientist, author, and adviser to the presidents—made the same observation a generation ago. These words from his book, *Public Opinion*, bear repeating:

Every newspaper when it reaches the reader is the result of a whole series of selections.... In order that [the reader] shall enter he must find a familiar foothold in the story, and this is supplied to him by the use of stereotypes. They tell him that if an association of plumbers is called a "combine" it is appropriate to develop his hostility; if it is called a "group of leading businessmen" the cue is for a favorable reaction. It is in a combination of these elements that the power to create opinion resides.

Why is it so easy to lead people into new behaviors, desires, and attitudes? Why don't people think more critically and see through some of the airy media stories that have no real substance—the stories that are less news than public relations or marketing? As Lippman noted, it's the result of "apathy, preference for the curious trivial as against the dull important, and the hunger for sideshows and three-legged calves."

These days, sideshows and curious trivia have actually gained even greater importance in an industry that has become a confusing mix of news and entertainment. Still, there are people who would like to pay attention to the more consequential events and issues that used to be called news. These can be hard to discern when politics itself has become trivialized.[1] Hence the need to become intelligent news consumers: to learn how to pick through massive fields of information for substantive[2] and fair reporting.

This is a tall task. The manipulation of public opinion is of great importance to both the government and the media. And it takes on added urgency in the months before an election.

Last year [2001], veteran CBS newsman Bernard Goldberg shocked the media world with his book, *Bias: A CBS Insider Exposes How the Media Distort the News*. He minced no words in laying out the fundamental problem. "The old argument that the networks and other 'media elites' have a liberal bias is so blatantly true that it's hardly worth discussing anymore," he writes. "No, we don't sit around in dark corners and plan strategies on how we're going to slant the news. We don't have to. It comes naturally to most reporters.... When you get right down to it, liberals in the newsroom see liberal views as just plain ... sensible, reasonable, rational views, *which just happen to coincide with their own*" (emphasis added).

Consider this exchange from [Cable News Network] CNN's *American Morning* show. The panelists are talking about the quality of the reporting from the Middle East. Anderson Cooper says, "On both sides of this issue, people see this so clearly one way or the other. It's really fascinating." Paula Zahn: "And it clearly colors their reaction to reporting, and I think it's, you know, very difficult for people to separate their own personal views from the way they interpret the news." Jack Cafferty: "The news media is [sic] only objective if they report something you agree with." Zahn: "Right." Cafferty concludes: "Then they're objective. Otherwise they're biased if you don't agree, you know."

For these three CNN personalities, the news media themselves are impervious[3] to the predispositions and prejudice that afflict their audience. But contrary to what CNN might have us believe, bias is a real problem. You can see it in all the ways the media interpret, frame, and produce the great issues of our day. They slant the news according to their ideologies and find sources who will back them up. Over my 23 years with a newsmagazine, it often did a good—sometimes *very* good—job of reporting and analyzing news and its impact. But sometimes it didn't. Sometimes the editors assigned reporters to a story that had been preconceived in the New York headquarters—a story with a foregone conclusion. . . .

In a world of media spin, it's not easy to keep one's own balance. First, know what your core values are, what you hold to be objectively true. Be discriminating in your selection of news sources and carefully scrutinize

---

[1] **trivialized:** treated as unimportant
[2] **substantive:** having considerable quantity or importance
[3] **impervious:** incapable of being penetrated

> **LITERARY TERMS**
>
> A **stereotype** is an oversimplified, generalized conception, opinion, and/or image about particular groups of people.

My Notes

My Notes

everything you hear and read—see how it resonates with what you believe.

Note how news gatherers select subjects and how they cover them. What photographs do they choose? Do their accounts sound slanted, or do they present compelling voices from both sides of an issue?

Notice their sources: Do you hear from the same set of "experts" again and again? I find this especially annoying. The newsmagazine I worked for is still using some of the same old liberal "news analysts" they used when I first arrived in the Midwest bureau more than two decades ago. And you see them all over television news as well. When the topic is Catholicism, the networks all call on the same dissident priests and ex-priests, feminists, and "Catholics for a Free Choice": Andrew Greeley, Eugene Kennedy, Charles Curran, Richard Sipe, Frances Kissling, and so on. Paula Zahn has continually used Sipe as the go-to expert on the troubles within the Church, always describing him as a "retired priest." He's an ex-priest, Paula. There's a difference.

"They don't want our new, fresh sources when they've got the regulars who give them the quotes they want," Ruderman says, sharing my observation that the major media, like the newsmagazine we worked for, have all taken the easy route of using dog-eared Rolodexes to call on the same talking heads. "They never wanted my sources when they didn't fit the mold of what they wanted the story to say. They had a preconceived idea of the status quo[4], and so they would always go to the status-quo sources for their standard comments."...

It's interesting how much of Lippman's analysis from 70 years ago still applies to the media. In the foreword to the 1997 edition of *Public Opinion*, Ronald Steel recalls that from a young age, Lippman studied politics and the press. "In *Liberty and the News* he concluded that the newspaper stories of one of the seminal events of the century (the Russian Revolution) were distorted and inaccurate, based not on the facts but on the 'hopes of the men who composed the news organization.'"

Lippman then posed a more fundamental problem, as Steel relates: "How could the public get the information it needed to make rational political judgments if it could not rely on the press? Unbiased information had become essential, he argued, because 'decisions in a modern state tend to be made by the interaction, not of Congress and the executive, but of public opinion and the executive.'... For this reason the accuracy of news reporting, the protection of the sources of public opinion, had become the 'basic problem of democracy.'"

The power of public opinion, which is supposed to be the driving force behind most important decisions in a democracy, can itself be driven or steered by the prejudices of unofficial opinion-makers. Vigilance and self-awareness are its only protection. Which is why, wherever they get their news, intelligent citizens will take nothing for granted except their principles.

---

[4] **status quo:** the existing condition or state of affairs

Media Bias Comes from Viewers Like You

by Tyler Cohen

Both left-wing and right-wing commentators lament media bias. The right wing cites the predominant Democratic orientations—often 80 to 90 percent—of major journalists. The left wing cites the right wing pundits, such as Rush Limbaugh, or the growing success of Fox News.

Why do the major media sometimes slant to the left, and other times slant to the right? The answer is simple: viewers want them to. We look to the media for entertainment, drama, and titillation[1] before objectivity. Journalists, to get ahead, must produce marketable stories with some kind of emotional slant, which typically will have broader political implications. The result: it looks like media bias when in fact journalists, operating in a highly competitive environment, are simply doing their best to attract an audience.

Consider the [2003] war with Iraq. Leading up to the war, and during the fighting, CNN and other American media treated the Bush regime with kid gloves. We saw little of the civilian casualties that filled news screens around the world. Yet after the war the American media appear to be far more critical of the Bush plans. Almost every day [in late 2003] we hear about suicide bomb attacks, and until lately we have had little exposure to rebuilding progress in Iraq.

What happened? Has the media changed its collective mind about our foreign policy? Maybe, but a simpler explanation operates. In each case the media chose the presentation that made for the best story. "Heroic American fighters" was the best and most marketable story before and during the major fighting. "Suicide bomber attacks" has proven to be a forceful story in the last few months. "American soldiers rebuilding schools" doesn't draw as big a crowd. In fact recently the pro-war side has done better by pushing "outrage that war critics neglect progress in Iraq" as a slant.

The media appear obsessed with personal scandals, such as the victims of toxic waste dumps, or women whose breast implants have poisoned their bodies.... The media thus appear to be hard on corporations, sympathetic to government regulation, and, as a result, "left-wing." But again, they are looking for a good and marketable story, and yes this includes Monica Lewinsky.[2] Journalists are seeking to advance their careers more than a political agenda.

---

[1] **titillation:** excitement or stimulation
[2] **Monica Lewinsky:** the intern whose relationship with President Bill Clinton helped lead to Clinton's impeachment trial and subsequent acquittal

My Notes

_____

_____

_____

_____

_____

_____

GRAMMAR & USAGE

Writers use **rhetorical questions** to focus readers' attention. The writers do not expect answers from their readers: they intend to answer the questions themselves.

Note the rhetorical question that introduces the second paragraph in this article. The question identifies the topic of the paragraph and the second sentence begins to provide the answer.

The third paragraph begins with two questions—the first fairly open and the second more specific. This rhetorical technique is used to draw the reader to the topic of the paragraph one step at a time.

Constructing Public Opinion

My Notes

For purposes of contrast, look at crime. Crime, and crime victims, make among the most compelling stories. Remember the obsession with the [Washington] DC area sniper case? Not surprisingly, people who watch TV receive the impression that crime is very high, if only because they see so much crime on TV. The contrasting reality is that most people in America lead very safe lives. Nonetheless the "left-wing" media appear to take a "right-wing" stance when it comes to warning us about crime, again in search of a better story.

Media favor coverage that can be packaged. The OJ trial,[3] for instance, had dramatic developments with some frequency, regular characters, and a fairly simple plot line. It resembled a daily soap opera, and not surprisingly it was immensely popular on TV. For similar reasons, serial killers will receive attention disproportionate to their number of victims.

Some economic points have an especially hard time getting a fair shake from the media. It is easy to show how a government program put Joe Smith back to work. Arguably the expenditure was a waste, once we consider the "hidden costs of opportunities foregone," but this abstract concept does not make for an easy visual, much less a good interview. In similar fashion, the media do little to show the benefits of free trade.

In sum, media bias may not be as harmful as many people think. It is perhaps sad that we do not look much to the news for objective information, but this same fact limits the damage that slanted coverage can cause. Keep in mind that many *definitions* of media bias mean that the media think one way, and the citizenry thinks another way. So clearly the media have not succeeded in forcing us all into the same mold.

We should resist the temptation to think that the TV screen, or the newspaper Op-Ed page, or the blogosphere for that matter, is the critical arena deciding the fate of the world. In reality, these media are a sideshow to the more general human preoccupation with stories. We use TV and other media to suit our personal purposes, not vice versa. No, the media are not fair, but they are unfair in ways different than you might imagine. They are unfair because you, collectively, as viewers, want them to be unfair.

---

[3] **OJ trial:** O.J. Simpson, a famous retired football star and a movie actor, was tried and eventually acquitted of killing his wife and another person in 1994.

After discussing the two articles, reflect on the following questions.

1. How much did your opinion before reading the two essays influence your perspective on which author was **more persuasive** regarding media bias?

2. How much did your opinion before reading the two essays influence your perspective on which author was **more correct** regarding media bias?

3. What's the difference between being persuasive and being correct?

4. In general, to what extent does our perspective on what is correct influence our perspective on what is persuasive and vice versa?

5. Based on the two articles and on your previous experience analyzing media, what are some specific things you can look for that reveal bias in a text you are reading, watching, or listening to?

WORD CONNECTIONS

Vice versa means the reverse of the two things or people mentioned.

The term comes from the Latin *vice*, meaning "a turn" and *versus*, meaning "to turn about."

LITERARY TERMS

Rhetorical slanters are words chosen to put a negative or positive spin on what the speaker or writer is saying.

While writers and directors can influence our perspective on a subject through the use of selection and omission, source control, and other manipulations of content, rhetoric itself may be the most powerful tool through which our perceptions can be influenced. In addition to the use of titles and labeling (and loaded language in general), the following *rhetorical slanters* (adapted from Brooke Noel Moore and Richard Parker's *Critical Thinking*, 8th ed, 2007) identify key techniques often used by writers.

Rhetorical analogy: The use of a figurative comparison (sometimes a simile or a metaphor) to convey a positive or negative feeling toward the subject.

> **Example:** "The environment needs global warming like farmers need a drought."

Rhetorical definition: The use of emotively charged language to express or elicit an attitude about something.

> **Example:** Capital punishment is "government-sanctioned murder."

Rhetorical explanation: Expressing an opinion as if it were fact, and doing so in biased language.

> **Example:** Joe "didn't have the guts to fight back" as compared to Joe "did not take a swing."

Innuendo: The use of language to imply that a particular inference is justified, as if saying "go ahead and read between the lines."

> **Example:** "Think carefully about whom you choose; you want a president who will be ready to do the job on day one."

Downplayers: The use of qualifier words or phrases to make someone or something look less important or significant.

> **Example:** "She got her 'degree' from a correspondence school."

Hyperbole: The use of extravagant overstatement.

> **Example:** "This school administration is fascist!"

Truth Surrogates: Hinting that proof exists to support a claim without actually citing that proof.

> **Example:** "There's every reason to believe that . . ."

Ridicule/Sarcasm: The use of language that suggests the subject is worthy of scorn.

> **Example:** ". . .the news **media** themselves are impervious to the predispositions and prejudice that afflict their audience."

News Source 1 _____

Facts		News Source	
Who?		Bias by Headline?	
What?		Bias by Photos, Captions, Camera Angle?	
When?		Bias through Selection/Omission?	
Where?		Bias by Source Control?	
Why?		Bias by Placement? Statistics/Crowd Control?	
How?		Bias through Labels/Titles/Loaded Language?	

Writing Prompt: Write a response exposing the bias evident in the way the news story reported the event. Include relevant quotes and appropriate commentary to support your conclusions. As you draft your text, be sure to include an accurate and honest representation of divergent views represented in the story. Select an organizing structure appropriate for the purpose, audience, and context of this task.

News Source 2 _____

Facts	News Source
Who?	Bias by Headline?
What?	Bias by Photos, Captions, Camera Angle?
When?	Bias through Selection/Omission?
Where?	Bias by Source Control?
Why?	Bias by Placement? Statistics/Crowd Control?
How?	Bias through Labels/Titles/Loaded Language?

Writing Prompt: Write a response exploring the bias evident in the way the news story reported the event. Include relevant quotes and appropriate commentary to support your conclusions. As you draft your text, be sure to include an accurate and honest representation of divergent views represented in the story. Select an organizing structure appropriate for the purpose, audience, and context of this task.

Framing the Investigation

Reading Guide for "The Dixie Chicks," by Betty Clarke

Use the following questions as you analyze Clarke's review.

1. What is being reported (the who, what, where, when, why, and how of the event)?

2. How is it being reported? How subjective/objective is the coverage? Identify and list (or highlight in the article) specific textual details (titles, labeling, omission, etc.) that reveal bias in the article.

3. What is the target audience for the article? How does the text's rhetorical context affect what it talks about and how (its language and its tone)? What inferences can you draw about the writer's expectations regarding the audience's perspective on the subject covered?

> **LITERARY TERMS**
> **Rhetorical context** refers to the subject, purpose, audience, occasion, or situation in which writing occurs.

4. If you only read this article, what would you think is the key issue? In other words, how does the article frame the truth and/or significance of the news event (the Dixie Chicks controversy)? Is the controversial quote cited for its political implications or for some other reason?

5. What critical lens or lenses are evident in how the text approaches the issue? Which dominate or are absent? What specific language reveals the lens(es) at work?

Framing the Investigation

Article

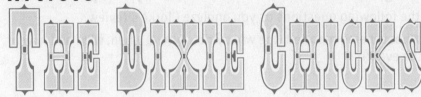

by Betty Clarke (March 2003)

The Dixie Chicks are the good-time girls the country establishment loves to hate. Too direct, too old-fashioned, too modern ... you name it, it's been slung at the Texan trio. The old vanguard[1] liked their women feisty but second-class, preferably wearing cowgirl outfits and a smile. But the Dixie Chicks were renegade[2] ladies of country who sung gleefully about killing abusive spouses and dressed like an older Britney Spears. Add the success they have had selling a progressive bluegrass sound to fans ignorant of banjos and whistles and you have an emasculating[3] threat.

And they don't know when to stop. "Just so you know," says singer Natalie Maines, "we're ashamed the president of the United States is from Texas." It gets the audience cheering – at a time when country stars are rushing to release pro-war anthems, this is practically punk rock.

Aside from courting controversy, the band has sold 25m LPs since their debut album, *Wide Open Spaces*, was released in 1998 and made the fiddle sexy. Featuring two sisters, Martie Maguire and Emily Robinson, along with the effervescent Maines, their passion for tradition and love for pop made the country genre a contender again. Their latest album, *Home*, won three Grammys.

Although their outfits are more New York than Nashville, the music is proud of its roots. "Long Time Gone" adopts the chatty style of Loretta Lynn and the poignancy of Hank Williams, Robinson's nifty banjo flowing beneath Maguire's sparky fiddle. "Tortured, Tangled Hearts" is similarly quick and quaint, Maines recalling Dolly Parton before she became Country Barbie.

Bluegrass's charm lies in its rawness, but the Dixie Chicks have polished the mountain sound and made it palatable[4] for a new audience. This does mean that "Truth No.2" creeps into Celine Dion territory, Maines grabbing each phrase and shaking her head like a puppy with a toy. But it's in the giddy "Sin Wagon," which turns religious worship into a hymn for sex, that the Dixie Chicks hit their stride, shrieking, shouting, unrepentant.[5]

---

[1] **vanguard:** the leaders of a movement
[2] **renegade:** a rebel, an outlaw
[3] **emasculating:** destroying strength, making less masculine
[4] **palatable:** agreeable, acceptable
[5] **unrepentant:** unashamed, unremorseful

WORD CONNECTIONS

The Latin word *palatum*, meaning "palate" forms the base of the word *palatable*. The addition of the suffix *–able*, meaning "able" or "likely," creates an adjective meaning "acceptable to the taste, or palate."

The following two statements were published on the Dixie Chicks' official website. What differences do you note in the tone and the content of the two messages?

Statement from the Dixie Chicks with respect to statements being reported in the British media, March 12, 2003:

We've been overseas for several weeks and have been reading and following the news accounts of our governments' position. The anti-American sentiment that has unfolded here is astounding. While we support our troops, there is nothing more frightening than the notion of going to war with Iraq and the prospect of all the innocent lives that will be lost." Maines further stated, "I feel the President is ignoring the opinions of many in the US and alienating the rest of the world. My comments were made in frustration and one of the privileges of being an American is you are free to voice your own point of view."

Statement from Natalie Maines of the Dixie Chicks, March 14, 2003:

As a concerned American citizen, I apologize to President Bush because my remark was disrespectful. I feel that whoever holds that office should be treated with the utmost respect. We are currently in Europe and witnessing a huge anti-American sentiment as a result of the perceived rush to war. While war may remain a viable option, as a mother, I just want to see every possible alternative exhausted before children and American soldiers' lives are lost. I love my country. I am a proud American.

Framing the Investigation

Developing Guiding Questions

In preparation for further investigation of the Dixie Chicks controversy, use the following process to develop focus questions to guide your research.

1. Review the description of the critical perspectives in Appendix 1. Which ones seem relevant to this topic? Why? Which ones do not? Why not?

2. Based on background knowledge and your preliminary investigation of the topic, brainstorm connections between each relevant lens and the topic.

3. Draft an initial closed (yes/no) question linking the lens to the subject.

4. Modify the question to make it open-ended by using one of the following stems:

   a. To what extent did X influence Y?

   b. In what ways did . . . ?

   c. What does the controversy surrounding (this topic) reveal about attitudes towards the (underlying issue)?

   d. What recurring story patterns are evoked by . . . ?

Throwing Light on the Situation

SUGGESTED LEARNING STRATEGIES: Close Reading, Discussion
Groups, Marking the Text, Think-Pair-Share

To prepare for the work you and your group members will do as you complete this unit's embedded assessments, you will complete two tasks.

1. **Analyzing a Text:** You will first analyze a text to see how it constructs the meaning and significance of the Dixie Chicks controversy. You will then present your findings to your classmates.

2. **Making Connections and Synthesizing Evidence:** Second, you will use the presentations of your peers to map connections with other texts, identifying textual evidence from those that are relevant which link to a lens of your choice. You will be expected to synthesize this evidence in support of an informal written analysis of what is revealed when looking at the controversy through that particular lens. *Note:* You will use the questions on the next page to guide your group's analysis of your article.

> **LITERARY TERMS**
> To **synthesize** is to combine ideas from different sources to create, express, or support a new idea.

Planning Your Presentation

Once you have completed your analysis, come up with a plan for how to present the article to the class. Your group's presentation to your peers should include:

- The most significant information from your article related to the who, what, when, where, why, and how of the event. In particular, include a discussion of how the article portrays the original incident. Does it defend, criticize, or objectively report what happened? What new insights or later events does it emphasize?

- A discussion of how the article frames the controversy. What issue(s) does it focus on? What does it say about the issue(s)? How biased is it in the way it discusses the Chicks, the music industry, country music fans, etc.? How slanted is the language?

- An analysis of what lens(es) you connected to the text. To construct your commentaries, begin with one of the following stems:

  a. When viewed as a(n) _____ text, this article reveals that _____. (*Use this stem if you think the article itself explicitly discusses the subject through a particular lens.*)

  b. When we read this article through a _____ lens, we notice that _____. (*Use this stem if you are applying the lens to the article to focus on reading it from a particular perspective.*)

- Quotes from the text to support your claims about its rhetoric and its perspective.

Questions for Analysis

Use the following questions as you analyze each of the articles in this activity.

1. What is being reported (the who, what, where, when, why and how of the event)? Summarize the information covered in the article and how it links to the original news event.

2. How is it being reported? How subjective/objective is its coverage? Identify and list (or highlight in the article) specific textual details (titles, labeling, omission, etc.) that reveal bias in the article.

3. What is the target audience for the article? How does the text's rhetorical context affect what it talks about and how (its language and its tone)? What inferences can you draw about the writer's expectations regarding the audience's perspective on the subject covered?

4. If you only read this article, what would you think is the key issue? In other words, how does the article frame the truth and/or significance of the news event (the Dixie Chicks controversy)?

5. What critical lens or lenses are evident in how the text approaches the issue? Which dominates or is absent? What specific language reveals the lens at work? How does this affect your reaction to the content covered?

My Notes

GRAMMAR & USAGE

An appositive is a word or clause that is in apposition to a noun or pronoun: that is, side by side with a noun. The purpose of an appositive is to identify or describe the noun or pronoun. If an appositive is nonessential, containing supplemental rather than essential information, it should be set off by commas. There are a number of appositives in this article.

Essential appositive:
Their albums "Wide Open Spaces" and "Fly" sold more than 10 million copies each.

Nonessential appositive:
... "Long Time Gone," the record's first song, includes a punning jab at radio playlists.

Article

The Dixie Chicks Keep the Heat on Nashville

by Bill Friskics-Warren (August 2002)

IN the early 1990's, the Dixie Chicks were a cowgirl revival troupe playing for tips on the Texas dance hall circuit. By the end of the decade, they were Nashville, and pop, superstars. Their albums "Wide Open Spaces" and "Fly" sold more than 10 million copies each. They won a clutch of Grammys. Their 2000 tour grossed more at the box office than those of Bruce Springsteen and Britney Spears. Most striking of all, the Dixie Chicks achieved success not by cleaving to the conservative dictates of the country music industry but by taking risks that could just as easily have been big mistakes.

The three women — Natalie Maines and the sisters Emily Robison and Martie Maguire — cultivated their own sense of fashion, favoring post-punk, neo-hippie styles over the more conventional ensembles worn by their female counterparts. They insisted on playing their own instruments instead of employing the usual session musicians. They played banjo (Ms. Robison) and fiddle (Ms. Maguire), instruments often dismissed as quaint by country radio programmers. They sang about dicey topics like "mattress dancing" and doing away with an abusive spouse. Displaying a "love it or leave it" attitude like that of Waylon Jennings, Willie Nelson and the other "outlaws" of the 70's, the Dixie Chicks reinvigorated the moribund[1] Nashville music scene of the late 90's.

"Home," the album they'll release on Tuesday on their new Open Wide Records label, an imprint of Sony Music, is likely to shake up and challenge the Nashville establishment further, suggesting that it has lost touch with its roots. Most of the record's 11 tracks will no doubt be deemed too long

---

[1] **moribund:** stagnant, near death

for airplay, some running as long as six minutes. There are no drums on this bluegrass-steeped album, something that is virtually unheard of in commercial country music, and "Long Time Gone," the record's first single, includes a punning jab at radio playlists.

Written by the Nashville singer-songwriter Darrell Scott, "Long Time Gone" all but dares country stations not to play it. "We listen to the radio to hear what's cookin'," goes one line. "But the music ain't got no soul/They sound tired but they don't sound Haggard/They got money but they don't got Cash."

The Dixie Chicks insist they weren't trying to force the hands of radio programmers by releasing "Long Time Gone" as a single. "I don't look at the song as a political statement," said Ms. Maguire, seated on a wraparound sofa with Ms. Robison and Ms. Maines in a Tuscan-style bed and breakfast off Nashville's Music Row. Ms. Maguire, 32, who was born in York, Pa., and Ms. Robison, 30, who was born in Pittsfield, Mass., spent their early childhood years in southeastern Pennsylvania, where they studied the violin using the Suzuki method of learning by ear. Ms. Maines, the lead singer, who will be 28 in October, was born and raised in Lubbock, Tex. Her father is Lloyd Maines, an esteemed producer and steel guitarist best known for his work with the charismatic roots rocker Joe Ely.

"We've had a lot of controversy in our career, and it's never been intentional," Ms. Maguire continued. "We didn't release 'Goodbye Earl'" — a comic tale of revenge akin to "Thelma and Louise" — "to get back at wife beaters. We're more lighthearted than that. Everyone has their own opinion about what should be on the radio, and I think there's room for all different people."

The Dixie Chicks also maintain that the bluegrass arrangements on "Home" don't constitute that much of a departure from the bold, expansive music on their last two albums. "We still have our core sound," Ms. Robison said. "We've peeled back a few layers, but I think people will still recognize it as us." Indeed, in contrast to the Appalachian cast of the soundtrack to "O Brother, Where Art Thou?," which despite sales of six million received a lukewarm response from country radio, the music on the Dixie Chicks' new album evinces[2] both traditional country and modern pop sensibilities.

Doubtless some will view the success of "Long Time Gone," which was No. 2 on the Billboard country chart this week, as a sign that the strictures[3] of country radio are loosening a bit. The Dixie Chicks' next single, a cover of Fleetwood Mac's "Landslide" done in the ambient bluegrass style of Alison Krauss and Union Station, will certainly test that notion.

---

[2] **evinces:** shows, demonstrates
[3] **strictures:** limits, restrictions

My Notes

But country stations can't afford to ignore any record the Dixie Chicks put out at this point. While Garth Brooks was feigning retirement and Shania Twain was off having a baby, the trio sold 21 million albums, doing more than any of their peers to see country music through its recent slump in sales.

"Do we have a choice not to play the Dixie Chicks?" asked Darren Davis, a program director for the Infinity Broadcasting network. "Sure, we have a choice, but one also has a choice to cut off one's nose to spite their face. The Dixie Chicks are the biggest of the big right now. We play their music as often as we can get it on the air."

Lon Helton, the Nashville bureau chief for the trade magazine Radio and Records, said he believes the ascendancy of the Dixie Chicks has as much to do with the integrity of their musical vision as with any demands of the market.

''The Chicks have to be given tremendous credit for knowing who they are musically, for saying, 'This is what we do; anyone who wants to do so is free to play it,'" Mr. Helton said.

For a while, it appeared that no one would be playing the Dixie Chicks' new album. Last summer, after the trio approached Sony about renegotiating their record deal, Sony filed a lawsuit against them for breach of contract. The Dixie Chicks responded with a suit of their own, charging that Sony had withheld $4.1 million in royalties. An 11-month legal battle ensued, along with speculation about whether the trio would leave Sony; then, surprisingly, the parties settled out of court. The terms of the agreement weren't made public, but The Los Angeles Times reported in June that the deal included a $20 million bonus for the group and an increase in its royalty rate to about 20 percent.

Had the Dixie Chicks' suit gone to court and been settled in their favor, the decision might have had far-reaching implications, perhaps making it easier for artists to renegotiate long-term contracts. "That would have been so awesome," said Ms. Maines. "We would have been in the history books if we'd have taken it to the end. We definitely meant to do more for the industry. It just got to the point where we had done as much as we could without jeopardizing our careers.

''We have families, we have kids now," added Ms. Maines, who is married to the actor Adrian Pasdar, with whom she has a 1-year-old son. Ms. Robison, who is married to the singer-songwriter Charlie Robison, is six months pregnant.

''We also didn't want to be the kinds of people who put our pride in front of our logic," Ms. Maguire said. "Sony had to swallow their pride, too, and I think they had to swallow a bigger dose of pride than we did."

Wrangling with a giant entertainment conglomerate is a long way from entertaining conventioneers on the street corners of Dallas, which is what Ms. Robison and Ms. Maguire did in 1989 as founding members of the Dixie Chicks. The original group, a neo-cowgirl quartet that took its name from "Dixie Chicken," a song by the funk-rock band Little Feat, also included Laura Lynch and Robin Macy on guitars and vocals.

That incarnation of the band enjoyed considerable popularity in Texas in the early 90's. The Dixie Chicks also played at Bill Clinton's 1993 inauguration and released three albums on an independent label, the first of which they titled "Thank Heavens for Dale Evans." Yet while amply talented, the group never really transcended its status as a regional or kitsch act until Ms. Maines replaced Ms. Lynch in 1995. (Ms. Lynch retired from performing and married a rancher and winner of the Texas state lottery. Ms. Lacy had left the group in 1992.)

Ms. Maines, who grew up watching her father play with Mr. Ely — who opened for the Clash during their 1980 tour — brought a rock 'n' roll swagger to the Dixie Chicks, and a big, brassy voice, that had been absent from the early edition of the group. Her arrival, however, didn't sit well with the trio's core fans or with the news media in the Dallas-Fort Worth area, both of which accused the women of selling out to a younger, pop-leaning audience. "We used to get hate messages on our voice mail," Ms. Robison said.

The burnished production that galvanized the first two albums the Dixie Chicks made for Sony might have struck some as a compromise. But no one can accuse them of selling out on "Home," a subtle but commanding record that is something of a return to the trio's Texas roots even as it casts judgment on the slick, crossover aesthetic that now defines country music. The women recorded the project not in Nashville but, as its title suggests, at home, in Austin. (Ms. Robison and her husband live in San Antonio.) They produced the album, do-it-yourself style, with Ms. Maines's father, who first introduced his daughter to Ms. Robison and Ms. Maguire.

Similarly, the updated mountain sound of "Home" recalls the albums the Dixie Chicks made before Ms. Maines joined the group. The sisters had sung behind Ms. Maines on the previous two albums, but this time the women recorded their vocals as a trio, in the fashion of the early Dixie Chicks. They also worked with first-call bluegrass musicians, including the guitarist Bryan Sutton, late of Ricky Skaggs's band, as well as the mandolinists Adam Steffey and Chris Thile, the latter of the trio Nickel Creek.

My Notes

Throwing Light on the Situation

The Dixie Chicks arranged most of the material on the album, much of it consisting of thoughtful and thought-provoking compositions from left-of-center singer-songwriters like Patty Griffin, Radney Foster and the team of Tim O'Brien and Gary Nicholson. Although they weren't credited as producers on "Wide Open Spaces" and "Fly," "they had a real good idea of how they wanted things to sound," said Mr. Maines, who played steel guitar on the two earlier albums.

"They definitely know what they're doing," he said. "They're really savvy about what they want to sing and how they want it to sound."

In many respects, making "Home" validated the risk-taking ethos the trio has always embraced. "It was nice to test our producing skills and realize how involved we were in that aspect of the making of 'Wide Open Spaces' and 'Fly,'" said Ms. Robison. "We knew we were, but we were still so new to Nashville. It was nice, this time, to know that we could trust our ears, and that we had total freedom to go anywhere we wanted."

Article

Chicks reap whirlwind

by Mike Rosen (May 2003)

McCarthyism, as the term was originally coined, was meant to describe the abuse and distortion of information by a government committee at the expense of an individual's rights and reputation.

McCarthyism is characterized by false accusations, smears and extracting a pound of lie from an ounce of truth. Although a demagogue, Sen. Joseph McCarthy had the goods on some of his targets; others were innocent victims.

Whatever the Dixie Chicks are, they are not innocent victims.

They said what they said where they said it. Holding people to account for their words and actions isn't McCarthyism. The Chicks are certainly free to oppose the Iraq war and to tell the world that they're ashamed to hail from the same state as President Bush. Just as the rest of us are free to tell the Chicks that we think they're idiots.

We're also free to not buy their CDs and to not pay to see them in concert. Radio stations are in business to attract and please listeners in order to sell their advertisers' products. If listeners are sufficiently turned off by the Chicks to tune out stations when they play their music, you can expect stations to play less of it. This is known as commerce, not McCarthyism.

The Dixie Chicks have no constitutional right to have their music played on commercial stations. And Tim Robbins and Susan Sarandon have no "right" to be invited to private functions like the Baseball Hall of Fame Dinner. Freedom of disassociation and freedom of association are opposite sides of the same coin. After Michael Moore's boorish behavior at the Oscars, it's understandable that the baseball folks would be leery of trusting this duo to refrain from indulging their anti-Bush, anti-war activism at a festive, nonpolitical affair.

Boycotting is a common tool of leftists and practitioners of racial politics. Conservative targets of such campaigns have included Rush Limbaugh, Laura Schlesinger and Anita Bryant.

My Notes

Jesse Jackson has amassed a fortune extorting corporations. Gay activists organized a boycott of the entire state of Colorado after voters approved Amendment 2. Why is it a legitimate tactic when lefties do it, but McCarthyism when country music fans turn their backs on the Dixie Chicks?

When Wyoming Sen. Alan Simpson questioned Anita Hill at Clarence Thomas' Supreme Court confirmation hearings, one columnist accused him of using McCarthy-like tactics. To which Simpson replied, "Accusing someone of McCarthyism is a McCarthyist tactic itself."

It wasn't just that the Chicks voiced their opposition to the war and dissed the president of the United States. Others have done that with impunity. It was how and where they did it. It might have been a principled, courageous act had they taken on a patriotic, flag-waving crowd in Lubbock, Texas. Instead, they pandered to an anti-American audience in London. When word got back home, all hell broke loose.

Then, the Chicks made matters worse with a pathetic, damage-control exercise, talking out of all sides of their three mouths in an incoherent interview with Diane Sawyer on ABC's Primetime.

Robbins' and Sarandon's politics might cost them a gig or two while gaining them some new ones, but they haven't damaged their careers.

They're still heroes to the Hollywood left and the white wine-and-brie crowd that supports the arts and contributes to National Public Radio.

But unlike Robbins and Sarandon, the Dixie Chicks aren't all that political - they're probably not smart enough. They're in over their heads. And they made the perfectly stupid business move of alienating their core audience.

They angered white males from Texas, Oklahoma, Mississippi and Alabama who drive pickup trucks with bumper stickers emblazoned with American flags, the kind of people who admire the Marine Corps more than Jane Fonda.

Popularity is fleeting, and aspiring country groups are lined up around the block. The Dixie Chicks might have to wash off their makeup, swap the spiked high heels for sandals, learn some folksy protest songs and start working the coffee houses in Greenwich Village.

Free speech has consequences - good and bad - as well it should.

No More Whistlin' Dixie

Diane Sawyer's Indecorous Performance with the Dixie Chicks

by Jim Lewis (April 2003)

> **ABOUT THE WRITER**
> Jim Lewis writes regularly about art for *Slate* and is the author of the forthcoming novel, *The King Is Dead*. He lives in Austin, Texas.

Last night's *Primetime Thursday*, which featured Diane Sawyer interviewing the Dixie Chicks about their recent woes, was one of those broadcast moments that make you want to put your foot through the television. In case you've been out working in the garden this past month, the occasion for the show was a relatively innocuous[1] remark the Chicks' lead singer, Natalie Maines, made at a concert in London just before the war. "Just so you know," she said from the stage, "we're ashamed that the president of the United States is from Texas." The Associated Press picked up the line; country music stations fanned the flames; and within a few weeks the Dixie Chicks' newest record, *Home*, which had been No. 1 on both the country and pop charts, was being boycotted across the country.

This is silly but not unpredictable. What followed was disgusting: CD-crushing radio promo events, vandalism of Chick Emily Robison's home, threats on the Chicks' lives, and a campaign of hatred directed at three of the most talented women in the music industry. Bruce Springsteen occasionally gets flack for his political remarks, but he doesn't get called a slut.

The Chicks themselves may have inadvertently made things worse. When Jonathan Franzen ticked off the Oprah folks, it was as distressing to see his furious backpedaling as it was to see the arrant frenzy that his remarks occasioned. It would have been easier on him—and probably shortened the story's news life—if he'd just insisted, "Yeah, I said it. Yeah, I meant it. If you want to talk about it, we can do that. If you want to scream at me, I'm going to have to tune you out and get on with my life." God knows Maines and her two bandmates might have saved themselves a little heartache if they'd done the same.

---

[1] **innocuous:** harmless

Still, they have the burden to bear of being from Dallas, where women tend to be a) spirited and b) polite. Not always an easy balance to maintain, but last night Maines did her best. When Sawyer prompted the three of them to ask for forgiveness, in a gruesome moment of utterly fake primetime piety, the trio paused. You could see them struggling with their pride, their conviction, and their desire to get along. Instead, Maines kept her cool and her dignity. "Accept us," she said. "Accept an apology that was made ... but to forgive us, don't forgive us for who we are." And she went on to point out, as if it needed to be said, that the practice of dissent is fundamental to democracy.

That wasn't good enough for Sawyer. She spent an hour trying to bend the Chicks with a combination of false sympathy and crass sensationalism. Time and again, she cut back to a typeset insert of Maines' original remark, as if Maines had called for the pillage of Crawford. "Ashamed?" Sawyer said, incredulously. "Ashamed?" In the tradition of a Stalinist show trial, the women were forced to affirm their patriotism and their support for the troops. At every point they—who are, after all, entertainers with no particular training in political science—were thoughtful, modest, and firm. At every point Sawyer tried to force them into a crude, Manichean[2] choice. "Do you feel awful about using that word about the president of the United States?" she asked at the start of the interview—in a prime example of the sort of leading question no self-respecting first year AP stringer would ask. "Well," replied Maines, carefully, " 'awful' is a really strong word." Later, when Maines was trying to apologize and clarify, Sawyer said, "I hear something not quite, what, wholehearted. ..."

Well, I heard something not quite—what—honorable in Sawyer's presentation of the affair: an attempt to take a trivial matter that had blown up into an absurd controversy, and blow it up even more under the guise of simply covering the story. Essentially, she asked the women to choose between abasing[3] themselves on national television or stirring up more hatred against themselves. It was a depressing moment in an ugly time.

For what it's worth, I have profoundly mixed feelings about the war, and if I were to sit down with Natalie Maines, I'm sure we'd have much to disagree about. But, just so you know, I'm proud that the Dixie Chicks are from Texas. What's more, I'm embarrassed that Diane Sawyer is a member of my profession.

---

[2] **Manichean:** a world view that divides things into either good or evil, allowing no ambiguity
[3] **abasing:** humiliating

Is Dixie Chicks protest a conspiracy?

by John Kiesewetter (March 2003)

Are the Dixie Chicks victims of a right-wing conspiracy?

That's what their manager, Simon Renshaw, has told country music stations being pressured to drop the Chicks' music after lead singer Natalie Maines criticized President Bush last week.

In an e-mail to stations distributed by Sony Music, their label, Renshaw says the protest has been orchestrated by the Free Republic, a Web site "for independent, grassroots conservatives," according to founder Jim Robinson of Fresno, Calif. The Web site also alleges that recent anti-war protests are "communist-organized demonstrations."

"Your company is being targeted by a radical right-wing online forum," Renshaw says in the e-mail. "You are being `Freeped,' which is the code word for an organized e-mail/telephone effort attempting to solicit a desired response."

On March 10, Maines told a London audience: "Just so you know, we're ashamed the president of the United States is from Texas."

Four days later, the Lubbock native apologized by saying, "I apologize to President Bush because my remark was disrespectful. I feel that whoever holds that office should be treated with the utmost respect."

Country music stations in Dallas-Fort Worth and Kansas City have been deluged with e-mails and calls demanding that the Dixie Chicks be dropped from the airwaves.

Complaints didn't arrive at WUBE-FM (105.1) until Monday. Only one person called Thursday when the B105 morning show read the story, says Tim Closson, operations manager.

"We broke the story on Thursday, and got very little reaction to it. We mentioned it again on Friday, and only got a few calls," he says.

The Chicks remain on B105. Closson says he "seriously considered indefinitely pulling all Dixie Chicks music... (but) our decision came down to one thing: We believe in the constitution. We believe in the freedom of speech."

At Middletown's WPFB-FM (105.9),the Dixie Chicks were dropped Monday for the week by Mark Evar, operations director.

GRAMMAR & USAGE

When they want to repeat what someone else has said, writers may use a direct quote or an indirect quote. The direct quote lends more authority to what is written. An indirect quote has the advantage of creating a more efficient progression from one idea to the next. In this article, Boliek uses both direct and indirect quotations:

Direct: *"This is an extremely active and well-organized group."*

Indirect: *That's what their manager, Simon Renshaw, has told country music stations being pressured to drop the Chicks' music....*

My Notes

_____

_____

_____

_____

_____

_____

_____

"They're telling us that the minute the Dixie Chicks come on, they're going to change the station - and we don't want to lose any listeners," Evar says.

The Chicks' manager, in his e-mail, says the group's Web site "was totally overrun (Sunday) and had to be closed down, and our publicist's servers and telephone system failed under the weight of the calls."

"This is an extremely active and well-organized group. As always the 'squeaky wheel gets the grease' and these weasels know how to squeak," Renshaw says.

Renshaw apparently used the word "weasel" because the Free Republic Web site uses that term.

Says the Free Republic home page: "As war with Iraq becomes imminent, more and more of the 'useful idiot' leftist weasels are crawling out of the woodwork. So-called 'anti-war' protests are popping up in cities all across the nation.

"We will not allow these communist organized demonstrations (to) go unanswered. Patriotic Americans are countering these terrorist supporting leftists wherever and whenever they pop up."

THE DIXIE CHICKS:

America Catches Up with Them

by Jon Pareles (May 2006)

THE DIXIE CHICKS call it "the Incident": the anti-Bush remark that Natalie Maines, their lead singer, made onstage in London in 2003. "Just so you know, we're ashamed the president of the United States is from Texas," said Ms. Maines, a Texan herself.

It led to a partisan firestorm, a radio boycott, death threats and, now, to an album that's anything but repentant: "Taking the Long Way" (Open Wide/ Monument/ Columbia). The Dixie Chicks – Ms. Maines, Emily Robison and Martie Maguire – were the top-selling country group of the late 1990's and early 2000's. After country's gatekeepers disowned them over politics, they decided to keep their politics and let country music fend for itself.

The Incident is very much at the center of "Taking the Long Way." The album could have been "way safe and scared," Ms. Maines said. "We could have pandered." They didn't. The new songs are filled with reactions, direct and oblique[1], to the Incident. There are no apologies.

"We had to make this album," Ms. Maines said. "We could not have gotten past any of this without making this album. Even if nobody ever heard it."

The Dixie Chicks were in New York this month to make media appearances and to perform at the party for this year's Time 100, the magazine's list of influential people, which includes them. Sitting around a dinner table in a Chelsea loft that Ms. Maines owns but hasn't used much – a former gallery with artist friends' paintings parked on the brick walls – the three Dixie Chicks dug into takeout Italian food and sipped red wine. "I've thought about all this way too much," Ms. Maines said.

"Taking the Long Way," due out on Tuesday, is the first Dixie Chicks album on which group members collaborated in writing all the songs. The first single, "Not Ready to Make Nice," declares, "I'm not ready to back down/I'm still mad as hell," and starts with a tolling guitar more suitable for a Metallica dirge than a honky-tonk serenade. The Dixie Chicks and their manager insisted to their record company that "we need to approach everything like not one radio station is going to play one single song," Ms. Maines said. Asked about country radio, she said, "Do you really think we're going to make an album for you and trust the future of our career to people who turned on us in a day?"

---

[1] **oblique:** indirect

Instead the album wraps gleaming California rock around its raw emotions. Although there's plenty of country in the music, "Taking the Long Way" reaches not for the lucrative yet insular country airwaves but for an adult pop mainstream. Meanwhile the core country audience may not be so hostile anymore. The album arrives at a time when approval for President Bush has dropped to as low as 29 percent, in a recent Harris Interactive poll.

On Amazon.com, preorders recently placed "Taking the Long Way" at No. 5 in a Top 10 that also includes albums with antiwar songs by Bruce Springsteen, Neil Young, Paul Simon and Pearl Jam.

For those who expect knee-jerk Republicanism from country singers, the Dixie Chicks never fit the stereotype to begin with. "I always knew people thought that about us, and it bugged me," Ms. Maines said. "Because I knew who we were, and I knew who I've been my whole life. So to me it was such a relief for people to know."

The Incident occurred on March 10, 2003, 10 days before the United States invaded Iraq. "It felt pretty trite to me to be doing a show on what was supposed to be the eve before war," Ms. Maines said, "and not say anything about it. At that stage too everyone in Europe, or everyone outside of the U.S., talked about the U.S. like we all thought one way. So it was important for me to let them know that you can't group us all into one."

Her remark was reported in Britain and quickly picked up. Right-wing blogs and talk shows vilified[2] the Dixie Chicks as unpatriotic and worse, and the Incident reached the nightly news. . . .

The complaint that she criticized the president on foreign soil has been a talk-radio talking point. Ms. Maines dismisses it. "It wasn't like we played 20 shows in America and I was saving up this comment for London," she said. "I was in London when the war was about to start. That's where I said it. I would have said it anywhere, because I didn't think that it was a bad thing to say or a controversial thing to say."

. . . Ms. Maines's free speech was costly. Country radio stations were bombarded with calls demanding that the Dixie Chicks be dropped from playlists. Within days, songs from the Chicks' 2002 album, "Home," virtually disappeared from American airwaves. They had the No. 1 country single that week with "Travelin' Soldier," which mourns a soldier killed in Vietnam; it plummeted to No. 63.

---

2 vilified: defamed or slandered

The Dixie Chicks' two previous albums, "Wide Open Spaces" (1998) and "Fly" (1999), had each been certified "diamond" for shipping more than 10 million copies in the United States. Without airplay, "Home" stalled that March at six million.

"I understand everybody was in a place of fear, and everybody's nerves were on edge, and mothers were sending their sons and daughters off to war, and tensions were high," Ms. Maguire said. "But you know when it continues and continues and people are still mad about it, I think back to those words and think: How is that bad, what she said? It's so harmless. It's so nothing."

The United States concerts on the Dixie Chicks' tour were already sold out. Promoters offered refunds, although there were more requests for new tickets than there were returns. Protesters showed up outside concerts; others burned Dixie Chicks albums.

"We have video footage of this lady at one of the shows protesting, holding her 2-year-old son," Ms. Maines said. The woman commanded her son to shout along with an angry chant. "And I was just like, that's it right there. That's the moment that it's taught. She just taught her 2-year-old how to hate. And that broke my heart."

The band received death threats, including at least one, in Dallas, that the F.B.I. considered credible. A newspaper printed Ms. Maines's home address in Austin, Tex., and she ended up moving first outside the city and then to Los Angeles. On the American tour a handful of boos were drowned out by fervent cheers. Suddenly there was more at stake than toe-tapping tunes.

In a way there always had been. The Dixie Chicks were never a typical country act. They got started in Texas, not Nashville. And their music is built around a country rarity: female instrumentalists. Ms. Robison plays banjo, and Ms. Maguire plays fiddle; they are sisters, and they helped found the Dixie Chicks as a bluegrass band in Dallas in 1989. After Ms. Maines replaced the group's lead singer in 1995, the Dixie Chicks became a voice of assertive, irreverent femininity in mainstream country. They also brought the sound of the banjo, once considered "too country," back to country radio.

While the Dixie Chicks' music was never confrontational, each album grew bolder. In the upbeat "Goodbye Earl," a hit from "Fly," an abused wife murders her husband and gets away with it. The album "Home" — made in Austin and produced by the Dixie Chicks themselves along with Lloyd

My Notes

WORD CONNECTIONS

The word **resentment** contains both a commonly used prefix, *re-*, and a commonly used suffix, *-ment*. *Re-* means "again" and *–ment* means "result" or "action." The root comes from Old French *sentir*, meaning "to feel."

My Notes

Maines, Natalie's father — deliberately set aside the slick, electric sound of current country for a largely acoustic, bluegrass-rooted production and some haunted songs back to country radio.

After their own tour ended — it was the top-grossing country music tour of 2003 — the Dixie Chicks joined the Vote for Change concert series supporting John Kerry. They had babies; Ms. Maguire and Ms. Robison both had twins. And they decided to record their next album in Los Angeles. The producer they chose was Rick Rubin, who has made albums with the Beastie Boys, the Red Hot Chili Peppers, Johnny Cash and Shakira. The Incident had sparked Mr. Rubin's interest.

"After the Incident everyone started taking what they said seriously," Mr. Rubin said by telephone from Los Angeles. "To take a band that's popular not for that reason and give them that power seemed very exciting.

"It's the biggest thing that's ever happened to them, and it rattled them and it changed them," he added. "The pain of it is really lingering. I thought they needed to somehow address what happened in a way that was truthful about how they felt, whatever that was. I just wanted it to be an honest reflection of that, but also told in a way that if you didn't know what happened to them and just heard the songs, you might relate to it anyway."

On previous albums the Dixie Chicks wrote the more lighthearted songs and got serious material from other songwriters. This time, Ms. Maines said, "We knew we had things to write about." Mr. Rubin brought in co-writers including Gary Louris, from the Jayhawks, and Dan Wilson, from Semisonic. "They took the fear out of us," said Ms. Maines. "You know, 'You need to say that because that's the truth and that's the way you feel.'"

. . . The Dixie Chicks sound determined not to whine on "Taking the Long Way," and they focus on personal reactions, not protests. The album is a defiant autobiography of their career, and "Not Ready to Make Nice" mentions the death threats after the Incident. But until it does, the song could be about the resentment following any breakup or betrayal.

"Lubbock or Leave It," a fierce country-rocker, describes Ms. Maines's Texas hometown as a hypocritical[3] "fool's paradise" with "more churches than trees," blind to its own problems. But there aren't many other specifics on the album. Without the Dixie Chicks' back story, the songs work as meticulous[4] pop vows of loyalty and determination.

Still, the Incident keeps peeking through the pretty arrangements. The countryish mandolin and pedal steel guitar of "Everybody Knows" carry the confession: "All the things I can't erase from my life/Everybody knows." An affectionate ballad, "Easy Silence," praises a companion who provides a refuge when "Anger plays on every station/Answers only make more questions." In the fiddle-topped waltz "Bitter End," one verse mocks fair-weather supporters: "As long as I'm the shiniest star,/Oh there you are." The album's finale, a gospel-soul anthem called "I Hope," insists, "I don't wanna hear nothin' else/About killin' and that it's God's will."

Three years after the Incident the Dixie Chicks insist that it liberated them. "When, no matter what you do, everybody's going to punch holes in it, then you just go and you do what you want," Ms. Maguire said. "And that's the most freeing place to be."

Ms. Maines added: "It will mean a lot to me if people buy the album just sort of out of protest. The naysayers and the people who were so organized to take us down did a really good job. And they succeeded. So it feels good to let the music win out in the end and say, 'Even your hatred can't stop what people want to listen to.'"

A smiling Ms. Maguire had the last word. "See you at the diamond record party," she said.

---

[3] **hypocritical:** insincere
[4] **meticulous:** careful and precise

© 2011 College Board. All rights reserved.

My Notes

Online Column

Speaking Up and Speaking Out

by Melissa Silverstein (November 2006)

Three years into the Iraq War, the American public is making next week's election a national referendum on the policies that got us there and seem to offer no end in sight. In a democratic culture with free speech at its core, one of the earliest challenges to those policies came from an unlikely source: three Texas-bred women called the Dixie Chicks. They may not have seen themselves as a political band, or even political people, when they made their antiwar feelings clear on the eve of the invasion at a March 2003 concert in London. But they put themselves squarely against the momentum growing in the country music/red state community, which was lining up behind the government's march to war.

The story of what happened to the band after lead vocalist Natalie Maines' fateful comment — "just so you know, we're ashamed the President of the United States is from Texas" — is the subject of *Shut Up and Sing* , the latest documentary from Barbara Kopple and co-director Cecilia Peck. To tell their story, the band made sure their experience would be treated seriously by teaming up with Kopple, whose films include the Oscar-winning *Harlan County USA* (striking coal miners in Kentucky) and *Bearing Witness* (women war correspondents in Iraq). On her part, Kopple was drawn to a story that, she says, has "become the center of a larger political debate. Their personal transformation in so many ways has come to represent the political climate we have in the U.S. right now."

The Dixie Chicks were country music superstars in 2003 and the best selling women's band ever. Having been named entertainers of the year by the Academy of Country Music two years before, their Top of the World tour sold out $49 million worth of tickets in one day, and they won eight Grammies including the 2003 best country album. But once Maines' comment became known, and when the band refused to back down, the country community quickly turned against them.

Did the Dixie Chicks pay a higher price for speaking out because they were women? Kopple believes women get into trouble for speaking their minds when the expectation is that "men are the ones to speak out, to take a stand, and a woman's role is to stand with her man. I think these ideas still permeate our culture." Apparently to the country music world, seeming unpatriotic in a time of war is a far worse sin than being a convicted wife batterer like Tracy Lawrence, who has been able to rehabilitate himself with his fans.

The least discussed piece of this story is how the continuing consolidation of media into the hands of a few large corporations created a situation that allowed the Dixie Chicks to be literally erased from the airwaves. "Travelin' Soldier" was the number one single when it was removed from playing rotation. Cumulus Media, a consortium of 306 radio stations, told their affiliates not to play the Chicks' music. Several disc jockeys who broke the ban were fired according to press reports. First denying there was a blacklist against the band, Cumulus CEO Lewis Dickey was forced to admit the truth during a Senate Commerce Committee hearing on July 8, 2003. Commenting on the dangerous effect of media consolidation, with enormous power and influence falling into very few hands, Kopple says, "too often those hands are attached to men more interested in the bottom line and blind 'patriotism' than creativity, risk-taking and progress."

The hate pouring onto these women was clearly sexist. Fans trashed their cds. At arenas, protestors' signs and slogans ranged from the ugly to the ridiculous — "strap her to a bomb and drop her over Baghdad" and "try the chicks for treason" to "free speech is ok except in public." Kopple points out an irony: "Women's voices are often considered dangerous. Ours are often the voices of change, of peace, of moderation, and of forgiveness."

While shut off from their country fan base, the Dixie Chicks were propelled into a completely different musical and political universe. On the cover of Entertainment Weekly and interviewed by Diane Sawyer, the band was introduced to an audience that fell in love with the music and the message. The recording of their new "comeback" album is highlighted throughout the film. Recording it and writing their own songs for the first time functioned as a catharsis[1] for the hell they went through. Their dismay with the country world is clear in the first single, "Not Ready to Make Nice," an anthem of unrepentant anger.

Theirs is the best sort of feminist story: all about what happens when women stand up for what they believe in. At the end of the documentary, Kopple shows the Dixie Chicks returning to the arena in London where the controversy began. Maines restates her comment, this time with a big smile on her face. Kopple got to know her subjects well while following them around for over a year. "I think, more than anything," she says, "their experience has highlighted that — although the cost of speaking your mind and being yourself can be high — the cost of being silenced is much higher."

---

[1] **catharsis:** release, cleansing

GRAMMAR & USAGE

An introductory adverbial or participial phrase at the beginning of a sentence is usually followed by a comma.

First denying there was a blacklist against the band, Cumulus CEO Lewis Dickey was forced to … .

At the end of the documentary, Kopple shows the Dixie Chicks returning… .

My Notes

My Notes

Article

Dixie Chicks
AMONG ESTEEMED OUTLAWS

by Ashley Sayeau (February 2007)

On Sunday night at the 49th annual Grammy awards, the Dixie Chicks took home five awards, including best album, record and song of the year.

It was a long road, indeed, for the Chicks, whose enormous fan base and ticket sales famously plummeted[1] in 2003 after lead singer Natalie Maines remarked on the eve of the Iraq war that the group was "ashamed the president of the United States is from Texas." Within days, radio stations were refusing to play their music, and fans were demanding refunds. Death threats were later issued.

Throughout the ordeal, the group remained admirably unapologetic, insisting that dissent is (or at least should be) a vital liberty in America. They further maintained this position in their album *Taking the Long Way* (which won the Grammy for best album) and especially in the song "Not Ready To Make Nice," in which they directly addressed their critics: "It's too late to make it right/ I probably wouldn't if I could/ Cause I'm mad as hell/ Can't bring myself to do what it is/ You think I should."

Despite the group's successes, the grudge has held, particularly among the Nashville music establishment. The Country Music Association completely snubbed the Chicks at its awards ceremony in May.

Such an affront[2] on the part of country music is not only cowardly, but also quite antithetical to the genre's history. For, while country music today is often equated with pickup trucks, rebel flags, and men with mullets, it also has a brave and, dare I say, liberal streak in its closet.

Take Johnny Cash, for instance. Not only did many of his most famous lyrics center on "the poor and the beaten down," including a poignant attack on this country's treatment of American Indians, but also Cash was a vocal critic of the Vietnam War, as in his famous song "Man in Black": "I wear the black in mourning for the lives that could have been/ Each week we lose a hundred fine young men."

---

[1] **plummeted:** declined suddenly and steeply
[2] **affront:** insult

WORD CONNECTIONS

The word *antithetical* begins with the Greek prefix *anti-*, which means "against" or "opposed to." English has many words that begin with this prefix, including *antidote*, *antifreeze*, *antifungal*, and *anti-inflammatory*.

And then there is Willie Nelson, who on Valentine's Day 2006 released a love song about gay cowboys, titled, "Cowboys Are Frequently, Secretly (Fond of Each Other)." Perhaps more seriously, he has been an avid supporter of presidential hopeful Dennis Kucinich, who, while arguing for universal health care and a swift withdrawal from Iraq, is probably the furthest left of any Democratic candidate.

Women in country music – like the Dixie Chicks – have a long tradition of being particularly bold in speaking out against some of the very conventions their record labels and conservative fan base celebrate. Back in 1933, the Carter Family, which consisted of A.P. Carter; his wife, Sara Doughtery Carter; and her cousin, the groundbreaking guitar player Maybelle Addington Carter, sang about a young woman who chose to commit suicide rather than marry. In Sara's sorrowful croon, we hear her say, "I never will marry/ I'll be no man's wife/ I expect to live single all the days of my life." Needless to say, she later divorced A.P.

Perhaps most memorable are some of Loretta Lynn's lyrics, particularly from the 1960s and 1970s. Released in 1966, her song "Dear Uncle Sam" was an early anti-Vietnam protest song. And though she once feigned[3] dozing off while listening to feminist advocate Betty Friedan speak as a fellow guest on *The David Frost Show*, Lynn was a pretty controversial women's advocate. In "I Wanna Be Free," she wrote of the liberating effect of divorce: "I'm gonna take this chain from around my finger/ And throw it just as far as I can sling 'er." She did the same thing for birth control in "The Pill": "The feelin' good comes easy now/ Since I've got the pill."

As daring as some outlaw artists have been, the country music establishment has often proved even more dogged in its conservative views. Lynn has purportedly had more songs banned than any other country music singer. And Cash, never completely at home in the country music world, once said that "the very idea of unconventional or even original ideas ending up on 'country' radio" was "absurd." No wonder, then, that in his gay cowboy song, Willie Nelson lamented that "you won't hear this song on the radio/ Not on your local TV."

With the November election, particularly with strong Democratic gains in Virginia and Missouri, Republican politicians may have to rethink their long-standing Southern strategy. Similarly, with last Sunday night's awards, country music should embrace the fact that its greatest assets have never been scared of controversy or doing the right thing.

To quote the great Dolly Parton – who has sung a few feminist, antiwar, and progressive anthems herself – "You'll never do a whole lot unless you're brave enough to try."

My Notes

---

[3] **feigned:** pretended

My Notes

© 2011 College Board. All rights reserved.

Article

A Tired Old Song

by Jonah Goldberg (March 2007)

WHAT do Jimmy Carter and the Dixie Chicks have in common? They're southerners who've traded "up" on their southernness. They hit their best moments long ago, but have ridden positive press far beyond their natural shelf life. They think a lot of themselves. Good teeth. What else, what else ...? Oh, right—they're all 2007 Grammy winners!

Jimmy Carter won the Grammy for the Best Spoken Word Album of 2006, sharing the honor with actress Ruby Dee. Carter and Dee beat out nominees Al Franken and Bill Maher for this year's Grammy. Yet Carter isn't the first ex-president to win this cutthroat competition. Bill Clinton actually won two Grammys back to back in 2004 and 2005, the first for his memoirs, *My Life*, sharing the second with Mikhail Gorbachev in the coveted Best Spoken Word Album for Children category.

In 1997, Clinton's wife of record, Hillary, won a Grammy for reading aloud her book *It Takes a Village*; last year that honor went to Barack Obama for his memoirs. In 2004, Franken won for his book Lying Liars, and the year before that Maya Angelou won her third Grammy in the category. Other winners include Jesse Jackson and Garrison Keillor.

But let me stop you right there. Politics has nothing to do with the selection process. This was a straightforward judgment based solely on merit, damn it. So if you're listening, Ted Kennedy, you'd better bring your A-game if you hope to beat the likes of Rush Limbaugh!

Which brings me to the Greatest Band of All Time. The Dixie Chicks won five Grammys in the Stick It to the Fascists category, including for their Best Song, "Not Ready to Make Nice," a poignant reminder that the Chicks weren't going to be cowed by the war-lusting American public.

Recall that in 2003, on the eve of war, Natalie Maines, the middle one in most pictures, said in London that she was "ashamed" President Bush was from her native Texas. She quickly apologized, saying, "As a concerned American citizen, I apologize to President Bush because my remark was disrespectful." "I love my country," she continued. "I am a proud American."

GRAMMAR & USAGE

Writers have available a number of rhetorical devices they can use to make their writing more effective. In this essay, Goldberg uses these two:

Rhetorical Questions:
- *What do Jimmy Carter and the Dixie Chicks have in common?*
- *What else? What else?*

Fragments:
- *Which brings me to the greatest band of all time.*
- *Good teeth.*

When this didn't improve sagging sales among the bloody jingoists[1] who made them rich in the first place, the Chicks decided to appeal to a different audience. "The entire country may disagree with me," Maines told Britain's Daily Telegraph, "but I don't understand the necessity for patriotism." Through "gritted teeth" she asked, "Why do you have to be a patriot? ... You can like where you live and like your life, but as for loving the whole country ... I don't see why people care about patriotism."

On Grammy night, Maines proclaimed, "I think people are using their freedom of speech with all these awards. We get the message." Of course, the "people" in question were members of the record industry, and only someone with a thumbless grasp of free speech would think it was at issue in the first place. The people who criticized the Dixie Chicks in the first place were people too, exercising their free speech. They just weren't the ones who mattered — at least to those nonpartisan[2] adjudicators[3] of raw talent who award Grammys.

---

[1] **jingoists:** extreme, aggressive patriots
[2] **nonpartisan:** free from bias
[3] **adjudicators:** judges

My Notes

Throwing Light on the Situation

Analyzing Presentations

As you listen to the presentations of the other groups, use the space below to create a concept map. Record titles, ideas, and page numbers as you make connections between your guiding question and the information presented in the other groups' presentations.

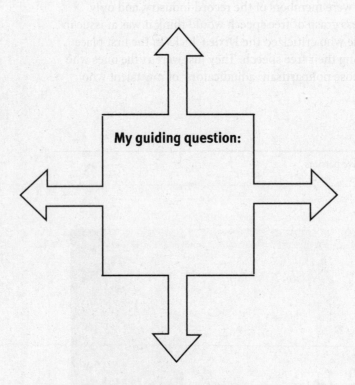

My guiding question:

Writing Prompt: Now that you have heard all the other presentations on the Dixie Chicks controversy, write an argumentative essay in which you use evidence from the various articles you have discussed to answer your guiding question and to persuade others to your own position. Include relevant quotes and appropriate commentary to support your conclusions, as well as information on the complete range of relevant perspectives on this controversy. Be sure to represent the divergent views from the various articles accurately and honestly. Select an organizing structure that is appropriate for the purpose, audience, and context of this task.

Considering the Medium

Documentary films may use both primary and archival footage.
Primary footage refers to footage shot by the filmmaker for the text
at hand. **Archival footage** is footage taken from another, previously
recorded, source.

Nonfiction Film Viewing Guide

Director: **Title:**   **Year:**

What Do You See (primary or archival footage, interviews, still images, the filmmaker)?

What Do You Hear (dialogue, narration, diegetic and nondiegetic sound)?

What Do You Read (subtitles, graphics, labels, etc.)?

How Is It Put Together (editing sequence, transition devices, etc.)?

What Is the Effect (what is the theme/message of the video, what "truth" does it convey about the subject)?

Considering the Medium

Modes and Styles in Nonfiction Film and Television

When we watch films and television shows that are fictional, we are aware that the creators/writers are not showing us reality. However, when we watch nonfiction films and television shows, we tend to assume that what we see is absolute reality and truth. Yet nonfiction films and television shows, as well as nonfiction books and articles, are shaped by their creators.

One way to analyze nonfiction films and television shows is to look at the documentary modes, or methods, the creators use to shape their creation. One critic has identified four modes—*expository, observational, interactive,* and *reflexive*—that the creators of nonfiction films and television shows use. Read the explanation of each mode below and consider the questions that follow each explanation.

Expository Mode The film explains a subject to the viewer. Think of a historical documentary or nature show. In "Direct Address," a voice-over narrative tells us information about the subject. In "Indirect Address," no central narrator talks directly to the audience, but we are shown (or hear) other people talking about the subject as we look at images of it. With either form of address, the filmmaker/creator is making choices about what to explain and how to explain it, but the viewer is not necessarily aware of those choices.

- How does the speaker's tone influence perception of the subject?
- What do you notice when comparing what is heard with what is being shown at the same time?

Observational Mode This is a "fly on the wall" mode, in which the camera seems to follow the subject without commenting on it. This mode features minimal editing or cutting, little or no use of non-diegetic sound, and no voice over or interaction between the filmmaker and what is being filmed. It comes across as exclusively "showing," rather than "telling," which suggests extreme objectivity. The camera is merely recording reality instead of constructing it. Nevertheless, the filmmaker/creator chooses what reality the camera will record.

- What is not shown?
- How do framing, angle, and lighting potentially influence our perceptions of the subject?

Interactive Mode The filmmaker/creator's presence is evident; we may hear the questions being asked or see the filmmakers engaging with the subjects. We also get the sense that those on film are aware of being filmed and are perhaps modifying how they present themselves as a result of this awareness. Think reality TV: the situations themselves only exist because the film/show is provoking them into existence. Again, the filmmaker/creator is making the choices, though the viewer may be a little more aware that those choices are being made.

- Is the filmmaker provoking reactions for the sake of entertainment or to make a persuasive point? Or both?

- How much does the filmmaker's presence affect our sense of reality?

Reflexive Mode The text calls attention to itself as a constructed text, through deliberate editing or sound effects or satirical self-examination. It may expose its own apparatus via shots of the film crew at work. When using this mode, the filmmaker/creator is saying, "Look, I'm creating this film/show. Watch me." The viewer is aware of some, if not all, of the choices being made.

- How does the text's reflection on itself impact our willingness to consider the film's message?

- Can a text be reflexive and still claim to be objective? Truthful?

Considering the Medium

Modes of Nonfiction Film/Television: As you watch each of the clips listed in this chart, try to determine which documentary mode is most prevalent. The modes may change between and within scenes, but which one seems to be dominant in the clip? Then identify a list of stylistic features you notice in the clip, before ending with an analysis of how the clip's mode contributes to its interpretation of the subject.

Title	Mode and Stylistic Features	Effect on Viewer's Perspective of the Subject
ABC News		
Shut Up and Sing, Chap. 8		
Shut Up and Sing, Chap. 10		
News War		

Writing Prompt: How did each mode influence the way you felt as you watched the information being presented? Based on your answer, write an explanation identifying which mode you might use in your group's project and why you might use it.

Looking for Trouble

SUGGESTED LEARNING STRATEGIES: Discussion Groups, Brainstorming

To define a preliminary topic and issue for your individual and group assessment, work with your group members to complete the following steps.

1. Based on the different ways in which the class exploration approached the Dixie Chicks controversy in this unit, generate a list of criteria for evaluating potential issues as topics for your own essay.

2. With these criteria in mind, brainstorm a list of potential topics and issues. Consider topics and issues that are of broad interest and that provoke inconsistent or opposing reactions.

Looking for Trouble

3. With your group members, discuss the possible topics and issues you might explore. Then use the chart below to consider what approaches each of you might individually take to complete Embedded Assessment 1. Help one another craft guiding questions.

Criticism	Relevant to this topic/issue?	What elements of the issue/topic does criticism link to?	What could be the guiding question?
Historical			
Cultural			
Archetypal			
Marxist			
Feminist			

Research Proposal Template

The research proposal is a one-page expository essay that informs the reader about your group's chosen "event" or issue, discusses information you have already learned, explains which critical perspective you plan to use to examine the issue and why, defines your guiding question, and indicates where and how you will continue to conduct research to answer it.

Components of the Proposal

Event/ Topic:

Review of the Issue: Write a summary of what you currently know about your chosen event or issue.

Which **critical perspective** will you apply while exploring the issue? What are some ways in which it links to your topic?

Initial Guiding Question (open-ended or specific):

Research Plan: Where and how will you further explore or research the issue?

Evaluating Sources

SUGGESTED LEARNING STRATEGIES: Graphic Organizer, Summarizing/
Paraphrasing, Discussion Groups, Sharing and Responding

When choosing sources for your research, consider both primary and
secondary sources that will provide multiple relevant perspectives on
your research topic and major research question. Evaluate the validity,
reliability, and relevance of each source you plan to use.

Criteria for Evaluating Sources

Who is this author? How can you determine the credibility of this author? Consider the author's
occupation, reputation, or credentials.

To what extent and it what ways does the author establish credibility in the text; e.g., Is the writing
objective? Is there a clear presence of logic? Is there personal testimony? Are other examples or experts
cited to support the author's position?

Is bias evident in the language of the text? Consider the author's rhetoric: Are slanters used (page 278)?
To what effect? To what extent? How does this impact the author's credibility?

How does the text link to your critical perspective? How might you use it to support your analysis?
Explain. What quotes might you cite as support for your claims?

What does the text's publication context reveal about its agenda? How might you use its context to
reinforce your claims about the text or about your subject itself?

Use the sample below as a model for the annotations you write for your five sources. Note that the example includes a summary of the source, an assessment of the usefulness of the source in providing information about the topic, and a reflection on how the source might be used to help inform research.

Book Entry

Author(s). <u>Title of Book.</u> Place of Publication: Publisher, Year of Publication: pages.

Golden, John. <u>Reading in the Reel World: Teaching Documentaries and Other Nonfiction Texts</u>. Urbana, IL: National Council of Teachers of English, 2006.

> The author provides a rationale as well as concrete lesson plans for teaching documentary film and narrative modes in the high school classroom. An explanation of modes and styles as well as practical guidelines for investigating them in a high school language arts class are included. This source challenges teachers to incorporate documentary film into their curriculum. The suggestions are accessible to teachers from different contexts and provide a valuable teaching tool.

Web Site Entry

Author(s). <u>Name of Page.</u> Date of Posting/Revision. Name of institution/organization affiliated with the site. Date of access <electronic address>.

Spader, Corrine. <u>Undergraduate Guide to MLA Format.</u> 10 Dec. 2003. Red Tide University. 15 Nov. 2004 <http://www.redtide.edu>.

> The author gives a comprehensive discussion of the MLA format and provides numerous examples of entries for readers to model. This source is an invaluable tool for the novice researcher as it provides step-by-step explanations. The examples of electronic forms are especially helpful when documenting sources from the Internet.

Examining How an Issue Is Presented in Media Texts

SUGGESTED LEARNING STRATEGIES: Discussion Groups, Drafting, Self-Editing/Peer Editing, Sharing and Responding

Assignment

Your assignment is to write an argumentative essay asserting a particular critical interpretation of an "event" using evidence from at least five of the texts you have gathered alone and with your group members to support your argument. As needed, conduct additional research to gain multiple perspectives on the topic. Refer to the information on page 318 as you evaluate both secondary and primary sources and the information you have collected for validity, reliability, and relevance to your topic.

Steps:

Planning

1. Based on your research plan, you have been collecting articles and other resources about a topic that you and your group will be presenting to the class. This individual assignment asks you to show your insights regarding your topic by using quotes and observations from your sources to present a particular critical interpretation of the issue. Evaluate the validity, relevance, and reliability of the information you have collected. Discard information and sources you deem unreliable.

2. In preparation for writing the essay, reread each text critically, marking it for evidence that links to the critical interpretation you are making. Consider both the article's content and the rhetoric the writer uses to discuss the subject. Identify quotations to use in your essay, and write commentary about the quotations you plan to use. Incorporate the quotes and commentary into your essay.

Drafting/Preparing

3. Define your thesis, paying careful attention to how your own reaction to your "event"or issue is influencing your response to the texts you are analyzing. Your thesis may be stated as a direct response to the guiding question you have used throughout your research.

4. Select an organizational pattern that reveals your perspective and presents accurate information that is relevant to your central thesis and your supporting concepts and themes. As you draft your essay, analyze the multiple views and evidence from your research. Identify the views that support your thesis, and accurately quote and cite evidence from those sources. Anticipate and respond to contradictory views and information. Analyze opposing viewpoints and their supporting evidence, and acknowledge them as part of your counter-argument. Anticipate readers' questions about your thesis, evidence, and counter-argument and provide a response. Incorporate a variety of rhetorical strategies to argue for your thesis. Conclude your essay with an effective summary and call to action.

Revising/Presenting

5. Within your group, review one another's essays using the Peer Review guidelines on the next page. As you read the essays of your peers, focus on each writer's rhetoric and his or her use of textual evidence as support for the interpretive claims made in the essay.

6. Proofread and edit your paper for final publication. Refer to a style manual to document sources and format your paper appropriately.

In preparation for receiving a peer review, use the questions below to self-evaluate your own work. You might also review the scoring guide to ensure that you are fully addressing the expectations for the assignment.

Peer Review

At various stages in the writing process, you have benefited from interacting with your peers, who have given feedback on your guiding question for research and your prewriting. Now you will receive feedback on the first draft of your argumentative essay, and you will provide feedback on the essays written by your peers. As you read one of your classmates' essay drafts, you will serve as a peer reviewer. Your classmate will use the feedback you provide to revise his or her thoughts and compose a second draft of the essay. Similarly, you will be provided with feedback on your draft from several classmates. Please read carefully and be specific in your response as you review your peer's work. Suggestions to guide your responses are provided.

Guide for Peer Review

1. What is the writer's thesis?

2. How well has the writer developed the thesis?

3. What suggestions would you make to improve the argumentative essay? Be specific.

4. What evidence is there that the material was carefully chosen?

5. How has the writer made the topic understandable to the reader?

6. Is the material/information in the essay well documented? Explain.

7. What evidence is there that the writer is dealing with a specific critical perspective?

SCORING GUIDE

Scoring Criteria	Exemplary	Proficient	Emerging
Ideas	The essay effectively combines the sources and the writer's position to argue how a particular lens can be used to interpret a single issue or controversy in multiple texts. The cohesive, sustained argument includes: • a thesis that contextualizes the issue and presents the critical lens; • support and commentary that convincingly links the citation of a variety of source material to a demonstration of the writer's position; • a conclusion that goes beyond a summary of the thesis by suggesting the larger significance of the writer's position in understanding the issue.	The essay adequately combines the sources and the writer's position to argue how a particular lens can be used to interpret a single issue or controversy in multiple texts. The sound argument includes: • a straightforwad thesis that briefly contextualizes the issue and identifies the critical lens; • support and commentary that clearly connects the various source material to the writer's position; • a conclusion that is logical yet may be somewhat repetitive of the thesis.	The essay tries to combine the sources and the writer's position yet inadequately argues how a particular lens can be used to interpret a single issue or controversy in multiple texts. The attempted argument includes: • a weak thesis or one that is lost in a summary of sources; • support that paraphrases source material with no commentary or analysis linking to the writer's position; sources may be misunderstood; • a conclusion that returns directly to the attempted thesis or is missing.
Organization	The essay's organization aptly reinforces the ideas of the argument. Ideas move smoothly and logically with successful use of transitions enhancing the essay's coherence.	The essay's clear organization supports the ideas of the argument. Ideas are easy to follow. Transitions are used to move between ideas.	The essay's lack of organization detracts from the argument, making the ideas difficult to follow. It may lack transitions and jump too rapidly between ideas.
Use of Language	The essay demonstrates a mature style that advances the writer's ideas. Precise diction and skillful use of syntax help to create a convincing voice. Standard writing conventions (including spelling and accurate citation of sources) are followed.	The essay demonstrates a style that adequately supports the writer's ideas. Logical diction and syntax help to create a suitable voice. Standard writing conventions (including spelling and accurate citation of sources) are followed; errors do not seriously impede readability.	The essay demonstrates a limited style that ineffectively supports the writer's ideas. Lapses in diction or syntax may not allow a suitable voice to sustain throughout the essay. Errors in spelling and standard writing conventions impede readability and sources may be inaccurately cited.

SCORING GUIDE

Scoring Criteria	Exemplary	Proficient	Emerging
Evidence of Writing Process	The essay demonstrates thoughtful planning (including an extensive annotated bibliography), significant revision, and careful editing in preparing a publishable draft.	The essay demonstrates adequate planning (including a complete annotated bibliography), revision, and editing in preparing a publishable draft.	The essay lacks evidence of planning (annotated bibliography may be incomplete or missing), revision, and/or editing. The draft is not ready for publication.
Additional Criteria			

Comments:

Learning Focus:

Creating Perspectives

Twelve words are casually referenced in a concert review. The words are picked up by a blog half way around the world that encourages its readers to call radio stations demanding the offender's music be pulled from rotation. Within days, the result is a firestorm of backlash against the performers, including CD burnings, plummeting sales, a ban from radio play by a major radio conglomeration, and even death threats. Three years of soul searching later, the band rises like a phoenix from the ashes, releasing a critically hailed and briskly selling CD and garnering major awards from the music industry. True story. Sounds like a movie, though, doesn't it? And, indeed, it became one in the documentary, *Shut Up and Sing*.

Documentaries present powerful accounts of stories such as this one, but there are many other **media channels** that are growing increasingly popular for the way they record and present "true" stories. In the first part of this unit, you were exposed to many such **channels: documentary film, television, investigative journalism, television interviews, online magazines and Web sites, radio newscasts, and various traditional print genres.** Analyzing these media channels is only one half of understanding how media impacts our understanding of issues and information. Becoming a producer of one of these media texts, using the **conventions** of a selected **media channel** to present an exposé on a controversial subject is another way to understand the power of media presentations. By presenting ideas via a media production, you exercise the power to influence how your viewers understand a subject. In this way, you will be responsible for creating others' perspective on the truth as you think it should be seen.

That Sounds Just Right

SUGGESTED LEARNING STRATEGIES: Quickwrite, Think-Pair-Share, SOAPSTone, Close Reading, Graphic Organizer

You will be watching a film clip twice. The first time you will view it without sound, and the second time the visuals will be accompanied by the sound track.

1. As you watch the film clip, make a list of the visual images you see.

2. Based on these images, what do you think the tone of this scene is? Brainstorm some possible tone words. Choose the one that seems to fit best, then describe what kind of music you would expect to hear that would support this tone.

3. As you watch the clip a second time, make a descriptive list of all sound elements in the scene (music, dialogue, background sounds, etc.).

4. How has the addition of the sound elements affected the tone of the scene? How is the resulting tone similar to or different from what you expected?

Quickwrite: After closely analyzing the musical and visual elements of the scene, write a paragraph on your own paper beginning with the following stem: In the opening scene of *(film title)* _____ the director establishes a _____ tone in order to suggest _____ . Develop the paragraph with specific examples from both the sounds and images in the scene.

That Sounds Just Right

Planning a Documentary Media Text

Long before you actually develop your documentary, you have to begin thinking about some of the basic components of a good plan. You need to focus on your topic or issue, your audience, and why you chose this particular topic or issue. Below are some questions you should ask and answer before you go further in planning your documentary.

- **Topic/Issue** What is your topic/issue? What event, person, text, conflict, etc., are you focusing on? What critical lenses are you using to illuminate that subject for your audience? What messages or interpretation of the topic/issues do you wish to convey?

- **Purpose** What is your purpose? What do you want your audience to think/feel/know/do as a result of viewing your text?

- **Audience** Decide on an audience to whom you'd like to address your argument. You must settle on an identifiable audience that you expect will have some interest in your topic. Your audience may not be "my teacher" or the other students in your class.

- **Tone** What tone will best help you achieve your desired purpose? What specific music, visual text, voice-over narrative, sound effects, etc., could you use to advance your tone? What images will best evoke the desired response in your viewers?

- **Speaker** Who are you as the speaker? Think about the various documentary modes: will you be observational, expository, interactive, or reflexive in your text? To what extent? Why?

- **Occasion** What is the occasion for your media text? Are you developing it in response to an incident or event, or to celebrate or acknowledge a situation? Would this be screened in a theater or shown on a television channel of some kind?

Turning Facts into Narrative

SUGGESTED LEARNING STRATEGIES: Discussion Groups,
Brainstorming, Rereading, Graphic Organizer

Developing Your Media Text

Working in groups, you have generated several questions to guide your investigation of media and media channels. Now you're ready to create a central question on a topic and write thesis statements relating to the question.

Revisiting Your Guiding Questions: Review the guiding questions you previously generated as a group, and write the questions each of you used in the space below.

Defining a Common Question: Work together to define a common guiding question. The goal is to identify a question that is broad enough to be an umbrella under which each of your individual questions falls.

Writing Thesis Statements: Once you have your central question, write thesis statements that answer the questions for each of the lenses that will be used by members of your group.

Turning Facts into Narrative

© 2011 College Board. All rights reserved.

ACADEMIC VOCABULARY

Media, collectively, refers to the organizations that communicate information in a public way. A **media channel** is one method an organization uses to communicate, such as radio, television, Internet, newspaper, magazine.

Identifying Characters and Roles: Using your collective research on your issue, decide who will be your "main characters." These may be actual people who were involved in or influenced by the event, or they may be composite characters that represent particular points of view. Decide in your group who will play each character as well as who will be the narrator/host/interviewer, if one or more will be included. Write the roles and responsibilities here.

Choosing a Media Channel and Identifying Its Conventions: Brainstorm a list of **media channels** that you might use to present your various points of view. Choose the option you think would best allow your group to explore your subject. Then make a list of typical structural and stylistic conventions of that channel. You might dissect a professional model to help you identify key features to emulate.

Nonfiction Film Treatment

Our thesis:

Our media channel/format:

Conventions of this format:

What will the audience see? What images/"characters" will be shown? What mode(s) will be used? What angles, framing, composition, etc., will be used to show our subjects?	**What will the audience hear?** (include dialogue/voice-over, music, diegetic sounds, etc.). What tone are we striving for?	**What will the audience think/feel?** What perspective will each lens provide? What will they learn about the subject? What will they believe/know after each segment?

Voir Dire: Facing a Jury of Your Peers

SUGGESTED LEARNING STRATEGIES: Double-Entry Journal,
Summarizing/Paraphrasing, Quickwrite

WORD CONNECTIONS

Voir dire is derived from the Anglo French and means "to speak the truth."

Juror Ballot

You will view a documentary provided by your teacher, and will complete a Juror Ballot as a **model of your task** as an audience member for your peers' media presentation. Your task as a juror is to assess the quality of the argumentative text you're viewing and the degree to which you find it successful in reaching the intended audience.

Section 1: Dialectical Journal

As you encounter evidence of the critical perspective(s) the presenter (in this case, the director) uses, make a note of what you see or hear and record a response using the same reading skills that you would normally bring to bear on a written text.

Critical Perspective(s)

Provide evidence based on what you see or hear.	Your response

Section 2: Argumentative Thesis

Paraphrase the group's thesis statement. If there are more than one, be sure to include each.

Section 3: Quickwrite

After viewing the film, respond with your overall impressions in the form of a quickwrite, with an emphasis on providing due praise for the parts of the presentation that are done well.

Section 4: Evaluating the Text

For each of the areas listed below, discuss the choices made by the group. How effective were these choices at supporting the presentation of their argument to their target audience?

Mode(s)

Style and Conventions

Tone (images and sound)

Section 5: Suggestions for Improvement

Make suggestions for improvement of the presentation's content.

Creating a Media Text

SUGGESTED LEARNING STRATEGIES: Visualizing, Mapping,
Self-Editing/Peer Editing, Sketching, Sharing and Responding,
Discussion Groups, Rehearsal

Assignment

Your assignment is to create a documentary text in a media channel of your choice
(TV news magazine, documentary film, news broadcast, pod cast, etc.) in which
you transform the information you gathered into an argument concerning the
topic or issue you have chosen. Your presentation should last 10 to 15 minutes.
It may be recorded or presented live. Each group member will take on a role (or
roles), research that role, and use the research to write his or her portion of the
presentation. Refer to page 318 as you evaluate both primary and secondary sources
and your researched information for validity, reliability, and relevance to your topic.

Steps:

1. With your film treatment as a general guide, use the information and quotations
   you have gathered from your research and your individual essays to create a
   script for your text. Each person will be responsible for creating the voice of his
   or her character(s). Keep in mind the conventions of the documentary model you
   have selected as you draft your script.

2. Much of what you write will be based on the information you have gathered
   from your research. Summarize, paraphrase, and quote information as needed.
   Document sources in the script by using footnotes or endnotes according
   to format guidelines provided by your teacher. Synthesize information from
   multiple points of view, and use that information as you write your script and
   design your multimedia presentation. Remember to collect and use appropriate
   graphics and other images to support your argument.

3. Edit your individual portions into a coherent script for the program.

4. As a group, you must submit a written annotated bibliography with your
   presentation. Your annotated bibliography will be a list of citations of books,
   articles, and documents your group consulted. Each citation should be followed
   by an annotation that briefly describes the source, including what lens it links to,
   how it frames the event, and how you are using it in your script/performance.

5. Depending on the approach you have chosen (live or recorded), rehearse or film
   your performance. If filming, factor in time for editing, which is generally far
   more time-consuming than the filming itself.

6. Present your documentary media text to the class. You will evaluate, and be
   evaluated by, a jury of your peers using the Juror Ballots.

7. You will complete a self-reflection using the feedback provided in the juror
   ballots you receive.

⟋**TECHNOLOGY TIP** Use available technology to help you create your media text. You
may want to reserve time in the computer lab. If needed, ask for help in learning
to use presentation software, video equipment, or graphics programs.

Juror Ballot

As you view a group's documentary media presentation, you will complete this Juror Ballot. Your task as a juror is to assess the quality of the media text you're viewing and the degree to which you find it successful in reaching the intended audience.

Section 1: Dialectical Journal

As you encounter evidence of the critical perspective(s) the presenter (in this case, the director) uses, make a note of what you see or hear and record a response using the same reading skills that you would normally bring to bear on a written text.

Critical Perspective(s)

Provide evidence based on what you see or hear.	Your response

Section 2: Argumentative Thesis

Paraphrase the group's thesis statement. If there are more than one, be sure to include each.

Section 3: Quickwrite

After viewing the film, respond with your overall impressions in the form of a quickwrite, with an emphasis on providing due praise for the parts of the presentation that are done well.

Section 4: Evaluating the Text

For each of the areas listed below, discuss the choices made by the group. How effective were these choices at supporting the presentation of their argument to their target audience?

Mode(s)

Style and Conventions

Tone (images and sound)

Section 5: Suggestions for Improvement

Make suggestions for improvement of the content of the documentary media text or presentation.

Guided Self-Reflection

Based on the feedback you received from your peers, to what extent did you succeed in presenting your argument persuasively? Quote peer comments to support your assessment.

What could you revise about your presentation to improve its effectiveness? Be specific.

How has your engagement with nonfiction media in this unit affected your understanding of how it functions? Do you approach reading/viewing any differently now? Explain.

How has your study of critical theory this year impacted the way you view literature, media, and the world around you? Explain.

SCORING GUIDE

Scoring Criteria	Exemplary	Proficient	Emerging
Preparatory Texts	The scripts and annotated bibliography reveal an insightful analysis and mature understanding of the event.	The scripts and annotated bibliography demonstrate careful analysis and clear understanding of the event.	The scripts and annotated bibliography reveal a limited analysis and understanding of the event.
Performance	The documentary demonstrates thorough investigation, insightful application of the lenses, and thoughtful understanding of the event. Its organizational structure is precisely appropriate to the media channel and enhances the intended message to the audience. Participants demonstrate a polished performance that creates focus and maintains energy.	The documentary demonstrates adequate investigation, application of the lenses, and clear understanding of the event. Its organizational structure is appropriate to the media channel and makes clear the intended message to the audience. Participants demonstrate an organized performance that creates coherence.	The documentary demonstrates inadequate investigation and/or misunderstanding of the lenses or how they apply to the event. Its organizational structure is inappropriate to the media channel and may convey an unclear message to the audience. Participants demonstrate a disorganized performance.
Evidence of Collaboration	Throughout the entire process of planning and presenting, the group cooperates and works successfully to maintain purpose and to achieve goals. Equal sharing of responsibility is evident.	Throughout the process of planning and presenting, the group works together adequately to maintain purpose and achieve goals. Sharing of responsibility is mostly balanced.	Throughout the process of planning and presenting, the group's cooperation is lacking, which impedes their ability to maintain a purpose or achieve goals. Responsibilities may not be equally divided.

SCORING GUIDE

Scoring Criteria	Exemplary	Proficient	Emerging
Reflective Text	The reflective text demonstrates a thorough and detailed analysis of the entire process including planning, rehearsing, and performing/ recording the scene. It includes insightful commentary based on the audience's evaluation of the final performance.	The reflective text demonstrates adequate analysis of the process of planning, rehearsing, and performing/ recording the scene. It includes commentary based on the audience's evaluation of the final performance.	The reflective text demonstrates inadequate analysis of the process of planning, rehearsing, and performing/recording the scene. Commentary based on the audience's evaluation of the final performance may be weak or missing. Analysis and evaluation may be replaced by summary.
Additional Criteria			

Comments:

Timed Writing

Critical Perspectives Timed Writing

Compose an expository essay in response to the following writing prompt. Take a moment to prewrite and plan your essay before beginning. Your essay will be assessed as a first draft with an emphasis on the development of your ideas. You will have 50 minutes to draft your essay.

Writing Prompt: Consider your favorite film or television program. How are your perceptions, opinions, conclusions, or enjoyment of this film or program altered when you apply different critical perspectives? Be sure to identify the critical perspectives in your response. Use rhetorical devices as needed to convey meaning to your readers.

Reflection

An important aspect of growing as a learner is to take the time to reflect. It is important to take into account where you have been, what you have accomplished, what helped you to learn, and how you will apply your new knowledge in the future. Use the following process to record your thinking and to identify evidence of your learning.

Thinking about Concepts

1. Using specific examples from this unit, respond to the Essential Questions:

    • How do media sources impact our understanding of the truth and significance of an issue?

    • How can media texts be constructed to support an agenda or interpretation?

2. Consider the new academic vocabulary from this unit (**Media Channel**) as well as academic vocabulary from previous units and select 2–3 terms of which your understanding has grown. For each term, answer the following questions:

    • What was your understanding of the word prior to the unit?

    • How has your understanding of the word evolved throughout the unit?

    • How will you apply your understanding in the future?

Thinking about Connections

3. Review the activities and products (artifacts) you created. Choose those that most reflect your growth or increase in understanding.

4. For each artifact that you choose, record, respond to, and reflect on your thinking and understanding, using the following questions as a guide:

    a. What skill/knowledge does this artifact reflect, and how did you learn this skill/knowledge?

    b. How did your understanding of the power of language expand through your engagement with this artifact?

    c. How will you apply this skill or knowledge in the future?

5. Create this reflection as Portfolio pages—one for each artifact you choose. Use the model in the box for your headings and commentary on questions.

Thinking About Thinking

Portfolio Entry

Concept:

Description of Artifact:

Commentary on Questions:

During the year, you will be asked to review and apply the following literary theories to the works you study and create. You may use this page as a reference for definitions, characteristics, and examples of different literary perspectives. This list is not intended to be an exhaustive representation of these complex theoretical perspectives, but rather a brief introduction. Your teacher may expect you to do further research on one or more of these literary theories.

Archetypal Criticism

Archetypes are universal symbols—images, characters, motifs, or patterns that recur in the myths, dreams, oral traditions, songs, literature, and other texts of peoples widely separated by time and place. Archetypal criticism deals with the similarities of these patterns in the literature of widely diverse cultures. For example, most cultures have stories that present the hero's journey.

Some common assumptions in the use of Archetypal Criticism are:

▶ Certain images recur in texts from diverse cultures that share a common interpretation—water, sun, colors, the tree, settings such as the garden, the desert.

▶ Certain characters recur—the hero, the trickster, the great mother, the wise old man, the prodigal son.

▶ Certain motifs and patterns recur—creation stories, the quest, voyage to the underworld, journey, and initiation.

Historical Criticism

While acknowledging the importance of the literary text, the Historical approach recognizes the significance of historical information in interpreting literature. This perspective assumes that texts both influence and are influenced by the times in which they were created. For example, an interpretation of *Things Fall Apart* by Chinua Achebe may be enhanced by an understanding of the effects of colonialism in present-day African life.

Some common assumptions in the use of Historical Criticism are:

▶ A text cannot be separated from its historical context, which is a web of social, cultural, personal, and political factors.

▶ An understanding of a text is enhanced by the study of beliefs and artifacts such as diaries, films, paintings, and letters in existence when the text was created.

Feminist Criticism

Feminist interpretation focuses on relationships between genders. It examines the patterns of thought, behavior, values, enfranchisement, and power in relations between and within the sexes. A feminist reading of *Their Eyes Were Watching God*, for example, may examine the novel as an example of a heroine's journey.

Some common assumptions in the use of Feminist Criticism are:

▶ A pervasively patriarchal society conveys the notion of male dominance through the images of women in its texts.

▶ Many literary texts lack complex female figures and deem the female reader as an outsider or require her to assume male values in terms of perception, feelings, and actions.

▶ Issues of gender and sexuality are central to artistic expression.

▶ Fictional portrayals of female characters often reflect and create stereotypical social and political attitudes toward women.

▶ Texts authored by women may have different viewpoints than texts authored by men.

Marxist Criticism

Marxist criticism asserts that economics provides the foundation for all social, political, and ideological reality. The presence of economic inequalities in a power structure drives history and influences differences in religion, race, ethnicity, and gender. For example, status in the community of *Their Eyes Were Watching God* can be examined from an economic point of view.

Some common assumptions in the use of Marxist Criticism are:

▶ All aspects of humanity are based on the struggle for economic power.

▶ The basic struggle in human society is between the haves and the have-nots.

Reader Response Criticism

Reader Response criticism focuses on a reader's active engagement with a piece of print or nonprint text. The reader's response to any text is shaded by the reader's own experiences, social ethics, moral values, and general views of the world. For example, the response to *To Kill a Mockingbird* may depend on the reader's sense of outrage on behalf of someone unjustly accused of a crime.

Some common assumptions in the use of Reader Response Criticism are:

▶ When encountering a text, the reader not only seeks the meaning that inherently lies within the text, but also creates meaning from a personal interaction with the text.

▶ It is important to the discussion of the text to take into account the reader as well as the reading situation.

▶ Different readers formulate different acceptable interpretations because a text allows for a range of acceptable interpretations for which textual support is available.

Cultural Criticism

Cultural criticism examines how differing religious beliefs, ethnicities, class identifications, political beliefs, and individual viewpoints affect how texts are created and interpreted. What it means to be a part of—or excluded from—a specific group contributes to and impacts our understanding of texts in relation to culture. For example, in *Things Fall Apart*, the way the missionaries treat the natives suggests they see the native culture as inferior.

Some common assumptions in the use of Cultural Criticism are:

▶ Ethnicity, religious beliefs, social class, and so on are crucial components in formulating plausible interpretations of text.

▶ While the emphasis is on diversity of approach and subject matter, Cultural criticism is not the only means of understanding ourselves and our art.

▶ An examination or exploration of the relationship between dominant cultures and the dominated is essential.

Grammar Handbook

Part 1: Using Pronouns Clearly

Because a pronoun REFERS BACK to a noun or TAKES THE PLACE OF that noun, you have to use the correct pronoun so that your reader clearly understands which noun your pronoun is referring to. Therefore, pronouns should:

1. Agree in number

If the pronoun takes the place of a singular noun, you have to use a singular pronoun.

> If a student parks a car on campus, he or she has to buy a parking sticker.
> (**NOT:** If a student parks a car on campus, they have to buy a parking sticker.)

Remember: the words **everybody, anybody, anyone, each, neither, nobody, someone, a person**, etc. are singular and take singular pronouns.

> Everybody ought to do his or her best. (NOT: their best)
> Neither of the girls brought her umbrella. (NOT: their umbrellas)

NOTE: Many people find the construction "his or her" wordy, so if it is possible to use a plural noun as your antecedent so that you can use "they" as your pronoun, it may be wise to do so. If you do use a singular noun and the context makes the gender clear, then it is permissible to use just "his" or "her" rather than "his or her."

2. Agree in person

If you are writing in the "first person" (I), don't confuse your reader by switching to the "second person" (you) or "third person" (he, she, they, it, etc.). Similarly, if you are using the "second person," don't switch to "first" or "third."

> When a person comes to class, he or she should have his or her homework ready.
> (**NOT:** When a person comes to class, you should have your homework ready.)

3. Refer clearly to a specific noun.

Don't be vague or ambiguous.

> **NOT:** Although the motorcycle hit the tree, it was not damaged. (Is "it" the motorcycle or the tree?)
> **NOT:** I don't think they should show violence on TV. (Who are "they"?)
> **NOT:** Vacation is coming soon, which is nice. (What is nice, the vacation or the fact that it is coming soon?)
> **NOT:** George worked in a national forest last summer. This may be his life's work. (What word does "this" refer to?)
> **NOT:** If you put this sheet in your notebook, you can refer to it. (What does "it" refer to, the sheet or your notebook?)

Pronoun Case

Pronoun case is really a very simple matter. There are three cases.

- Subjective case: pronouns used as subject.
- Objective case: pronouns used as objects of verbs or prepositions.
- Possessive case: pronouns which express ownership.

Pronouns as Subjects	Pronouns as Objects	Pronouns that show Possession
I	me	my (mine)
you	you	your (yours)
he, she, it	him, her, it	his, her (hers), it (its)
we	us	our (ours)
they	them	their (theirs)
who	whom	whose

The pronouns **this, that, these, those,** and **which** do not change form.

Some problems of case:

1. **In compound structures, where there are two pronouns or a noun and a pronoun, drop the other noun for a moment. Then you can see which case you want.**

   Not: Bob and me travel a good deal.
   (Would you say, "me travel"?)
   Not: He gave the flowers to Jane and I.
   (Would you say, "he gave the flowers to I"?)
   Not: Us men like the coach.
   (Would you say, "us like the coach"?)

2. **In comparisons. Comparisons usually follow than or as:**

   He is taller than I (am tall).
   This helps you as much as (it helps) me.
   She is as noisy as I (am).

Comparisons are really shorthand sentences which usually omit words, such as those in the parentheses in the sentences above. If you complete the comparison in your head, you can choose the correct case for the pronoun.

   Not: He is taller than me.
   (Would you say, "than me am tall"?)

3. **In formal and semiformal writing:**

Use the subjective form after a form of the verb to be.

   Formal: It is I.
   Informal: It is me.

Use whom in the objective case.

   Formal: To whom am I talking?
   Informal: Who am I talking to?

Part 2: Appositives

An appositive is a noun or pronoun — often with modifiers — set beside another noun or pronoun to explain or identify it. Here are some examples of appositives (the **noun or pronoun will be in blue**, the **appositive will be in boldface**).

> Your friend **Bill** is in trouble.
>
> My brother's car, **a sporty red convertible with bucket seats**, is the envy of my friends.
>
> The chief surgeon, **an expert in organ-transplant procedures**, took her nephew on a hospital tour.

An appositive phrase usually follows the word it explains or identifies, but it may also precede it.

> **A bold innovator**, Wassily Kadinsky is known for his colorful abstract paintings.
>
> **The first state to ratify the U. S. Constitution**, Delaware is rich in history.
>
> **A beautiful collie**, Skip was my favorite dog.

Punctuation of Appositives

In some cases, the noun being explained is too general without the appositive; the information is essential to the meaning of the sentence. When this is the case, do not place commas around the appositive; just leave it alone. If the sentence would be clear and complete without the appositive, then commas are necessary; place one before and one after the appositive. Here are some examples.

> The popular US president **John Kennedy** was known for his eloquent and inspirational speeches.

Here we do not put commas around the appositive, because it is essential information. Without the appositive, the sentence would be, "The popular US president was known for his eloquent and inspirational speeches." We wouldn't know which president was being referred to.

> John Kennedy, **the popular US president**, was known for his eloquent and inspirational speeches.

Here we put commas around the appositive because it is not essential information. Without the appositive, the sentence would be, "John Kennedy was known for his eloquent and inspirational speeches." We still know who the subject of the sentence is without the appositive.

Part 3: What is the Difference Between Adjectives and Adverbs?

The Basic Rules: Adjectives

Adjectives modify nouns. To modify means to change in some way. For example:

- "I ate a meal." *Meal* is a noun. We don't know what kind of meal; all we know is that someone ate a meal.
- "I ate an enormous lunch." *Lunch* is a noun, and *enormous* is an adjective that modifies it. It tells us what kind of meal the person ate.

Adjectives usually answer one of a few different questions: "What kind?" or "Which?" or "How many?" For example:

- "The *tall* girl is riding a *new* bike." *Tall* tells us which girl we're talking about. *New* tells us what kind of bike we're talking about.
- "The *tough* professor gave us the *final* exam." *Tough* tells us what kind of professor we're talking about. *Final* tells us which exam we're talking about.
- "*Fifteen* students passed the midterm exam; *twelve* students passed the final exam." *Fifteen* and *twelve* both tell us how many students; *midterm* and *final* both tell us which exam.

So, generally speaking, adjectives answer the following questions: Which? What kind of? How many?

The Basic Rules: Adverbs

Adverbs modify verbs, adjectives, and other adverbs. (You can recognize adverbs easily because many of them are formed by adding -ly to an adjective, though that is not always the case.) The most common question that adverbs answer is **how.**

Let's look at verbs first.

- "She sang *beautifully.*" *Beautifully* is an adverb that modifies *sang.* It tells us **how** she sang.
- "The cellist played *carelessly.*" *Carelessly* is an adverb that modifies *played.* It tells us **how** the cellist played.

Adverbs also modify adjectives and other adverbs.

- "That woman is *extremely* nice." *Nice* is an adjective that modifies the noun *woman. Extremely* is an adverb that modifies *nice;* it tells us **how** nice she is. **How** nice is she? She's extremely nice.
- "It was a *terribly* hot afternoon." *Hot* is an adjective that modifies the noun *afternoon. Terribly* is an adverb that modifies the adjective *hot.* **How** hot is it? Terribly hot.

So, generally speaking, adverbs answer the question **how.** (They can also answer the questions **when**, **where**, and **why.**)

Part 4: Verbals

Gerunds

A gerund is a verbal that ends in *-ing* and functions as a noun. The term *verbal* indicates that a gerund, like the other two kinds of verbals, is based on a verb and therefore expresses action or a state of being. However, since a gerund functions as a noun, it occupies some positions in a sentence that a noun ordinarily would, for example: subject, direct object, subject complement, and object of preposition.

Gerund as subject:

- Traveling might satisfy your desire for new experiences. (**Traveling** is the gerund.)
- The study abroad program might satisfy your desire for new experiences. (The gerund has been removed.)

Gerund as direct object:

- They do not appreciate my singing. (The gerund is **singing**.)
- They do not appreciate my assistance. (The gerund has been removed)

Gerund as subject complement:

- My cat's favorite activity is sleeping. (The gerund is **sleeping**.)
- My cat's favorite food is salmon. (The gerund has been removed.)

Gerund as object of preposition:

- The police arrested him for speeding. (The gerund is **speeding**.)
- The police arrested him for criminal activity. (The gerund has been removed.)

A Gerund Phrase is a group of words consisting of a gerund and the modifier(s) and/or (pro)noun(s) or noun phrase(s) that function as the direct object(s), indirect object(s), or complement(s) of the action or state expressed in the gerund, such as:

The gerund phrase functions as the subject of the sentence.

Finding a needle in a haystack would be easier than what we're trying to do.

Finding (gerund) **a needle** (direct object of action expressed in gerund) **in a haystack** (prepositional phrase as adverb)

The gerund phrase functions as the direct object of the verb *appreciate*.

I hope that you appreciate **my** offering you *this opportunity*.

my (possessive pronoun adjective form, modifying the gerund)
offering (gerund)
you (indirect object of action expressed in gerund)
this opportunity (direct object of action expressed in gerund)

The gerund phrase functions as the subject complement.

Ned's favorite tactic has been **lying to** his constituents.

lying to (gerund)
his constituents (direct object of action expressed in gerund)

The gerund phrase functions as the object of the preposition *for*.

You might get in trouble for **faking** an illness *to avoid work*.

faking (gerund)
an illness (direct object of action expressed in gerund)
to avoid work (infinitive phrase as adverb)

The gerund phrase functions as the subject of the sentence.

Being the boss made Jeff feel uneasy.

Being (gerund)
the boss (subject complement for Jeff, via state of being expressed in gerund)

Punctuation
A gerund virtually never requires any punctuation with it.

Points to remember:
1. A gerund is a verbal ending in -ing that is used as a noun.
2. A gerund phrase consists of a gerund plus modifier(s), object(s), and/or complement(s).
3. Gerunds and gerund phrases virtually never require punctuation.

Participles
A participle is a verbal that is used as an adjective and most often ends in -ing or -ed. The term *verbal* indicates that a participle, like the other two kinds of verbals, is based on a verb and therefore expresses action or a state of being. However, since they function as adjectives, participles modify nouns or pronouns. There are two types of participles: present participles and past participles. Present participles end in -ing. Past participles end in -ed, -en, -d, -t, or -n, as in the words *asked*, *eaten*, *saved*, *dealt*, and *seen*.

- The *crying* baby had a wet diaper.
- *Shaken*, he walked away from the *wrecked* car.
- The *burning* log fell off the fire.
- *Smiling*, she hugged the *panting* dog.

A participial phrase is a group of words consisting of a participle and the modifier(s) and/or (pro)noun(s) or noun phrase(s) that function as the direct object(s), indirect object(s), or complement(s) of the action or state expressed in the participle, such as:

Example: Removing his coat, Jack rushed to the river.

The participial phrase functions as an adjective modifying *Jack*.

Removing (participle)
his coat (direct object of action expressed in participle)

> **Example:** Delores noticed her cousin **walking** **along the shoreline**.

The participial phrase functions as an adjective modifying *cousin*.
walking (participle)
along the shoreline (prepositional phrase as adverb)

> **Example:** Children **introduced to** music <u>early</u> develop strong intellectual skills.

The participial phrase functions as an adjective modifying *children*.
introduced (to) (participle)
music (direct object of action expressed in participle)
<u>early</u> (adverb)

> **Example: Having been** a gymnast, Lynn knew the importance of exercise.

The participial phrase functions as an adjective modifying *Lynn*.
Having been (participle)
a gymnast (subject complement for Lynn, via state of being expressed in participle)

Placement: In order to prevent confusion, a participial phrase must be placed as close to the noun it modifies as possible, and the noun must be clearly stated.

- *Carrying a heavy pile of books,* his foot caught on a step.
- *Carrying a heavy pile of books,* he caught his foot on a step.

In the first sentence there is no clear indication of who or what is performing the action expressed in the participle carrying. Certainly foot can't be logically understood to function in this way. This situation is an example of a <u>dangling modifier</u> error since the modifier (the participial phrase) is not modifying any specific noun in the sentence and is thus left "dangling." Since a person must be doing the carrying for the sentence to make sense, a noun or pronoun that refers to a person must be in the place immediately after the participial phrase, as in the second sentence.

Punctuation: When a participial phrase begins a sentence, a comma should be placed after the phrase.

- *Arriving at the store,* I found that it was closed.
- *Washing and polishing the car,* Frank developed sore muscles.

If the participle or participial phrase comes in the middle of a sentence, it should be set off with commas only if the information is not essential to the meaning of the sentence.

- Sid, *watching an old movie,* drifted in and out of sleep.
- The church, *destroyed by a fire,* was never rebuilt.

Note that if the participial phrase is essential to the meaning of the sentence, no commas should be used:

- The student *earning the highest grade point average* will receive a special award.
- The guy *wearing the chicken costume* is my cousin.

If a participial phrase comes at the end of a sentence, a comma usually precedes the phrase if it modifies an earlier word in the sentence but not if the phrase directly follows the word it modifies.

- The local residents often saw Ken wandering through the streets.
  (The phrase modifies *Ken*, not *residents*.)
- Tom nervously watched the woman, alarmed by her silence.
  (The phrase modifies *Tom*, not *woman*.)

Points to remember

1. A participle is a verbal ending in *-ing* (present) or *-ed*, *-en*, *-d*, *-t*, or *-n* (past) that functions as an adjective, modifying a noun or pronoun.

2. A participial phrase consists of a participle plus modifier(s), object(s), and/or complement(s).

3. Participles and participial phrases must be placed as close to the nouns or pronouns they modify as possible, and those nouns or pronouns must be clearly stated.

4. A participial phrase is set off with commas when it:
   (a) comes at the beginning of a sentence
   (b) interrupts a sentence as a nonessential element
   (c) comes at the end of a sentence and is separated from the word it modifies.

Infinitives

An infinitive is a verbal consisting of the word *to* plus a verb (in its simplest "stem" form) and functioning as a noun, adjective, or adverb. The term *verbal* indicates that an infinitive, like the other two kinds of verbals, is based on a verb and therefore expresses action or a state of being. However, the infinitive may function as a subject, direct object, subject complement, adjective, or adverb in a sentence. Although an infinitive is easy to locate because of the *to* + verb form, deciding what function it has in a sentence can sometimes be confusing.

- *To wait* seemed foolish when decisive action was required. (subject)
- Everyone wanted *to go*. (direct object)
- His ambition is *to fly*. (subject complement)
- He lacked the strength *to resist*. (adjective)
- We must study *to learn*. (adverb)

Be sure not to confuse an infinitive—a verbal consisting of *to* plus a verb—with a prepositional phrase beginning with *to*, which consists of *to* plus a noun or pronoun and any modifiers.

- **Infinitives:** to fly, to draw, to become, to enter, to stand, to catch, to belong
- **Prepositional Phrases:** to him, to the committee, to my house, to the mountains, to us, to this address

An Infinitive Phrase is a group of words consisting of an infinitive and the modifier(s) and/or (pro)noun(s) or noun phrase(s) that function as the actor(s), direct object(s), indirect object(s), or complement(s) of the action or state expressed in the infinitive, such as:

We intended **to leave <u>early</u>**.

The infinitive phrase functions as the direct object of the verb *intended*.

to leave (infinitive)
<u>early</u> (adverb)

I have a paper **to write <u>before class</u>**.

The infinitive phrase functions as an adjective modifying *paper*.

to write (infinitive)
<u>before class</u> (prepositional phrase as adverb)

Phil agreed **to give <u>me</u> *a ride***.

The infinitive phrase functions as the direct object of the verb *agreed*.

to give (infinitive)
<u>me</u> (indirect object of action expressed in infinitive)
a ride (direct object of action expressed in infinitive)

They asked **me** to bring *some food*.

The infinitive phrase functions as the direct object of the verb *asked*.

> **me** (actor or "subject" of infinitive phrase)
> **to bring** (infinitive)
> *some food* (direct object of action expressed in infinitive)

Everyone wanted **Carol** to be <u>the captain</u> *of the team*.

The infinitive phrase functions as the direct object of the verb *wanted*.

> **Carol** (actor or "subject" of infinitive phrase)
> **to be** (infinitive)
> <u>the captain</u> (subject complement for Carol, via state of being expressed in infinitive)
> *of the team* (prepositional phrase as adjective)

Actors: In these last two examples the actor of the infinitive phrase could be roughly characterized as the "subject" of the action or state expressed in the infinitive. It is somewhat misleading to use the word *subject*, however, since an infinitive phrase is not a full clause with a subject and a finite verb. Also notice that when it is a pronoun, the actor appears in the objective case (*me*, not *I*, in the fourth example). Certain verbs, when they take an infinitive direct object, require an actor for the infinitive phrase; others can't have an actor. Still other verbs can go either way, as the charts below illustrate.

Verbs that take infinitive objects without actors:			
agree	begin	continue	decide
fail	hesitate	hope	intend
learn	neglect	offer	plan
prefer	pretend	promise	refuse
remember	start	try	

Examples:

- Most students *plan* to study.
- We *began* to learn.
- They *offered* to pay.
- They *neglected* to pay.
- She *promised* to return.

In all of these examples no actor can come between the italicized main (finite) verb and the infinitive direct-object phrase.

Verbs that take infinitive objects with actors:			
advise	allow	convince	remind
encourage	force	hire	teach
instruct	invite	permit	tell
implore	incite	appoint	order

Examples:

- He *reminded* me to buy milk.
- Their fathers *advise* them to study.
- She *forced* the defendant to admit the truth.
- You've *convinced* the director of the program to change her position.
- I *invite* you to consider the evidence.

In all of these examples an actor is required after the italicized main (finite) verb and before the infinitive direct-object phrase.

Verbs that use either pattern:				
ask	expect	(would) like	want	need

Examples:

- I *asked* to see the records.
- I *asked* him to show me the records.
- Trent *expected* his group to win.
- Trent *expected* to win.
- Brenda *likes* to drive fast.
- Brenda *likes* her friend to drive fast.

In all of these examples the italicized main verb can take an infinitive object with or without an actor.

Punctuation: If the infinitive is used as an adverb and is the beginning phrase in a sentence, it should be set off with a comma; otherwise, no punctuation is needed for an infinitive phrase.

- To buy a basket of flowers, John had to spend his last dollar.
- To improve your writing, you must consider your purpose and audience.

Points to remember:

1. An infinitive is a verbal consisting of the word *to* plus a verb; it may be used as a noun, adjective, or adverb.
2. An infinitive phrase consists of an infinitive plus modifier(s), object(s), complement(s), and/or actor(s).
3. An infinitive phrase requires a comma only if it is used as an adverb at the beginning of a sentence.

Split infinitives

Split infinitives occur when additional words are included between *to* and the verb in an infinitive. Many readers find a single adverb splitting the infinitive to be acceptable, but this practice should be avoided in formal writing.

Examples:

- I like *to* on a nice day *walk* in the woods. (unacceptable)
  On a nice day, I like *to walk* in the woods. (revised)
- I needed *to* quickly *gather* my personal possessions. (acceptable in informal contexts)
  I needed *to gather* my personal possessions quickly. (revised for formal contexts)

Part 5: Prepositions for Time, Place, and Introducing Objects

One point in time

On is used with days:

- I will see you **on** Monday.
- The week begins **on** Sunday.

At is used with noon, night, midnight, and with the time of day:

- My plane leaves **at** noon.
- The movie starts **at** 6 p.m.

In is used with other parts of the day, with months, with years, with seasons:

- He likes to read **in** the afternoon.
- The days are long **in** August.
- The book was published **in** 1999.
- The flowers will bloom **in** spring.

Extended time

To express extended time, English uses the following prepositions: **since, for, by, from–to, from–until, during, (with)in**

- She has been gone **since** yesterday. (*She left yesterday and has not returned.*)
- I'm going to Paris **for** two weeks. (*I will spend two weeks there.*)
- The movie showed **from** August **to** October. (*Beginning in August and ending in October.*)
- The decorations were up **from** spring **until** fall. (*Beginning in spring and ending in fall.*)
- I watch TV **during** the evening. (*For some period of time in the evening.*)
- We must finish the project **within** a year. (*No longer than a year.*)

Place

To express notions of place, English uses the following prepositions: to talk about the point itself: **in**, to express something contained: **inside**, to talk about the surface: **on**, to talk about a general vicinity, **at**.

- There is a wasp **in** the room.
- Put the present **inside** the box.
- I left your keys **on** the table.
- She was waiting **at** the corner.

To introduce objects of verbs

English uses the following prepositions to introduce objects of the following verbs.

At: glance, laugh, look, rejoice, smile, stare
- She took a quick glance **at** her reflection.
  (*exception with **mirror**: She took a quick glance **in** the mirror.*)
- You didn't laugh **at** his joke.
- I'm looking **at** the computer monitor.
- We rejoiced **at** his safe rescue.
- That pretty girl smiled **at** you.
- Stop staring **at** me.

Of: approve, consist, smell
- I don't approve of his speech.
- My contribution to the article consists of many pages.
- He came home smelling of garlic.

Of (or about): dream, think
- I dream of finishing college in four years.
- Can you think of a number between one and ten?
- I am thinking about this problem.

For: call, hope, look, wait, watch, wish
- Did someone call for a taxi?
- He hopes for a raise in salary next year.
- I'm looking for my keys.
- We'll wait for her here.
- You go buy the tickets and I'll watch for the train.
- If you wish for an "A" in this class, you must work hard.

Part 6: Identifying Independent and Dependent Clauses

When you want to use commas and semicolons in sentences and when you are concerned about whether a sentence is or is not a fragment, a good way to start is to be able to recognize dependent and independent clauses. The definitions offered here will help you with this.

Independent Clause

An independent clause is a group of words that contains a subject and verb and expresses a complete thought. An independent clause is a sentence.

Jim studied in the Sweet Shop for his chemistry quiz.

Dependent Clause

A dependent clause is a group of words that contains a subject and verb but does not express a complete thought. A dependent clause cannot be a sentence. Often a dependent clause is marked by a **dependent marker word**.

When Jim studied in the Sweet Shop for his chemistry quiz . . . (What happened when he studied? The thought is incomplete.)

Dependent Marker Word

A dependent marker word is a word added to the beginning of an independent clause that makes it into a dependent clause.

When Jim studied in the Sweet Shop for his chemistry quiz, it was very noisy.

Some common dependent markers are: **after, although, as, as if, because, before, even if, even though, if, in order to, since, though, unless, until, whatever, when, whenever, whether,** and **while.**

Connecting Dependent and Independent Clauses

There are two types of words that can be used as connectors at the beginning of an independent clause: coordinating conjunctions and independent marker words.

1. Coordinating Conjunction

The seven coordinating conjunctions used as connecting words at the beginning of an independent clause are **and, but, for, or, nor, so,** and **yet.** When the second independent clause in a sentence begins with a coordinating conjunction, a comma is needed before the coordinating conjunction:

Jim studied in the Sweet Shop for his chemistry quiz, **but** it was hard to concentrate because of the noise.

2. Independent Marker Word

An independent marker word is a connecting word used at the beginning of an independent clause. These words can always begin a sentence that can stand alone. When the second independent clause in a sentence has an independent marker word, a semicolon is needed before the independent marker word.

Jim studied in the Sweet Shop for his chemistry quiz; **however**, it was hard to concentrate because of the noise.

Some common independent markers are: **also**, **consequently**, **furthermore**, **however**, **moreover**, **nevertheless**, and **therefore**.

Some Common Errors to Avoid

Comma Splices

A comma splice is the use of a comma between two independent clauses. You can usually fix the error by changing the comma to a period and therefore making the two clauses into two separate sentences, by changing the comma to a semicolon, or by making one clause dependent by inserting a dependent marker word in front of it.

Incorrect: I like this class, it is very interesting.

Correct: I like this class. It is very interesting.
- (or) I like this class; it is very interesting.
- (or) I like this class, and it is very interesting.
- (or) I like this class because it is very interesting.
- (or) Because it is very interesting, I like this class.

Fused Sentences

Fused sentences happen when there are two independent clauses not separated by any form of punctuation. This error is also known as a run-on sentence. The error can sometimes be corrected by adding a period, semicolon, or colon to separate the two sentences.

Incorrect: My professor is intelligent I've learned a lot from her.

Correct: My professor is intelligent. I've learned a lot from her.
- (or) My professor is intelligent; I've learned a lot from her.
- (or) My professor is intelligent, and I've learned a lot from her.
- (or) My professor is intelligent; moreover, I've learned a lot from her.

Sentence Fragments

Sentence fragments happen by treating a dependent clause or other incomplete thought as a complete sentence. You can usually fix this error by combining it with another sentence to make a complete thought or by removing the dependent marker.

Incorrect: Because I forgot the exam was today.

Correct: Because I forgot the exam was today, I didn't study.
- (or) I forgot the exam was today.

Part 7: Parallel Structure

Parallel structure means using the same pattern of words to show that two or more ideas have the same level of importance. This can happen at the word, phrase, or clause level. The usual way to join parallel structures is with the use of coordinating conjunctions such as "and" or "or."

Words and Phrases

With the -ing form (gerund) of words:

> **Parallel:** Mary likes hiking, swimming, and bicycling.

With infinitive phrases:

> **Parallel:** Mary likes to hike, to swim, and to ride a bicycle.
> OR
> Mary likes to hike, swim, and ride a bicycle.

(Note: You can use "to" before all the verbs in a sentence or only before the first one.)

Do not mix forms.

Example 1

> **Not Parallel:**
> Mary likes hiking, swimming, and **to ride** a bicycle.

> **Parallel:**
> Mary likes hiking, swimming, and riding a bicycle.

Example 2

> **Not Parallel:**
> The production manager was asked to write his report quickly, accurate ly, and **in a detailed manner**.

> **Parallel:**
> The production manager was asked to write his report quickly, accurately, and thoroughly.

Example 3

> **Not Parallel:**
> The teacher said that he was a poor student because he waited until the last minute to study for the exam, completed his lab problems in a careless manner, and **his motivation was** low.

> **Parallel:**
> The teacher said that he was a poor student because he waited until the last minute to study for the exam, completed his lab problems in a careless manner, and lacked motivation.

Clauses

A parallel structure that begins with clauses must keep on with clauses. Changing to another pattern or changing the voice of the verb (from active to passive or vice versa) will break the parallelism.

Example 1

> **Not Parallel:**
> The coach told the players that they should get a lot of sleep, that they should not eat too much, and to do some warm-up exercises before the game.

> **Parallel:**
> The coach told the players that they should get a lot of sleep, that they should not eat too much, and that they should do some warm-up exercises before the game.

OR

Parallel:
The coach told the players that they should get a lot of sleep, not eat too much, and do some warm-up exercises before the game.

Example 2

Not Parallel:
The salesman expected that he would present his product at the meeting, that there would be time for him to show his slide presentation, and **that questions would be asked** by prospective buyers. **(passive)**

Parallel:
The salesman expected that he would present his product at the meeting, that there would be time for him to show his slide presentation, and **that prospective buyers would ask** him questions.

Lists After a Colon

Be sure to keep all the elements in a list in the same form.

Example 1

Not Parallel:
The dictionary can be used for these purposes: to find word meanings, pronunciations, correct spellings, and **looking up irregular verbs**.

Parallel:
The dictionary can be used for these purposes: to find word meanings, pronunciations, correct spellings, and irregular verbs.

Proofreading Strategies to Try:

- Skim your paper, pausing at the words "and" and "or." Check on each side of these words to see whether the items joined are parallel. If not, make them parallel.
- If you have several items in a list, put them in a column to see if they are parallel.
- Listen to the sound of the items in a list or the items being compared. Do you hear the same kinds of sounds? For example, is there a series of "-ing" words beginning each item? Or do your hear a rhythm being repeated? If something is breaking that rhythm or repetition of sound, check to see if it needs to be made parallel.

Part 8: Introduction and General Usage in Defining Clauses

Relative pronouns are **that, who, whom, whose, which, where, when,** and **why.** They are used to join clauses to make a complex sentence. Relative pronouns are used at the beginning of the subordinate clause which gives some specific information about the main clause.

This is the house *that* Jack built.
I don't know the day *when* Jane marries him.
The professor, *whom* I respect, was tenured.

In English, the choice of the relative pronoun depends on the type of clause it is used in. There are two types of clauses distinguished: *defining* (*restrictive*) relative clauses and *non-defining* (*non-restrictive*) relative clauses. In both types of clauses the relative pronoun can function as a subject, an object, or a possessive.

Relative Pronouns in Defining Clauses

Defining relative clauses (also known as *restrictive relative clauses*) provide some essential information that explains the main clause. The information is crucial for understanding the sentence correctly and cannot be omitted. Defining clauses are opened by a relative pronoun and **ARE NOT** separated by a comma from the main clause.

The table below sums up the use of relative pronouns in defining clauses:

Function in the sentence	Reference to				
	People	Things/concepts	Place	Time	Reason
Subject	who, that	which, that			
Object	(that, who, whom)	(which, that)	where	when	why
Possessive	whose	whose, of which			

Examples

Relative pronoun used as a subject:

This is the house *that* had a great Christmas decoration.

It took me a while to get used to people *who* eat popcorn during the movie.

Relative pronoun used as an object:

1. As can be seen from the table, referring to a person or thing, the relative pronoun **may be omitted** in the object position:

   This is the man (who / that) I wanted to speak to and whose name I'd forgotten.

   The library didn't have the book (which / that) I wanted.

   I didn't like the book (which / that) John gave me.

   This is the house *where* I lived *when* I first came to the US.

2. In American English, *whom* is not used very often. **Whom** is more formal than *who* and is very often omitted in **speech**:

   Grammatically Correct: The woman to *whom* you have just spoken is my teacher.

   Common in Speech: The woman (*who*) you have just spoken to is my teacher.

However, *whom* may not be omitted if preceded by a preposition:

   I have found you the tutor <u>for</u> *whom* you were looking.

Relative pronoun used as a possessive:

Whose is the only possessive relative pronoun in English. It can be used with both people and things:

   The family *whose* house burnt in the fire was immediately given a suite in a hotel.

   The book *whose* author is now being shown in the news has become a bestseller.

General remarks: That, Who, Which compared

The relative pronoun *that* can only be used in defining clauses. It can also be substituted for *who* (referring to persons) or *which* (referring to things). *That* is often used in speech; *who* and *which* are more common in written English.

   William Kellogg was the man *that* lived in the late 19th century and had some weird ideas about raising children. (spoken, less formal)

William Kellogg was the man *who* lived in the late 19th century and had some weird ideas about raising children. (written, more formal)

Although your computer may suggest to correct it, referring to things, *which* may be used in the defining clause to put additional emphasis on the explanation. Again, the sentence with *which* is more formal than the one with *that*: Note that since it is the defining clause, there is NO comma used preceding *which*:

The café *that* sells the best coffee in town has recently been closed. (less formal)
The café *which* sells the best coffee in town has recently been closed. (more formal)

Some special uses of relative pronouns in defining clauses

that / who
Referring to people, both *that* and *who* can be used. *That* may be used to refer to someone in general:

He is the kind of person *that/who* will never let you down.
I am looking for someone *that/who* could give me a ride to Chicago.

However, when a particular person is being spoken about, *who* is preferred:

The old lady *who* lives next door is a teacher.
The girl *who* wore a red dress attracted everybody's attention at the party.

that / which
There are several cases when *that* is more appropriate and is preferred to *which*.

After the pronouns *all, any(thing), every(thing), few, little, many, much, no(thing), none, some(thing)*:

The police usually ask for every detail *that* helps identify the missing person. (*that* used as the subject)
Marrying a congressman is *all* (that) she wants. (*that* used as the object)

After verbs that answer the question **WHAT?** For example, *say, suggest, state, declare, hope, think, write*, etc. In this case, the whole relative clause functions as the object of the main clause:

Some people *say* (that) success is one percent of talent and ninety-nine percent of hard work.
The chairman *stated* at the meeting (that) his company is part of a big-time entertainment industry.

After the noun modified by an adjective *in the superlative degree*:

This is the *funniest* story (that) I have ever read! (*that* used as the object)

After ordinal numbers, e.g., *first, second, etc.*:

The first draft (that) we submitted was really horrible. (*that* used as the object)

If the verb in the main clause is a form of *BE*:

This is a claim that has absolutely no reason in it. (*that* used as the subject)

Relative Pronouns in Non-Defining Clauses
Non-defining relative clauses (also known as non-restrictive, or parenthetical, clauses) provide some additional information which is not essential and may be omitted without affecting the contents of the sentence. All relative pronouns EXCEPT "that" can be used in non-defining clauses; however, the pronouns MAY NOT be omitted. Non-defining clauses ARE separated by commas.

The table below sums up the use of relative pronouns in non-defining clauses:

Function in the sentence	Reference to				
	People	Things/concepts	Place	Time	Reason
Subject	who	which			
Object	who, whom	which	where	when	why
Possessive	whose	whose, of which			

a. **Relative pronoun used as a subject:**

The writer, **who** lives in this luxurious mansion, has just published his second novel.

b. **Relative pronoun used as an object:**

The house at the end of the street, **which** my grandfather built, needs renovating.

c. **Relative pronoun used as a possessive:**

William Kellogg, **whose** name has become a famous breakfast foods brand-name, had some weird ideas about raising children.

Some Special Uses of Relative Pronouns in Non-Defining Clauses

a. **which**
If you are referring to the previous clause as a whole, use **which**:
My friend eventually decided to get divorced, **which** upset me a lot.

b. **of whom, of which**
Use **of whom** for persons and **of which** for things or concepts after numbers and words such as *most, many, some, both, none*:
I saw a lot of new people at the party, <u>some</u> **of whom** seemed familiar.
He was always coming up with new ideas, <u>most</u> **of which** were absolutely impracticable.

Part 9: Sentence Types and Punctuation Patterns

To punctuate a sentence, you can use and combine some of these patterns.

Pattern One: Simple Sentence

This pattern is an example of a simple sentence:

Independent clause [.]

Example: Doctors are concerned about the rising death rate from asthma.

Pattern Two: Compound Sentence

This pattern is an example of a compound sentence with a coordinating conjunction:

Independent clause [,] coordinating conjunction independent clause [.]

There are seven coordinating conjunctions: and, but, for, or, nor, so, yet.

Example: Doctors are concerned about the rising death rate from asthma, but they don't know the reasons for it.

Pattern Three: Compound Sentence

This pattern is an example of a compound sentence with a semicolon.

Independent clause [;] independent clause [.]

Example: Doctors are concerned about the rising death rate from asthma; they are unsure of its cause.

Pattern Four: Compound Sentence

This pattern is an example of a compound sentence with an independent marker.

Independent clause [;] independent marker [,] independent clause [.]

Examples of independent markers are the following: therefore, moreover, thus, consequently, however, also.

Example: Doctors are concerned about the rising death rate from asthma; therefore, **they have called for more research into its causes.**

Pattern Five: Complex Sentence

This pattern is an example of a complex sentence with a dependent marker.

Dependent marker dependent clause [,] **Independent clause** [.]

Examples of dependent markers are as follows: because, before, since, while, although, if, until, when, after, as, as if.

Example: *Because* doctors are concerned about the rising death rate from asthma, **they have called for more research into its causes.**

Pattern Six: Complex Sentence

This pattern is an example of a complex sentence with a dependent marker following the independent clause.

Independent clause dependent marker dependent clause [.]

Example: Doctors are concerned about the rising death rate from asthma because it is a common, treatable illness.

Pattern Seven

This pattern includes an independent clause with an embedded <u>non-essential</u> clause or phrase. A non-essential clause or phrase is one that can be removed without changing the meaning of the sentence or making it ungrammatical. In other words, the non-essential clause or phrase gives additional information, but the sentence can stand alone without it.

First part of an independent clause [,] non-essential clause or phrase, **rest of the independent clause** [.]

Example: Many doctors, including both pediatricians and family practice physicians, **are concerned about the rising death rate from asthma.**

Pattern Eight

This pattern includes an independent clause with an embedded <u>essential</u> clause or phrase. An essential clause or phrase is one that cannot be removed without changing the overall meaning of the sentence.

First part of an independent clause essential clause or phrase **rest of the independent clause** [.]

Example: Many doctors who are concerned about the rising death rate from asthma **have called for more research into its causes.**

Part 10: Making Subjects and Verbs Agree

1. When the subject of a sentence is composed of two or more nouns or pronouns connected by *and*, use a plural verb.

   She and **her friends are** at the fair.

2. When two or more singular nouns or pronouns are connected by *or* or *nor*, use a singular verb.

   The book or **the pen is** in the drawer.

3. When a compound subject contains both a singular and a plural noun or pronoun joined by *or* or *nor*, the verb should agree with the part of the subject that is nearer the verb.

   The boy or **his friends run** every day.
   His friends or **the boy runs** every day.

4. *Doesn't* is a contraction of *does not* and should be used only with a singular subject. *Don't* is a contraction of *do not* and should be used only with a plural subject. The exception to this rule appears in the case of the first person and second person pronouns *I* and *you*. With these pronouns, the contraction *don't* should be used. [Note that formal writing generally avoids the use of contractions.]

   He doesn't **like** it.
   They don't **like** it.

5. Do not be misled by a phrase that comes between the subject and the verb. The verb agrees with the subject, not with a noun or pronoun in the phrase.

   One of the boxes **is** open
   The people who listen to that music **are** few.
   The team captain, as well as his players, **is** anxious.
   The book, including all the chapters in the first section, **is** boring.
   The woman with all the dogs **walks** down my street.

6. The words *each*, *each one*, *either*, *neither*, *everyone*, *everybody*, *anybody*, *anyone*, *nobody*, *somebody*, *someone*, and *no one* are singular and require a singular verb.

   Each of these hot dogs **is** juicy.
   Everybody knows Mr. Jones.
   Either is correct.

7. Nouns such as *civics*, *mathematics*, *dollars*, *measles*, and *news* require singular verbs.

   The news is on at six.

   Note: The word **dollars** is a special case. When talking about an amount of money, it requires a singular verb, but when referring to the dollars themselves, a plural verb is required.

   Five dollars is a lot of money.
   Dollars are often used instead of rubles in Russia.

8. Nouns such as *scissors*, *tweezers*, *trousers*, and *shears* require plural verbs. (There are two parts to these things.)

   These scissors are dull.
   Those trousers are made of wool.

9. In sentences beginning with *there is* or *there are*, the subject follows the verb. Since *there* is not the subject, the verb agrees with what follows.

There **are** many questions.
There **is** a question.

10. Collective nouns are words that imply more than one person but that are considered singular and take a singular verb, such as: *group, team, committee, class,* and *family*.

The team **runs** during practice.
The committee **decides** how to proceed.
The family **has** a long history.
My family **has never been able to agree**.

In some cases, a sentence may call for the use of a plural verb when using a collective noun.

The crew **are preparing** to dock the ship.

This sentence is referring to the individual efforts of each crew member.

11. Expressions such as *with, together with, including, accompanied by, in addition to,* or *as well* do not change the number of the subject. If the subject is singular, the verb is too.

The President, accompanied by his wife, **is** traveling to India.
All of the books, including yours, **are** in that box.

Sequence of Tenses

Simple Present: They walk.

Present Perfect: They have walked.

Simple Past: They walked.

Past Perfect: They had walked.

Future: They will walk.

Future Perfect: They will have walked.

Problems in sequencing tenses usually occur with the perfect tenses, all of which are formed by adding an auxiliary or auxiliaries to the past participle, the third principal part.

> ring, rang, rung
> walk, walked, walked

The most common auxiliaries are forms of "be," "can," "do," "may," "must," "ought," "shall," "will," "has," "have," "had," and they are the forms we shall use in this most basic discussion.

Present Perfect

The present perfect consists of a past participle (the third principal part) with "has" or "have." It designates action which began in the past but which continues into the present or the effect of which still continues.

1. Betty taught for ten years. (simple past)
2. Betty has taught for ten years. (present perfect)

The implication in (1) is that Betty has retired; in (2), that she is still teaching.

1. John did his homework. He can go to the movies.
2. If John has done his homework, he can go to the movies.

Infinitives, too, have perfect tense forms when combined with "have," and sometimes problems arise when infinitives are used with verbs such as "hope," "plan," "expect," and "intend," all of which usually point to the future (I wanted to go to the movie. Janet meant to see the doctor.) The perfect tense sets up a sequence by marking the action which began and usually was completed before the action in the main verb.

1. I am happy to have participated in this campaign!
2. John had hoped to have won the trophy.

Thus the action of the main verb points back in time; the action of the perfect infinitive has been completed.

The past perfect tense designates action in the past just as simple past does, but the action of the past perfect is action completed in the past before another action.

1. John raised vegetables and later sold them. (past)
2. John sold vegetables that he had raised. (past perfect)

The vegetables were raised before they were sold.

1. Renee washed the car when George arrived. (simple past)
2. Renee had washed the car when George arrived. (past perfect)

In (1), she waited until George arrived and then washed the car. In (2), she had already finished washing the car by the time he arrived.

In sentences expressing condition and result, the past perfect tense is used in the part that states the condition.

1. If I had done my exercises, I would have passed the test.
2. I think George would have been elected if he hadn't sounded so pompous.

Future Perfect Tense
The future perfect tense designates action that will have been completed at a specified time in the future.

1. Saturday I will finish my housework. (simple future)
2. By Saturday noon, I will have finished my housework. (future perfect)

Part 11: Using Active Versus Passive Voice

In a sentence using **active voice**, the subject of the sentence performs the action expressed in the verb.

The dog *bit* the boy.

The arrow points from the subject performing the action (the dog) to the individual being acted upon (the boy). This is an example of a sentence using the active voice.

Scientists *have conducted* experiments to test the hypothesis.

Sample active voice sentence with the subject performing the action described by the verb.

Watching a framed, mobile world through a car's windshield *reminds* me of watching a movie or TV.

The active voice sentence subject (watching a framed, mobile world) performs the action of reminding the speaker of something.

Each example above includes a sentence subject performing the action expressed by the verb.

Examples:

	Active	Passive
Simple Present	• The company ships the computers to many foreign countries.	• Computers are shipped to many foreign countries
Present Progressive	• The chef is preparing the food.	• The food is being prepared.
Simple Past	• The delivery man delivered the package yesterday.	• The package was delivered yesterday.
Past Progressive	• The producer was making an announcement.	• An announcement was being made.
Future	• Our representative will pick up the computer.	• The computer will be picked up.
Present Perfect	• Someone has made the arrangements for us.	• The arrangements have been made for us.
Past Perfect	• They had given us visas for three months.	• They had been given visas for three months.
Future Perfect	• By next month we will have finished this job.	• By next month this job will have been finished.

Part 12: Irregular Verbs: Overview and List

In English, regular verbs consist of three main parts: the root form (present), the (simple) past, and the past participle. Regular verbs have an *-ed* ending added to the root verb for both the simple past and past participle. Irregular verbs do not follow this pattern, and instead take on an alternative pattern.

The following is a partial list of irregular verbs found in English. Each listing consists of the present/ root form of the verb, the (simple) past form of the verb, and the past participle form of the verb.

List of Irregular Verbs in English						
Present	Past	Past Participle		Present	Past	Past Participle
be	was, were	been		deal	dealt	dealt
become	became	become		do	did	done
begin	began	begun		drink	drank	drunk
blow	blew	blown		drive	drove	driven
break	broke	broken		eat	ate	eaten
bring	brought	brought		fall	fell	fallen
build	built	built		feed	fed	fed
burst	burst	burst		feel	felt	felt
buy	bought	bought		fight	fought	fought
catch	caught	caught		find	found	found
choose	chose	chosen		fly	flew	flown
come	came	come		forbid	forbade	forbidden
cut	cut	cut		forget	forgot	forgotten

Present	Past	Past Participle
forgive	forgave	forgiven
freeze	froze	frozen
get	got	gotten
give	gave	given
go	went	gone
grow	grew	grown
have	had	had
hear	heard	heard
hide	hid	hidden
hold	held	held
hurt	hurt	hurt
keep	kept	kept
know	knew	known
lay	laid	laid
lead	led	led
leave	left	left
let	let	let
lie	lay	lain
lose	lost	lost
make	made	made
meet	met	met
pay	paid	paid
quit	quit	quit
read	read	read
ride	rode	ridden
run	ran	run
say	said	said

Present	Past	Past Participle
see	saw	seen
seek	sought	sought
sell	sold	sold
send	sent	sent
shake	shook	sent
shine	shone	shone
sing	sang	sung
sit	sat	sat
sleep	slept	slept
speak	spoke	spoken
spend	spent	spent
spring	sprang	sprung
stand	stood	stood
steal	stole	stolen
swim	swam	swum
swing	swung	swung
take	took	taken
teach	taught	taught
tear	tore	torn
tell	told	told
think	thought	thought
throw	threw	thrown
understand	understood	understood
wake	woke (waked)	woken (waked)
wear	wore	worn
win	won	won
write	wrote	written

Commonly Confused Verbs

LIE versus LAY

Lie vs. Lay Usage		
Present	Past	Past Participle
lie, lying (to tell a falsehood)	I lied to my mother.	I have lied under oath.
lie, lying (to recline)	I lay on the bed because I was tired.	He has lain in the grass.
lay, laying (to put, place)	I laid the baby in her cradle.	We have laid the dishes on the table.

Example sentences:

After **laying** down his weapon, the soldier **lay** down to sleep.
Will you **lay** out my clothes while I **lie** down to rest?

SIT versus SET

Sit vs. Set Usage		
Present	Past	Past Participle
sit (to be seated or come to resting position)	I sat in my favorite chair.	You have sat there for three hours.
set (to put or place)	I set my glass on the table.	She has set her books on my desk again.

Example sentence:

Let's **set** the table before we **sit** down to rest.

RISE versus RAISE

Rise vs. Raise Usage		
Present	Past	Past Participle
rise (steady or customary upward movement)	The balloon rose into the air.	He has risen to a position of power.
raise (to cause to rise)	They raised their hands because they knew the answer.	I have raised the curtain many times.

Example sentence:

The boy **raised** the flag just before the sun **rose**.

Part 13: Capitalization and Punctuation

A Little Help with Capitals

If you have a question about whether a specific word should be capitalized that doesn't fit under one of these rules, try checking a dictionary to see if the word is capitalized there.

Use capital letters in the following ways:

The first words of a sentence

When he tells a joke, he sometimes forgets the punch line.

The pronoun "I"

The last time I visited Atlanta was several years ago.

Proper nouns (the names of specific people, places, organizations, and sometimes things)

Worrill Fabrication Company
Golden Gate Bridge
Supreme Court
Livingston, Missouri
Atlantic Ocean
Mothers Against Drunk Driving

Family relationships (when used as proper names)

I sent a thank-you note to Aunt Abigail, but not to my other aunts.

Here is a present I bought for Mother.

Did you buy a present for your mother?

The names of God, specific deities, religious figures, and holy books

God the Father
the Virgin Mary
the Bible
the Greek gods
Moses
Shiva
Buddha
Zeus

Exception: Do not capitalize the non-specific use of the word "god."

The word "polytheistic" means the worship of more than one god.

Titles preceding names, but not titles that follow names

She worked as the assistant to Mayor Hanolovi.

I was able to interview Miriam Moss, mayor of Littonville.

Directions that are names (North, South, East, and West when used as sections of the country, but not as compass directions)

The Patels have moved to the Southwest.

Jim's house is two miles north of Otterbein.

The days of the week, the months of the year, and holidays (but not the seasons used generally)

Halloween
October
Friday
winter
spring
fall

Exception: Seasons are capitalized when used in a title.

The Fall 1999 Semester

The names of countries, nationalities, and specific languages

Costa Rica
Spanish
French
English

The first word in a sentence that is a direct quote

Emerson once said, "A foolish consistency is the hobgoblin of little minds."

The major words in the titles of books, articles, and songs (but not short prepositions or the articles "the," "a," or "an," if they are not the first word of the title)

One of Jerry's favorite books is *The Catcher in the Rye*.

Members of national, political, racial, social, civic, and athletic groups

Green Bay Packers
African-Americans
Democrats
Friends of the Wilderness
Chinese

Periods and events (but not century numbers)

Victorian Era
Great Depression
Constitutional Convention
sixteenth century

Trademarks

Pepsi
Honda
IBM
Microsoft Word

Words and abbreviations of specific names (but not names of things that came from specific things but are now general types)

Freudian   UN
NBC   french fries
pasteurize   italics

Comma

Use a comma to join two independent clauses by a comma and a coordinating conjunction (*and, but, or, for, nor, so*).

Road construction can be inconvenient, but it is necessary.

The new house has a large fenced backyard, so I am sure our dog will enjoy it.

Use a comma after an introductory phrase, prepositional phrase, or dependent clause.

To get a good grade, you must complete all your assignments.

Because Dad caught the chicken pox, we canceled our vacation.

After the wedding, the guests attended the reception.

Use a comma to separate elements in a series. Although there is no set rule that requires a comma before the last item in a series, it seems to be a general academic convention to include it. The examples below demonstrate this trend.

On her vacation, Lisa visited Greece, Spain, and Italy.

In their speeches, many of the candidates promised to help protect the environment, bring about world peace, and end world hunger.

Use a comma to separate nonessential elements from a sentence. More specifically, when a sentence includes information that is not crucial to the message or intent of the sentence, enclose it in or separate it by commas.

John's truck, a red Chevrolet, needs new tires.

When he realized he had overslept, Matt rushed to his car and hurried to work.

● Use a comma between coordinate adjectives (adjectives that are equal and reversible).

> The irritable, fidgety crowd waited impatiently for the rally speeches to begin.

> The sturdy, compact suitcase made a perfect gift.

Use a comma after a transitional element (*however, therefore, nonetheless, also, otherwise, finally, instead, thus, of course, above all, for example, in other words, as a result, on the other hand, in conclusion, in addition*)

> For example, the Red Sox, Yankees, and Indians are popular baseball teams.

> If you really want to get a good grade this semester, however, you must complete all assignments, attend class, and study your notes.

Use a comma with quoted words.

> "Yes," she promised. Todd replied, saying, "I will be back this afternoon."

Use a comma in a date.

> October 25, 1999
> Monday, October 25, 1999
> 25 October 1999

Use a comma in a number.

> 15,000,000
> 1614 High Street

● Use a comma in a personal title.

> Pam Smith, MD
> Mike Rose, Chief Financial Officer for Operations, reported the quarter's earnings.

Use a comma to separate a city name from the state.

> West Lafayette, Indiana
> Dallas, Texas

Avoid comma splices (two independent clauses joined only by a comma). Instead, separate the clauses with a period, with a comma followed by a coordinating conjunction, or with a semicolon.

Semicolon

Use a semicolon to join two independent clauses when the second clause restates the first or when the two clauses are of equal emphasis.

> Road construction in Dallas has hindered travel around town; streets have become covered with bulldozers, trucks, and cones.

Use a semicolon to join two independent clauses when the second clause begins with a conjunctive adverb (*however, therefore, moreover, furthermore, thus, meanwhile, nonetheless, otherwise*) or a transition (*in fact, for example, that is, for instance, in addition, in other words, on the other hand, even so*).

> Terrorism in the United States has become a recent concern; in fact, the concern for America's safety has led to an awareness of global terrorism.

● Use a semicolon to join elements of a series when individual items of the series already include commas.

> Recent sites of the Olympic Games include Athens, Greece; Salt Lake City, Utah; Sydney, Australia; Nagano, Japan.

Colon

Use a colon to join two independent clauses when you wish to emphasize the second clause.

> Road construction in Dallas has hindered travel around town: parts of Main, Fifth, and West Street are closed during the construction.

Use a colon after an independent clause when it is followed by a list, a quotation, an appositive, or other idea directly related to the independent clause.

> Julie went to the store for some groceries: milk, bread, coffee, and cheese.

> In his Gettysburg Address, Abraham Lincoln urges Americans to rededicate themselves to the unfinished work of the deceased soldiers: "It is for us the living rather to be dedicated here to the unfinished work which they who fought here have thus far so nobly advanced. It is rather for us to be here dedicated to the great task remaining before us — that from these honored dead we take increased devotion to that cause for which they gave the last full measure of devotion — that we here highly resolve that these dead shall not have died in vain, that this nation under God shall have a new birth of freedom, and that government of the people, by the people, for the people shall not perish from the earth."

> I know the perfect job for her: a politician.

Use a colon at the end of a business letter greeting.

> To Whom It May Concern:

Use a colon to separate the hour and minute(s) in a time notation.

> 12:00 p.m.

Use a colon to separate the chapter and verse in a Biblical reference.

> Matthew 1:6

Parentheses

Parentheses are used to emphasize content. They place more emphasis on the enclosed content than commas. Use parentheses to set off nonessential material, such as dates, clarifying information, or sources, from a sentence.

> Muhammed Ali (1942-present), arguably the greatest athlete of all time, claimed he would "float like a butterfly, sting like a bee."

Use parentheses to enclose numbered items in a sentence.

> He asked everyone to bring (1) a folding tent, (2) food and water for two days, and (3) a sleeping bag.

Also use parentheses for literary citations embedded in text or to give the explanation of an acronym.

> Research by Wegener and Petty (1994) supports...
> The AMA (American Medical Association) recommends regular exercise.

Dash

Dashes are used to set off or emphasize the content enclosed within dashes or the content that follows a dash. Dashes place more emphasis on this content than parentheses.

> Perhaps one reason why the term has been so problematic—so resistant to definition, and yet so transitory in those definitions—is because of its multitude of applications.

> In terms of public legitimacy—that is, in terms of garnering support from state legislators, parents, donors, and university administrators—English departments are primarily places where advanced literacy is taught.

The U.S.S. *Constitution* became known as "Old Ironsides" during the War of 1812—during which the cannonballs fired from the British H.M.S. *Guerriere* merely bounced off the sides of the *Constitution.*

To some of you, my proposals may seem radical—even revolutionary.

Use a dash to set off an appositive phrase that already includes commas. An appositive is a word that adds explanatory or clarifying information to the noun that precedes it.

The cousins—Tina, Todd, and Sam—arrived at the party together.

Quotation Marks

Use quotation marks to enclose direct quotations. Note that commas and periods are placed inside the closing quotation mark, and colons and semicolons are placed outside. The placement of question and exclamation marks depends on the situation.

He asked, "When will you be arriving?" I answered, "Sometime after 6:30."

Use quotation marks to indicate the novel, ironic, or reserved use of a word.

History is stained with blood spilled in the name of "justice."

Use quotation marks around the titles of short poems, song titles, short stories, magazine or newspaper articles, essays, speeches, chapter titles, short films, and episodes of television or radio shows.

"Self-Reliance," by Ralph Waldo Emerson
"Just Like a Woman," by Bob Dylan
"The Smelly Car," an episode of Seinfeld

Do not use quotation marks in indirect or block quotations. Indirect quotations are not exact wordings but rather rephrasings or summaries of another person's words. In this case, it is not necessary to use quotation marks. However, indirect quotations still require proper citations, and you will be committing plagiarism if you fail to do so.

Mr. Johnson, a local farmer, reported last night that he saw an alien spaceship on his own property.

Italics

Underlining and Italics are often used interchangeably. Before word-processing programs were widely available, writers would underline certain words to indicate to publishers to italicize whatever was underlined. Although the general trend has been moving toward italicizing instead of underlining, you should remain consistent with your choice throughout your paper. To be safe, you could check with your teacher to find out which he/she prefers. Italicize the titles of magazines, books, newspapers, academic journals, films, television shows, long poems, plays of three or more acts, operas, musical albums, works of art, websites, and individual trains, planes, or ships.

Time
Romeo and Juliet by William Shakespeare
The Metamorphosis of Narcissus by Salvador Dali
Amazon.com
Titanic

Italicize foreign words.

Semper fi, the motto of the U.S. Marine Corps, means "always faithful."

Italicize a word or phrase to add emphasis.

The *truth* is of utmost concern!

Italicize a word when referring to that word.

The word *justice* is often misunderstood and therefore misused.

Hyphen

Two words brought together as a compound may be written separately, written as one word, or connected by hyphens. For example, three modern dictionaries all have the same listings for the following compounds:

> hair stylist
> hairsplitter
> hair-raiser

Another modern dictionary, however, lists *hairstylist*, not *hair stylist*. Compounding is obviously in a state of flux, and authorities do not always agree in all cases, but the uses of the hyphen offered here are generally agreed upon.

1. Use a hyphen to join two or more words serving as a single adjective before a noun:

    > a one-way street
    > chocolate-covered peanuts
    > well-known author

    However, when compound modifiers come after a noun, they are not hyphenated:

    > The peanuts were chocolate covered.
    > The author was well known.

2. Use a hyphen with compound numbers:

    > forty-six
    > sixty-three
    > Our much-loved teacher was sixty-three years old.

3. Use a hyphen to avoid confusion or an awkward combination of letters:

    > re-sign a petition (vs. resign from a job)
    > semi-independent (but semiconscious)
    > shell-like (but childlike)

4. Use a hyphen with the prefixes *ex-* (meaning former), *self-*, *all-*; with the suffix *-elect*; between a prefix and a capitalized word; and with figures or letters:

    > ex-husband
    > self-assured
    > mid-September
    > all-inclusive
    > mayor-elect
    > anti-American
    > T-shirt
    > pre-Civil War
    > mid-1980s

5. Use a hyphen to divide words at the end of a line if necessary, and make the break only between syllables:

    > pref-er-ence
    > sell-ing
    > in-di-vid-u-al-ist

6. For line breaks, divide already hyphenated words only at the hyphen:

    > mass-
    > produced

Apostrophe

The apostrophe has three uses:

- to form possessives of nouns
- to show the omission of letters
- to indicate certain plurals of lowercase letters

Forming Possessives of Nouns

To see if you need to make a possessive, turn the phrase around and make it an "of the..." phrase. For example:

> the boy's hat = the hat of the boy
> three days' journey = journey of three days

If the noun after "of" is a building, an object, or a piece of furniture, then **no** apostrophe is needed!

> room of the hotel = hotel room
> door of the car = car door
> leg of the table = table leg

Once you've determined whether you need to make a possessive, follow these rules to create one.

- **add 's to the singular form of the word (even if it ends in -s):**

  the owner's car
  James's hat (James' hat is also acceptable. For plural, proper nouns that are possessive, use an apostrophe after the 's': "The Eggles' presentation was good." The Eggles are a husband and wife consultant team.)

- **add 's to the plural forms that do not end in -s:**

  the children's game
  the geese's honking

- **add ' to the end of plural nouns that end in -s:**

  houses' roofs
  three friends' letters

- **add 's to the end of compound words:**

  my brother-in-law's money

- **add 's to the last noun to show joint possession of an object:**

  Todd and Anne's apartment

Showing omission of letters

Apostrophes are used in contractions. A contraction is a word (or set of numbers) in which one or more letters (or numbers) have been omitted. The apostrophe shows this omission. Contractions are common in speaking and in informal writing. To use an apostrophe to create a contraction, place an apostrophe where the omitted letter(s) would go. Here are some examples:

> don't = do not
> I'm = I am
> he'll = he will
> who's = who is
> could've = could have (NOT "could of"!)
> '60 = 1960

Don't use apostrophes for possessive pronouns or for noun plurals.

Apostrophes should not be used with possessive pronouns because possessive pronouns already show possession — they don't need an apostrophe. *His, her, its, my, yours, ours* are all possessive pronouns. Here are some examples:

> **wrong:** his' book
> **correct:** his book

> **wrong:** The group made it's decision.
> **correct:** The group made its decision.

(Note: *Its* and *it' s* are not the same thing. *It' s* is a contraction for "it is" and *its* is a possessive pronoun meaning "belonging to it." It's raining out= it is raining out. A simple way to remember this rule is the fact that you don't use an apostrophe for the possessive *his* or *hers*, so don't do it with *its*!)

> **wrong:** a friend of yours'
> **correct:** a friend of yours

Proofreading for apostrophes

A good time to proofread is when you have finished writing the paper. Try the following strategies to proofread for apostrophes:

- If you tend to leave out apostrophes, check every word that ends in *-s* or *-es* to see if it needs an apostrophe.
- If you put in too many apostrophes, check every apostrophe to see if you can justify it with a rule for using apostrophes.

Ellipsis

An ellipsis (a row of three dots: ...) must be used whenever anything is omitted from within a quoted passage—word, phrase, line, or paragraph-- regardless of its source or use. It would, therefore, apply to all usage, including technical, non-technical, medical, journalistic, fiction, etc. The usual form is a "bare" ellipsis (just the three dots, preceded and followed by a space), although the MLA Handbook for Writers of Research Papers recommends that the writer enclose an ellipsis in brackets [...] when omitting part of an original quotation, to differentiate instances of deleted text from ellipses included in the original text. In all cases, the entire quoted passage, including ellipses, is preceded and followed by quotation marks and the source properly cited.

Two things to consider: 1) using ellipses is a form of "editing" the source material, so be certain that the final outcome does not change the original meaning or intent of the quoted passage; and 2) if quoted text ends up with more ellipses than words, consider paraphrasing rather than using direct quotes.

Brackets

Brackets are most often used to clarify the meaning of quoted material. If the context of your quote might be unclear, you may add a few words to provide clarity. Enclose the added material in brackets.

> **Added Material:** The quarterback told the reporter, "It's quite simple. They [the other team] played a better game, scored more points, and that's why we lost."

Resources

SpringBoard Learning Strategies

READING STRATEGIES

STRATEGY	DEFINITION	PURPOSE
Close Reading	Accessing small chunks of text to read, reread, mark, and annotate key passages, word-for-word, sentence-by-sentence, and line-by-line	To develop comprehensive understanding by engaging in one or more focused readings of a text
Diffusing	Reading a passage, noting unfamiliar words, discovering meaning of unfamiliar words using context clues, dictionaries, and/or thesauruses, and replacing unfamiliar words with familiar ones	To facilitate a close reading of text, the use of resources, an understanding of synonyms, and increased comprehension of text
Double-Entry Journal	Creating a two-column journal (also called Dialectical Journal) with a student-selected passage in one column and the student's response in the second column (e.g., asking questions of the text, forming personal responses, interpreting the text, reflecting on the process of making meaning of the text)	To respond to a specific passage with comments, questions, or insights to foster active involvement with a text and to facilitate increased comprehension
Graphic Organizer	Using a visual representation for the organization of information	To facilitate increased comprehension and discussion
KWHL Chart	Setting up discussion with use of a graphic organizer. Allows students to activate prior knowledge by answering "What do I *know*?" sets a purpose by answering "What do I *want* to know?" helps preview a task by answering "*How* will I learn it?" and reflects on new knowledge by answering "What have I *learned?*"	To organize thinking, access prior knowledge, and reflect on learning to increase comprehension and engagement
Marking the Text	Selecting text by highlighting, underlining, and/or annotating for specific components, such as main idea, imagery, literary devices, and so on	To focus reading for specific purposes, such as author's craft, and to organize information from selections; to facilitate reexamination of a text
Metacognitive Markers	Responding to text with a system of cueing marks where students use a ? for questions about the text; a ! for reactions related to the text; and an * for comments about the text and underline to signal key ideas	To track responses to texts and use those responses as a point of departure for talking or writing about texts
Predicting	Making guesses about the text by using the title and pictures and/or thinking ahead about events which may occur based on evidence in the text	To help students become actively involved, interested, and mentally prepared to understand ideas
Previewing	Examining a text's structure, features, layout, and so on, prior to reading	To gain familiarity with the text, make connections to the text, and extend prior knowledge to set a purpose for reading
QHT	Expanding prior knowledge of vocabulary words by marking words with a Q, H, or T (Q signals words students do not know; H signals words students have heard and might be able to identify; T signals words students know well enough to teach to their peers.)	To allow students to build on their prior knowledge of words, to provide a forum for peer teaching and learning of new words, and to serve as a pre-reading exercise to aid in comprehension

STRATEGY	DEFINITION	PURPOSE
Questioning the Text*	Developing literal, interpretive, and universal questions about the text while reading a text	To engage more actively with texts, read with greater purpose and focus, and ultimately answer questions to gain greater insight into the text
Quickwrite	Responding to a text by writing for a short, specific amount of time about a designated topic or idea related to a text	To activate background knowledge, clarify issues, facilitate making connections, and allow for reflection
RAFT	Responding to and analyzing text by brainstorming various roles (e.g., self, characters from other texts), audiences (e.g., a different character, a real person), formats (e.g., letter, brochure, essay, travel guide), and topics; readers may choose one particular role, audience, format, and topic to create a new text	To initiate reader response; to facilitate an analysis of a text to gain focus prior to creating a new text
Rereading	Encountering the same text with more than one reading	To identify additional details; to clarify meaning and/or reinforce comprehension of texts
SIFT*	Analyzing a fictional text by examining stylistic elements, especially symbol, images, and figures of speech, in order to show how all work together to reveal tone and theme.	To focus and facilitate an analysis of a fictional text by examining the title and text for symbolism, identifying images and sensory details, analyzing figurative language and identifying how all these elements reveal tone and theme
Skimming/Scanning	Skimming by rapid or superficial reading of a text to form an overall impression or to obtain a general understanding of the material; scanning by focusing on key words, phrases, or specific details to provide speedy recognition of information	To quickly form an overall impression prior to an in-depth study of a text; to answer specific questions or quickly locate targeted information or detail in a text

*AP strategy

READING STRATEGIES (Continued)

STRATEGY	DEFINITION	PURPOSE
SMELL*	Analyzing a persuasive speech or essay by asking five essential questions: • **S**ender-receiver relationship—What is the sender-receiver relationship? Who are the images and language meant to attract? Describe the speaker of the text. • **M**essage—What is the message? Summarize the statement made in the text. • **E**motional Strategies—What is the desired effect? • **L**ogical Strategies—What logic is operating? How does it (or its absence) affect the message? Consider the logic of the images as well as the words. • **L**anguage—What does the language of the text describe? How does it affect the meaning and effectiveness of the writing? Consider the language of the images as well as the words.	To analyze a persuasive speech or essay by focusing on five essential questions
SOAPSTone*	Analyzing text by discussing and identifying *Speaker, Occasion, Audience, Purpose, Subject,* and *Tone*	To use an analytical process to understand the author's craft
Summarizing/ Paraphrasing	Restating in one's own words the main idea or essential information expressed in a text, whether it be narration, dialogue, or informational text	To facilitate comprehension and recall of a text
Think Aloud	Talking through a difficult passage or task by using a form of metacognition whereby the reader expresses how he/she has made sense of the text	To reflect on how readers make meaning of challenging texts
TP-CASTT*	Analyzing a poetic text by identifying and discussing *Title, Paraphrase, Connotation, Attitude, Shift, Theme,* and *Title* again	To use an analytical process to understand the author's craft
Visualizing	Forming a picture (mentally and/or literally) while reading a text	To increase reading comprehension and promote active engagement with text
Word Maps	Using a clearly defined graphic organizer such as concept circles or word webs to identify and reinforce word meanings	To provide a visual tool for identifying and remembering multiple aspects of words and word meanings

*AP strategy

WRITING STRATEGIES

STRATEGY	DEFINITION	PURPOSE
Adding	Making conscious choices to enhance a text by adding additional words, phrases, sentences, or ideas	To refine and clarify the writer's thoughts during revision and/or drafting
Brainstorming	Using a flexible but deliberate process of listing multiple ideas in a short period of time without excluding any idea from the preliminary list	To generate ideas, concepts, or key words that provide a focus and/or establish organization as part of the prewriting or revision process
Deleting	Providing clarity and cohesiveness for a text by eliminating words, phrases, sentences, or ideas	To refine and clarify the writer's thoughts during revision and/or drafting
Double-Entry Journal	Creating a two-column journal (also called Dialectical Journal) with a student-selected passage in one column and the student's response in the second column (e.g., asking questions of the text, forming personal responses, interpreting the text, reflecting on the process of making meaning of the text)	To assist in organizing key textual elements and responses noted during reading in order to generate textual support that can be incorporated into a piece of writing at a later time
Drafting	Composing a text in its initial form	To incorporate brainstormed or initial ideas into a written format
Free writing	Using a fluid brainstorming process to write without constraints in order to solidify and convey the writer's purpose	To refine and clarify the writer's thoughts, spark new ideas, and/or generate content during revision and/or drafting
Generating Questions	Clarifying and developing ideas by asking questions of the draft. May be part of self-editing or peer editing	To clarify and develop ideas in a draft. Used during drafting and as part of writer response
Graphic Organizer	Representing ideas and information visually (e.g., Venn diagrams, flowcharts, cluster maps)	To provide a visual system for organizing multiple ideas, details, and/or textual support to be included in a piece of writing
Looping	Focusing on one section of a text and generating new ideas from that section and then repeating the process with the newly generated segments	To refine and clarify the writer's thoughts, spark new ideas, and/or generate new content during revision and/or drafting
Mapping	Creating a graphic organizer that serves as a visual representation of the organizational plan for a written text	To generate ideas, concepts, or key words that provide a focus and/or establish organization during the prewriting, drafting, or revision process

STRATEGY	DEFINITION	PURPOSE
Marking the Draft	Interacting with the draft version of a piece of writing by highlighting, underlining, color-coding, and annotating to indicate revision ideas.	To encourage focused, reflective thinking about revising drafts
Outlining	Using a system of numerals and letters in order to identify topics and supporting details and ensure an appropriate balance of ideas	To generate ideas, concepts, or key words that provide a focus and/or establish organization prior to writing an initial draft and/or during the revision process
Quickwrite	Writing for a short, specific amount of time about a designated topic related to a text	To generate multiple ideas in a quick fashion that could be turned into longer pieces of writing at a later time (May be considered as part of the drafting process)
RAFT	Generating and/or transforming a text by identifying and/or manipulating its component parts of *Role, Audience, Format,* and *Topic*	To consider the main elements of the writer's own work in order to generate a focus and purpose during the prewriting and drafting stages of the writing process
Rearranging	Selecting components of a text and moving them to another place within the text and/or modifying the order in which the author's ideas are presented	To refine and clarify the writer's thoughts during revision and/or drafting
Revisiting Prior Work	Looking through a collection of previously completed work to identify successes and challenges that may have been encountered with particular formats, conventions, style, word choice, and so on	To build on prior experience in preparation for a new piece of writing and/or to revise a previous piece of writing
Self Editing/Peer Editing	Working with a partner to examine a text closely in order to identify areas that might need to be corrected for grammar, punctuation, spelling	To provide a systematic process for editing a written text to ensure correctness of identified components such as conventions of standard English
Sharing and Responding	Communicating with another person or a small group of peers who respond to a piece of writing as focused readers (not necessarily as evaluators)	To make suggestions for improvement to the work of others and/or to receive appropriate and relevant feedback on the writer's own work, used during the drafting and revision process
Sketching	Drawing or sketching ideas or ordering of ideas. Includes storyboarding, visualizing	To generate and/or clarify ideas by visualizing them; may be part of prewriting
Substituting	Replacing original words or phrases in a text with new words or phrases that achieve the desired effect	To refine and clarify the writer's thoughts during revision and/or drafting
Transformation of Text	Providing opportunities for students to create new text from a studied text by changing the genre, vernacular, time period, culture, point of view, and so on	To highlight the elements of a genre, point of view and so on; to illustrate how elements of style work together
TWIST*	Arriving at a thesis statement that incorporates the following literary elements: tone, word choice (diction), imagery, style and theme	To craft an interpretive thesis in response to a prompt about a passage
Webbing	Developing a graphic organizer that consists of a series of circles connected with lines to indicate relationships among ideas	To generate ideas, concepts, or key words that provide a focus and/or establish organization prior to writing an initial draft and/or during the revision process

*AP strategy

SPEAKING AND LISTENING STRATEGIES

STRATEGY	DEFINITION	PURPOSE
Notetaking	Creating a record of information while listening to a speaker	To facilitate active listening; to record and organize ideas that assist in processing information
Oral Interpretation	Reading a text orally while providing the necessary inflection and emphasis that demonstrate an understanding of the meaning of the text	To share with an audience the reader's personal insight into a text through voice, fluency, tone, and purpose
Oral Reading	Reading aloud one's own text or the texts of others (e.g., echo reading, choral reading, paired readings).	To share one's own work or the work of others; build fluency and increase confidence in presenting to a group
Role Playing	Assuming the role or persona of a character	To develop the voice, emotions, and mannerisms of a character to facilitate improved comprehension of a text
Rehearsal	Encouraging multiple practices of a piece of text prior to a performance	To provide students with an opportunity to clarify the meaning of a text prior to a performance as they refine the use of dramatic conventions (e.g., gestures, vocal interpretations, facial expressions)

COLLABORATIVE STRATEGIES

STRATEGY	DEFINITION	PURPOSE
Think-Pair-Share	Considering and thinking about a topic or question and then writing what has been learned; pairing with a peer or a small group to share ideas; sharing ideas and discussion with a larger group	To construct meaning about a topic or question; to test thinking in relation to the ideas of others; to prepare for a discussion with a larger group
Discussion Groups	Engaging in an interactive, small group discussion, often with an assigned role; to consider a topic, text, question, and so on	To gain new understanding or insight of a text from multiple perspectives

Web Organizer

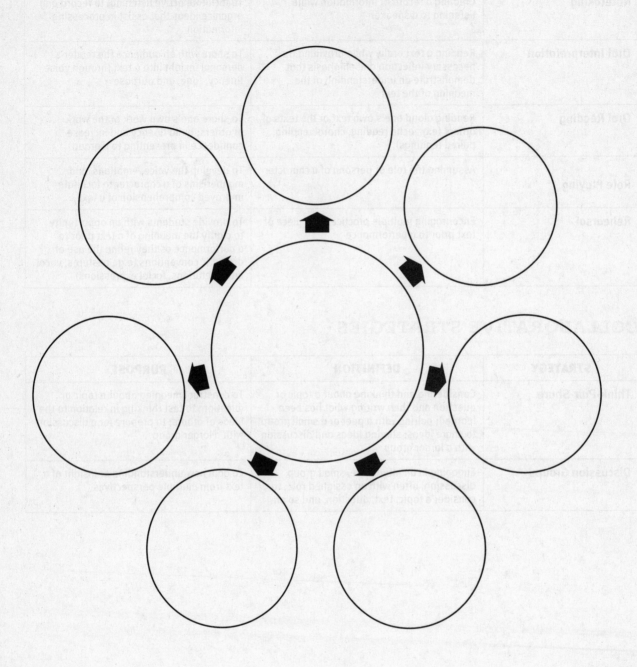

Concept Circle

Directions: Place your Academic Vocabulary word in the middle of the circle. Next, identify four concepts that closely relate to this concept, and place one in each quadrant. Finally, use words and/or pictures to show the relationship between the outer concepts and the Academic Vocabulary concept.

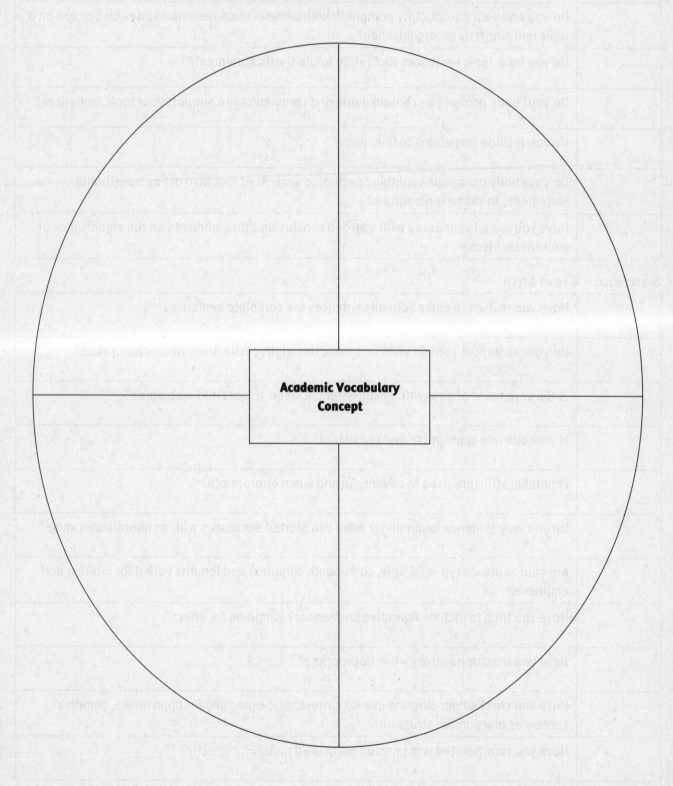

Academic Vocabulary Concept

Editor's / Writer's Checklist

Organizational Elements

	Does your title express the topic and engage the reader?
	Do you have an engaging hook or lead to open your essay?
	Do you end your introductory paragraph with a thesis statement that states an opinion on a topic and suggests an organization?
	Do you have topic sentences that relate to the thesis statement?
	Do your body paragraphs contain detail and commentary to support your topic sentences?
	Do you include transitions to link ideas?
	Do your body paragraphs contain concluding sentences that also act as transitional statements to the next paragraph?
	Have you ended your essay with a strong conclusion that comments on the significance of your thesis ideas?

Sentence Elements

	Have you revised to make sure all sentences are complete sentences?
	Do your sentences contain vivid verbs and descriptive adjectives when appropriate?
	Is the verb tense of your writing consistent? Do the subject and verb agree?
	Is pronoun use appropriate and consistent?
	Is parallel structure used to advantage and when appropriate?
	Do you vary sentence beginnings? Have you started sentences with a subordinate clause?
	Are your sentence types (simple, compound, complex) and lengths varied for interest and emphasis?
	Have you tried to include figurative and sensory language for effect?
	Have you used appositives when appropriate?
	Have you checked punctuation use for correctness, especially for appositives, complex sentences and parallel structure?
	Have you incorporated and punctuated quoted material correctly?

Compare and Contrast Diagram

Concept 1		Concept 2

HOW ALIKE?

HOW DIFFERENT?

	with regard to	

Glossary
Glosario

A

active-voice verbs: a verb form indicating that the subject performs the action
verbos en voz activa: forma verbal que indica que el sujeto realiza la acción

advertising techniques: specific methods used in print, graphics, or videos to persuade people to buy a product or use a service
técnicas publicitarias: métodos específicos usados en impresos, gráfica o videos para persuadir a las personas a comprar un producto o usar un servicio

alliteration: the repetition of initial consonant sounds in words that are close together
aliteración: repetición de sonidos consonánticos iniciales en palabras cercanas

allusion: a reference to a well-known person, event, or place from history, music, art, or another literary work
alusión: referencia a una persona, evento o lugar muy conocidos de la historia, música, arte u otra obra literaria

anaphora: the repetition of the same word or group of words at the beginnings of two or more clauses or lines
anáfora: repetición de la misma palabra o grupo de palabras al comienzo de una o más cláusulas o versos

anecdotal evidence: evidence based on personal accounts of incidents
evidencia anecdótica: evidencia basada en relatos personales de los hechos

annotated bibliography: a list of sources used in research along with comments about each source
bibliografía anotada: lista de fuentes utilizadas en la investigación, junto con comentarios acerca de cada fuente

antagonist: the character who opposes or struggles again the main character
antagonista: personaje que se opone o lucha contra el personaje principal

aphorism: a succinct statement expressing an opinion or general truth
aforismo: afirmación breve que expresa una opinión o verdad general

archetypes: universal symbols—images, characters, motifs, or patterns—that recur in myths, art and literature through the world
arquetipos: símbolos universales —imágenes, personajes, motivos o patrones— reiterativos en los mitos, el arte y la literatura alrededor del mundo

archival footage: film footage taken from another, previously recorded, source
cortometraje de archivo: fragmento de película tomada de otra fuente grabada previamente

argument: a form of writing that presents a particular opinion or idea and supports it with evidence
argumento: forma de redacción que presenta una opinión o idea particular y la apoya con evidencia

argumentation: the structure of an argument includes the *hook* (quotation, example, or idea that catches readers' attention), *claim* (the opinion or thesis statement), *support* (evidence in the form of facts, statistics, examples, anecdotes, or expert opinions), *concession* (the writer's admission that the other side of the argument has a valid point), *refutation* (a well-reasoned denial of an opponent's point, based on solid evidence), and *call to action* (an inspired request of readers)
argumentación: la estructura de una argumentación incluye el gancho (cita, ejemplo o idea que capta la atención del lector), afirmación (declaración de opinión o tesis), apoyo (evidencia en forma de hechos, estadísticas, ejemplos, anécdotas u opiniones de expertos), concesión (admisión por parte del escritor de que la otra parte del debate tiene un punto válido), refutación (negación bien razonada de una opinión del oponente, basada en evidencia sólida) y llamado a la acción (petición inspirada de lectores)

argument by analogy: a comparison of two similar situations, implying that the outcome of one will resemble the outcome of the other
argumento por analogía: comparación de dos situaciones semejantes, infiriendo que el resultado de será parecido al resultado de la otra

aside: a short speech spoken by an actor directly to the audience and unheard by other actors on stage
aparte: alocución breve dicha por un actor directamente al público y que no escuchan los demás actores que están en el escenario

assonance: the repetition of similar vowel sounds in accented syllables, followed by different consonant sounds, in words that are close together
asonancia: repetición de sonidos vocálicos similares en sílabas acentuadas, seguida de diferentes sonidos consonánticos, en palabras que están cercanas

audience: the intended readers, listeners, or viewers of specific types of written, spoken or visual texts
público: lectores objetivo, oyentes o espectadores de tipos específicos de textos escritos, hablados o visuales

audience analysis: determining the knowledge, beliefs, and needs of a target audience in order to reach them successfully
análisis del público: determinar los conocimientos, creencias y necesidades de una audiencia objetivo de modo de llegar a ella con éxito

author's purpose: the specific reason or reasons for the writing; what the author hopes to accomplish
propósito del autor: razón específica para escribir; lo que el autor espera lograr

B

balanced sentence: a sentence that presents ideas of equal weight in similar grammatical forms to emphasize the similarity or difference between the ideas
oración balanceada: oración que representa ideas de igual peso en formas gramaticales similares para enfatizar la semejanza o diferencia entre las ideas

bias: an inclination or mental leaning for or against something, which prevents impartial judgment
sesgo: inclinación o tendencia mental a favor o en contra de algo, lo que impide una opinión imparcial

blank verse: unrhymed verse
verso libre: verso que no tiene rima

blocking: in drama, how actors position themselves in relation to one another, the audience, and the objects on the stage
bloqueo: en drama, el modo en que los actores se sitúan entre sí, con el público y los objetos en el escenario

C

caricature: a visual or verbal representation in which characteristics or traits are exaggerated or distorted for emphasis
caricatura: representación visual o verbal en la que las características o rasgos se exageran o se distorsionan para dar énfasis

characterization: the methods a writer uses to develop characters
caracterización: métodos que usa un escritor para desarrollar personajes

characters: people, animals, or imaginary creatures that take part in the action of a story. A short story usually centers on a *main character*, but may also contain one or more *minor characters*, who are not as complex, but whose thoughts, words, or actions move the plot along. A character who is *dynamic* changes in response to the events of the narrative; a character who is *static* remains the same throughout the narrative. A *round* character is fully developed—he or she shows a variety of traits; a *flat* character is one-dimensional, usually showing only one trait.
personajes: personas, animales o criaturas imaginarias que participan en la acción de un cuento. Un cuento corto normalmente se centra en un *personaje principal*, pero puede también contener uno o más *personajes secundarios*, que no son tan complejos, pero cuyos pensamientos, palabras o acciones hacen avanzar la trama. Un personaje que es *dinámico* cambia según los eventos del relato; un personaje que es *estático* permanece igual a lo largo del relato. Un personaje *complejo* está completamente desarrollado: muestra una diversidad de rasgos; un personaje *simple* es unidimensional, mostrando normalmente sólo un rasgo.

chorus: in traditional or classic drama, a group of performers who speak as one and comment on the action of the play
coro: en el drama tradicional o clásico, grupo de actores que hablan al unísono y comentan la acción de la obra teatral

cinematic elements: the features of cinema—movies, film, video—that contribute to its form and structure: *angles* (the view from which the image is shot); *framing* (how a scene is structured); *lighting* (the type of lighting used to light a scene); and *mise en scène* (the composition, setting, or staging of an image, or a scene in a film); *sound* (the sound effects and music accompanying each scene)
elementos cinematográficos: las características del cine—películas, filmaciones, video—que contribuyen a darle forma y estructura: *angulación* (vista desde la cual se toma la imagen); *encuadre* (cómo se estructura una escena); *iluminación* (tipo de iluminación que se usa para una escena); y *montaje* (composición, ambiente o escenificación de una imagen o escena en una película); *sonido* (efectos sonoros y música que acompañan cada escena)

claim: a position statement (or thesis) that asserts an idea or makes an argument
afirmación: declaración de opinión (o tesis) que asevera una idea o establece un debate

cliché: an overused expression or idea
cliché: expresión o idea que se usa en exceso

climax: the point at which the action reaches its peak; the point of greatest interest or suspense in a story; the turning point at which the outcome of the conflict is decided
clímax: punto en el que la acción alcanza su punto culminante; punto de mayor interés en un cuento; punto de inflexión en el que se decide el resultado del conflicto

coherence: the quality of unity or logical connection among ideas; the clear and orderly presentation of ideas in a paragraph or essay
coherencia: calidad de unidad o relación lógica entre las ideas; presentación clara y ordenada de las ideas en un párrafo o ensayo

commentary: in an expository essay or paragraph, the explanation of the importance or relevance of supporting detail and the way the details support the larger analysis
comentario: ensayo o párrafo expositivo, explicación de la importancia o relevancia de los detalles de apoyo, y la manera en que los detalles apoyan el análisis principal

complex sentence: a sentence containing one independent clause and one or more subordinate clauses
oración compleja: oración que contiene una cláusula independiente y una o más cláusulas subordinadas

complications: the events in a plot that develop the conflict; the complications move the plot forward in its rising action
complicaciones: sucesos de una trama que desarrollan el conflicto; las complicaciones hacen avanzar la trama en su acción ascendente

compound sentence: a sentence containing two independent clauses
oración compuesta: oración que contiene dos cláusulas independientes

concession: an admission in an argument that the opposing side has valid points
concesión: admitir en un debate que el lado opositor tiene opiniones válidas

conflict: a struggle or problem in a story. An *internal conflict* occurs when a character struggles between opposing needs or desires or emotions within his or her own mind. An *external conflict* occurs when a character struggles against an outside force. This force may be another character, a societal expectation, or something in the physical world.

conflicto: lucha o problema en un cuento. Un *conflicto interno* ocurre cuando un personaje lucha entre necesidades o deseos o emociones que se contraponen dentro de su mente. Un *conflicto externo* ocurre cuando un personaje lucha contra una fuerza externa. Esta fuerza puede ser otro personaje, una expectativa social o algo del mundo físico.

connotation: the associations and emotional overtones attached to a word beyond its literal definition or denotation. A connotation may be positive, negative, or neutral.

connotación: asociaciones y alusiones emocionales unidas a una palabra más allá de su definición literal o denotación. Una connotación puede ser positiva, negativa o neutra.

consonance: the repetition of final consonant sounds in stressed syllables with different vowel sounds

consonancia: repetición de sonidos consonánticos finales en sílabas acentuadas con diferentes sonidos vocálicos

context: the circumstances or conditions in which something takes place

contexto: circunstancias o condiciones en las que algo ocurre

conventions: standard practices and forms

convenciones: prácticas y formas usuales

couplet: two consecutive lines of verse with end rhyme; a couplet usually expresses a complete unit of thought

copla: dos líneas de versos consecutivos con rima final; una copla normalmente expresa una unidad de pensamiento completa

credibility: the quality of being trusted or believed

credibilidad: calidad de ser confiable o creíble

critical lens: a particular identifiable perspective as in Reader Response Criticism, Cultural Criticism, etc., through which a text can be analyzed and interpreted

ojo crítico: punto de vista particular identificable como por ejemplo Teoría de la recepción, Crítica sociocultural, etc., por medio del que se puede analizar e interpretar un texto

cultural conflict: a struggle that occurs when people with different cultural expectations or attitudes interact

conflicto cultural: lucha que ocurre cuando interactúan personas con diferentes expectativas o actitudes culturales

culture: the shared set of arts, ideas, skills, institutions, customs, attitude, values and achievements that characterize a group of people, and that are passed on or taught to succeeding generations

cultura: conjunto de artes, ideas, destrezas, instituciones, costumbres, actitud, valores y logros compartidos que caracterizan a un grupo de personas, y que se transfieren o enseñan a las generaciones siguientes

cumulative (or loose) sentence: a sentence in which the main clause comes first, followed by subordinate structures or clauses

oración acumulativa (o frases sueltas): oración cuya cláusula principal viene primero, seguida de estructuras o cláusulas subordinadas

D

deductive reasoning: a process of using general information from which to draw a specific conclusion

razonamiento deductivo: proceso en que se usa información general para sacar una conclusión específica

denotation: the exact literal meaning of a word

denotación: significado literal exacto de una palabra

detail: a specific fact, observation, or incident; any of the small pieces or parts that make up something else

detalle: hecho, observación o incidente específico; cualquiera de las pequeñas piezas o partes que constituyen otra cosa

dialect: the distinctive language, including the sounds, spelling, grammar, and diction, of a specific group or class of people

dialecto: lenguaje distintivo, incluyendo sonidos, ortografía, gramática y dicción, de un grupo o clase específico de personas

dialogue: the words spoken by characters in a narrative or film

diálogo: palabras que dicen los personajes en un relato o película

diction: the writer's choice of words; a stylistic element that helps convey voice and tone

dicción: selección de palabras por parte del escritor; elemento estilístico que ayuda a transmitir voz y tono

diegetic sound: actual noises associated with the shooting of a scene, such as voices and background sounds

sonido diegético: sonidos reales asociados con la filmación de una escena, como por ejemplo voces y sonidos de fondo

discourse: the language or speech used in a particular context or subject

discurso: lenguaje o habla usada en un contexto o tema en particular

documentary or nonfiction film: a genre of filmmaking that provides a visual record of factual events, using photographs, video footage, and interviews

documental o película de no-ficción: género cinematográfico que realiza un registro visual de sucesos basados en hechos por medio del uso de fotografías, registro en videos y entrevistas

drama: a play written for stage, radio, film, or television, usually about a serious topic or situation

drama: obra teatral escrita para representar en un escenario, radio, cine o televisión, normalmente sobre un tema o situación seria

E

editorial: an article in a newspaper or magazine expressing the opinion of its editor or publisher

editorial: artículo de periódico o revista, que expresa la opinión de su editor

effect: the result or influence of using a specific literary or cinematic device

efecto: resultado o influencia de usar un recurso literario o cinematográfico específico

empirical evidence: evidence based on experiences and direct observation through research
evidencia empírica: evidencia basada en experiencias y en la observación directa por medio de la investigación

epigram: a short witty saying
epigrama: dicho corto e ingenioso

ethos: (ethical appeal) a rhetorical appeal that focuses on ethics, or the character or qualifications of the speaker
ethos: (recurso ético) recurso retórico centrado en la ética o en el carácter o capacidades del orador

evidence: the information that supports or proves an idea or claim; forms of evidence include facts, statistics (numerical facts), expert opinions, examples, and anecdotes; *see also*, anecdotal, empirical, and logical evidence
evidencia: información que apoya o prueba una idea o afirmación; formas de evidencia incluyen hechos, estadística (datos numéricos), opiniones de expertos, ejemplos y anécdotas; *ver también* evidencia anecdótica, empírica y lógica

exaggeration: representing something as larger, better, or worse than it really is
exageración: representar algo como más grande, mejor o peor que lo que realmente es

explicit theme: a theme that is clearly stated by the writer
tema explícito: tema que está claramente establecido por el escritor

exposition: events that give a reader background information needed to understand a story. During exposition, characters are introduced, the setting is described, and the conflict begins to unfold.
exposición: sucesos que dan al lector los antecedentes necesarios para comprender un cuento. Durante la exposición, se presentan los personajes, se describe el ambiente y se comienza a revelar el conflicto.

extended metaphor: a metaphor extended over several lines or throughout an entire poem
metáfora extendida: metáfora que se extiende por varios versos o a través de un poema completo

F

falling action: the events in a play, story, or novel that follow the climax, or moment of greatest suspense, and lead to the resolution
acción descendente: sucesos de una obra teatral, cuento o novela posteriores al clímax, o momento de mayor suspenso, y que conllevan a la resolución

fallacy: a false or misleading argument
falacia: argumento falso o engañoso

figurative language: imaginative language not meant to be taken literally; figurative language uses figures of speech
lenguaje figurativo: lenguaje imaginativo que no pretende ser tomado literalmente; el lenguaje figurativo usa figuras literarias

flashback: an interruption in the sequence of events to relate events that occurred in the past
flashback: interrupción en la secuencia de los sucesos para relatar sucesos ocurridos en el pasado

fixed form: a form of poetry in which the length and pattern are determined by established usage of tradition, such as a sonnet
forma fija: forma de poesía en la que la longitud y el patrón están determinados por el uso de la tradición, como un soneto

foil: a character whose actions or thoughts are juxtaposed against those of a major character in order to highlight key attributes of the major character
antagonista: personaje cuyas acciones o pensamientos se yuxtaponen a los de un personaje principal con el fin de destacar atributos clave del personaje principal

folk tale: a story without a known author that has been preserved through oral retellings
cuento folclórico: cuento sin autor conocido que se ha conservado por medio de relatos orales

footage: literally, a length of film; the expression is still used to refer to digital video clips
metraje: literalmente, la longitud de una película; la expresión aún se usa para referirse a video clips digitales

foreshadowing: the use of hints or clues in a narrative to suggest future action
presagio: uso de claves o pistas en un relato para sugerir una acción futura

free verse: poetry without a fixed pattern of meter and rhyme
verso libre: poesía que no sigue ningún patrón, ritmo o rima regular

G

genre: a kind or style of literature or art, each with its own specific characteristics. For example, poetry, short story, and novel are literary genres. Painting and sculpture are artistic genres.
género: tipo o estilo de literatura o arte, cada uno con sus propias características específicas. Por ejemplo, la poesía, el cuento corto y la novela son géneros literarios. La pintura y la escultura son géneros artísticos.

genre conventions: the essential features and format that characterize a specific genre
convenciones genéricas: características básicas y el formato que caracterizan un género específico

graphics: images or text used to provide information on screen
gráfica: imágenes o texto que se usa para dar información en pantalla

graphic novel: a book-length narrative, or story, in the form of a comic strip rather than words
novela gráfica: narrativa o cuento del largo de un libro, en forma de tira cómica más que palabras

H

hamartia: a tragic hero's fatal flaw; an ingrained character trait that causes a hero to make decisions that ultimately lead to his or her death or downfall
hamartia: error fatal de un héroe trágico; característica propia de un personaje que causa que un héroe tome decisiones que finalmente llevan a su muerte o caída

hero: the main character or protagonist of a play, with whom audiences become emotionally invested
héroe: personaje principal o protagonista de una obra teatral, con el que el público se involucra emocionalmente

hook: an interesting quotation, anecdote, or example at the beginning of a piece of writing that grabs readers' attention
gancho: cita, anécdota o ejemplo interesante al comienzo de un escrito, que capta la atención del lector

humor: the quality of being amusing
humor: calidad de ser divertido

hyperbole: exaggeration used to suggest strong emotion or create a comic effect
hipérbole: exageración que se usa para sugerir una emoción fuerte o crear un efecto cómico

I

iamb: a metrical foot that consists of an unstressed syllable followed by a stressed syllable
yambo: pie métrico que consta de una sílaba átona seguida de una sílaba acentuada

iambic pentameter: a rhythmic pattern of five feet (or units) of one unstressed syllable followed by a stressed syllable
pentámetro yámbico: patrón rítmico de cinco pies (o unidades) de una sílaba átona seguida de una sílaba acentuada

image: a word or phrase that appeals to one of more of the five senses and creates a picture
imagen: palabra o frase que apela a uno o más de los cinco sentido y crea un cuadro

imagery: the verbal expression of sensory experience; descriptive or figurative language used to create word pictures; imagery is created by details that appeal to one or more of the five senses
imaginería: lenguaje descriptivo o figurativo utilizado para crear imágenes verbales; la imaginería es creada por detalles que apelan a uno o más de los cinco sentidos

implied theme: a theme that is understood through the writer's diction, language construction, and use of literary devices
tema implícito: tema que se entiende a través de la dicción del escritor, construcción lingüística y uso de recursos literarios

inductive reasoning: a process of looking at individual facts to draw a general conclusion
razonamiento inductivo: proceso de observación de hechos individuales para sacar una conclusión general

interior monologue: a literary device in which a character's internal emotions and thoughts are presented
monólogo interior: recurso literario en el que se presentan las emociones internas y pensamientos de un personaje

irony: a literary device that exploits readers' expectations; irony occurs when what is expected turns out to be quite different from what actually happens. *Dramatic irony* is a form of irony in which the reader or audience knows more about the circumstances or future events in a story than the characters within it; *verbal irony* occurs when a speaker or narrator says one thing while meaning the opposite; *situational irony* occurs

when an event contradicts the expectations of the characters or the reader.
ironía: recurso literario que explota las expectativas de los lectores; la ironía ocurre cuando lo que se espera resulta ser bastante diferente de lo que realmente ocurre. La *ironía dramática* es una forma de ironía en la que el lector o la audiencia saben más acerca de las circunstancias o sucesos futuros de un cuento que los personajes del mismo; la *ironía verbal* ocurre cuando un orador o narrador dice una cosa queriendo decir lo contrario; la *ironía situacional* ocurre cuando un suceso contradice las expectativas de los personajes o del lector.

J

justice: the quality of being reasonable and fair in the administration of the law; the ideal of rightness or fairness
justicia: calidad de ser razonable e imparcial en la administración de la ley; ideal de rectitud o equidad

juxtaposition: the arrangement of two or more things for the purpose of comparison
yuxtaposición: ordenamiento de dos o más cosas con el objeto de compararlas

L

literary theory: attempts to establish principles for interpreting and evaluating literary texts
teoría literaria: intento de establecer principios para interpretar y evaluar textos literarios

logical evidence: evidence based on facts and a clear rationale
evidencia lógica: evidencia basada en hechos y una clara fundamentación

logos: (logical appeal) a rhetorical appeal that uses logic to appeal to the sense of reason
logos: (apelación lógica) apelación retórica que usa la lógica para apelar al sentido de la razón

M

metacognition: the ability to know and be aware of one's own thought processes; self-reflection
metacognición: capacidad de conocer y estar consciente de los propios procesos del pensamiento; introspección

metaphor: a comparison between two unlike things in which one thing is spoken of as if it were another; for example, the moon was a crisp white cracker
metáfora: comparación entre dos cosas diferentes en la que se habla de una cosa como si fuera otra; por ejemplo, la luna era una galletita blanca crujiente

meter: a pattern of stressed and unstressed syllables in poetry
métrica: patrón de sílabas acentuadas y átonas en poesía

monologue: a dramatic speech delivered by a single character in a play
monólogo: discurso dramático que hace un solo personaje en una obra teatral

montage: a composite picture that is created by bringing together a number of images and arranging them to create a connected whole

montaje: cuadro compuesto que se crea al reunir un número de imágenes y que al organizarlas se crea un todo relacionado

mood: the atmosphere or general feeling in a literary work
carácter: atmósfera o sentimiento general en una obra literaria

motif: a recurrent image, symbol, theme, character type, subject, or narrative detail that becomes a unifying element in an artistic work.
motivo: imagen, símbolo, tema, tipo de personaje, tema o detalle narrativo recurrente que se convierte en un elemento unificador en una obra artística.

myth: a traditional story that explains the actions of gods or heroes or the origins of the elements of nature
mito: cuento tradicional que explica las acciones de dioses o héroes, o los orígenes de los elementos de la naturaleza

N

narration: the act of telling a story
narración: acto de contar un cuento

non-diegetic sound: voice-overs and commentary, sounds that do not come from the action on screen.
sonido no diegético: voces y comentarios superpuestos, sonidos que no provienen de la acción en pantalla.

O

objective: based on factual information
objetivo: basado en información de hechos

objectivity: the representation of facts or ideas without injecting personal feelings or biases
objetividad: representación de los hechos o ideas sin agregar sentimientos o prejuicios personales

ode: a lyric poem expressing feelings or thoughts of a speaker, often celebrating a person, event, or a thing
oda: poema lírico que expresa sentimientos o pensamientos de un orador, que frecuentemente celebra a una persona, suceso o cosa

onomatopoeia: words whose sound suggest their meaning
onomatopeya: palabras cuyo sonido sugiere su significado

oral tradition: the passing down of stories, tales, proverbs, and other culturally important stories and ideas through oral retellings
tradición oral: traspaso de historias, cuentos, proverbios y otras historias de importancia cultural por medio de relatos orales

oxymoron: words that appear to contradict each other; e.g., cold fire
oxímoron: palabras que parecen contradecirse mutuamente; por ejemplo, fuego frío

P

parallel structure (parallelism): refers to a grammatical or structural similarity between sentences or parts of a sentence, so that elements of equal importance are equally developed and similarly phrased for emphasis
estructura paralela (paralelismo): se refiere a una similitud gramatical o estructural entre oraciones o partes de una

oración, de modo que los elementos de igual importancia se desarrollen por igual y se expresen de manera similar para dar énfasis

paraphrase: to briefly restate ideas from another source in one's own words
parafrasear: volver a presentar las ideas de otra fuente en nuestras propias palabras

parody: a literary or artistic work that imitates the characteristic style of an author or a work for comic effect or ridicule
parodia: obra literaria o artística que imita el estilo característico de un autor o una obra para dar un efecto cómico o ridículo

passive-voice verbs: verb form in which the subject receives the action; the passive voice consists of a form of the verb be plus a past participle of the verb
verbos en voz pasiva: forma verbal en la que el sujeto recibe la acción; la voz pasiva se forma con el verbo ser más el participio pasado de un verbo

pathos: (emotional appeal) a rhetorical appeal to readers' or listeners' senses or emotions
pathos: (apelación emocional) apelación retórica a los sentidos o emociones de los lectores u oyentes

periodic sentence: a sentence that makes sense only when the end of the sentence is reached; that is, when the main clause comes last
oración periódica: oración que tiene sentido sólo cuando se llega al final de la oración; es decir, cuando la cláusula principal viene al final

persona: the voice assumed by a writer to express ideas or beliefs that may not be his or her own
personaje: voz que asume un escritor para expresar ideas o creencias que pueden no ser las propias

personification: a figure of speech that gives human qualities to an animal, object, or idea
personificación: figura literaria que da características humanas a un animal, objeto o idea

persuasive argument: an argument that convinces readers to accept or believe a writer's perspective on a topic
argumento persuasivo: argumento que convence a los lectores a aceptar o creer en la perspectiva de un escritor acerca de un tema

perspective: a way of looking at the world or a mental concept about things or events, one that judges relationships within or among things or events
perspectiva: manera de visualizar el mundo o concepto mental de las cosas o sucesos, que juzga las relaciones dentro o entre cosas o sucesos

photo essay: a collection of photographic images that reveal the author's perspective on the subject
ensayo fotográfico: recolección de imágenes fotográficas que revelan la perspectiva del autor acerca del tema

plagiarism: the unattributed use of another writer's words or ideas
plagio: usar como propias las palabras o ideas de otro escritor

plot: the sequence of related events that make up a story or novel
trama: secuencia de sucesos relacionados que conforman un cuento o novela

poetic structure: the organization of words, lines, and images as well as ideas
estructura poética: organización de las palabras, versos e imágenes, así como también de las ideas

point of view: the perspective from which a narrative is told; i.e., first person, third person limited, third person omniscient
punto de vista: perspectiva desde la cual se cuenta un relato; es decir, primera persona, tercera persona limitada, tercera persona omnisciente

precept: a rule, instruction, or principle that guides somebody's actions and/or moral behavior
precepto: regla, instrucción o principio que guía las acciones y/o conducta moral de alguien

primary footage: film footage shot by the filmmaker for the text at hand
metraje principal: filmación hecha por el cineasta para el texto que tiene a mano

primary source: an original document containing firsthand information about a subject
fuente primaria: documento original que contiene información de primera mano acerca de un tema

prologue: the introduction or preface to a literary work
prólogo: introducción o prefacio de una obra literaria

prose: ordinary written or spoken language using sentences and paragraphs, without deliberate or regular meter or rhyme; not poetry or song
prosa: forma común del lenguaje escrito o hablado, usando oraciones y párrafos, sin métrica o rima deliberada o regular; ni poesía ni canción

protagonist: the central character in a work of literature, the one who is involved in the main conflict in the plot
protagonista: personaje central de una obra literaria, el que participa en el conflicto principal de la trama

Q

quatrain: a four-line stanza in a poem
cuarteta: en un poema, estrofa de cuatro versos

R

reasoning: the thinking or logic used to make a claim in an argument
razonamiento: pensamiento o lógica que se usa para hacer una afirmación en un argumento

refrain: a regularly repeated line or group of lines in a poem or song, usually at the end of a stanza
estribillo: verso o grupo de versos que se repiten con regularidad en un poema o canción, normalmente al final de una estrofa

refutation: the reasoning used to disprove an opposing point
refutación: razonamiento que se usa para rechazar una opinión contraria

reliability: the extent to which a source provides good quality and trustworthy information
confiabilidad: grado en el que una fuente da información confiable y de buena calidad

repetition: the use of any element of language—a sound, a word, a phrase, a line, or a stanza—more than once
repetición: uso de cualquier elemento del lenguaje—un sonido, una palabra, una frase, un verso o una estrofa—más de una vez

resolution (denouement): the end of a play, story, or novel in which the main conflict is finally resolved
resolución (desenlace): final de una obra teatral, cuento o novela, en el que el conflicto principal finalmente se resuelve

résumé: a document that outlines a person's skills, education, and work history
currículum vitae: documento que resume las destrezas, educación y experiencia laboral de una persona

rhetoric: the art of using words to persuade in writing or speaking
retórica: arte de usar las palabras para persuadir por escrito o de manera hablada

rhetorical appeals: the use of emotional, ethical, and logical arguments to persuade in writing or speaking
recursos retóricos: uso de argumentos emocionales, éticos y lógicos para persuadir por escrito o de manera hablada

rhetorical context: the subject, purpose, audience, occasion, or situation in which writing occurs
contexto retórico: sujeto, propósito, audiencia, ocasión o situación en que ocurre el escrito

rhetorical devices: specific techniques used in writing or speaking to create a literary effect or enhance effectiveness
dispositivos retóricos: técnicas específicas que se usan al escribir o al hablar para crear un efecto literario o mejorar la efectividad

rhetorical question: a question that is asked for effect or one for which the answer is obvious
pregunta retórica: pregunta hecha para producir un efecto o cuya respuesta es obvia

rhyme: the repetition of sounds at the ends of words
rima: repetición de sonidos al final de las palabras

rhyme scheme: a consistent pattern of rhyme throughout a poem
esquema de la rima: patrón consistente de una rima a lo largo de un poema

rhythm: the pattern of stressed and unstressed syllables in spoken or written language, especially in poetry
ritmo: patrón de sílabas acentuadas y no acentuadas en lenguaje hablado o escrito, especialmente en poesía

rising action: the movement of a plot toward a climax or moment of greatest excitement; the rising action is fueled by the characters' responses to the conflict
acción ascendente: movimiento de una trama hacia el clímax o momento de mayor emoción; la acción ascendente es impulsada por las reacciones de los personajes ante el conflicto

S

satire: a manner of writing that mixes a critical attitude with wit and humor in an effort to improve mankind and human institutions

sátira: manera de escribir que mezcla una actitud crítica con ingenio y humor en un esfuerzo por mejorar a la humanidad y las instituciones humanas

scenario: an outline, a brief account, a script, or a synopsis of a proposed series of events

escenario: bosquejo, relato breve, libreto o sinopsis de una serie de sucesos propuestos

secondary source: discussion about or commentary on a primary source; the key feature of a secondary source is that it offers an interpretation of information gathered from primary sources

fuente secundaria: discusión o comentario acerca de una fuente primaria; la característica clave de una fuente secundaria es que ofrece una interpretación de la información recopilada en las fuentes primarias

sensory details: details that appeal to or evoke one or more of the five senses--sight, sound, smell, taste, touch

detalles sensoriales: detalles que apelan o evocan uno o más de los cinco sentidos: vista, oído, gusto, olfato, tacto

sensory images: images that appeal to the reader's senses—sight, sound, smell, taste, touch

imágenes sensoriales: imágenes que apelan a los sentidos del lector: vista, oído, olfato, gusto, tacto

setting: the time and place in which a story happens

ambiente: tiempo y lugar en el que ocurre un relato

simile: a comparison of two or more unlike things using the words *like or as*; for example, the moon was as white as milk

símil: comparación entre dos o más cosas diferentes usando las palabras *como o tan*; por ejemplo, la luna estaba tan blanca como la leche

slanters: rhetorical devices used to present the subject in a biased way.

soslayo: recursos retóricos para presentar el tema de modo sesgado.

slogan: a short, catchy phrase used for advertising by a business, club, or political party

eslogan: frase corta y tendenciosa que usa como publicidad para un negocio, club o partido político

social commentary: an expression of an opinion with the goal of promoting change by appealing to a sense of justice

comentario social: expresión de una opinión con el objeto de promover el cambio al apelar a un sentido de justicia

soliloquy: a long speech delivered by an actor alone on the stage

soliloquio: discurso largo realizado por un actor sobre el escenario

sonnet: a fourteen-line lyric poem, usually written in iambic pentameter and following a strict pattern of rhyme

soneto: poema lírico de catorce versos, normalmente escrito en un pentámetro yámbico y que sigue un patrón de rima estricto

speaker: the imaginary voice or persona of the writer or author

orador: voz o persona imaginaria del escritor o autor

stakeholder: a person motivated or affected by a course of action

participante: persona motivada o afectada por el curso de una acción

stanza: a group of lines, usually similar in length and pattern, that form a unit within a poem

estrofa: grupo de versos, normalmente similares en longitud y patrón, que forman una unidad dentro de un poema

stereotype: an oversimplified, generalized conception, opinion, and/or image about particular groups of people.

estereotipo: concepto generalizado, opinión y/o imagen demasiado simplificada acerca de grupos específicos de personas.

structure: the way a literary work is organized; the arrangement of the parts in a literary work

estructura: manera en que la obra literaria está organizada; disposición de las partes en una obra literaria

style: the distinctive way a writer uses language, characterized by elements of diction, syntax, imagery, etc.

estilo: manera distintiva en que un escritor usa el lenguaje, caracterizada por elementos de dicción, sintaxis, lenguaje figurado, etc.

subculture: a smaller subsection of a culture; for example, within the culture of a high school may be many subcultures

subcultura: subsección más pequeña de una cultura; por ejemplo, dentro de la cultura de una escuela secundaria puede haber muchas subculturas

subjectivity: based on one's personal point of view, opinion, or values

subjetividad: en base en nuestro punto de vista, opinión o valores personales

subtext: the underlying or implicit meaning in dialogue or the implied relationship between characters in a book, movie, play or film. The subtext of a work is not explicitly stated.

subtexto: significado subyacente o implícito en el diálogo o la relación implícita entre los personajes de un libro, película, u obra teatral. El subtexto de una obra no se establece de manera explícita.

survey: a method of collecting data from a group of people; it can be written, such as a print or online questionnaire, or oral, such as an in-person interview

encuesta: método para recolectar datos de un grupo de personas; puede ser escrita, como un impreso o cuestionario en línea, u oral, como en una entrevista personal

symbol: anything (object, animal, event, person, or place) that represents itself but also stands for something else on a figurative level

símbolo: cualquier cosa (objeto, animal, evento, persona o lugar) que se representa a sí misma, pero también representa otra cosa a nivel figurativo

symbolic: serving as a symbol; involving the use of symbols or symbolism

simbólico: que sirve como símbolo; que implica el uso de símbolos o simbolismo

syntax: the arrangement of words and the order of grammatical elements in a sentence; the way in which words are put together to make meaningful elements, such as phrases, clauses, and sentences

sintaxis: disposición de las palabras y orden de los elementos gramaticales en una oración; manera en que las palabras se juntan para formar elementos significativos, como frases, cláusulas y oraciones

synthesis: the act of combining ideas from different sources to create, express, or support a new idea

síntesis: acto de combinar ideas de diferentes fuentes para crear, expresar o apoyar una nueva idea

T

target audience: the intended group for which a work is designed to appeal or reach

público objetivo: grupo al que se pretende apelar o llegar con una obra

thematic statement: an interpretive statement articulating the central meaning or message of a text

oración temática: afirmación interpretativa que articula el significado o mensaje central de un texto

theatrical elements: elements employed by dramatists and directors to tell a story on stage. Elements include *costumes* (the clothing worn by actors to express their characters), *makeup* (cosmetics used to change actors' appearances and express their characters), *props* (objects used to help set the scene, advance a plot and make a story realistic), *set* (the place where the action takes place, as suggested by objects, such as furniture, placed on a stage), *acting choices* (gestures, movements, staging, and vocal techniques actors use to convey their characters and tell a story).

elementos teatrales: elementos que utilizan los dramaturgos y directores para contar una historia en el escenario. Los elementos incluyen *vestuario* (ropa que usan los actores para expresar sus personajes), *maquillaje* (cosméticos que se usan para cambiar la apariencia de los actores y expresar sus personajes), *elementos* (objetos que se usan para ayudar a montar la escena, avanzar la trama y crear una historia realista), *plató* (lugar donde tiene lugar la acción, según lo sugieren los objetos, como muebles, colocados sobre un escenario), *opciones de actuación* (gestos, movimientos, representación y técnicas vocales que se usan para transmitir sus personajes y narrar una historia).

theme: a writer's central idea or main message about life; *see also*, explicit theme, implied theme

tema: idea central o mensaje principal acerca de la vida de un escritor; *véase también*, tema explícito, tema implícito

thesis: the main idea or point of an essay or article; in an argumentative essay the thesis is the writer's position on an issue

tesis: idea o punto principal de un ensayo o artículo; en un ensayo argumentativo, la tesis es la opinión del autor acerca de un tema

topic sentence: a sentence that states the main idea of a paragraph; in an essay, it also makes a point that supports the thesis statement

oración principal: oración que establece la idea principal de un párrafo; en un ensayo, también establece una proposición que apoya el enunciado de la tesis

tone: a writer's or speaker's attitude toward a subject

tono: actitud de un escritor u orador acerca de un tema

tragedy: a dramatic play that tells the story of a character, usually of a noble birth, who meets an untimely and unhappy death or downfall, often because of a specific character flaw or twist of fate

tragedia: obra teatral dramática que cuenta la historia de un personaje, normalmente de origen noble, que encuentra una muerte o caída imprevista o infeliz, con frecuencia debido a un defecto específico del personaje o una vuelta del destino

tragic hero: an archetypal hero based on the Greek concept of tragedy; the tragic hero has a flaw that makes him vulnerable to downfall or death

héroe trágico: héroe arquetípico basado en el concepto griego de la tragedia; el héroe trágico tiene un defecto que lo hace vulnerable a la caída o a la muerte

U

understatement: the representation of something as smaller or less significant than it really is; the opposite of exaggeration or hyperbole

subestimación: representación de algo como más pequeño o menos importante de lo que realmente es; lo opuesto a la exageración o hipérbole

V

valid: believable or truthful

válido: creíble o verídico

validity: the quality of truth or accuracy in a source

validez: calidad de verdad o precisión en una fuente

vignette: a picture or visual or a brief descriptive literary piece

viñeta: ilustración o representación visual o pieza literaria descriptiva breve

vocal delivery: the way words are expressed on stage, through volume, pitch, rate or speed of speech, pauses, pronunciation, and articulation

presentación vocal: manera en que se expresan las palabras en el escenario, por medio del volumen, tono, rapidez o velocidad del discurso, pausas, pronunciación y articulación

voice: the way a writer or speaker uses words and tone to express ideas as well as his or her personas

voz: manera en que el escritor u orador usa las palabras y el tono para expresar ideas, así como también su personaje

Index of Skills

Literary Skills

Adversaries, 217
Allusions, 121
Analogies, 9, 91, 106, 131, 248
Aphorisms, 6, 52
Archetypal criticism, 88, 94, 108, 109,
111, 142, 161, 198, 245
Asides, 188
Audience, 34, 53, 102, 114, 115, 170,
188, 195, 227, 247, 248, 312, 326
Bias, 272, 273, 277, 278, 279, 318
Characterization, 99, 100, 136, 176, 179
Characters, 94, 99, 107, 140, 142, 171,
176, 179, 180, 188, 189, 192, 199,
200, 328
antagonist, 217
protagonist, 217, 235, 237, 241, 245,
247
tragic hero, 217
Chronological order, 202, 203
Comics, 229
Compare and contrast, 48, 107, 200
Conflict, 102, 107
Credibility, 319
Critical perspective, 143–144, 146, 148,
150, 152, 154, 156, 158, 191, 193,
198, 241, 245, 246
Cultural criticism, 1, 45, 46, 53, 57, 123,
161, 168, 169, 177, 191, 193, 198,
225, 231, 236, 237, 259, 282, 296,
297, 299, 300, 302, 306, 308, 309
Details, textual, 10, 19, 21, 37, 109, 242,
243, 270, 279, 280, 281, 287
Dialogue, 68, 102, 103, 104, 105, 107,
170, 177, 187, 188
Diction, 19, 21, 22, 30, 34, 71
Downplayers, 278, 293, 309
Feminist criticism, 89, 120, 123, 124,
129, 131, 138, 139, 140, 161, 187,
191, 193, 198, 243, 244, 287, 288,
295, 301
Film interpretation, 65, 91, 92, 93, 108,
109, 140, 180, 190, 191, 196, 197,
311, 325
Flashback, 243
Flashpoint, in hero's journey, 217
Flourishing, in hero's journey, 217
Foil, to heroic character, 217
Folk tales, 124
Graphic novels, 227, 229, 230–233, 256
Historical criticism, 163, 182, 191, 198,
282, 288, 293, 296, 297, 300
Hyperbole, 278, 293
Idioms, 70
Imagery, 19, 20, 37

Innuendo, 278
Irony
dramatic, 170, 188
situational, 170
verbal, 170
Literary theory, 4, 12
Literature circles, 257
Marxist criticism, 89, 113, 114, 115,
142, 161, 171, 191, 193, 198, 200,
243, 244
Metaphors, 33
Mise en scène, 9, 95
Monologue, 8, 109
interior, 241
Montage, 135
Mood, 58, 242
Motifs, 94
Myths, 97
Narratives, 234–235, 236, 244
New literacies, 227
Parody, 51
Perception, 6
Perspective, 7
Play scripts, 102
Plot, 142, 189, 230, 237
Poetry, 22
fixed form, 16
free verse, 16
Point of view, 1, 11, 21, 34, 37, 44, 278
Prologue, 23
Protagonist, 217
Reader response critical theory, 1, 4, 9,
11, 12, 14, 16, 18, 34, 44, 161, 168,
191, 193, 198, 233
Reflective essays, 57
Rhetorical analogy, 278
Rhetorical context, 281
Rhetorical definition, 278
Rhetorical explanation, 278
Rhetorical slanters, 278
Ridicule/sarcasm, 278
Satire, 52, 101
Sensory details, 19
Sensory images, 241
Setting, 237
Soliloquies, 188
Stereotypes, 129, 272, 273
Structure, of literary text, 230
Style, 230
Subplot, 141, 245
Subtext, 103, 170
Symbols, 18
Syntax, 27
Themes, 245
Thesis, 34

Thesis statement, 37, 193
Title, 242, 245
Tone, 8, 21, 34, 37, 108, 109, 174, 325
Tragic hero, 217
Truth surrogates, 278
Vignettes, 29, 30
Voice, 21

Reading Skills

Anticipation guide, 113
Choral reading, 55
Close reading, 5, 9, 23, 37, 44, 90, 91,
103, 108, 120, 135, 164, 171, 178,
188, 190, 201, 216, 228, 234–235,
236, 244, 248, 269, 287, 311, 324
Compare and contrast, 48, 107, 140, 200
Comparisons, 201
Context clues, 135
Diffusing the text, 35, 57, 187, 229
Double-entry journal, 187, 330
Independent reading, 4, 88, 163, 227,
268
KWHL chart, 54
KWL chart, 218, 228, 269
Mark the text, 2, 4, 5, 11, 12, 14, 15, 20,
22, 29, 34, 44, 45, 57, 61, 63, 67, 71,
72, 75, 86, 88, 90, 97, 99, 101, 120,
121, 133, 164, 172, 173, 174, 181,
187, 189, 202, 216, 226, 228, 230,
252, 266, 269, 272, 282, 287, 324
Metacognitive markers, 15, 35, 36, 37
Paired reading, 62, 71, 73
Predicting, 48, 95, 96, 97, 99, 107, 181,
195, 203, 230, 235
Previewing, 171, 216, 230, 245
Questioning the text, 46, 48, 62, 193
Read aloud, 20, 58, 61, 64, 75, 121, 122,
131
Rereading, 15, 63, 107, 111, 129, 130,
143, 181, 188, 192, 201, 235, 257, 328
Scanning, 5, 75, 176, 186, 187, 228, 230,
269
Scripts, 201
Shared reading, 34, 237, 241
Sketching, 15, 18, 24
Skimming, 5, 57, 75, 117, 130, 202, 269
SOAPSTone strategy, 49, 81, 114, 121,
123, 178, 179, 180, 181, 286
Socratic seminar, 53, 64, 79
Summarizing, 14, 26, 128, 195, 230,
232, 241, 245, 258, 287, 317
Think aloud, 104, 106, 172, 234–235
TP-CASTT, 15

Writing Skills

Alternate endings, 107
Annotated bibliography, 319
Annotation, 22
Aphorisms, 6
Argumentative text, 121
Character sketches, 176, 177, 181
Concept visualization, 24
Critical perspectives timed writing, 338
Descriptive writing, 10
Details, 10, 19, 21, 37, 109, 242, 243, 270, 279, 280, 281, 287
Dialogue, 68, 170
Drawing conclusions, 176
Editing, 68, 104, 107, 112, 144
Essays, 18, 32, 34, 37, 38, 122, 191, 199, 200, 202
   expository, 314, 317
   informative, 171
   reflective, 40, 57, 254
Free writing, 11, 19, 22, 39
Generating questions, 55
Interpretative responses, 7, 14, 15, 18, 34
Life story, 25
Looping, 19, 39
Media text, 332–333, 334–335, 336–337
Monologue, 100, 109, 241
Narratives, 234–235, 236
New literacies, 227
On-demand writing, 37
OPTIC strategy, 10, 32
Outlines, 193
Paraphrasing, 5, 6, 45, 90, 114, 133, 164, 182, 269
Peer review, 321
Perspective, 7
Persuasive text, 246, 310
   bias in, 279, 318
Play scripts, 110, 117
Presentation, 40, 262, 320–321
Prewriting, 57, 80, 143, 192, 214, 233, 254, 320
Prologues, 23
Publishing, 81, 117
Quickwriting, 6, 14, 18, 25, 28, 47, 53, 91, 94, 98, 99, 102, 132, 168, 169, 229, 244, 272, 281, 325, 331
Revising, 22, 28, 30, 39, 64, 67, 68, 80–81, 101, 107, 140, 143–144, 181, 308, 320–321
Staging notebook, 219–220
Summarizing, 5, 14, 90, 97, 105, 111, 128, 131, 164, 181, 192, 195, 203, 218, 228, 230, 235, 257, 269
Synopsis, 142
Thesis statements, 327
Timed writing, 37

TWIST strategy, 142
Vignettes, 29, 30
Visualizing, 29, 172, 201
Writing prompt, 9, 22, 28, 30, 37, 66, 110, 123, 138, 139, 140, 142, 191, 201, 214, 233, 246, 247, 254, 256, 279, 310, 314

Media Skills

Acting company
   actors, 165
   director, 165
   dramaturge, 165
Blocking a scene, 194, 195
Camera angles
   eye level, 31, 133, 243
   high angle, 31, 133, 243
   low angle, 31, 133, 243
Camera movements
   boom/crane, 134
   dolly/tracking, 134
   pan, 133, 137
   tilt, 133, 137
   zoom, 133
Cinematic techniques, 120, 180, 196, 268
Composition, 234
Designing media communication, 251
Documentary films, 311
   archival footage, 311
   primary footage, 311
Documentary media text, 326, 327, 329
Editing techniques
   cross cutting, 134
   cut, 134, 137
   dissolve, 134
   eye-line-match, 134, 137
   fade, 134, 137
   flashback, 134
   point of view, 134
   shot-reverse-shot, 134, 137
   wipe, 134
Filters, 268
First screening, 91, 92, 93
Form, of scripts, 102
Framing, 234
Internet, 6, 227
   blogs, 268, 275
   chat rooms, 268
   online essays, 275
Lighting
   back lighting, 31, 134
   bottom lighting, 31, 134
   front lighting, 31, 134
   high key, 31, 134
   low key, 31, 134
   side lighting, 31, 134
Magazines, 268

Media channels, 328
Nonfiction film and television, 312, 314
   expository mode, 312
   interactive mode, 313
   observational mode, 312
   reflexive, 313
Photographic elements
   composition, 9
   cropping, 9
   frame, 9
   image, 9
   lighting, 9
   space, 9
   subject, 9
Print newspapers, 268
Production elements, 246, 247, 251
Rhetorical context, 281, 287
Rhetorical questions, 275, 308
Rhetorical slanters, 278
Second screening, 91, 92, 93
Shots and framing
   close up, 31, 133, 137
   establishing shot, 31, 133, 137, 242
   extreme close up, 31, 133
   long shot, 31, 133, 137
   medium shot, 31, 133, 137
   mise en scène, 133
   shot, 31, 133
   two shot, 31, 133
Sound
   diegetic, 134, 137, 227
   nondiegetic, 134, 227
Stage directions, 102
Target audience, 271, 182, 287, 326, 329
Television news networks, 268
Tone, 325

Listening and Speaking Skills

Active skills, 330
Adapting for audience, 247, 248
Audio/visual prompts, 168, 180
Choral reading, 55
Debating, 107
Dialogue, 11, 68, 103, 104, 105, 107, 170, 177, 187, 188
Diction, 19, 21, 22
Drama game, 65
Dramatic performance, 165, 166, 191
Group presentations, 248
Listening responsively, 230, 243, 246, 252, 259
Oral interpretation, 11, 47, 53, 103, 219–220
Oral presentations, 116, 130, 188, 203, 286, 310
Rehearsing, 170, 174, 219, 220

Index of Authors and Titles

Text Credits:

"My Papa's Waltz," copyright 1942 by Hearst Magazines, Inc., from *Collected Poems of Theodore Roethke* by Theodore Roethke. Used by permission of Doubleday, a division of Random House, Inc.

"in Just-". Copyright 1923, 1951, © 1991 by the Trustees for the E. E. Cummings Trust. Copyright © 1976 by George James Firmage, from *Complete Poems: 1904-1962* by E. E. Cummings, edited by George J. Firmage. Used by permission of Liveright Publishing Corporation.

"The Last Word" from *The Poems of Peter Davison* by Peter Davison, copyright © 1995 by Peter Davison. Used by permission of Alfred A. Knopf, a division of Random House, Inc.

"Mushrooms" from *The Colossus and Other Poems* by Sylvia Plath, copyright © 1957, 1958, 1959, 1960, 1961, 1962 by Sylvia Plath. Used by permission of Alfred A. Knopf, a division of Random House, Inc.

"I Remember" by Edward Montez, California Poetry Project.

"Prologue," from *Invisible Man* by Ralph Ellison, copyright 1952 by Ralph Ellison. Used by permission of Random House, Inc.

From *The House on Mango Street*. Copyright © by 1984 by Sandra Cisneros. Published by Vintage Books, a division of Random House, Inc., and in hardcover by Alfred A. Knopf in 1994. By permission of Susan Bergholz Literary Services, New York, NY and Lamy, NM. All rights reserved.

"On Seeing England for the First Time," originally published in *Harper's*. Copyright © 1991 by Jamaica Kincaid, reprinted with permission of The Wylie Agency, LLC.

"Speaking with Hands" from *The Concrete River*, copyright 1993 by Luis J. Rodriguez. Reprinted with permission of Curbstone Press.

"Shooting an Elephant" from *Shooting an Elephant and Other Stories* by George Orwell, copyright 1950 by Sonia Brownell Orwell and renewed 1978 by Sonia Pitt-Rivers, reprinted by permission of Houghton Mifflin Harcourt Publishing Company.

"Lindo-Jong: Double-Face" from *The Joy Luck Club* by Amy Tan. Copyright © 1989 by Amy Tan. Used by permission of G.P. Putnam's Sons, a division of Penguin Group (USA) Inc.

Notes of a Native Son by James Baldwin, Copyright © 1955, renewed 1983, by James Baldwin. Reprinted by permission of Beacon Press, Boston.

The Metamorphoses of Ovid translated with an introduction by Mary M. Innes (Penguin Classics, 1955). Copyright © Mary M. Innes, 1955. Used by permission of Penguin Group (UK) Ltd.

"Cinderella, the Legend," from *Kiss Sleeping Beauty Good-bye* by Madonna Kolbenschlag. Used by permission of Women & Leadership Archives, Loyola University Chicago.

From "Why Women Always Take Advantage of Men," from *Mules and Men* by Zora Neale Hurston. Copyright © 1935 by Zora Neale Hurston; renewed © 1963 by John C. Hurston and Joel Hurston. Reprinted by permission of HarperCollins Publishers.

"A Rose for Emily," copyright 1930 and renewed 1958 by William Faulkner, from *Collected Stories of William Faulkner* by William Faulkner. Used by permission of Random House, Inc.

The Moor in English Renaissance Drama by Jack D'Amico. Copyright 1991 by University of South Florida Press. Reproduced by permission of the University Press of Florida.

"Othello on Stage and Screen" by Sylvan Barnet, copyright © 1963, 1986, 1998 by Sylvan Barnet, from *The Tragedy of Othello* by William Shakespeare, edited by Alvin Kernan. Used by permission of Phyllis Fogelman Books, a division of Penguin Group (USA) Inc.

From *Understanding Comics: The Invisible Art* by Scott McCloud. Copyright © 1993, 1994 by Scott McCloud. Reprinted by permission of HarperCollins Publishers.

"Immigrant Song," words and music by Jimmy Page and Robert Plant. © 1970 (Renewed) Flames of Albion Music, Inc. All rights administered by WB Music Corp. Exclusive print rights for the world excluding Europe administered by Alfred Publishing Co, Inc. All rights reserved. Used by permission of Alfred Publishing Co., Inc.

"Comments on *The Arrival*" by Shaun Tan. Courtesy of Shaun Tan.

"How the Media Twist the News," by Sheila Gribben Liaugminas, originally published in *Crisis* in October 2002. Reprinted by permission of InsideCatholic.com.

"Media Bias Comes from Viewers Like You" by Tyler Cowen, published on TCS Daily, Nov. 11, 2003. Used by permission of the author.

"The Dixie Chicks" by Betty Clarke as appeared in *The Guardian,* March 12, 2003. Used by permission of the author.

"The Dixie Chicks Keep the Heat on Nashville" from *The New York Times,* Aug. 25, 2002, © 2002 The New York Times All rights reserved. Used by permission and protected by the Copyright Laws of the United States. The printing, copying, redistribution, or retransmission of the Material without express written permission is prohibited.

"Chicks reap whirlwind" by Mike Rosen as appeared in *Rocky Mountain News,* May 2, 2003. Reprinted by permission of Mike Rosen, talk show host, KOA Radio, Denver. *Denver Post* Columnist.

"No More Whistlin' Dixie" by Jim Lewis, originally published by Slate.com, April 25, 2003. Reprinted by permission.

"Is Dixie Chicks protest a conspiracy?" by John Kiesewetter from *The Cincinnati Enquirer,* March 18, 2003, © The Cincinnati Enquirer.

"The Dixie Chicks: America Catches Up with Them" from *The New York Times,* May 21, 2006 © 2006 The New York Times All rights reserved. Used by permission and protected by the Copyright Laws of the United States. The printing, copying, redistribution, or retransmission of the Material without express written permission is prohibited.

"Speaking Up and Speaking Out" by Melissa Silverstein, posted to Women's Media Center, Nov. 1, 2006 for the Women's Media Center (www.womensmediacenter.com) Used by permission.

"Dixie Chicks Among Esteemed Outlaws" by Ashley Sayeau, *The Philadelphia Inquirer,* Feb. 16, 2007 Reprinted by permission of the YGS Group.

"A Tired Old Song" by Jonah Goldberg, *The National Review,* March 5, 2007. Copyright © 2007 by National Review, Inc., 215 Lexington Avenue, New York, NY 10016. Reprinted by permission.

Photo credits:

11 thephotoguy/BigStockPhoto.com; 15 Dicdesign/ BigStockPhoto.com; 17 mjp/BigStockPhoto.com; 20 CzERTik/BigStockPhoto.com; 37 kjpargeter/ BigStockPhoto.com; 47 Terry Morris/BigStockPhoto. com; 52 Kelpfish/BigStockPhoto.com; 55 elenathewise/ BigStockPhoto.com; 59 Travelshots/BigStockPhoto. com; 60 Tootles/BigStockPhoto.com; 63 Four Oaks/ BigStockPhoto.com; 64 ginaellen/BigStockPhoto.com; 67 Harald/BigStockPhoto.com; 70 ajn/BigStockPhoto. com; 72 jirkaejc/BigStockPhoto.com; 74 davinci/ BigStockPhoto.com; 77 Jacques Kloppers/BigStockPhoto. com; 79 soupstock/BigStockPhoto.com. 98 p.lange/ BigStockPhoto.com; 123 cosma/BigStockPhoto. com; 127 Tiniiiii/BigStockPhoto.com; 147 Elnur/ BigStockPhoto.com; 151 South12th/BigStockPhoto. com; 153 vladacanon/BigStockPhoto.com; 155 DLeonis/ BigStockPhoto.com; 157 palmer530/BigStockPhoto. com. 175 kentoh/BigStockPhoto.com; 184 mtrommer/ BigStockPhoto.com; 185 fotomy/BigStockPhoto.com; 186 ELITE-PHOTO/BigStockPhoto.com; 203 Lance Bellers/ BigStockPhoto.com; 205 Orlando/BigStockPhoto.com; 207 voiceover/BigStockPhoto.com; 208 Lance Bellers/ BigStockPhoto.com; 211 T.A. Byrne/BigStockPhoto. com; 213 jgroup/BigStockPhoto.com. 249 (B) drx / BigStockPhoto.com, (T) goce/BigStockPhoto.com; 250 donna57/BigStockPhoto.com; 253 Swartz Photography/BigStockPhoto.com; 254 RazvanPhotography/BigStockPhoto.com. 273 Yakobchuk/BigStockPhoto.com; 276 volare2004/ BigStockPhoto.com; 309 Domen Colja/ BigStockPhoto.com.